T0191976

GRID-BASED PROBLEM SOLVING ENVIRONMENTS

IFIP – The International Federation for Information Processing

IFIP was founded in 1960 under the auspices of UNESCO, following the First World Computer Congress held in Paris the previous year. An umbrella organization for societies working in information processing, IFIP's aim is two-fold: to support information processing within its member countries and to encourage technology transfer to developing nations. As its mission statement clearly states,

> *IFIP's mission is to be the leading, truly international, apolitical organization which encourages and assists in the development, exploitation and application of information technology for the benefit of all people.*

IFIP is a non-profitmaking organization, run almost solely by 2500 volunteers. It operates through a number of technical committees, which organize events and publications. IFIP's events range from an international congress to local seminars, but the most important are:

• The IFIP World Computer Congress, held every second year;
• Open conferences;
• Working conferences.

The flagship event is the IFIP World Computer Congress, at which both invited and contributed papers are presented. Contributed papers are rigorously refereed and the rejection rate is high.

As with the Congress, participation in the open conferences is open to all and papers may be invited or submitted. Again, submitted papers are stringently refereed.

The working conferences are structured differently. They are usually run by a working group and attendance is small and by invitation only. Their purpose is to create an atmosphere conducive to innovation and development. Refereeing is less rigorous and papers are subjected to extensive group discussion.

Publications arising from IFIP events vary. The papers presented at the IFIP World Computer Congress and at open conferences are published as conference proceedings, while the results of the working conferences are often published as collections of selected and edited papers.

Any national society whose primary activity is in information may apply to become a full member of IFIP, although full membership is restricted to one society per country. Full members are entitled to vote at the annual General Assembly, National societies preferring a less committed involvement may apply for associate or corresponding membership. Associate members enjoy the same benefits as full members, but without voting rights. Corresponding members are not represented in IFIP bodies. Affiliated membership is open to non-national societies, and individual and honorary membership schemes are also offered.

GRID-BASED PROBLEM SOLVING ENVIRONMENTS

IFIP TC2/ WG 2.5 Working Conference on Grid-Based Problem Solving Environments: Implications for Development and Deployment of Numerical Software
July 17-21, 2006, Prescott, Arizona, USA

Edited by

Patrick W. Gaffney
Bergen Software Services International AS
Norway

James C. T. Pool
California Institute of Technology
USA

 Springer

Grid-Based Problem Solving Environments

Edited by P. W. Gaffney and J.C.T. Pool

p. cm. (IFIP International Federation for Information Processing, a Springer Series in Computer Science)

ISSN: 1571-5736 / 1861-2288 (Internet)

ISBN: 13: 978-1-4419-4466-5   eISBN: 13: 978-0-387-73659-4
Printed on acid-free paper

9 8 7 6 5 4 3 2 1
springer.com

INTRODUCTION

PART 1

WORKFLOW TOOLS

PART 2

APPLICATION EXPERIENCE

PART 3

INFRASTRUCTURE: SERVICES

PART 4

INFRASTRUCTURE: NUMERICAL SOFTWARE

PART 5

EVENT DRIVEN APPLICATIONS

PART 6

APPLICATIONS I

PART 7

APPLICATIONS II

PART 8

GRID-BASED IMAGING

PART 9

CONFERENCE SUMMARY; STRATEGY FOR FUTURE ACTIVITIES

The Conference

1 Introduction

The conference was held July 17-21, 2006 at the Hassayampa Inn in Prescott, Arizona, USA. Prescott, "Everybody's Hometown", was selected to provide an environment with minimal distractions during the event, while providing pre- and post-conference opportunities for family vacations and, hence, stimulating participation during the usually busy summer months. Prescott is a convenient starting point for vacations, including trips to the Grand Canyon, the Navajo Nation, and numerous state and federal parks. Built in 1927 as a "Southwestern luxury hotel" and recently renovated, the Hassayampa Inn, listed in the National Register of Historic Places and a member of the National Trust Historic Hotels of America, provided ample space for both the conference plenary sessions and quiet retreats to stimulate impromptu discussions.

While interaction was emphasized throughout the conference by a format emphasizing questions and answers, Wednesday afternoon and evening provided a break from the intense immersion. Informal interactions were stimulated through an introduction to Arizona's Frontier Days, including a tour of the Sharlot Hall Museum featuring the early days of Prescott as the capital of the Arizona Territory, a visit to The Palace - the oldest frontier saloon in Arizona, and finally "An Evening with Mr. and Mrs. Wyatt Earp" presented by Wyatt Earp, a grandnephew of the Wyatt Earp of Tombstone fame, and his playwright/actress wife, Terry Earp.

2. Program

Following the successful patterns of past WG2.5 working conferences, the conference was scheduled for a full week with presentations grouped by topic. Scheduled presentations were made by twenty seven speakers in eight topical sessions. Twenty one presentations have been expanded to papers included in these Proceedings. Each speaker was allocated thirty minutes plus fifteen minutes for questions and answers. An additional thirty minute discussion period concluded each topical session. The questions and answers were recorded by discussants in each session and are included in these proceedings. Speakers provided abstracts made available to participants via the conference website prior to the event. These abstracts, slides from most presentations, and other information about the conference can be accessed at http://www.nsc.liu.se/wg25/woco9/.

Monday, July 17
8:45 Opening Session: J. Pool, Chair
9:00 **Workflow Tools**: W. Gropp, Session Chair; R. Boisvert, Discussant
      D. Gannon: *Scientific Gateways and Workflow Tools*
9:45 K. Kennedy: *Why Performance Models Matter for Grid Computing*
10:30 Break
11:00 M. Vouk: *Automation of Large-scale Network-Based Scientific Workflows using Kepler: Tools and Case Studies*
11:45 Discussion
12:15 Lunch
13:30 **Application Experience**: R. Boisvert, Session Chair; B. Einarsson, Discussant
      P. Gaffney & T. Hopkins: *Virtual Manufacturing - The Vision for Virtual Paint Operations*
14:15 D. Schissel: *Service-oriented Computation in Magnetic Fusion Research*
15:00 Break
15:30 D. Walker: *Lessons Learned from the GECEM Portal*
16:15 A. Trefethen: *e-Research and Applications*
17:00 Discussion
18:30 Reception
19:30 Conference Dinner

Tuesday, July 18
8:45 Opening Session: J. Pool, Chair
9:00 **Infrastructure: Services**: A. Trefethen, Session Chair; M. Mu, Discussant
      J. Treadwell: *Open Grid Services Architecture*
9:45 B. Norris: *Computational Quality of Service for Scientific Component Applications*
10:30 Break
11:00 T. Jackson: *A Middleware Webservice Architrecture for Distributed Search Applications*
11:45 Discussion
12:15 Lunch
13:30 **Infrastructure: Numerical Software**: W. Enright, Session Chair; T. Hopkins, Discussant
      X. Wang: *THCORE: A Component Runtime for Service Oriented Numerical Software*

9:00 **Grid-based Imaging**: B. Ford, Session Chair; M. Vouk, Discussant
      V. Boccia: *MedIGrid: A Medical Imaging PSE for Computational Grids*
9:45 D. Keyes: *Grid-based Image Registration*
10:30 Break
11:00 Discussion
11:30 **Conference Summary; Strategy for Future Activities**
12:15 Lunch

3. Organization

The conference was sponsored by IFIP, organized by the IFIP Working Group on Numerical Software (IFIP WG2.5) and the Center for Advanced Computing Research at the California Institute of Technology in cooperation with the Society for Industrial and Applied Mathematics. General plans for the conference and the following organizational structure were approved by WG2.5 during its annual meeting in 2004:

- **Chair**
  - James C. T. Pool, Center for Advanced Computing Research, California Institute of Technology
- **Deputy Chair**
  - Brian Ford, Mathematics Faculty, Oxford University and Founding Director, Numerical Algorithms Group
- **Executive Committee**
  - Conference Chair
  - Deputy Conference Chair
  - Program Committee Chair
  - WG2.5 Chair: Ronald F. Boisvert, Mathematical and Computational Sciences Division, National Institute of Standards and Technology
- **Program Committee**
  - Chair: William D. Gropp, Mathematics and Computer Science Division, Argonne National Laboratory
  - Dennis Gannon, Department of Computer Science, Indiana University
  - Jennifer Schopf, Mathematics and Computer Science Division, Argonne National Laboratory and UK National e-Science Centre, University of Edinburgh
  - Masaaki Shimasaki, Department of Electrical Engineering, Kyoto University
  - Michael Thuné, Department of Information Technology, Uppsala University
  - Anne Trefethen; Interdisciplinary e-Research Centre; Oxford University and UK e-Science Core Programme, Engineering and Physical Sciences Research Council

- o Conference Chair
- o Conference Deputy Chair
- o Proceedings Co-Editors
- **Proceedings Co-Editors**
  - o Patrick W. Gaffney, Bergen Software Services International A/S, Bergen, Norway
  - o Conference Chair
- **Local Arrangements and Conference Support**
  - o Sarah Emery Bunn, Center for Advanced Computing Research, California Institute of Technology
  - o Charles Chapman, Center for Advanced Computing Research, California Institute of Technology
  - o Santiago Lombeyda, Center for Advanced Computing Research, California Institute of Technology
  - o Doris M. Pool
  - o Susan Powell, Center for Advanced Computing Research, California Institute of Technology

4. Attendees

The forty six attendees, including eighteen members of WG 2.5, came from ten different countries:

Jay Alameda, National Center for Supercomputing Applications, United States

Gabrielle Allen, Louisiana State University, United States

Mutsumi Aoyagi, Kyushu University, Japan

Bill Applebe, Victorian Partnership for Advanced Computing, Australia

Vania Boccia, University Of Naples & Southern Partnership for Advanced Computational Infrastructures, Italy

Ronald Boisvert, National Institute of Standards and Technology, United States

Pasquale Caruso, University Of Naples & Southern Partnership for Advanced Computational Infrastructures, Italy

Craig Douglas, University of Kentucky, United States

Bo Einarsson, Linkoping University, Sweden

Wayne Enright, University of Toronto, Canada

Brian Ford, Oxford University, United Kingdom

Pat Gaffney, Bergen Software Services International, Norway

Dennis Gannon, Indiana University, United States

Marc Garbey, University of Houston, United States

Sebastien Goasguen, Purdue University, United States

William D. Gropp, Argonne National Laboratory, United States

Richard J. Hanson, Visual Numerics, Inc., United States

Pieter Hemker, Centrum voor Wiskunde en Informatica, Netherlands

Tim Hopkins, University of Kent, United Kingdom

Keith Jackson, Lawrence Berkeley National Laboratory, United States
Tom Jackson, University of York, United Kingdom
Ken Kennedy, Rice University, United States
David Keyes, Columbia University, United States
Osni A. Marques, Lawrence Berkeley National Laboratory, United States
Robert Meersman, Vrije Universiteit Brussel, Belgium
Mo Mu, Hong Kong University of Science and Technology, China
Sara Murphy, Hewlett-Packard, United States
Suman Nadella, Argonne National Laboratory, United States
Boyana Norris, Argonne National Laboratory, United States
Julian Padget, University of Bath, United Kingdom
Beth Plale, Indiana University, United States
Jim Pool, California Institute of Technology (Retired), United States
Ian Reid, Numerical Algorithms Group Ltd, United Kingdom
David Schissel, General Atomics, United States
Masaaki Shimasaki, Kyoto University, Japan
Brian Smith, Numerica 21 Inc & University Of New Mexico, United States
Mark Stalzer, California Institute of Technology, United States
Mary Thomas, San Diego State University, United States
Michael Thuné, Uppsala University, Sweden
Jem Treadwell, Hewlett-Packard, United States
Anne Trefethen, Oxford e-Research Centre, United Kingdom
Hitohide Usami, National Institute of Informatics, Japan
Mladen A. Vouk, North Carolina State University, United States
David Walker, University of Cardiff, United Kingdom
Xiaoge Wang, Tsinghua University, China
Asim YarKhan, University of Tennessee at Knoxville, United States

Preface

In 1984 W. J. Cody, an early member of the IFIP Working Group on Numerical Software (WG 2.5), reviewed progress in numerical software during the previous two decades and then identified future challenges posed by the rapid advances in computing technology[1]:

- decline of the local central computing facility
    - isolated from research
    - libraries neglected
- rise of personal computing
    - isolated from everyone
    - poor software
- rise of remote computing facilities
    - good libraries
    - resident specialists

Cody's foresight was remarkable. The establishment of supercomputer centers coupled with development of distributed computing, including the recent development of grid infrastructure, has resulted in users being increasingly dependent on software resources on remote systems.

Indeed, the use of the Internet to bring together providers and users of resources has become commonplace. One of the earliest such tools was Netlib, which started in the 1980's as an email-based application for distributing numerical software. Other services, such as NetSolve (for linear algebra) and NEOS (for nonlinear and optimization problems) have demonstrated the potential of grid-based problem solving environments (PSEs)[2]. Domain specific PSEs, such as Cactus (developed for numerical relativity) and PYRE (developed for shock physics), have been applied outside their original discipline to generate new PSEs and are being extended to exploit grid technology.

The development and deployment of numerical software for grid-based problem solving environments must ultimately be driven by the needs of scientists and engineers. However, the major changes in the computing environment during the past few years and the advances, both anticipated and unforeseen, during the next few years pose new challenges to the numerical software community as it responds to these needs. There is more to making use of a grid-based service than simply knowing its web address. Does the service work reliably? What are its limitations? Can it be combined with other services? There are also opportunities for improving

---

[1] W. J. Cody, "Second Thoughts on the Mathematical Software Effort: A Perspective", Proceedings of the Symposium on Computational Mathematics – State of the Art – Held at Argonne National Laboratory September 20-21, 1984 in Honor of James H. Wilkinson, ANL/MCS-TM-42, December, 1984.

[2] In this context, the phrase "Grid-Based Problem Solving Environments" is, in many cases, synonymous with "science gateways" or "science portals", nomenclature introduced recently by the grid community.

the ability of applications to use the best numerical software, for example, by simplifying the acquisition and use of high-quality numerical software. The development of numerical software can benefit from the experience of the scientific and engineering communities using and developing new grid-based PSEs, for example, defining interfaces more appropriate for integrating numerical software into grid-oriented applications and exploiting test sets and tools for comparing different methods.

The IFIP Working Conference on Grid-based Problem Solving Environments: Implications for Development and Deployment of Numerical Software was, therefore, planned to bring together four communities:

- users of both grid-based and traditional problem solving environments;
- developers of both grid-based and traditional problem solving environments;
- developers of grid infrastructure; and
- developers of numerical software

for a week of intensive interaction to address issues including, but not limited to:

- accuracy contracts and software services;
- standards for problem specification;
- service models for the use of numerical software;
- using the grid to link numerical and other services together;
- experiences with web-based numerical services;
- application-oriented numerical interfaces such as web portals;
- software deployment issues including updates and bug fixes;
- large data (including data security) and grid-based numerical software;
- grid-based services as an alternative to deployment; and
- evaluation and comparison of both production and research software.

The conference, WG2.5's ninth working conference since 1978, built upon the experience and insights gained during past working conferences organized by WG2.5, in particular, "WoCo4: Problem Solving Environments for Scientific Computing"[3]; "WoCo6 Programming Environments for High-Level Scientific Problem Solving"[4]; and "WoCo8: Software Architectures for Scientific Computing Applications"[5].

The conference was sponsored by IFIP, organized by the IFIP Working Group on Numerical Software and the Center for Advanced Computing Research at the California Institute of Technology in cooperation with the Society for Industrial and Applied Mathematics. The conference was supported by a major contribution from Hewlett-Packard and additional contributions from Intel, Numerical Algorithms

[3] Editors: B. Ford, F. Chatelin; Problem Solving Environments for Scientific Computing; North Holland, Amsterdam; 1987; ISBN 0-444-70254-7

[4] Editors: P. W. Gaffney, E. N. Houstis; Programming Environments for High-Level Scientific Problem Solving; North-Holland, Amsterdam; 1992; ISBN-0-444-89176-5

[5] Editors: R. F. Boisvert, P. Tang; The Architecture of Scientific Software; Kluwer Academic Publishers, Boston; 2001; ISBN 0-7923-7339-1

Group, and Visual Numerics. Caltech's Center for Advanced Computing Research contributed staff effort necessary for planning and implementing the conference.

Twenty one of the twenty seven presentations at the conference have been expanded into papers included in these Proceedings. The presentations were scheduled in topical groups. A feature distinguishing the conference is the question/answer sessions both after each presentation and after a topical group – the discussions in these sessions are included in these proceedings. Two particular contributions are also included. *Observations on WoCo9*, offers a summary of the meeting, from the perspective of the Program Committee Chair, William D. Gropp. Discussions during the conference stimulated Brian T. Smith to prepare a brief paper, *Future Directions for Numerical Software Research*, emphasizing the need for "software that evaluates the accuracy of the computed results or more importantly the sensitivity of the numerical results to the data and the platforms on which the computation occurs". Abstracts, slides from most presentations, and other information about the conference can be accessed at http://www.nsc.liu.se/wg25/woco9/.

The success of the conference was the result of the Program Committee's guidance and selection of speakers; therefore, we wish to thank: William D. Gropp; Dennis Gannon; Jennifer Schopf; Masaaki Shimasaki; Michael Thuné; and Anne Trefethen. We also wish to thank the members of WG 2.5 who contributed nominations of speakers and participants. We thank the speakers for their efforts to delineate and address the challenges to the numerical software community by the rapidly emerging and changing grid technology and the participants for their insightful questions that stimulated discussions throughout the week. The session chairs and discussants deserve recognition for the difficult task of maintaining the conference schedule while stimulating discussion and recording the questions and answers included in these proceedings. The staff of the Center for Advanced Computing Research at the California Institute of Technology, Sarah Emery Bunn, Santiago Lombeyda, Charles Chapman, and Susan Powell, provided excellent support for the conference planning and implementation.

We thank Ronald F. Boisvert, WG 2.5 Chair, for his support and guidance during the conference planning. We especially thank Brian Ford, Conference Deputy Chair, for his assistance from the earliest planning through the conference implementation to the preparation of these proceedings. Patrick Gaffney, the principal editor of these proceedings, deserves special thanks and acknowledgement for his continuing and persistent efforts to obtain and prepare the papers and discussion dialogues for these proceedings.

Finally, I wish to thank my wife, Doris M. Pool, for her assistance both before and during the conference and for her patience during the months prior to the conference when a multitude of tasks for our new home near Prescott were "temporarily delayed".

James C. T. Pool
Conference Chair

PART 1

WORKFLOW TOOLS

W. Gropp, Session Chair; R. Boisvert, Discussant

D. Gannon: *Programming Paradigms for Scientific Problem Solving Environments*

K. Kennedy: *Why Performance Models Matter for Grid Computing*

M. Vouk: *Automation of Network-Based Scientific Workflows*

Panel Discussion

Programming Paradigms for Scientific Problem Solving Environments

Dennis Gannon, Marcus Christie, Suresh Marru, Satoshi Shirasuna, Aleksander Slominski

Department of Compute Science, School of Informatics,
Indiana University,
Bloomington, IN 47401
gannon@cs.indiana.edu

Summary. Scientific problem solving environments (PSEs) are software platforms that allow a community of scientific users the ability to easily solve computational problems within a specific domain. They are designed to hide the details of general purpose programming by allowing the problem to be expressed, as much as possible, in the scientific language of the discipline. In many areas of science, the nature of computational problems has evolved from simple desktop calculations to complex, multidisciplinary activities that require the monitoring and analysis of remote data streams, database and web search and large ensembles of supercomputer-hosted simulations. In this paper we will look at the class of PSE that have evolved for these "Grid based" systems and we will consider the associated programming models they support. It will be argued that a hybrid of three standard models provides the right programming support to handle the majority of the applications of these PSEs.

1 Introduction

Domain specific problem solving environments have a long history in computing and there are several examples of widely used tools that are also commercial successes. For example Mathematica [1] provides a platform for doing symbolic mathematics and related visualization tasks using a programming language that is designed with mathematical primitives as a basic component of the type system. Another example is Matlab [2], which is widely used in the scientific community to study problems requiring matrix manipulations or other linear algebra operations. In the area of computer graphics PSE like AVS and Explorer [3] pioneered the use of programming by component composition to build visualization pipelines. This same approach is used in SciRun [4] and many of the other systems described below.

In recent years, we have seen a shift in the nature of the problems scientists are trying to solve and this is changing the way we think about the design of PSEs. Specifically, many contemporary computational science applications require the integration of resources that go beyond the desktop. Remote data sources including on-line instruments and databases and high-end supercomputing platforms are among

Please use the following format when citing this chapter:

Gannon, D., Christie, M., Marru, S., Shirasuna, S., Slominski, A., 2007, in IFIP International Federation for Information Processing, Volume 239, Grid-Based Problem Solving Environments, eds. Gaffney, P. W., Pool, J.C.T., (Boston: Springer), pp. 3-15.

the standard tools of modern science. In addition multidisciplinary collaborations involving a distributed team of researchers are becoming a very common model of scientific discovery. Grid computing was invented to make it easier for applications and research teams to pool resources to do science in such a distributed setting. Grids are defined as a service oriented architecture that allows a group of collaborators, known as a virtual organization (VO), to share access to a set of distributed resources. There are three primary classes of core services that Grids provide that make it easier to build PSEs that use distributed systems. These services are:

- Security - authentication and authorization
- Virtualization of Data Storage
- Virtualization of Computation

The PSE that is built on top of a Grid service framework is often called a science gateway, because it provides a portal for a community to access a collection of resources without requiring them to be trained in the distributed systems and security technology that the Grid is built upon. As illustrated in Figure 1, the user's desktop interaction is through a browser and other tools which can be started with a mouse click in the browser. A remote server mediates the user's interaction with the Grid security services, the virtual data storage and metadata catalogs and application resources. The user's programs are represented as workflows that are executed by a remote execution engine.

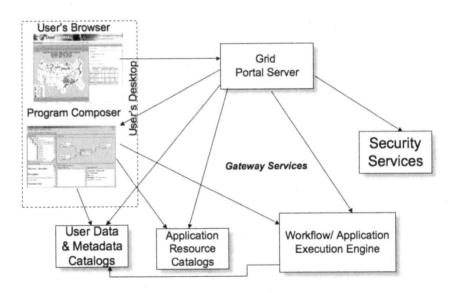

Figure 1. The organization of top level services in a science gateway PSE.

In this paper we will look at the problem solving programming model that is evolving for these Grid science gateway PSEs and suggest ways in which it can be extended in the future.

2 Programming in a Science Gateway PSE

The access point to a science gateway is usually based on a web portal that allows users access to the collective computational and data management resources of the underlying Grid. There are many examples of these gateway portals currently in use. The TeraGrid web site (http://www.teragrid.org) has links to many of these. They include

- The National Virtual Observatory (NVO), a gateway for astronomical sciences.
- Linked Environments for Atmospheric Discovery (LEAD), a PSE portal for mesoscale weather prediction.
- Network for Earthquake Engineering Simulation (NEES), a gateway for earthquake hazard mitigation.
- The GEOsciences Network (GEON), a geophysics gateway.
- Network for Computational Nanotechnology and nanoHUB, a PSE for access to nanotechnology tools.
- The Earth System Grid (ESG), a portal for global atmospheric research.
- The National Biomedical Computation Resource (NBCR), a gateway focused on integrative biology and neuroscience
- The Virtual Laboratory for Earth and Planetary Materials (VLAB), which focuses on materials research.
- The Biology and Biomedicine Science Gateway (The Renci Bioportal) which provides resources and tools for molecular biosciences.
- The Telescience Project, a gateway for neuroscience biology.

This is only a small sample. There are many other significant gateway projects in the U.S., Europe and Japan. While there are many unique features supported by these gateways, they also share many common attributes. Perhaps the most important feature they all share are mechanisms that provide access to community data. Science has become more data driven. The Scientists and engineers need to be able to search for, discover, analyze and visualize the data produced by instruments and computational experiments. They need to have mechanisms to discover new data based on searchers of metadata catalogs and they need tools to extract this data and save it in a gateway workspace for later use.

Once a scientist has collected the data (or identified the required data sources), he or she must begin the process of analyzing it. The data is frequently used as the input to a large simulation, a data mining computation or other analysis tool. A simple approach to the design of a PSE is to wrap up all the important application components and present a web portal user-interface page to the user for each one. For example, a simulation program may require one or two standard input files and a desired name for the output file or files. These may be exactly what is required to run the simulation program from the command line. The advantage of providing the input parameters in a portal web page is that we can transfer the complexity of selecting the best computer to run the application and establishing all the needed libraries and environment variables to the back-end Grid system. The user need only identify the input and output data set names.

While a simple web interface to individual applications is useful, life is seldom this simple. Specifically, the data is seldom in exactly the form that the analysis tools expect, so transformations must be applied to make it fit. These transformations may be format conversions, data sub-sampling, or interpolation. The task may also involve data assimilation, where multiple data sources must be merged or aligned in a particular way to meet the requirements of the simulation task. There may be many such preprocessing tasks and the analysis/simulation part of the activity may require the use of more than one package. Finally, there may be post-processing to create visualizations or other reports. And, as with most scientific experiments, the sequence of transformations, data analysis, mining, simulation, and post processing must be repeated in exactly the same way for many different input data samples. Programming the sequence of steps required to do such an analysis scenario is known as workflow design and this term is now in common use in the e-Science community.

The second most important feature of any science gateway PSE is to provide a mechanism for users to create workflow scripts that can be saved and later bound to input files and executed automatically using the remote grid resources. A recent study [5] has identified a dozen popular workflow tools used by these PSEs. The four most commonly used tools are Kepler [6], which is used in a variety of application domains, Taverna [7], a common tool for life-science workflows, Pegasus [8], used by many large physics applications, and BPEL [9], the industry standard for web service orchestration. In a later section of this paper we describe how BPEL has been integrated into the LEAD science gateway.

3 Compositional Programming Models in e-Science

To see how these tools work we need to look at the semantics of their graphical composition. Within the e-Science community, the primary model of workflow composition is based largely on macro-dataflow concepts. The idea is very simple. Scientific analysis is based upon transformation of data. An experiment begins with raw data. These data are often derived from experimental measurement, such as from a collection of instruments. The data must be pre-processed or "assimilated" into a coherent set of inputs to analysis or simulation packages. The output is then routed to final analysis or visualization tools. This is "programmed" by using a graphical tool which uses icons to represent the individual tasks as components in a workflow. As illustrated in Figure 2, each workflow component has one or more inputs and one or more outputs. Each input represents a data object or "message" that is required to enact the component and each output represents a result data message. The data

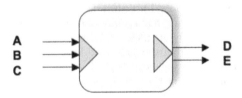

Figure 2. Each icon represents a process "component" with one or more required inputs and one or more output data objects.

object may be a numerical value, a string or the URI of a file. In some systems the data object may be a continuous stream of data to be processed. As illustrated in Figure 3, two components may be composed if the output of one component can serve as a valid input to another component. "Unbound" inputs represent the data sources for the workflow and the unbound outputs are the final data products.

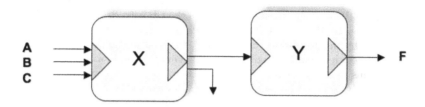

Figure 3. The components may be composed. In this case one result from component X is used as an input to component Y. A, B, and C are unbound inputs which must be supplied by the user at runtime.

In the typical system based on this model, the programmer drags icons onto a pallet and wires together the dataflow for the experiment. Figure 4 illustrates the interface to the XBaya system used in the Linked Environments for Atmospheric Discovery (LEAD) project [10, 11].

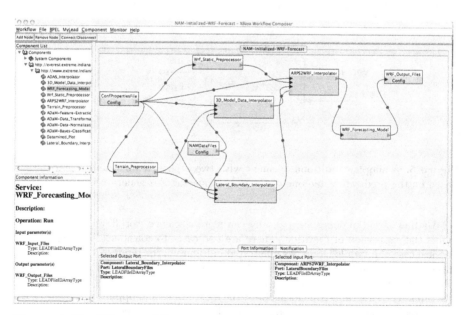

Figure 4. The XBaya workflow composition tool used to build a storm forecasting workflow.

Unfortunately, there are several problems with this basic model of dataflow driven workflow as described above. The first problem relates to the way components are connected. When is the output of one component suitable as an input to another component? Clearly, if they have conflicting simple types, such as providing a String as an input to something that is expecting a Float, then it is easy for a rudimentary type system to detect the error. But most problems are due to subtle semantic differences between the content of the message that is passed. For example, in large systems, the message often only contains the URI of a data file that is stored on a remote resource. How do we know if the data file has the right format or content to be used by the destination component? The solution to this problem lies in providing complete information about the exact semantics and format of each input and output. This metadata needs to be attached to the component and some form of metadata analysis would be required to check compatibility. Without a common metadata schema, a component provided by one group of researchers cannot be used by another group. Consequently, it is up to the scientist composing the workflow to understand this issue.

The second problem with this simple model is that it does not take into account the control dependencies that a typical computer program uses. For example, conditionals and iteration are difficult to express in a language where the only operation is the composition of directed acyclic graphs. However, it is not difficult to overlay additional control operations over the dataflow. For example, a conditional can be expressed by a component (Figure 5) that takes two inputs, a value message, and a conditional predicate that the message must satisfy. There are two outputs. If the predicate evaluates to true, then the value is forwarded out one output. If the value is false, the other message is generated.

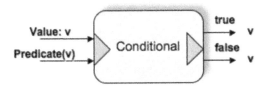

Figure 5. A simple conditional element with two inputs: a value and a predicate. Based on the predicate value one of the output messages is generated.

Another essential component of any complete e-science workflow programming tool is the expression of iteration. There are two cases to consider. The first is the classical case of a "while" loop. As illustrated in Figure 6, the input is a predicate, an initial iterate value and a set of data values. The predicate is applied to the iterate value and if the result is true, the iterate value and data values are passed to a subgraph. The subgraph transforms both the data values and applies some function to the iterate value. These are fed back to the while control node and the test is repeated.

The second form is a parallel "for each" that can be used when you wish to execute a subgraph for each element of a set of data values. In this case the subgraph

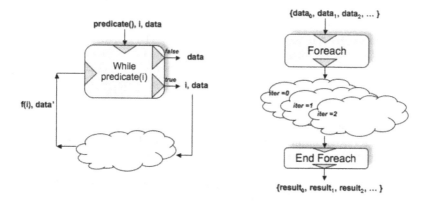

Figure 6. A "while" loop and a parallel "for each" element.

is also supplied with an additional "iteration" index so the different invocations of the subgraph can be uniquely identified. This additional index is important when the subgraph must create a side-effect outside the body of the workflow. For example, when an element of the workflow creates a file, it must be distinguished from the file generated by the other instances. However, the exact semantics of how such an iteration index is propagated to the body of a "for each" loop is non-trivial and not a topic for this paper.

There are other standard features of workflow composition tools in this category. For example, it is important to be able to encapsulate any valid composed workflow as a component which can be used in other workflows.

Finally a topic that is always overlooked by e-Science workflow systems is that of exceptions. An exception occurs when a specific component realizes that it cannot correctly process an incoming message. As with any modern programming language, it is essential that the system have a mechanism to capture these runtime exceptions and deal with them. The model often used in programming languages, where a block of code is encapsulated in a "try" block which is followed by a "catch" block which is responsible for handling the exceptional conditions, can be used in graphical dataflow-based systems. In the graphical case we can simply identify a subgraph that may throw an exception and provide a description for a replacement "catch" subgraph. The exceptions that are the most frequent are those that are related to access to remote resources. For example, a remote service that fails to respond because of a network or other resource failure. In these cases it is often better to handle the problem at a lower, resource allocation level than at the abstract workflow graph level. A situation that may be handled at the graph level could be one where a request to an application component is simply too large or, for some other reason, too difficult to process. In these cases, the workflow designer may know that an alternative service exists that can be used in special cases like this.

4 The Service Architecture of a Science Gateway PSE.

The science gateway PSE programming model we have described so far is based on building applications by composing application services. The LEAD gateway is like many others in that the components services are implemented as Web services. This allows us to use standard robust middleware concepts and tooling that is widely used in the commercial sector. However, large-scale computational science is still the domain of big Fortran applications that run from the command line. To use these applications in a Web service based workflow we need to encapsulate them as services. To accomplish this we use an Application Factory Service [12], which when given a description of an application deployment and execution shell script, automatically generates a web service that can run the application. As illustrated in Figure 7, the service takes as input command-line parameters and the URLs of any needed input files. The service automatically fetches the files and stages

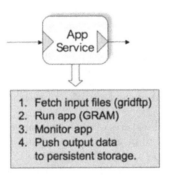

Figure 7. The application services provide a mechanism to execute applications on behalf of the user on remote resources.

them in a subdirectory on the machine where the application is to run. It then uses a remote job execution tool (Globus GRAM [13]) to run and monitor the application. Finally the output files are pushed to the data storage facilities. During the invocation of the service the progress of the data transfers and the monitoring of the application are published as "events" to a message notification bus. The bus relays the messages to listening processes including the user's private application metadata catalog. This allows the user to consult the catalog from the portal to see the status of the execution.

To tie this all together we need to fill out a more complete service oriented archi-tecture (SOA). The portal and workflow composer are only one piece of the system. One important component is the workflow engine. While most e-Science workflow tools also double as the execution engine, the XBaya system is actually a compiler. It can either directly execute the workflow or it can compile a python program which, when run, does the execution, or it can generate a BPEL document. BPEL is the industry standard for web service orchestration and many commercial and open source execution engines exist. The importance of having an execution engine that is separate from the composition tool cannot be understated. Science workflows can take a very long time to execute. This is especially true in the case where a workflow is driven by data from instruments where an event from the instrument may not come for months! The execution engine must be able to retain the state of the workflow in persistent storage so that it can survive substantial system failures. Even the workflow engine may need rebooting. Figure 8 illustrates the parts of the SOA that are directly involved in the execution of the workflows. The only detail of the

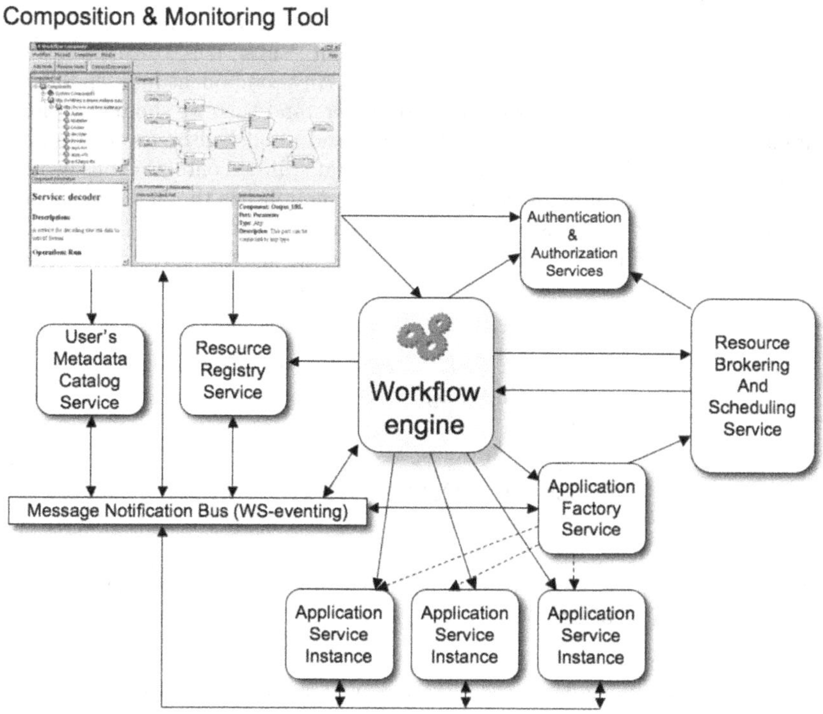

Figure 8. The organization of services in a science gateway PSE.

SOA workflow execution we have not discussed is the process of resource allocation and brokering. When a workflow is composed it is in an abstract form: the specific application services used in the graph are not bound to specific instances of services ready to run the application on specific hosts. The application factory service is responsible for instantiating the application services, but the specific instances are selected by a resource brokering and workflow configuration service. There are many ways to do resource brokering and this topic is far beyond the scope of this paper.

It should also be noted that we have not described the complete picture of the the SOA for an e-Science PSE. A major component not discussed here is the data subsystem. e-Science revolves around data. The workflow system only transforms the data. This topic is treated in another paper in this workshop and elsewhere [14, 15].

5 Event Bus based PSE organization.

There are other approaches to building a PSE programming system that are often overlooked because the dataflow graph model is so intuitive for scientists. Rather than thinking in terms of composing applications as explicit dataflow/control flow graphs, we can consider the possibility of program components that respond to their own environment in productive ways. The concept is based on an information bus as illustrated in Figure 9. In this model a component "subscribes" to messages of some type or "topic" or containing certain content. Any component may "publish" messages on some topics for others to hear. To understand this, we should consider an example. Data from an instrument is gathered and published by an instrument component sitting on the bus. The user inserts data filters onto the bus which captures the data events and transforms them and republishes them. These events are captured by a data analysis component, which publishes results. The results are captured by different rendering tools. This type of system, which resembles a blackboard model [11], is extremely flexible and dynamic.

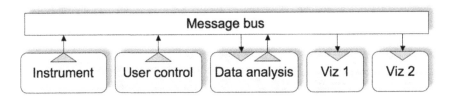

Figure 9. The message bus architecture allow a more dynamic organization than the fixed dataflow model of execution.

This information bus model is the most flexible for integrating user interaction into the system. Future systems will likely contain a combination of bus-based and dataflow approaches.

6 Discussion.

As part of this workshop a series of questions were posed to the authors from other participants. In the spirit of the workshop we will devote our conclusion to a discussion of the points they raised.

- Q1: Anne Trefethen. You mentioned MATLAB as one of the classic PSEs. Have you looked at MATLAB Simulink, SimBiology, or SimEvents, which seem to have the same kind of graphical interface? Have they solved any of the issues you raise?

Yes. These tools all use a graphical interface similar to the ones we have discussed here. There are many more examples. This model of programming is certainly not new. Many domain specific composition tools are able to reduce the complexity of the problem by simplifying the semantic space. SImBiology is an excellent example. However, most of these systems are not designed to operate in the wide area as web service workflow engines. However MATLAB does have support for Web service integration, so it is possible to integrate web services into a MATLAB-based application framework.

- Q2: Tom Jackson. How do you deal with the problem of integrating legacy user code into portals (which are typically non-Java), particularly for visualization?

As discussed in Section 4 of this paper, legacy application integration is accomplished by wrapping the application as a web service. This is a semi-automatic process. In the case of visualization, it is possible to wrap an off-line rendering system as a web service and we have done that. A more complex problem is to invoke a "live" desktop application as part of a workflow. This is a general problem many systems have with inserting a human action into the workflow. The best solution is to combine the dataflow model with the event-bus model described above.

- Q3: Gabrielle Allen. How do you deal with resource allocation and/or resource scheduling in these scenarios?

As mentioned in section 5, resource allocation and scheduling is handled by a "call-out" to a resource allocation service from the workflow configuration service. This use of late binding of the resources with the workflow script allows for very great flexibility. If the workflow engine is also able to catch exceptions and listen to the event notification bus, it is possible to change the resource allocation while the workflow execution is continuing.

- Q4: Tom Jackson. Where you referring to Enterprise Service Bus architectures when you discussed message bus solutions?

Yes. Although Enterprise Service Bus is often associated with a specific technology such as an EJB/JMS solution. However the concept is identical.

- Q5: Gabrielle Allen. What is the difference between event-driven and data-driven architectures, and can you integrate these with a centralized component which allows decision making and control to only need to be implemented in one place?

A workflow or computation can be data-driven and implemented with an event-driven bus framework or with a dataflow framework. There is a big difference between dataflow (as described here) and an event-driven bus. In the case of dataflow the workflow designer implements control based on a graph of dependencies that must be satisfied. Messages from one service are explicitly routed to the graphically connected services. In the even-driven bus case each service can hear all messages and respond to any of them. We control chaos by selecting services that only respond to messages that are of the appropriate topic.

- Q6: Bill Gropp. Have formal methods for verifying correctness been applied to graphical workflows?

Yes and No. There is ample work in the theoretical literature about the semantics and correctness of these graphical models, but we know of no system in use that implements any of these idea in practice.

- Q7. Richard Hanson. Libraries of software routines are well established as a programming model and tool. What do you visualize as an execution model for grid computing and workflows?

In many ways, what we have described here is a way to deploy application software libraries in a distributed context. But there is an important and subtle difference between software components and traditional software libraries. Most software libraries are not well encapsulated: they rely on the runtime environment of the program invoking them and they often operate by side-effecting common data structures. The behavior of component systems is completely defined by the interfaces they present to their clients.

- Q8: (Mo Mu) What do you think is the role of APIs in the composition of workflows as a mechanism/standards to ensure the proper fitting of components/services?

In a Web service oriented system, interfaces are defined by the Web Service Definition Language. This provides a programming language neutral way to describe the messages sent to a service and the types of messages that are returned. Also, Web service systems have evolved considerably from the days of remote procedure calls. The stand now is message oriented, where the message is an XML document defined by an XML schema. The reply is defined similarly. By using WSDL and XML schemas, the services become completely programming language neutral. Services built from Java or C++ or .Net or Perl or Python can all interoperate. This was not possible with programming language based APIs because they all have different type systems.

- Q9 : (Keith Jackson) What role dows semantic information play in a component architecture? What kinds of semantic information should a service expose?

Semantics are critical. Current service models do not provide enough semantics about the content of messages and responses. As discussed above this is one of the greatest challenges to making a truly interoperable system of service components.

- Q10: (Anne Trefethen) How do we get community agreement on the semantics?

This is perhaps the most important question. The first step is to get a community to agree upon an ontology. This is starting to happen in many scientific domains. Once there is a common ontology, one can start defining common scientific metadata. Again this is happening in atmospheric science, oceanography, physics, geology, and many more areas. But there is a long way to go. Once you have a common ontology and common scientific metadata, then wrapping community codes to work as services in general e-Science PSE frameworks is relatively easy.

References

1. S. Wolfram, Mathematica: a system for doing mathematics by computer, 1991, Adison Wesley Co.
2. D. Hanselman, B. Littlefield, Mastering MATLAB 5: A Comprehensive Tutorial and Reference, 1997 - Prentice Hall PTR Upper Saddle River, NJ, USA

3. C. Upson , T. Faulhaber, Jr. , D. Kamins , D. H. Laidlaw, D. Schlegel, J. Vroom, R. Gurwitz, A. van Dam, The Application Visualization System: A Computational Environment for Scientific Visualization, IEEE Computer Graphics and Applications archive Vol. 9 , no. 4, July 1989, pp. 30 - 42

4. S. Parker, C. Johnson, SCIRun: a scientific programming environment for computational steering, Proceedings of the 1995 ACM/IEEE conference on Supercomputing, San Diego, California, United States Article No. 52, 1995.

5. I. Taylor, E. Deelman, D. Gannon, M. Shields (Eds.) , Workflows for e-Science Scientific Workflows for Grids, Springer, 2007.

6. D. Pennington, D. Higgins, A. Townsend Peterson, M. Jones, B. Ludascher, S. Bowers, Ecological Niche Modeling Using the Kepler Workflow System. in Workflows for e-Science Scientific Workflows for Grids, Springer, 2007.

7. T. Oinn, P. Li, D. Kel l, C. Goble, A. Goderis, M. Greenwood, D. Hul l, R. Stevens, D. Turi and J. Z hao, Taverna / myGrid: aligning a workflow system with the life sciences community, in Workflows for e-Science Scientific Workflows for Grids, Springer, 2007.

8. E. Deelman, G. Mehta, G. Singh, M-H. Su, K. Vahi, Pegasus: Mapping Large-Scale Workflows to Distributed Resources, in Workflows for e-Science Scientific Workflows for Grids, Springer, 2007.

9. A.Slominski, Adapting BPEL to Scientific Workflows, in Workflows for e-Science Scientific Workflows for Grids, Springer, 2007.

10. K. Droegemeier, D. Gannon, D. Reed, B. Plale, J. Alameda, T. Baltzer, K. Brewster, R. Clark, B. Domenico, S. Graves, E. Joseph, D. Murray, R. Ramachandran, M. Ramamurthy, L. Ramakkrisshnan, J. Rushing, D. Webeer, R. Wilhelmson, A. Wilson, M. Xue, S. Yalda, Service-Oriented Environments for Dynamically Interacting with Mesoscale Weather, CiSE, Computing in Science & Engineering – November 2005, vol. 7, no. 6, pp. 12-29.

11. B. Plale, D. Gannon, J. Brotzge, K. Droegemeier, J. Kurose, D. McLaughlin, R. Wilhelmson, S. Graves, M. Ramamurthy, R. Clark, S. Yalda, D. Reed, E. Joseph, V. Chandrasekar, CASA and LEAD: Adaptive Cyberinfrastructure for Real-Time Multiscale Weather Forecasting, IEEE Computer, November 2006 (Vol. 39, No. 11) pp. 56-64

12. Gopi Kandaswamy, Dennis Gannon, Liang Fang, Yi Huang, Satoshi Shirasuna, Suresh Marru, Building Web Services for Scientific Applications, IBM Journal of Research and Development, Vol 50, No. 2/3 March/May 2006.

13. I Foster, C Kesselman, Globus: A metacomputing infrastructure toolkit, International Journal of Supercomputer Applications, 1997

14. Y. Simmhan, S. Lee Pallickara, N. Vijayakumar, and B. Plale, Data Management in Dynamic Environment-driven Computational Science, IFIP Working Conference on Grid-Based Problem Solving Environments (WoCo9) August 2006, to appear as Springer-Verlag Lecture Notes in Computer Science (LNCS).

15. Beth Plale, Dennis Gannon, Yi Huang, Gopi Kandaswamy, Sangmi Lee Pallickara, and Aleksander Slominski, Cooperating Services for Data-Driven Computational Experimentation", CiSE, Computing in Science & Engineering – September 2005 vol. 7 issue 5, pp. 34-43

Q&A – Dennis Gannon

Questioner: Anne Trefethen

You mentioned MATLAB as one of the classic PSEs. Have you looked at MATLAB Simulink, SimBiology, or SimEvents, which seem to have the same kind of graphical interface? Have they solved any of the issues you raise?

Dennis Gannon:

For our application domains, MATLAB is not a primary tool, but we do get requests to support it. Part of the problem is MATLAB is not completely Grid friendly. However, it does now support Web Services. Hence it should be possible to integrate MATLAB based tools into Grid workflows.

Questioner: Tom Jackson

How do you deal with the problem of integrating user code into portals (which are typically non-Java), particularly for visualization?

Dennis Gannon:

We have an application service factory that is capable of "wrapping" a command line application and turning it into a Web service. This is described in the talk. However, a big challenge is integrating legacy desktop tools. In some cases it is possible to create a service which listens for an event of a specific type. This service runs on the user's desktop. When the service gets the event, it can fetch data and then launch the legacy application with the data. This allows the tool to exist at the end points of the workflow. The difficulty is putting the legacy desktop application in the critical loops of a workflow. More work needs to be done in this area. It is very important.

Questioner: Tom Jackson

Were you referring to Enterprise Service Bus architectures when you discussed message bus solutions?

Dennis Gannon:

ESB is one solution. However, we prefer a Web services solution and find ws-notification and ws-eventing to be very powerful and general solutions to the message bus.

Questioner: Gabrielle Allen

How do you deal with resource allocation and/or resource scheduling in these scenarios?

Dennis Gannon:

Poorly. However, we are working with the VGrADS project which is focused on scheduling and resource allocation. In general, this is a service that the workflow engine and other services can invoke in advance of execution or on-the-fly.

Questioner: Gabrielle Allen

What is the difference between event-driven and data-driven architectures, and can you integrate these with a centralized component which allows decision making and control to only need to be implemented in one place?

Dennis Gannon:

Event-driven is based on a bus organization where components subscribe to event by type, and publish other events back to the bus. Data-driven are worklfows that behave like dataflow graphs. Data arrives at the source components and the work propagates through the graph. It can be pipelined. Purely event-driven workflows are harder to manage with a central control, while data-driven is manageable by a centralized workflow engine.

Questioner: Bill Gropp

Have formal methods for verifying correctness been applied to graphical workflows?

Dennis Gannon:

There is not much work that I know about on this for e-science workflows but there may be lots of work I am unaware of. One natural place to look is the work that has been done on circuit simulation.

Questioner: Bill Gropp

How do you handle relationships between elements or hierarchy in representation?

Dennis Gannon:

This is a big problem. Many of the legacy applications have complex, interdependent input files. Often a change in one input file to an upstream service may require a change to a downstream service. The only want to handle this is to propagate change information downstream with the other data. It is a hard problem in general.

Why Performance Models Matter for Grid Computing

Ken Kennedy[1]

Rice University `ken@rice.edu`

1 Introduction

Global heterogeneous computing, often referred to as "the Grid" [5, 6], is a popular emerging computing model in which high performance computers linked by high-speed networks are used to solve technical problems that cannot be solved on any single machine. The vision for Grid computing is that these interconnected computers form a global distributed problem-solving system, much as the Internet has become a global information system. However, to achieve this vision for a broad community of scientists and engineers, we will need to build software tools that make the job of constructing Grid programs easy. This is the principle goal of the *Virtual Grid Application Development Software (VGrADS) Project*, an NSF-supported effort involving 11 principal investigators at 7 institutions: Rice, Houston, North Carolina, Tennessee, UCSB, UCSD, and USC Information Sciences Institute.

The eventual goal, shared by most researchers working in the field, is for Grid computing to be transparent. A user should be able to submit a job to the Grid, with the understanding that the Grid software system would find and schedule the appropriate resources and compile and run the job in such a way that the time to completion would be minimized, subject to the user's budget. The current situation is far from that ideal. There exist some simple and useful tools, such as Globus [4], which provides a mechanism for resource discovery and handles distributed job submission, and Condor DAGMan [12], which manages the execution of job workflow structured as a directed acyclic graph (DAG) by scheduling each job step when all its predecessors have been completed. However, the application developer must still do a lot of work by hand. For example, he or she must manage the complexity of heterogeneous resources, schedule computation and data movement (if something more sophisticated than DAGMan is desired), and manage fault tolerance and performance adaptability.

To address these issues, the VGrADS Project is carrying out research on software that separates application development from resource management

Please use the following format when citing this chapter:

Kennedy, K., 2007, in IFIP International Federation for Information Processing, Volume 239, Grid-Based Problem Solving Environments, eds. Gaffney, P. W., Pool, J.C.T., (Boston: Springer), pp. 19-29.

through an abstraction called a "virtual grid." In addition it is exploring tools to bridge the gap between conventional and Grid computation. These include generic scheduling algorithms, resource management tools, mechanisms for transparent distributed launch, simple programming models, mechanisms to incorporate fault tolerance, and strategies for managing the exchange of computation time on different platforms (sometimes called "grid economies").

2 VGrADS Overview

The current research of the VGrADS Project is focused on two major themes: virtualization of Grid resources and generic in-advance scheduling of application workflows. In this section we describe these two themes in more detail.

2.1 Virtualization

The key motivation behind virtualization within the VGrADS software stack is that, eventually, the Grid will consist of hundreds of thousands, or even millions, of heterogeneous computing resources interconnected with network links of differing speeds. In addition, these resources may be configured through software to provide a variety of specialized services. For an end user, or even an application scheduler, the task of sorting through such a huge resource base to find the best match to application needs will be nearly intractable. To simplify this task, the VGrADS *Virtual Grid Execution System (vgES)* provides an abstract interface called the *Virtual Grid Definition Language (vgDL)*, that permits the application to specify, in simple terms, what kinds of resources are needed. Specifications in this language are quite high level. For example, an application might say "give me a loose bag of 1000 processors, each with at least one gigabyte of memory, and with the fastest possible processors" or "give me a tight bag of as many AMD Opteron processors as possible." Here the distinction between a "loose bag" and "tight bag" is qualitative: a loose bag has substantively lower interconnection bandwidth than a tight bag. The user can also specify a "cluster" of processors, which means that all processors have to be in the same physical machine, interconnected at extremely high bandwidths.

In response to a query of this sort, the vgES does a fast search of a database of global resources and produces one or more configurations, or *virtual grids*, that best match the specification. This search can be thought of as a first step in a two-step resource allocation and scheduling procedure. The second step applies a more complex scheduling algorithm, as described in the next section, to the returned virtual grid. VGrADS experiments have shown that this approach produces application schedules that are nearly as good those produced by complex global algorithms, at a tiny fraction of the scheduling cost [7, 15].

In addition to resource screening, the vgES provides many other services, including job launch and support for fault tolerance, but this paper will not further discuss these facilities.

2.2 Scheduling

Most Grid problems are formulated as *workflows*, directed acyclic graphs (DAGs) in which the vertices represent job steps and the edges represent data transfers (or dependencies). As described in Section 1, Condor DAGMan and other Grid scheduling mechanisms map a particular step onto available resources only when all of its input data sets are ready. In contrast, in-advance, or off-line, scheduling looks at the entire workflow before the job begins to ensure that each step is assigned to a resource that is able to execute it efficiently, while keeping the data transfer times between steps to a minimum. This approach has many advantages over demand scheduling. First, it should do a better job of matching resources to computations by exploring the space of possible assignments in advance, rather than just using whatever is available when a step is ready to execute. Second, it streamlines the data movement process and reduces delays between computations because, at the end of each step, we already know where the data needs to be sent and no inter-step scheduling is necessary. Finally, as we will see in Section 4.2, it makes it possible to incorporate estimated batch queue waiting times into the schedule as extra delays between job steps. Our experiments have shown that off-line scheduling can produce dramatically better workflow completion times, in many cases by factors greater than 2, than dynamic approaches [2, 9].

On the other hand, there is a major impediment to the use of any off-line scheduling algorithm: to do a good job, it must have accurate performance models for each job step in the workflow. A performance model is needed estimate the time for a step to complete as a function of the size of the input data sets and the nature of the computing platform on which it is executed. In an off-line scheduler, performance models serve as surrogates for the actual execution times of different job steps. Dynamic scheduling schemes do not need such models because steps are scheduled only when all predecessor steps have completed. Thus, the actual execution time of a step is its performance model.

The need for performance models is a real problem because accurate models are notoriously difficult to construct. Furthermore, our experiments demonstrate that inaccurate performance models lead to bad schedules [9]. The goal of the VGrADS Project is to make Grid programming *easier* rather than more difficult, so requiring that the developer construct performance models by hand is out of the question. To address this issue, VGrADS researchers are exploring new methods for automatic construction of accurate performance models. This work, which produces remarkably accurate models for uniprocessor performance will be discussed in Section 3.

Since the scheduling problem for DAGs is NP-complete, VGrADS uses heuristics to schedule workflows onto virtual grids. Each of the heuristics employs an affinity matrix that is constructed by using performance models to estimate how efficiently each job step will run on each resource. Data transfer times between resources are estimated as data volumes divided by average bandwidths from the Network Weather Service [14]. From these inputs, the actual mapping can be computed using one of two different kinds of heuristic scheduling algorithms. A *level-based scheduler* operates by moving from the start of a workflow forward, considering at each stage all the computation steps that are ready to execute after the previous echelon of compute steps finishes. At a given stage, the scheduler maps each job step to the best available resource, where "best" is determined by a heuristic measure. For example, it might pick the resources that minimize the maximum completion time of steps in the echelon, the so-called *min-max* strategy. Currently, the standard VGrADS strategy is level-based, but it uses three different heuristic measures and picks the shortest of the three resulting schedules [9].

The alternative *critical path* scheduling strategy is similar to list scheduling: it picks the next step to be scheduled by some heuristic measure based on time from the start of the workflow or time to completion of the workflow. This has the advantage of starting workflow steps when they are ready, instead of waiting until all steps in the previous echelon have completed. Our experiments show that critical path heuristics are usually better than level-based approaches and we plan to switch the standard scheduler to use one of these in the near future.

Because VGrADS scheduling algorithms are applied to the virtual grids returned by the vgES, which are limited to sizes approximating what the user needs rather than the space of total resources, the scheduling times are reasonable, even for complex scheduling heuristics, such as the ones described above, that are quadratic or worse in the number of resources.

3 Construction of Performance Models

Given that most of the applications of interest to the VGrADS project consist of workflows in which each computational step is executed on a single processor, our research on construction of performance models has focused on accurate, and non-intrusive ways, to model performance on modern commodity processors.

The base strategy of the VGrADS-supported performance model construction research, due to John Mellor-Crummey and his student Gabriel Marin [10], uses instrumentation of application binaries to determine the memory hierarchy behavior of each data reference in a program. Based on trial runs with a few data sets, the approach constructs, for each static memory reference in a program, a histogram of the number of different cache lines touched since the last touch of the referenced cache line: this quantity is often

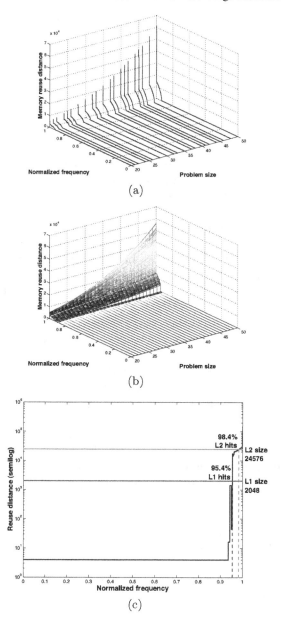

Fig. 1. (a) Reuse distance data collected for one reference in the application Sweep3D; (b) Final model for the data in (a); (c) Model evaluation at problem size 70 on a logarithmic y axis, and predictions for a 2048-block level 1 cache and 24576-block level 2 cache. (Figure reprinted with permission from a paper by Marin and Mellor-Crummey [11].)

called *reuse distance*. The reuse distance histogram, depicted in Figure 1(a), is parameterized by the size of the input data set and the percentage of the time that the reuse distance achieves this value. For most array references, the reuse distance will be a small constant most of the time, but it may be linear in the data set size in some cases and occasionally non-linear in data set size. This is because a static reference that touches to the next element in an array column (constant reuse distance) most of the time can also refer to the first element in a column (linear reuse distance) or even the first element referenced in the array (non-linear reuse distance).

From the data histogram for each reference, a model is constructed by fitting curves to the different regions of the histogram (constant distance, linear distance, quadratic distance, etc.), as depicted in Figure 1(b). From these models, which are machine-independent, we can compute the memory hierarchy delays for a given cache size and data set size by examining where the plane for a given cache size intersects the model (see Figure 1(c)), determining the number of misses above the plane, and multiplying by the miss penalty for that level of cache. This must be done for each reference and each level in the memory hierarchy. The result is the aggregate miss penalty for a given memory hierarchy.

The remainder of the execution costs can be estimated by carrying out a speculative scheduling exercise for the loops in the program with the specific machine's delays. Here we can assume that all data is found in cache, because miss penalties are accounted for in the memory-hierarchy analysis.

This strategy has proved extremely accurate in practice and has been used in VGrADS to estimate the performance of individual computations in the EMAN application [8].

In the future, we hope to extend this methodology to more complex computations that can be carried out on tightly-coupled multiprocessors. Of course there are a number of other approaches to performance estimation and modeling available in the literature and individual applications may come with such models already built in.

4 Value of Performance Models

In addition to being an integral part of the VGrADS scheduling methodology, performance models have many other important roles to play in the Grid. In this section we review several applications that are the focus of new work in VGrADS.

4.1 Grid Economy and Global Resource Utilization

It is fair to say that we will not be able to deploy a truly global Grid until we can establish exchange agreements and exchange rates among different types of computing resources. Success will depend on maintaining floating exchange rates that permit machine cycles on one platform to be exchanged for cycles on another. These rates could be established by estimate, then adjusted through experience: As different applications are run on different resources, we could collect data on relative performance and adjust the exchange rate accordingly. I will not elaborate further on how such a process might work, because that is the subject of substantive ongoing research. However, suffice it to say that the exchange rates at any given moment accurately reflect the recent average relative performance of a wide variety of applications.

Because an established exchange rate represents *average* relative performance over many applications, accurate performance models can be used to procure the most cost-effective computation for a *particular* application. For example, suppose that the exchange rate indicates that, over all applications, processor X is worth about twice as much as processor Y at the same clock frequency. However, the performance models for application A indicates that A will run three times as fast on X as on Y. In that case, it is always more economical to run A on processor X. To put it another way, if A is perfectly partitionable, it will need three times as many of processor Y to get the same work done in the same time. Thus, if A can be done in an hour with n of processor X, but only $n - k$ are available, it will need $3k$ of processor Y if it is still to finish in an hour. Given that the total cost is $(n - k)r_X + 3kr_Y$, where r_X is the cost in dollars per hour of time on processor X, r_Y is the cost per hour of processor Y and $r_X = 2r_Y$, the total cost for a run with $n - k$ of processor X and k of processor Y is:

$$2(n - k)r_Y + 3kr_Y = (2n + k)r_Y \tag{1}$$

Since this increases linearly with k, it is always best to use as few of processor Y as possible.

The important observation is this: If every application has its own performance model, it can use this model to select the most cost effective resources for its execution. If all applications do this and the exchange rate is set to correctly reflect the mix of applications, this strategy will have the beneficial effect of optimizing the utilization of global Grid resources. Of course, for this to happen, the exchange rate will need to be continually adjusted as the application mix evolves.

4.2 Scheduling around Batch Queues

If the Grid is to be truly universal, it will need to incorporate machines, like those in the NSF TeraGrid, that are scheduled via batch queues. This presents a new problem for global application schedulers: how to predict and account for delays that are incurred waiting in batch queues. The VGrADS project has developed a capability to predict batch queue wait times by using statistical methods applied to queue histories [3]. This has been used to schedule Grid workflows by adding wait times to data transfer times in the scheduling algorithm [13].

The problem with the VGrADS approach described above is that the time spent waiting in batch queues is essentially wasted. If the batch queue systems supported *resource reservations*, in which a time slot could be reserved in advance, then the scheduler might be able to predict when these slots would be needed and reserve them at scheduling time, thus eliminating batch queue delays. In the absence of explicit reservations, such a facility might be simulated by using estimates of batch queue waiting times to put jobs in the queue far enough in advance to reach the front of the queue by the time the data for a given job step arrives. In its most recent research, the VGrADS project has been experimenting with both of these approaches.

The use of resource reservations for specific time slots presents another problem, namely how to determine the required slot reservation times. If a slot is allocated before the input data for the associated job step arrives, costly resources will be wasted. On the other hand, if the data arrives before the slot is available, completion of the workflow will be delayed. In order to accurately estimate when a slot is needed for a particular job step without knowing which resources will be assigned to the workflow by the vgES, the scheduler must have some way to normalize the time used every step in the workflow.

To address this problem, VGrADS is introducing vgDL queries that support equivalences between different resource types. A query with equivalence might take the form: "Give me the equivalent of 1000 processors of type X using a mixture of X and Y, where $X = 3Y$ for this application step." Such a request allows us to normalize the time for a particular job step by asking for enough processors of each available type so that the step can finish in a predetermined time. Using these equivalences should dramatically reduce the variance in the scheduled time for any given job step and hence increase the reliability of a request for a specific time slot, independent of the type of machine on which that time slot and others before it are allocated.

Of course, accurate performance models are what makes it possible to generate accurate equivalences of the sort described above.

4.3 Scheduling to a Deadline

In a recent collaboration with the *Linked Environmental and Atmospheric Discovery (LEAD) Project*, the VGrADS team has been exploring how to schedule application workflows to a deadline. LEAD performs mesoscale weather analysis and prediction, needed to track tornados and hurricanes, using inputs from adjustable Doppler radars. The LEAD workflow is executed repetitively and, after each workflow iteration, which involves both data integration and simulation, the outputs are used to adjust the orientation of the Doppler radars prior to running another iteration. Thus the deadlines are essential to maintaining the accuracy of storm tracking.

Deadlines present another issue for scheduling: How many resources of what size do we need to meet the deadline with a high degree of confidence?

Performance models can help answer this question through a process of iterative scheduling. The idea is to perform a first scheduling pass by requesting an initial set of resources and scheduling onto these resources. If the schedule completes before the deadline, we are done. If not, we can use a strategy called *automatic differentiation* [1], to compute sensitivities of the performance models for the computationally intensive steps to resource sizes. We can then use these derivatives to predict the resource set sizes needed to reduce the workflow running time by enough to meet the deadline.

In some cases, it may not be possible to meet the deadline, no matter how many resources are used. For LEAD, an alternative is to reduce the computation done in some of the steps, as a less accurate computation performed on time may still be adequate to reorient the radars accurately enough for the next cycle. Performance models are useful in this case as well, because they can help determine when the deadline is effectively unreachable.

If performance models have the capability of generating estimated variance in addition to estimated running time, the scheduler can increase the robustness of the schedule by putting more resources along the critical and near-critical paths of high aggregate variance, thus increasing the likelihood of meeting the deadline, though at a somewhat higher cost.

5 Summary and Conclusions

The Virtual Grid Application Development (VGrADS) Project has adopted a strategy for generic, off-line scheduling of application workflows that mandates the use of accurate performance models. Although performance models can be constructed by hand, this is a labor-intensive and error-prone process. Therefore, VGrADS is exploring methodologies for automatically constructing such performance models from trial runs and inspection of the application itself, typically through binary analysis.

Once good performance models are available, they can be used for a variety of other problems, including scheduling around batch queues and scheduling to deadlines. In addition, accurate application performance models can be used to increase the efficiency with which collections of applications use global Grid resources by mapping computations to the most cost-effective computing platforms within the Grid economy.

In summary, the construction and use of application performance models can help make the global Grid into an efficient system for general problem solving, because they allow for the accurate accounting of costs across diverse computing engines.

6 Acknowledgements

The VGrADS Project owes its success to a talented group of principle investigators who have developed its vision and supervised its implementation.

In addition to the author, these include: Keith Cooper, Charles Koelbel, and Linda Torczon (Rice), Rich Wolski (UCSB), Fran Berman, Henri Cassanova, and Andrew Chien (UCSD), Lennart Johnsson (Houston), Dan Reed (UNC RENCI), Karl Kesselman (USC Information Sciences Institute), and Jack Dongarra (Tennessee, Knoxville). John Mellor Crummey of Rice, though not an official PI, has directed the effort on performance model construction. In addition many graduate students and research staff members have contributed to the ideas and implementation.

The VGrADS Project has been supported by the National Science Foundation under Cooperative Agreement CCR-0331654 and Grant No. ACI0103759 (the GrADS Project). I would like to thank our NSF Program Managers, Frederica Darema, Kamal Abdali, Mike Foster, and Almadena Chtchelkanova for their support and encouragement.

Finally I would thank our collaborators, Wah Chiu and Steve Ludtke of the National Center for Macromolecular Imaging at Baylor College of Medicine, which maintains the EMAN application, and Kelvin Droegemeier, Dennis Gannon, and Bob Wilhelmson of the LEAD Project for their contributions to VGrADS research.

References

1. C. H. Bischof, P. Khademi, A. Mauer, and A. Carle. ADIFOR 2.0 — automatic differentiation of Fortran 77 programs. *IEEE Computational Science and Engineering*, 3(3):18–32, 1996.
2. J. Blythe, S. Jain, E. Deelman, Y. Gil, K. Vahi, A. Mandal, and K. Kennedy. Task scheduling strategies for workflow-based applications in grids. In *IEEE International Symposium on Cluster Computing and the Grid (CCGrid 2005)*. IEEE Press, 2005.
3. J. Brevik, D. Nurmi, and R. Wolski. Predicting bounds on queuing delay for batch-scheduled parallel machines. In *Proceedings of PPoPP 2006*, March 2006.
4. I. Foster and C. Kesselman. Globus: A metacomputing infrastructure toolkit. *International Journal of Supercomputer Applications*, 1997.
5. I. Foster and C. Kesselman. *The Grid: Blueprint for a New Computing Infrastructure*. Morgan Kaufmann Publishers, Inc., 1999.
6. I. Foster and C. Kesselman. *The Grid 2*. Morgan Kaufmann Publishers, Inc., 2003.
7. Y.-S. Kee, D. Logothetis, R. Huang, H. Casanova, and A. Chien. Efficient resource description and high quality selection for virtual grids. In *Proceedings of the 5th IEEE Symposium on Cluster Computing and the Grid (CCGrid'05)*, *Cardiff, U.K.*, May 2005.
8. S. Ludtke, P. Baldwin, and W. Chiu. EMAN: Semiautomated software for high resolution single-particle reconstructions. *J. Struct. Biol*, (128):82–97, 1999.
9. A. Mandal, K. Kennedy, C. Koelbel, G. Marin, J. Mellor-Crummey, B. Liu, and L. Johnsson. Scheduling strategies for mapping application workflows onto the grid. In *14-th IEEE Symposium on High Performance Distributed Computing (HPDC14)*, pages 125–134, 2005.

10. Gabriel Marin and John Mellor-Crummey. Cross architecture performance predictions for scientific applications using parameterized models. In *Proceedings of the Joint International Conference on Measurement and Modeling of Computer Systems*, June 2004.

11. Gabriel Marin and John Mellor-Crummey. Scalable cross-architecture predictions of memory hierarchy response for scientific applications. In *Proceedings of the Los Alamos Computer Science Institute Sixth Annual Symposium*, Santa Fe, NM, October 2005.

12. M. Mika, G.Waligora, and J.Weglarz. *Grid Resource Management: State of the Art and Future Trends*. Kluwer Academic Publishers, 2003.

13. Daniel Nurmi, Anirban Mandal, John Brevik, Rich Wolski, Charles Koelbel, and Ken Kennedy. Evaluation of a workflow scheduler using integrated performance modelling and batch queue wait time prediction. In *Proceedings of SC'06*, Tampa, FL, November 2006.

14. R. Wolski. Dynamically forecasting network performance to support dynamic scheduling using the network weather service. In *Proceedings 6th IEEE Symposium on High Performance Distributed Computing*, August 1997.

15. Yang Zhang, Anirban Mandal, Henri Casanova, Andrew Chien, Yang-Suk Kee, Ken Kennedy, and Charles Koelbel. Scalable Grid application scheduling via decoupled resource selection and scheduling. In *Proceedings of the 6th IEEE Symposium on Cluster Computing and the Grid (CCGrid'06)*, May 2006.

Q&A – Ken Kennedy

Questioner: David Walker

How can you apply performance models when the grid resources are shared with other users?

Ken Kennedy:

Much of the VGrADS research was done assuming that individual compute nodes in the Grid would be devoted to a single process. However, for many resource environments, this is unrealistic. In VGrADs, we hypothesized, and verified experimentally, that if a compute node is partially loaded to a fraction of x, the running time predicted by the performance model must be scaled by a factor of 1/x. If the load varies dramatically, of course, this simple correction will be inaccurate, which is one of the difficulties of optimizing in a highly dynamic environment.

Questioner: Gabrielle Allen

How could this system change to support applications which are hard to profile a priori, for example, applications modeling chaotic and nonlinear phenomena, or complex application systems able to dynamically invoke new libraries, etc?

Ken Kennedy:

It is true that, for some applications, performance will be difficult to predict a priori. (However, irregular scientific applications do yield reasonable predictions in our system.) Our GridSAT application has this characteristic. For workflows in which such an application is a step, we may want to employ a hybrid dynamic/ static scheduling strategy. This illustrates that there *are* situations in which the advantages of dynamic scheduling win out.

Questioner: Suman Nadella

How does VGrAds' "offline scheduling to meet deadlines" compare or contrast with priority scheduling such as the SPRUCE system in case of applications such as LEAD?

Ken Kennedy:

Although I was not familiar with SPRUCE until this meeting, I discussed it with the questioner after the meeting. From that discussion, I believe that the strategies are complementary. We have been working under the assumption that, in many cases, the applications we would be scheduling (including LEAD) would not, except in special cases, be able to command very high priorities. However, such a capability would be very useful in emergency situations. It could also be used to provide more reliable resource reservations within the VGrADS scheme.

Questioner: Xiaoge Wang

How do you model the network data transfer rate? Is it more complicated than memory hierarchy?

Ken Kennedy:

Right now, we are using a very rough model. We use services like Network Weather Service to estimate the instantaneous bandwidth between resources involved in a data transfer and divide bandwidth into data volume (adding latency) to estimate data transfer time. Of course, when loads vary dramatically, this can lead to inaccuracy. So far these have not been very troublesome.

Questioner: Xiaoge Wang

What if the resource provider could commit the resources and support the resource reservations? Will the performance prediction be more realistic and accurate?

Ken Kennedy:

Eventually, I think all providers will support resource reservations on a priority system. It may be the case that a request for reservations will fail, in which case our scheduling system will need to look elsewhere. With resource reservations, the scheduling should be more reliably accurate.

Questioner: Bill Applebe

In a grid economy, a lot of incentives can be given to reward accurate manual estimation of resources (e.g., do not schedule jobs without resource (time) estimate, or otherwise punish bad estimates). How can manual and automatic estimates be combined?

Ken Kennedy:

I believe that automatic estimates can replace manual estimates, but for the purpose of Bill's question, we may want to use very conservative estimates, as described in the next section. In other words, the estimates should be at the 95th percentile, or above, of assurance if you could be kicked off because of going over time.

Questioner: Bill Gropp

Should distributions or intervals be used instead of single numbers in the performance estimates, particularly given the uncertainties in the performance of applications and resources?

Ken Kennedy:

Absolutely. In fact you may wish to use different functions of the performance estimation distributions in different situations. For example, to minimize expected run time, you should use expectation. However, to ensure meeting a deadline, you may wish to use the 80th, 90th, or 95th percentile, based on an analysis of the criticality of meeting the deadline.

An interesting problem is that the estimates annotate nodes and edges of the workflow DAG. This raises the interesting question about how to compute the distribution of the makespan, given the distributions on the nodes and edges. As it happens, in a study I was involved with in the 1970s, it may be necessary to use empirical methods to approximate the aggregate distributions.

Questioner: Boyanna Norris

How extensible is the HPC Toolkit, i.e., can third-party tools operate on the architecture-independent performance models before they are mapped to a particular architecture by the scheduler?

Ken Kennedy:

This is a research project, so it may lack the robustness of a commercial system. However, the code is distributed with an open-source license, and the architecture-neutral description is encapsulated in a way that would permit it to be operated on.

Automation of Network-Based Scientific Workflows

M. A. Vouk[1], I. Altintas[2], R. Barreto[3], J. Blondin[4], Z.Cheng[1], T. Critchlow[5], A. Khan[6], S. Klasky[3], J. Ligon[1], B. Ludaescher[7], P. A. Mouallem[1], S. Parker[6], N. Podhorszki[7], A. Shoshani[8], C. Silva[6]

[1]Department of Computer Science, North Carolina State University, Box 8206, Raleigh, NC 27695, USA, {vouk, zcheng, jtligon, pmouall}@ncsu.edu
[2]San Diego Supercomputing Center, University of California, La Jolla, CA 92093, USA, altintas@sdsc.edu
[3]Oak Ridge National Laboratory, PO BOX 2008, MS6008, Oak Ridge, TN 37831, USA, {barreto, klasky }@ornl.gov
[4]Department of Physics, North Carolina State University, Box 8202, Raleigh, NC 27695, USA, John_Blondin@ncsu.edu
[5]Center for Applied Scientific Computing, Lawrence Livermore National Laboratory, Livermore, CA 94550, USA, critchlow1@llnl.gov
[6]Department of Computer Science, University of Utah, Salt Lake City, UT 84112, USA, {ayla, sparker,csilva }@cs.utah.edu
[7]Department of Computer Science, University of California Davis, Davis, CA 95616, USA {ludaesch, pnorbert}@ucdavis.edu
[8]Computing Research Division, Lawrence Berkeley National Laboratory, Berkeley, CA 94720, USA, shoshani@lbl.gov

Abstract. Comprehensive, end-to-end, data and workflow management solutions are needed to handle the increasing complexity of processes and data volumes associated with modern distributed scientific problem solving, such as ultra-scale simulations and high-throughput experiments. The key to the solution is an integrated network-based framework that is functional, dependable, fault-tolerant, and supports data and process provenance. Such a framework needs to make development and use of application workflows dramatically easier so that scientists' efforts can shift away from data management and utility software development to scientific research and discovery. An integrated view of these activities is provided by the notion of scientific workflows - a series of structured activities and computations that arise in scientific problem-solving. An information technology framework that supports scientific workflows is the Ptolemy II based environment called Kepler. This paper discusses the issues associated with practical automation of scientific processes and workflows and illustrates this with workflows developed using the Kepler framework and tools.

Please use the following format when citing this chapter:

Vouk, M. A., Altintas, I., Barreto, R., Blondin, J., Cheng, Z., Critchlow, T., Khan, A., Klasky, S., Ligon, J., Ludaescher, B., Mouallem, P. A., Parker, S., Podhorszki, N., Shoshani, A., Silva, C., 2007, in IFIP International Federation for Information Processing, Volume 239, Grid-Based Problem Solving Environments, eds. Gaffney, P. W., Pool, J.C.T., (Boston: Springer), pp. 35-61.

1   Introduction

Scientific research is exploratory in nature. Scientists carry out experiments, often in a trial and error manner, and they modify the steps of the tasks performed as exploration proceeds. As technology advances, more and more scientists are relying on computing systems to aide them in this process. In fact, some of the heaviest users of computing are in the sciences, and often it is no longer possible for scientists to carry out their day-to-day activities without heavy use of computing. This holds in the fields and problem areas as diverse as computational medicine, biology, chemistry, genetics, environment, fusion and combustion.

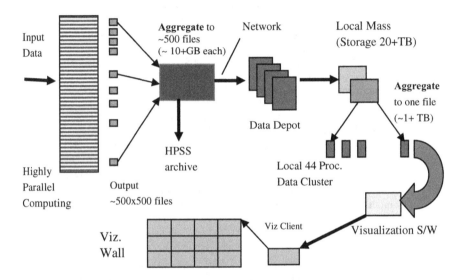

Fig. 1. Illustration of an astrophysics simulation workflow. Computations are done at a remote supercomputer, and the resulting data sets are transferred to NC State University via a high-speed internet link. This is followed by local "slicing and dicing" of the data, and their analysis and visualization.

We use the term *scientific workflow* to describe a series of structured activities and computations (we call them workflow components or *actors[1]*) that arise in scientific research and problem-solving process [11]. A scientist may divide the overall task into smaller sub-tasks, each of which can be considered to be an individual step in an experiment or a simulation. At each step, the results can be

---

[1] The term "actor" is the one used in the Kepler [2] workflow support system based on Ptolemy II framework [12] to describe process components interconnected by data flows and orchestrated by a "director" or a workflow control process. In general, a process oriented network can be described using generalized activity networks [13]. Activity oriented networks have nodes interconnected by data flows and their graph-based depictions are sometimes called actigrams, while data-oriented networks have data nodes interconnected by data transforming activity links and their graph-based depictions are sometimes called datagrams (not to be confused with internet protocol datagrams).

generated, managed, analyzed, stored, or otherwise processed, and then used as an input to the next step in the process. Such reuse of data can be done repeatedly until the overall task is completed to scientist's satisfaction. We use the term "workflow" to describe the chaining of smaller tasks to achieve the desired results using data from different source in combination with different transformation, analysis and visualization services, [1, 11]. Today, many – often all – of the steps involve support from or interaction with information technology. Scientific workflow includes actions performed (by actors), decisions made (control-flow), information transferred (data-flow), exception and interrupt handling (e.g., event-flows) and the underlying coordination and scheduling required to execute a workflow (orchestration). In its simplest case, a workflow is a linear sequence of tasks, each one implemented by an actor.

An example of a workflow is: a) transfer of executable simulation application code and computational and storage configuration information to a cluster or a high-performance computer, b) running of this application, and c) transferring of the results to a remote machines for further analysis and visualization. Figure 1 illustrates such a workflow.

Comprehensive end-to-end data and workflow management solutions are needed to handle the increasing complexity of processes and data volumes associated with modern distributed scientific problem solving, such as ultra-scale simulations and high-throughput experiments. The key to the solution is an integrated network-based framework that is functional, dependable, fault-tolerant, and supports data and process provenance. Such a framework needs to make application workflows dramatically easier to develop and use [36] so that scientists' efforts can shift away from data management and application development to scientific research and discovery. A Ptolemy II based environment called Kepler [2] is one such framework.

This paper discusses the issues associated with practical automation of scientific processes and workflows and illustrates this through workflows developed using the Kepler framework and tools.

2   Workflows

Workflow technologies have a long history in the databases and information systems communities [1]. Scientific community has developed a number of problem-solving environments, most of them as integrated solutions [24 and references there in]. However, more recently component-based solution support systems have become more popular [e.g., 14, 25, 26, 29, 30]. Scientific workflows merge advances in all these areas to automate support for sophisticated scientific information technology assisted exploration and problem-solving [e.g., 2 – 11, 46, 55, 61].

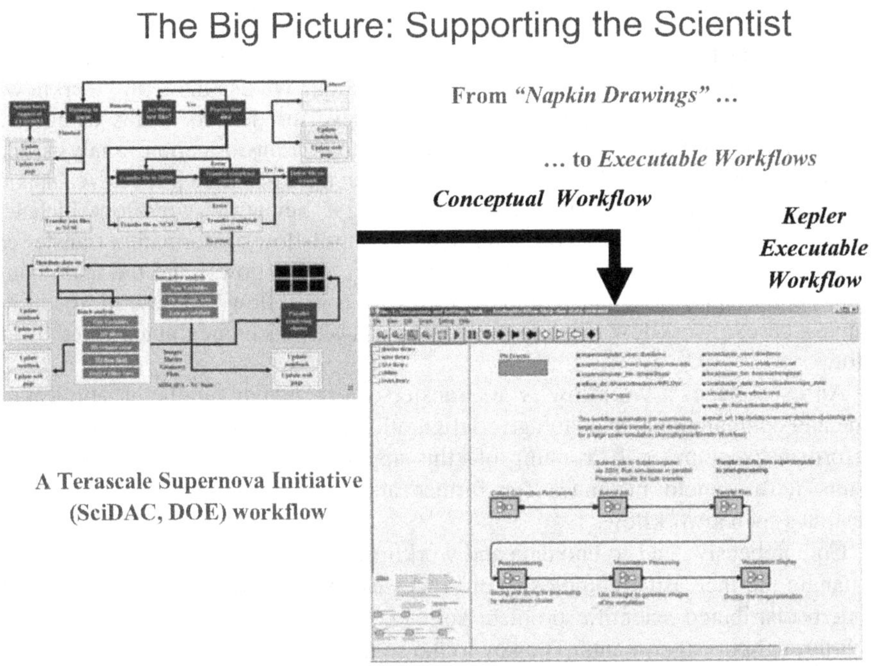

The Big Picture: Supporting the Scientist

Fig. 2. From a "napkin drawing" to an executable Kepler-based workflow.

Scientific workflows, as we understand them, are crucial to the success of major initiatives in high-performance computing. As parallel computing expands, their standards encourage scientists to construct complex distributed solutions that span the networks, and through web-based interfaces and virtualization invite incorporation into still more complex systems that may include interactions with economic and business flows. Workflows provide the necessary abstractions that enable effective usage of computational resources, and development of robust problem-solving environments that marshal high-performance computing resources.

Workflows have many synergies with web and network-based services. In fact, (web) service based workflows are quickly becoming a requirement of a wide range of new service-oriented applications. Many domain experts, particularly in life sciences, do not wish to construct workflows by coding them beyond what is necessary to do research in their domain, e.g., to develop appropriate algorithms. They would like to considerably reduce the overhead currently required by some information technology solutions. That overhead can be as much a 50% of the activity. Therefore, workflow automation and higher-level specification fits naturally into the trends towards increased domain specialization as application developers move to become (web) services providers, and computer scientists seek reusable libraries and tools, rather than custom made applications.

Of course, workflows such as the one shown in Figure 1 have much more depth and structure than shown in the Figure 1 diagram. Often they can be naturally mapped onto graph representations, e.g., [13, 30]. Typically, a scientist would like to go from a conceptual "napkin drawing" of a workflow to an executable version of it with as little overhead from the information technology tools and solutions as possible (Figure 2). Sometimes the best way to manage complexity of such structures is to nest the graphs (e.g., Figure 3). A graph can then be translated into executable form either manually or automatically. However, the process can be a reverse one – the code and some process scripts for an, in part, manually assisted workflow already exists, and the workflow technology is used to integrate these elements. In either case, it is beneficial to keep a high level graph representation of a workflow so that end-users can better understand and modify application logic.

An Astrophysics Workflow (using Kepler framework)

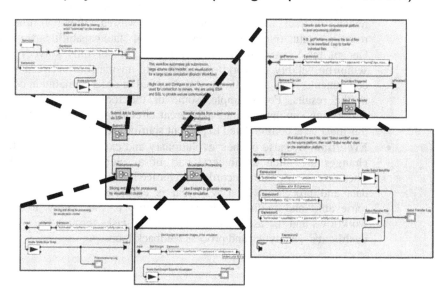

Fig. 3. Nesting can help manage complexity of workflows.

Scientific workflows can exhibit and exploit data-, task-, and pipeline-parallelism. In science and engineering workflow processes, tasks and computations are often large-scale, complex, and structured with intricate dependencies [7, 13, 14]. Information technology assisted scientific workflows have several common characteristics:

- **Composition**. Scientific workflows require invocation, interconnection and integration of multiple data collection, simulation, application or **analysis** elements, i.e., methods, approaches, tools and processes. While these elements are often invoked in a routine manner, there may also be changes in the workflow as scientists interactively explore new options. Developing an executable workflow requires resolving mismatches between what an element expects and what the previous step in the process generated.
- **Diversity**. Scientific workflows require significant **heterogeneous**, computational, storage and networking **resources**. Many large-scale

scientific workflows will execute for hours, often days, perhaps weeks and months, and may require user intervention at multiple times. If the workflow, or one of the associated computations or activities runs into trouble, **fault-tolerant behavior**, e.g., via human intervention or perhaps automated failover or recovery techniques must be attempted because returning to the initial starting point is usually not acceptable.

- **Verification and validation** of processes as well as intermediate and final results is essential in the domain of scientific problem solving. This ensures integrity of the data, processes and results, that the activity as a whole remains on track, and that resources are not wasted. Often real-time or near-real-time status tracking and preservation of state capabilities are required. One of the most difficult (and currently not yet fully solved) issues is **semantic** validity of workflows. Semantic mismatches between workflow components, tools and data must be handled in order to maintain confidence in the results. For example, some of the tools may be designed for performing simulations under different circumstances or assumptions, and this must be accommodated to prevent spurious results.

- **Evolution**. Because of their evolutionary and exploratory nature, **frequent changes** are often an integral part of a scientific workflow lifecycle. Therefore, is critical to record **provenance** information (e.g., the lineage of data and processes) in a way that is consistent, persistent, and easily retrievable and auditable. Related to this is the ability to **steer** the workflows and the associated computational tasks through use of run-time **dashboards**, analytics and process feedback loops.

3   Overhead

In the 21st century, a key differentiating characteristic of a successful information technology (IT) is its ability to become true and valuable contributor to cyberinfrastructure. Cyberinfrastructure [36] makes IT systems, applications and services dramatically easier to develop, deploy and use. This expands the scope of applications and services possible within budget and organizational constraints. It also increases efficiency, quality, and reliability by capturing commonalities and by facilitating efficient sharing of resources and services. Ultimately, cyberinfrastructure shifts the effort away from IT (overhead) concentrating it on the basic end-user mission and business.

Appropriate cyberinfrastructure is especially important for any business that in large part relies on IT to conduct its daily operations. Today, this is true of many financial, educational, research, government and retail organizations. From the perspective of an end-user IT must be enabling and appliance-like. End-users should be able to use the technology to improve their productivity and reduce technology-driven overhead, e.g., software installation or management. For example, unless IT is the primary business of an organization or an individual, less than 20% of its effort not directly connected to its primary business should have to do with IT issues, even though 80% of its business may be conducted using electronic means. In general, infrastructure installation and maintenance overhead must have the property of the economy-of-scale at all levels – hardware, software, provisioning, maintenance, etc.

A powerful cyberinfrastructure enabling concept is utility-computing through service-oriented architectures (SOA) [e.g., 50]. An SOA is an environment where end-users can request an IT service at the desired functional, quality and capacity level, and receive it either at the time requested or at a specified later time. A key enabler of SOA is component-based construction of services. Another key supporting technology is virtualization of IT resources and services. It is expected that in the next 10 years, service-based solutions will be a major vehicle for delivery of information and other IT assisted functions at both individual and organizational levels, e.g., software applications, web-based services, even personal and business "desktops" computing.

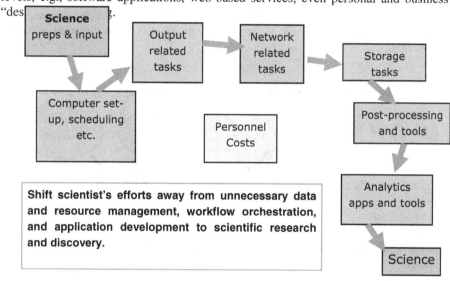

Fig. 4. A typical scientist is primarily interested in preparation of inputs and codes (green areas) related to his/her specific research domain and in doing "science," i.e., discovery. There is much less interest in tending computers, moving data or developing peripheral IT applications (orange areas).

Scientific computing is no different in this respect. Today a scientist involved with a large-scale scientific workflow, e.g., of the peta-scale class of problems, may spend a lot of time dealing with IT related activities they need, but often wish they did not have to do [37]. For example, a typical class of heavy-duty scientific simulation workflows may have abstraction steps shown in Figure 4. A typical scientist's primary interest is in preparation of inputs and codes related to her or his specific research domain and in doing domain specific scientific discovery. Unless IT is the research or development passion of the scientist, there is much less interest in tending computers, moving data or developing peripheral IT applications and support tools (e.g., visualization frameworks). Yet, as much as 50%, sometimes even more, of a scientist's time may be taken up by IT tasks that can be, but are not, automated and/or easy to use. Obviously, there is a need to improve on this. In fact, this has prompted a number of entities (including the US Department of Energy) to sponsor research and development projects[2] aimed at making scientists more productive.

4   Component-based Construction

Component-based construction of solutions, of course, is not a new concept. It has been one of the "holy grails" of software engineering since its earliest days. Results have been mixed so far. However, the advent of reliable and readily available networked resources, and especially of service-oriented architecting, makes truly component-based construction of large scale distributed software-based solutions viable reality.

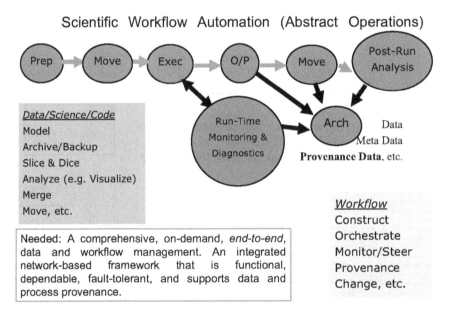

Fig. 5. Workflow abstraction.

Consider the Figure 4 abstraction in a somewhat different light (Figure 5). The flow starts with preparation of the domain-specific codes and inputs. In computationally very intense workflows, these preparatory activities may happen in environments that are different from the one where the code will actually execute. This is followed by moving of the data and codes to host (or grid) that will execute the simulation (e.g., a high-end supercomputer). Once the execution is scheduled (a request may wait in a queue for resources), the scientist may wish to monitor its run-time progress, handle run-time diagnostics, perhaps steer the computations, and certainly collect outputs and results. Outputs of large-scale computations may not remain where they are generated, but may move to a post-run data manipulation and

---

[2] For example, SciDAC (http://www.scidac.gov/)

analysis environment for slicing, dicing, analytics, visualization, and so on A lot of information, perhaps all, is archived in a permanent way. Furthermore, all through the process there is generation of meta-data (data about data and processes) that is either used directly (perhaps in "dashboards") or is part of the data and process lineage (provenance) information [57].

Implementation of workflow abstractions requires availability of a relevant set of IT-based operations in the form of either software applications or perhaps as commands built into operating systems used. In this context, it is very important to distinguish between a custom-made workflow solution (or a problem-solving environment), and a more canonical set of operations, methods, and solutions that can be composed into a scientific workflow. Former have been around for a long time [e.g., 24 and references therein], latter are emerging. For instance, sort, uniq, grep, ftp, ssh and so on, are typical unix operating system commands that scientists can rely on to be available for workflow construction. It is less certain that a complex tool like SAS (which can also sort data, but also does many other things) is available on all platforms of interest, or that some non-standard data moving utility application such as bbcp is readily available on all platforms of interest. Some, operations such as "slice and dice" or "visualize" data are usually available only in the form of specialized software packages or applications.

On the other hand, expectations are rising. *Scientific community now expects utility-like (appliance-like) on-demand access* to needed IT resources where use of IT-based solutions is not bound to a fixed location (such as a specific lab) and fixed resources (e.g., a particular operating system), but has moved to a (mobile) personal access device of a scientist (e.g., laptop or a PDA or a cell phone) and service-based delivery. Scientists would like to move away from the situation where they have to spend more time on IT development, support and workflow management (art) to a situation where IT support is a commodity and they can focus primarily on their basic scientific mission (Figure 6). They are looking for environment where application workflows are dramatically easier to develop and use. Yet, today a practical bottleneck is often still in the IT domain, i.e., in the *scientific workflow environment* of the end-user scientists.

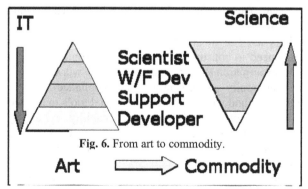

Fig. 6. From art to commodity.

The key to the solution, is an integrated scientific process support framework that is dependable, supports networked or distributed workflows, supports a range of couplings among its building blocks, provides fault-tolerant and data- and process-aware service-based delivery, and provides the capability to audit processes, data and results. Key characteristic of such a framework and its elements are [25, 26]: **reusability** (e.g., elements can be re-used in other workflows), **substitutability** (alternative implementations are easy to insert, very precisely specified interfaces are available, run-time component replacement mechanisms exist, there is ability to verify and validate substitutions, etc), **extensibility** (ability to readily extend system component pool, increase capabilities of individual components, have an extensible architecture that can automatically discover new functionalities and resources, etc), and **composability** (easy construction of more complex functional solutions using basic components, reasoning about such compositions, etc.).

Components are **assembled** according to the rules specified by a **component model.** Their **coupling** can range from **tight** to **loose,** from **synchronous** and blocking to **asynchronous.** Components are assembled using their **interfaces.** **Component composition** assembles components to form a larger component, an application, or a workflow. All parts must conform to the **component model** or they do not fit together. A **component technology** is a concrete implementation of a component model.

Interoperability among components, or workflows built from components, is a major practical issue. Unless component technologies allow for interoperation among different technologies and component models (perhaps through standardized inter-workflow interfaces), there is a danger that workflows from different groups and communities (who invariably use different component technologies) will create "stove-pipes" that will hamper disciplinary and multidisciplinary project, data exchange and scientific discovery. Steps in that direction are standardization efforts related to workflow description languages, web-services and similar [e.g., 51, 52, 53].

5   Complexity and Usability

A major issue of concern with new technologies, and general purpose scientific workflow support environments are no exception in this context, is complexity and usability. End-to-end workflows involve three types of interactions human-to-human, human-to-machine and vice versa, and machine-to-machine. Human-to-human communications have a relatively slow information exchange rate and are tolerant of both semantic and syntactic errors. Machine-to-machine communications are at the other end of the spectrum. They can take place at very high rates but must use very exact and unambiguous protocols.

Human-to-machine interactions are the most critical from the complexity and usability point of view. Humans need to construct the workflow at some point, and humans are the recipients of the information that emerges from those workflows. As already mentioned, scientific community expects utility-like (appliance-like) on-demand access to needed IT resources and workflow technology and tools must meet cost, complexity, skill level to implement, usability, maintainability, reliability, availability, and other expectations of its users. If it fails to do so, i.e., the overhead brought on by the technology does not exceed the potential value added by its use, technology is typically not be used.

This is illustrated in Figure 7. Some technologies never make the break-even point, some "arrive" at or past the break-even point. A good example of a technology that was widely accepted, because it made access to networked information much more acceptable for a general user, is the Web. Scientific workflow technologies are now approaching the break-even point through reduction in the complexity of workflow construction, increased operational reliability, and provision of a suite of support functionalities and packages scientists expect. One such environment is Kepler.

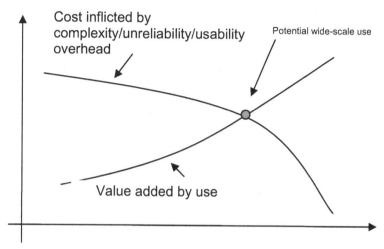

Fig. 7. The relationship between the value added by use of a technology and the overhead inflicted by complexity, reliability, usability and cost of the technology.

6   Kepler

Kepler [2] is an open source component-based scientific workflow support system based on the Ptolemy II framework [12]. Kepler is being developed through a large cross-project collaboration[3]. Basic components of the Kepler framework include: the Ptolemy II core, Kepler core extensions, Kepler object and repository manager, extensions for smart re-run and failure recovery, provenance support modules, a graphical user interface (GUI) layer based on the Ptolemy II Vergil GUI, an authentication layer, a library of generic, application and domain specific actors, and a repository for provenance information. While Kepler can operate without the GUI, it is a useful workflow construction and execution monitoring tool.

Figure 8 illustrates a GUI-level view of a simple workflow. In this case the director is called "PN Director" where PN stands for Process Networks, and as it name implies it implements the process network model. Actor icons can be dragged and dropped from the actor repository (shown on the left in the Figure 8) and connected together with dataflow arcs. Inputs can be parameterized (and their values automatically displayed on the desktop) or can come from files, or be hidden within icons. For example, one would change or input parameters by double clicking on an

[3] SEEK: Science Environment for Ecological Knowledge, SDM Center/SPA: SDM Center/Scientific Process Automation, Ptolemy II: Heterogeneous Modeling and Design, GEON: Cyberinfrastructure for the Geosciences, ROADNet: Real-time Observatories, Applications, and Data Management Network, EOL: Encyclopedia of Life, Resurgence, CIPRes: CyberInfrastructure for Phylogenetic Research, and others.

icon. Once workflow execution has started it can be paused, resumed or stopped, and the flow of information through the workflow can be monitored in real-time. Documentation is an integral part of the system.

Ptolemy II was originally developed to support modeling, simulation, and design of concurrent, real-time, embedded systems. Kepler project has extended this framework to provide access to and use of synchronous and asynchronous loosely and tightly coupled and networked resources and functionalities that are typically used in scientific workflows. From the end-user perspective, there are two principal groups of elements. One set are the computational models - represented by "directors", and the other set are the data-flow connected processing nodes called "actors".

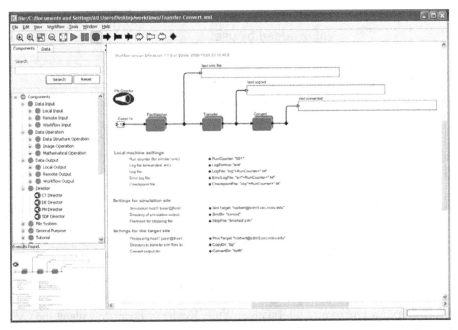

Fig. 8. Kepler GUI.

A director is an engine that controls the behavior and execution of the workflow components. In doing that, it implements different computational models, and thus it defines the semantics of the execution and of the interactions among the actors. While there are a number of open source and closed source scientific workflow support environments [e.g., 2, 3, 4, 42, 43, 55], a very unique and distinguishing feature of the Kepler framework is that (through Ptolemy II) it enables a very rich mixture of models of computation. Examples of realized computational domains range from continuous-time modeling, to dynamic data flow, to discrete-event modeling, to finite state machines, to process networks, to synchronous dataflow modeling, to discrete time and distributed discrete events, and so on.

Actors encapsulate parameterized actions and have interfaces define by ports and parameters. Ports are used to communicate input and output data and streams, but without call-return semantics. Communication semantics among ports is handled by the directors – one per workflow level – which provide flow control. Workflows can be nested (e.g., Figure 2), and different computational models can be used at different hierarchical levels so long the communication channels and actions that may cross level boundaries are compatible.

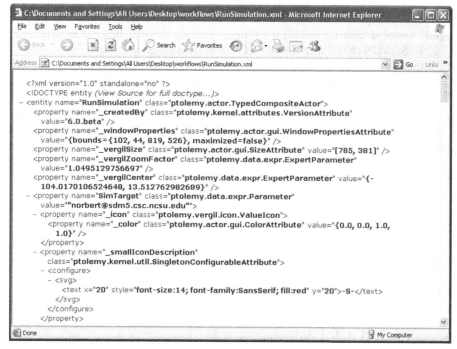

Fig. 9. Part of the XML-based description of the workflow shown in Figure 8.

Actors are typically collected in libraries, many of which are domain and data polymorphic. A number of supporting packages and actors are provided either as part of Ptolemy or as part of Kepler additions. This includes graph-theoretic manipulations, matrix and vector math, signal processing, data typing, handling of generic web services, customizable relational data-based management, command line wrappers for ssh, scp, ftp and similar, a level of Grid support (e.g., GridFTP, certificate generator), native R and Matlab support, SRB – the SDSC storage resource broker, communication with object resource brokers, image processing, visualization, textual and graphical outputs, etc. A number of functionalities are being added or improved, including large-scale robust data movers, more extensive provenance support, semantic-intensive actors, management for data-intensive and compute-intensive workflows, authentication and authorization, distributed execution, execution monitoring, fault tolerance, and scientific data management application-driven extensions such as access to or integration with parallel NetCDF, PVFS, MPI-IO, parallel-R, FastBit, and CCA.

Kepler workflows are recorded and can be exchanged as XML-based Modeling Markup Language (MoML) files [38]. Figure 9 shows part of the MoML description of the workflow shown in Figure 8. Kepler has many other desirable features. For example, if running in a distributed environment, it operates as a relatively loosely coupled system, while operating on a single platform it can operate as a very tightly coupled system. In addition, Kepler allows, using additional middleware that manipulates MoML files, dynamic construction of workflows. Kepler environment is very external-application friendly. It can invoke and communicate with existing tightly coupled external problem solving, analysis or visualization environments (e.g., R, SciRUN [62], Ensight [63]), as well as Grid-based resources..

Kepler is also very flexible in how far it extends into a workflow. It can contain the whole workflow and orchestrate it in a synchronous or asynchronous manner, or it can act only as a control layer, with separate provenance and "heavy lifting" computational, data movement and storage layers. The current implementation is primarily a single instance environment that virtualizes quite well. For example, NC State University Virtual Computing Laboratory [64] offers Kepler to its users as one of its images, and allows users to spawn multiple instances of Kepler workflows for simultaneous use by one or more end-users.

7   Run-Time Monitoring and Provenance

The need to provide run-time monitoring of scientific processes and collect provenance information has been recognized for some time now [e.g., 9, 10, 14, 39, 40 – 45, 57]. Provenance is the history of data, execution and conditions applied to a workflow run. Run-time monitoring may be part of the provenance meta-data, but it also may require collection of additional information and display of that information in a user-friendly format, for example on a "**dashboard**," so that run-time tracking, problem determination, computational steering, and other workflow-related feedback may take place. Such information may also be used to provide fault-tolerance related information (including check-point and recovery data and information), recreate of results and rebuilding of workflows, associate workflows with results it produced, create links between generated data in different runs, compare different runs, checkpoint a workflow and recover, debug and explain results. In general this information can attest to the lineage of the data (**data provenance**, such as intermediate and end results, file names and paths, data-base references, URLs, etc.), processes (**process provenance**, such as software version numbers, the actual workflow graphs or descriptions, events that occurred during a run, input data and parameters used, etc.), error and exception management (error and execution logs), and given the right tools, workflow design provenance.

Kepler currently implements an internal actor-based provenance mechanism [e.g., 2, 41, 54], and several optional portal-based and domain-oriented external process tracking and monitoring mechanisms and dashboards. Under consideration is incorporation of the VisTrails [55] provenance infrastructure into the Kepler framework. VisTrails has extensive support for process and data provenance [57, 58], including visual querying capabilities and multi-user support, which aids collaborative work.

8   Security

Authentication, authorization, access control and security are a major issue with almost any network-based solution available today. The issues take many shapes and forms. Practically all workflow support environments, including Kepler, face these problems. For example, actors need to manage data, programs, and computing resources in distributed and heterogeneous environments, and that has to happen under a variety of security conditions – from very stringent ones (possibly military grade) to relatively relaxed ones (e.g., academic institutions). While some of the components may be operating under "grid" authentication rules (e.g., via certificates, such as using the GAMA framework [59]), some may use LDAP [60] based authentication, while others may be using yet another approach. How does one reconcile these mechanisms to allow trusted exchange of information among the workflow components?

When accessing higher-security resources (e.g., in the National Laboratories) users are required to use encrypted connections (e.g., ssh-based, ssl-based, secure HTTP aided solutions, etc.) and often one-time passwords and other security devices. While secure connections are typically not an issue in workflow environments (e.g., Kepler has ssh and other appropriate actors), one time passwords can be an impediments since they may require use of special keys or security devices that prevent one-stop authentication paths, and in practice invariably require human intervention, thus slowing workflow related operations and communications that span authentication domains.

While workflow related security, authentication, authorization and associated access control have been studied extensively over the last 10 or more years, the problem is still here. A more encompassing solution remains work in progress when it comes to scientific workflow environments. Usable environments support different authentication mechanisms but until identity management and security are treated in a more uniform way, they may represent a major obstacle to interoperability among different workflow frameworks and solutions.

9   Fault-Tolerance

Application of the workflow technology to a specific domain or project, requires information about the domain, project content, participants (both developers and end-users), schedules, resources, other relevant technology, and development of the corresponding operational profiles for the scientific workflow system. Operational profile is the set of relative frequencies which tells us how often a particular scenario, function or capability occurs in practice [34]. Specifically, one would first identify and categorize workflow system users, functionalities and resources and frequency of use of each. This would allow mapping amongst them. This finally yields an operational profile that needs to be supported during the workflow system use. The mappings and the operational profile allow us to recognize functional alternatives and introduce adaptive or fault-tolerant behavior into the model.

There are two basic forms of run-time fault-tolerance: forward-recovery (which includes failure masking and redundancy based failover), and backward-recovery (which includes check-pointing) e.g. [15, 16, 31]. Exception handling is a very traditional way of managing run-time problems [e.g., 16, 31]. It is also used in the workflow-oriented environments [e.g., 48, 49]. Exception handling can involve forward-recovery, backward-recovery, or graceful termination. More recently web-services community has recognized the need for some form of standardized fault-tolerance in the service provisioning through replication [56].

A run-time failure of a system is often the result of a series of events – sometimes that of a set of very complex and unexpected interactions. Typically, a failure is a result of either a system fault – a design-time developer or researcher error that materializes at run-time, or it is a user error at execution time, or there is an issue with the underlying infrastructure (including invoked services). An initial design error can become a fault in the initial product. This fault can propagate (as a series of defects) to the final executable version of the workflow. When the workflow encounters that defect during execution, the workflow enters an error-state. If that error-state, or its result, becomes visible to the end-user, it becomes a failure that may have anywhere from no consequences to catastrophic consequences. Similarly, a call to a workflow component that fails at run-time may again force the workflow into an error-state, and manifest as a failure. So, run-time workflow failures can be caused by one or more of the following non-comprehensive set of events:

- Use errors caused by end user, for example entering incorrect data.
- Error-state caused by network difficulties, such as congestion.
- Error-state initiated by workflow component faults due to a programming issue.
- Hardware faults and failures
- Error-states caused by failures of services, such as the unavailability of a certain service (e.g., actual web service, or a remote computational or storage service)
- Failures in any underlying software components (e.g., operating system kernel bugs, device misconfigurations, etc.)

9.1   Illustration

In illustrating fault-tolerant solutions in the context of network-based workflows we do not plan to discuss the cost of the services, and we make some **assumptions**:

- Failures of redundant services are **not correlated**, or at least the probability of correlated failures is very low. This basically means that the failure of one service doesn't affect another functionally equivalent (or perhaps replicated) service. For example, we assume that redundant services are hosted on separate perhaps geographically distributed servers, so that in the case one server fails, only one service will be affected. However, assumption also implies that failures are not caused by a basic algorithmic flaw that may be present in both services and may result in identical but wrong responses from all redundant services [16].
- In discussing system reliability, we will make the assumption that all workflow services have the same failure and recovery **probability**. This, of course may not be a realistic assumptions, but it provides a vehicle for the model discussion. An enormous amount of work has been already done by others in modeling and simulation of redundant components under a variety

of conditions, e.g., see [31, 33] and references therein, and the reader should consult that literature before deciding on a particular solution.

The first assumption does not apply to the case when there are no redundant or replicated services, i.e., if we assume that different services used by the workflow are deployed in a serial fashion[4]. This is the worst-case scenario where failure of one service means the failure of the entire workflow since no alternative services are being provided. Of course, one could actually have different functions performed in parallel and at different locations, if the (data) flow model allows that (and this is sometimes done). But, in practical terms a failure of either of those services again fails the workflow. Therefore, serialization assumption can still be used. We also assume that services are atomic, i.e., we do not discuss the option of seamless fail-over once a service has been engaged, we assume that that issue is handled through re-start of that part of the workflow.

Today's web services appear to have a varying and broad range of failure probabilities depending on their implementation and quality, how they are being hosted, who is hosting them, where they are being reached from, etc. One value for average failure probability found in the literature is 0.045, this translates into more than one failure a month. [17, 18, 19]. During peak-time operation, that failure probability may become as high as 0.2, or more than two failures to deliver a service on request as day, depending on the request type and duration. Of course, there are services that do much better and much worse than this range indicates. The level to which improvements need to be made may be domain specific. For example, educational workflows need to have availability of at least 0.95 [35]. We use these two numbers to provide an illustration of a possible range of service failure probabilities upon which one would have to improve, and to illustrate the power of a simple redundancy-based fault-tolerance strategy.

Consider a scientific workflow that invokes serially 3 different network-based services before it is done. Let one of those services fail. Then, the workflow will not finish successfully unless mitigation is put in place. For example, at the point of failure we could recover back to the point where the workflow was check-pointed, and then we could re-run the remaining part. Alternatively, we could try to mask the failure of the component service. We focus on the latter. Given the assumptions above, the probability that the workflow fails is the probability that at least one of the services fails [16,31]. In other words:

$$P_F = 1 - \prod_{i=1}^{n} (1 - p_i) \tag{1}$$

Where p_F is the probability that the workflow will fail, p_i is the probability that service i fails, and n is the number of serial services in the workflow. Using the example numbers and Eq. 1, on the "average" $P_F = 1 - (1-0.045)^3 = 0.129$, and in the "heavy load" case $P_F = 1 - (0.8)^3 = 0.488$. Obviously, reliability R (which is one minus failure probability) is not too good. Figure 10 shows a graph of the failure probability for this example. System failure probability grows considerably with the

[4] However, physical co-location of serial or replicated services runs another risk – that of the whole site power or other type of outage.

number of serial services (Equation 1). In the "heavy load" situation, the failure probability is very close to one once the number of services in the workflow exceeds 15.

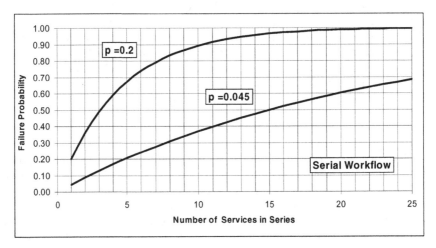

Fig. 10. Failure probability of a serial system without fault-tolerance

While the numbers in the graph may seem excessively pessimistic, it is clear that as the number of services in a complex workflow grows, service failures can have a dramatic effect on the whole system operation. A well known solution is to use multiple backup servers (service replication) in parallel to counter physical infrastructure and networking failures, and/or to use alternative but functionally equivalent services if other types of failures may be suspected. Then, if one of the services fails, the workflow can automatically switch to an alternative one.

Let's assume that the probability that a service, or any of its alternative fails, is p. Then, the probability that such redundant service fails is that of a group of parallel components, i.e., all of them need to fail before an end-user visible failure occurs. For example, the reliability of a service with 3 alternatives is the probability that at least one of the alternatives is operational, i.e., $R = (1-p) + p(1-p) + p^2(1-p) = 1 - p^3$ Generalizing:

$$R = 1 - p^m \qquad (2)$$

where m is the number of alternatives[5]. Applying (1) and (2) to the entire workflow, the failure probability of the workflow would be:

$$P_F = 1 - (\prod_{i=1}^{n} \sum_{j=0}^{m-1} p_i^{\,j}(1-p_i)) = 1 - \prod_{i=1}^{n}(1-p_i^m) \qquad (3)$$

[5] Note: $(1-p) + p(1-p) + p^2(1-p) + \ldots + p^{m-1}(1-p) = 1 - p + p - p^2 + p^2 - p^3 + \ldots + p^{m-2} - p^{m-1} + p^{m-1} - p^m = (1 - p^m)$

where P_F is the probability that the workflow fails, n is the number of service in the workflow, m is the number of replicas of each service in the workflow (in this example, we assume that the number of replicas is the same for all services), and p_i is the probability that service i fails.

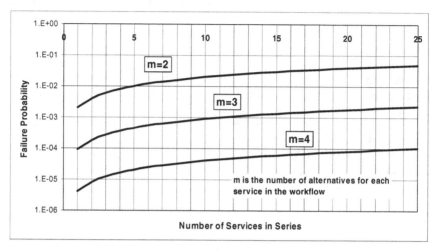

Fig. 11. Failure probability of a series – parallel model (p = 0.045)

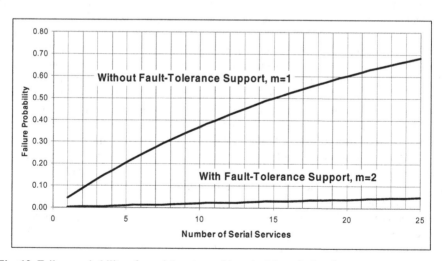

Fig. 12. Failure probability of a serial system with and without fault-tolerance.

Consider again our example with three "serial" services. Let each service have 2 backup services (m=3). Then the probability that at least one of the services fails (thus the workflow fails), and given our two illustration failures rates, $P_F = 1 - (1 - 0.045^3)^3 = 0.00027$ and $P_F = 1 - (1 - 0.2^3)^3 = 0.0238$. Figure 11 illustrates different failure probabilities based on this fault-tolerance model given the assumption that p=0.045 for all services. Different lines represent the number of alternatives available for each service. We notice that, even when there is only one alternative for each service (m=2), failure probability is significantly lower than that of a workflow without any fault-tolerance support. For example for a workflow with 25 services to invoke, the failure probability goes down from almost 0.7 to 0.05 for m=2, down to 0.002 for m=3, and down to 0.0001 for m=4. Notice that in this case and with our assumptions, every time we add an alternative service, the failure probability can go down by a factor of 20 or more.

In comparing the two models, we find the potential for considerable improvement using redundancy. Of course, the caveat is that the redundant services must not exhibit significantly correlated failures, either due to their (co-)location, or for algorithmic or other reasons. For example, with p=0.045, n=3 and m=3, workflow failure probability is reduced from 0.129 to less than 10^{-3}. Figure 12 compares failure probability of a workflow with no fault-tolerant support, and a workflow with redundancy-based service-level fault-tolerance, where each service has only one backup service. Notice again that, even with only one backup service, the reliability increases dramatically.

9.2   Implementations

To achieve some measure of fault-tolerance, there should be at least one backup server running identical copies of the services or there should be another implementation of the services. Also, the workflow should be able to switch to that server/service in the case the primary server/service fails. The most obvious method to implement that is to simply encode the extra service location (e.g., URL, IP number, or DNS name) within the code of the actors, i.e. hard code the location of the alternatives. This way, by using a simple control structure, the actor then tries to invoke the backup services when the primary service fails to respond. We should note that the mechanism of this method is transparent to the user. The only impact that it might have on the performance is a small delay, because the flow may have to wait to confirm timeout of the primary service before it tries the alternative, and the timeout may take a few seconds. The advantage of using hard-coded alternatives is that this provides very simple basic fault-tolerance. It makes the workflow more resilient with respect to simple failures of known services. But there are also several disadvantages. The most significant one is that when the location of the services changes, or when we want to add more backup services, then we need to change the code and recompile the actors and redistribute them. This complicates matters. One options it to provide an interface for the end user to input the location of the primary and alternative services. That also is not very efficient because it requires that the end user know the location of different servers. Thus, the need for a more versatile solution emerges. The next two solutions address that issue.

Instead of simply hard coding the location of different services, one could use a less intrusive and more dynamic approach. This approach stores all relevant information about the services in a file (the choice nowadays is an XML file). That XML file is then kept on a separate server to be accessed by the actors at run-time. An actor parses file, and stores the results in an internal data structure. An alternative is to provide the alternate service locations as actor parameters – this is what some Kepler actors do today. When the time comes to invoke a service, system retrieves the relevant information and invokes the service at the primary location. When this succeeds, system continues executing the rest of the workflow. If the invocation fails, system can try an alternative service from the list. This approach presents a more versatile solution than the previous one since it does not require that the location of services be hard coded. Thus it allows adding and modifying the location of the services without modifying the source code. The user would still need to know the location of the XML file, and which alternative service is to be invoked. Both can be passed as actor parameters.

A third approach is to use UDDI [20] based registry of services. Using this method, the end user needs only to supply the name of the service the user is trying to invoke, and the actor then searches the repository to find matching services. Note that there is an underlying assumption that a proper set of compatible keywords (and ontologies) exists for all registered services. That service is then invoked. If this is successful, the actor continues its execution. If invocation fails, another search can occur to find yet another alternative service. The advantage of using this method over the previous ones is that the repository can regularly check whether a service is still online by using the heartbeat approach. This feature isn't supported in the previous method, i.e. in the case one of the services isn't available, the XML file or parameter entry has to be manually corrected, or it would keep on returning the location of the unavailable service. Another advantage is the flexibility in adding or modifying existing services. In order to add an additional service, all that needs to be done is to add the service to the repository through an easy-to-use web interface. Thus no configuration files or parameters need to be modified.

Figure 13 shows a screenshot of the parameters required for a fault tolerant web service actor. Only a keyword, method name, username and password (if username and password are used) are required. The actor automatically extracts the namespace and location URL from the retrieved services lists.

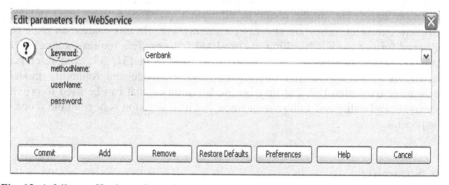

Fig. 13. A fail-over Kepler web-service actor.

It is possible that one of the services returned in the search isn't what we're looking for. This can be avoided by providing a more complex search phrase, for example in the case of the Genbank service illustration in Figure 13, the user could enter "SDM SPA Genbank" instead of just "Genbank". Another approach is to have a sample input and output, then invoke the service with that sample input and compare the outputs, to make sure that the service in question is indeed what we're looking for. This approach involves more computation and a comparison step, and thus might cause a slight delay. But it can also be looked at as a way to provide validation, since in the case the outputs didn't match; we can consider that the service in question is either an incorrect one, or is not behaving properly.

9.3   Further Improvements

A natural alternative worth emphasizing in this context is to simply just re-try one or more times services that appear to have failed. Sometimes services do not respond due to oversubscription or network glitches, and re-trying solves the problem. Re-trying a service is a general (and very common) approach that can be used in conjunction with all methods discussed above. An example of that (at the workflow execution level) is the fault-tolerant shell [32]. However, all discussed solutions have some inherent limitations. The most important one is that they do not deal with the case when the web service is operational but is not behaving properly, for example not returning correct results, or where the workflow is in the middle of a conversation with the service when the service fails and the state of the service matters. Solutions discussed above can only handle problems caused by initial unavailability of the services.

A more complex, perhaps voting based scheme may be needed to deal with comparison of results, with semantic differences among alternatives, and with state-recovery. Further improvements need to include validation of the results before proceeding with the rest of the workflow. That can be done, for example, by submitting an appropriately selected sample request and comparing the result with a saved result before submitting the rest of the results. That approach may require sophisticated comparison algorithms since services interfaces may be quire complex, but this may be able to mitigate a correctness failure. Yet, another approach could involve invoking several identical services and comparing their results, then choosing the consensus response. Both methods present a possible solution to the validation issue, but might result in additional processing time, thus delaying workflow execution. They are also not comprehensive. In this context an issue that will need further work is handling of correlated failures. This requires a much more complex model. Interested readers may wish to consult [31, 33], and references therein, for more information on different fault-tolerance and reliability models. Software rejuvenation [27, 28] may be another solution that can be used to provide increased availability and failure-avoidance, but its discussion is beyond the scope of this paper.

10 Summary

As scientific discovery and problem solving becomes more complex and more dependent on high-end information technology, comprehensive end-to-end data and process management solutions are needed to reduce the IT burden on the scientist. A group of technologies, called scientific workflow support frameworks, that do that is maturing and we expect to see an increased use of these solutions. One such technology is the Ptolemy II based environment called Kepler. This paper has discussed some of the issues associated with practical automation of scientific processes and workflows and has illustrated this with workflows developed using the Kepler framework and tools. The topics covered include general workflow development concepts, the impact of information technology overhead and complexity in this context, the structure of Kepler, and issues related to provenance and fault-tolerance. Open issues for high-end scientific workflow technologies include autonomic behavior (auto-recovery and fault-tolerance), authentication and security management, data and provenance management, run-time data and process monitoring and steering (e.g., via "dashboards"), semantic level verification and validation of workflows during construction and at run-time, and development of appropriate end-user visual and other interfaces (e.g., workflow construction "wizards" and persistent portals).

We expect that scientific workflow support technologies will play a critical role in the world of peta- and exa-scale computing supported research and discovery, and in the next 10 years will become a standard feature of the cyberinfrastructure. A key issue that will need to be resolved in this context will be **interoperability**. While many workflow related standardization efforts are under way, it is currently not trivial to exchange more complex information and service, not to mention workflows themselves, among for example Kepler, Taverna [61] and Windows Workflow Foundation [4] environments. In the future, there will be many scientific workflow support environments in operation – some open source, some not. But, unless there is a relatively widely accepted way of exchanging information and services among the workflows constructed in different environments, different scientific communities may be have difficulties collaborating. To avoid "stove-piping" and impediments to progress that that brings, it is very important that open interfaces be defined now and that the existing and new workflow environments be architected and implemented in the spirit of SOA [50].

11 Acknowledgments

We would like thank our colleagues working on the U.S. Department of Energy (DOE) Scientific Data Management Center project for their support and interest. This work has been supported in part by the DOE SciDAC grants DE-FC02-01ER25484 and DE-FC02-07ER25809, IBM Shared University Program, and StrikeIron Inc. The Kepler and Vistrails projects are also funded by grants from the National Science Foundation.

12 References

1. D. Georgakopoulos, M. Hornick, and A. Sheth, "An Overview of Workflow Management: From Process Modeling to Workflow Automation Infrastructure," Distributed and Parallel Databases, Vol. 3(2), April 1995.
2. "Kepler Project" Website, 2006. http://kepler-project.org
3. TRIANA Project, October 2006, http://www.trianacode.org/
4. Windows Workflow Foundation (http://msdn2.microsoft.com/en-us/netframework/aa663328.aspx) http://www.microsoft.com/windowsserversystem/virtualserver/default.mspx

5. B. Ludäscher, I. Altintas, C. Berkley, D. Higgins, E. Jaeger, M. Jones, E. A. Lee, J. Tao, and Y. Zhao. Scientific Workflow Management and the Kepler System. Concurrency and Computation: Practice & Experience, 18(10):1039-1065, 2006.
6. B. Ludäscher and C. A. Goble. "Guest Editors: Introduction to the Special Section on Scientific Workflows." SIGMOD Record, 34(3), 2005.
7. R. Mount et al., Department of Energy, Office of Science report, "Data Management Challenge". Nov 2004, http://www.er.doe.gov/ascr/Final-report-v26.pdf
8. Altintas, S. Bhagwanani, D. Buttler, S. Chandra, Z. Cheng, M. Coleman, T. Critchlow, A. Gupta, W. Han, L. Liu, B. Ludäscher, C. Pu, R. Moore, A. Shoshani, and M. Vouk, "A Modeling and Execution Environment for Distributed Scientific Workflows", demonstration track, 15th Intl. Conference on Scientific and Statistical Database Management (SSDBM), Boston, Massachussets, 2003.
9. R.I. Balay, Vouk M.A., Perros H., "Performance of Network-Based Problem-Solving Environments," Chapter 18, in Enabling Technologies for Computational Science Frameworks, Middleware and Environments, editors Elias N. Houstis, John R. Rice, Efstratios Gallopoulos, Randall Bramley, Hardbound, ISBN 0-7923-7809-1, 2000
10. M.A Vouk., and M.P. Singh, "Quality of Service and Scientific Workflows," in The Quality of Numerical Software: Assessment and Enhancements, editor: R. Boisvert, Chapman & Hall, pp.77-89 , 1997.
11. M.P. Singh, Vouk M.A., "Scientific workflows: scientific computing meets transactional workflows," Proceedings of the NSF Workshop on Workflow and Process Automation in Information Systems: State-of-the-Art and Future Directions, Univ. Georgia, Athens, GA, USA; 1996, pp.SUPL 28-34.
12. "The Ptolemy II Project" website, 2005. http://ptolemy.eecs.berkeley.edu/ptolemyII/
13. S.E. Elmaghraby, "On generalized activity networks," J. Ind. Eng., Vol. 17, 621-631, 1966.
14. R.L. Dennis, D.W. Byun, J.H. Novak, K.J. Galluppi, C.C. Coats, and M.A. Vouk, "The Next Generation of Integrated Air Quality Modeling: EPA's Models-3," Atmospheric Environment, Vol 30 (12), pp 1925-1938, 1996.
15. J.C. Laprie, and C. Beounes, "Definition and Analysis of Hardware- and Software-Fault-Tolerant Architectures", IEEE Computer Society Press, Volume 23, Issue 7, Pages: 39 – 51, July 1990.
16. D.F. McAllister, and M.A. Vouk, "Software Fault-Tolerance Engineering," Chapter 14 in Handbook of Software Reliability Engineering, McGraw Hill, pp. 567-614, January 1996.
17. ACME Laboratories, "Web Servers Comparison",, http://www.acme.com/software/thttpd/benchmarks.html, 1998.
18. Iyengar, A.; MacNair, E.; Nguyen, T. , "An analysis of Web server performance". Global Telecommunications Conference, 1997. GLOBECOM '97., IEEE Volume 3, 3-8 Nov. 1997 Page(s):1943 - 1947 vol.3
19. Lloyd Ian, "Government website failure – Is it so shocking?" March 06, http://www.webstandards.org/2006/03/31/government-web-site-failure-is-it-so-shocking-2/
20. "OASIS UDDI ", OASIS Open website 2005 http://www.uddi.org

21. "StrikeIron Web Services Business Directory", StrikeIron Inc. 2005. http://www.strikeiron.com
22. "Apache Web Services Project: jUDDI" website. 2005 http://ws.apache.org/juddi/
23. "Soap UDDI Project" website, 2005. http://soapuddi.sourceforge.net/
24. Elias N. Houstis, John R. Rice, Efstratios Gallopoulos, Randall Bramley, "Enabling Technologies for Computational Science Frameworks, Middleware and Environments", Hardbound, ISBN 0-7923-7809-1, 2000
25. Crnkovic and M. Larsson (editors), Building Reliable Component-Based Software Systems, Artech House Publishers, ISBN 1-58053-327-2, 2002, http://www.idt.mdh.se/cbse-book/
26. Common Component Architecture Forum, http://www.cca-forum.org/, accessed February 2006
27. Y. Huang, C. Kintala, N. Kolettis, and N. D. Fulton, "Software Rejuvenation: Analysis, Module and Applications", in Proc. of 25th Symposium on Fault Tolerant Computing, FTCS-25, pages 381–390, Pasadena, California, June 1995.
28. K. Vaidyanathan; Trivedi, K.S. "A comprehensive model for software rejuvenation". IEEE Transactions on Dependable and Secure Computing, Volume 2, Issue 2, April-June 2005 Page(s):124 - 137
29. S.E. Elmaghraby, Baxter E.I., and Vouk M.A., "An Approach to the Modeling and Analysis of Software Production Processes," Intl. Trans. Operational Res., Vol. 2(1), pp. 117-135, 1995.
30. G. Chin. Jr., Leung, L.R., Schuchardt, K.L., and Gracio, D.K. (2002). New Paradigms in Collaborative Problem Solving Environments for Scientific Computing. In Proceeding of the 2002 International Conference of Intelligent User Interfaces (IUI 2002), (Jan. 13-16, San Francisco, CA). ACM Press, New York.
31. M.A Vouk, "Software Reliability Engineering of Numerical Systems," Chapter 13, in Accuracy and Reliability in Scientific Computing, Editor: Bo Einarsson, ISBN 0-89871-584-9, SIAM, 2005, pp. 205-231 [PDF - Draft]
32. Cooperative Computing Lab at the University of Notre Dame (http://www.cse.nd.edu/~ccl/software/ftsh/)
33. M.R. Lyu (ed.), Software Fault Tolerance, Trends-in-Software Book Series, Wiley, 1994
34. J.D. Musa, ªOperational Profiles in Software-Reliability Engineering, IEEE Software, vol. 10, no. 2, pp. 14-32, Mar. 1993.
35. M. Vouk, R.L. Klevans, and D.L. Bitzer, "Workflow and End-User Quality of Service Issues in Web-Based Education," IEEE Trans. On Knowledge Engineering, to Vol 11(4), July/August 1999, pp. 673-687.
36. Report of the National Science Foundation Blue-Ribbon Advisory Panel on Cyberinfrastructure, January 2003, http://www.nsf.gov/od/oci/reports/atkins.pdf
37. Department of Energy, Office of Science, "Data Management Report". May 2004, http://ultralight.caltech.edu/gaeweb/portal/misc/2005/05DMW/Final-report.pdf
38. Edward A. Lee and Steve Neuendorffer. MoML — A Modeling Markup Language in XML — Version 0.4. Technical report, University of California at Berkeley, March, 2000.

39. International Provenance and Annotation Workshop (IPAW'06), Chicago, Illinois, May 3-5, 2006, http://www.ipaw.info/ipaw06/
40. Simmhan, Y. L., Plale, B., Gannon, D., A survey of data provenance in e-science. In *SIGMOD Rec.* 34(3): 31-36, 2005
41. Altinats, I., Barney O., Jaeger-Frank, E. "Provenance Collection Support in Kepler Scientific Workflow System," Proc. of the IPAW'06, www.ipaw.info/ipaw06/proceedings/CameraReady_s5_2.pdf
42. Foster, I., Voeckler, J., Wilde, M., Zhao, Y., "Chimera, A Virtual Data System for Representing, Querying, and Automating Data Derivation," In Proceedings of the 14th Conference on Scientific and Statistical Database Management, 2002
43. Greenwood, M., Goble, C., Stevens, R., Zhao, J., Addis, M., Marvin, D., Moreau, L., Oinn, T., "Provenance of e-Science Experiments - experience from Bioinformatics," In Proceedings of The UK OST e-Science second All Hands Meeting 2003 (AHM'03)
44. Groth, P., Luck, M., Moreau, L. "A protocol for recording provenance in service-oriented grids," In Proceedings of the 8th International Conference on Principles of Distributed Systems (OPODIS'04), 2004
45. Bavoil, L., Callahan, S., Crossno, P., Freire, J., Scheidegger, C., Silva, C., and Vo, H., "Vistrails: Enabling interactive multipleview visualizations." In IEEE Visualization 2005, pages 135–142, 2005
46. Some examples of open source scientific workflow solutions: BioPipe, BizTalk, BPWS4J, DAGMan, GridAnt, Grid Job Handler, GRMS (GridLab Resource Management System), GWFE (Gridbus Workflow Engine), GWES (Grid Workflow Execution Service), IT Innovation Enactment Engine, JIGSA, Kepler, Karajan, OSWorkflow, Pegasus (uses DAGMan), ScyFLOW, SDSC Matrix, SHOP2, Taverna, Triana, wftk, YAWL Engine, WebAndFlo, WFEE, etc. see http://www.gridworkflow.org/snips/gridworkflow/space/Workflow+Engines, http://www.extreme.indiana.edu/swf-survey/
47. Win Bausch, Cesare Pautasso, Reto Schaeppi, Gustavo Alonso, "BioOpera: Cluster-Aware Computing," CLUSTER 2002, pp. 99-106
48. Claus Hagen, Gustavo Alonso, "Flexible Exception Handling in the OPERA Process Support System," ICDCS 1998, pp. 526-533
49. Fabio Casati, Stefano Ceri, Stefano Paraboschi, and Giuseppe Pozzi, "Specification and Implementation of Exceptions in Workflow Management Systems," ACM Transactions on Database Systems 24(3), Sept. 1999
50. Service Oriented Architecture (SOA), Wikipedia, 2006 (http://en.wikipedia.org/wiki/Service-oriented_architecture), also http://www-306.ibm.com/software/solutions/soa/, and references therein.
51. OASIS, http://www.oasis-open.org/ (e.g., BPEL)
52. OWL, http://www.w3.org/TR/owl-features/
53. Web Services standards at http://www.w3.org/TR (e.g., WSDL and similar).
54. KEPLER provenance framework at http://kepler-project.org/Wiki.jsp?page=KeplerProvenanceFramework
55. VisTrails (http://www.vistrails.org)
56. J. Salas, F. Perez, M. Patia-Martinez, R. Jiminez-Peris, "WS-Replication: A Framework for Highly Available Web Services," WWW Conf., Edinburgh, Scotland, May 2006.

57. J. Freire, C. Silva, S. Callahan, E. Santos, C. Scheidegger and H. T. Vo, "Managing Rapidly-Evolving Scientific Workflows," International Provenance and Annotation Workshop (IPAW), LNCS 4145, pages 10-18, 2006. Springer.

58. C. Scheidegger, D. Koop, E. Santos, H. Vo, S. Callahan, J. Freire, and C.Silva. "Tackling the Provenance Challenge One Layer at a Time," submitted to Concurrency And Computation: Practice And Experience. (Special issue on the first Provenance Challenge.)

59. Grid Account Management Architecture (http://grid-devel.sdsc.edu/gridsphere/gridsphere?cid=gama), SDSC, 2005, and Mueller, GEON, 2006 (http://www.geongrid.org/presentations/webcasts/Mueller_GAMA_GEON_May 06.ppt)

60. LDAP, SEEK (http://seek.ecoinformatics.org/Wiki.jsp?page=CertificateAuthorityDesign)

61. Taverna Project Website (http://taverna.sourceforge.net/)

62. SciRUN (http://software.sci.utah.edu/scirun.html/)

63. Ensight (http://www.ensight.com/home/index.php)

64. Virtual Computing Laboratory (VCL) - http://vcl.ncsu.edu

Q&A – Mladen Vouk

Questioner: Bill Applebe

Component-based software architectures, like .NET and J2EE work well because they are component-based from top to bottom. A key problem for scientific component-based software is that components only extend down so far, and modifying a Kepler application may require modifying the wrapped legacy codes. What approaches might be used to overcome these problems?

Mladen Vouk

The approach we are taking is to identify similarities for classes of workflows (e.g., large scale simulations that may produce terabytes at a time at distributed locations, but analyze and steer results at a different locations), then develop a "template" workflow and data models that would serve these applications. We initially develop wrappers that are intelligent enough to avoid legacy code changes (if possible), but later we work with end-users to have them accept (develop) a workflow framework compliant data-model and interfaces (especially when they write new codes).

Here is where it would be very important to develop such plug-in capability in a broadly accepted open interface language/protocol/format so that compliant apps could "plug" into not just one, but any number of relevant workflow frameworks that support such an interface. This provides a lot of options for end-users and resolves potential monopoly and framework lock-in situations.

Questioner: Bill Gropp

Have techniques such as aspects been considered to address cross-cutting issues such as security and authentication in a workflow diagram?

Mladen Vouk

Not yet. Security and identity management are big issues and we are seriously pursuing several avenues. In our case, the issues are particularly complex when workflows cross framework boundaries, e.g., both grid-based and non-grid based resources are mixed in the same workflow.

Questioner: Dennis Gannon

Why not use Grid GSI security and capability-based authorization?

Mladen Vouk

Only a fraction of our platforms / clients use, or have, a Grid GSI compliant facility. We often have to deal with other than Grid GIS mechanisms, and mixing among these different mechanisms adds to the complexity.

Questioner: Bill Gropp

What can be done to reduce the fragmentation of many open source projects?

Mladen Vouk

Ideally, we would all agree on a common set of interoperability formats, protocols, semantics, interfaces, etc., so that the mixed-workflow programming would be possible before too much stove-piping sets in.

Questioner: Mary Thomas

What is the current state of compilers that can support workflows, e.g. compilers so I can run "fort -og" (optimize for the grid)?

Mladen Vouk

End-to-end workflow compilers that span different applications, platforms, layers, language frameworks, and models, etc., is the long-term goal, but unfortunately we have a long way to go before we get there.

Ken Kennedy

This is a very interesting question and a complex one. Right now, the VGrADS system and other Grid schedulers assume the vendor compiler will be used on each platform, so there is no active attempt to tailor the code in a workflow step or even a series of steps to the context of the actual Grid workflow. Nevertheless, there are many opportunities that could open up if grid-aware compilers were available. Many of these opportunities also arise in compilation for heterogeneous machines. An interesting idea would be to compose workflow steps that will run on a single resource into a single application which could avoid disk accesses, much as a UNIX pipe does this.

In the long term, it would be good if the compiler could translate a single program, written in Matlab, Python, C, or Fortran, into an optimized Grid computation. Many groups are working on this idea right now, but there is much left to be done.

Monday AM Panel Discussion

Panel:

- Dennis Gannon
- Ken Kennedy
- Mladen Vouk

Questioner: Richard Hanson

Libraries of software routines are well established as a programming model and tool. What do you visualize as an execution model for grid computing and workflows?

Dennis Gannon

As I outlined in my talk, I see the programming model for grids to be workflow by component composition of services. The service model is well suited to provide a virtualization layer above heterogeneous, distributed, unreliable resources. The execution model is invocation of services by a workflow engine and reliable delivery of events.

Ken Kennedy

In the long run, I would see the programming interface as being similar to the one that is used today in normal single-platform applications, except that invocations would be redirected to machines offering the services. All this is possible now, although the scheduling of communication and computation needs to take performance into account. As to how the services would be paid for, each service supplier would enhance the value of his/her resource by offering the library services, which would allow them to charge more.

Mladen Vouk

I expect that the workflow programming models of the future will allow a composite of the solutions ranging from network-delivered high-quality services of different granularity, with very well defined interfaces, and with good ability to interoperate both with other workflow models and with both grid and other than "grid" based communication and resource sharing solutions.

Questioner: Mo Mu

What do you think is the role of APIs in the composition of workflows as a mechanism/standards to ensure the proper fitting of components/services?

Dennis Gannon

API's play a very critical role. In a service based architecture, the interface to each component service in a workflow is an API. It is a precise specification of the types of messages a component can understand and act upon. It also provides a specification of the messages a component can generate.

Ken Kennedy

I think we will need very general API specifications that go beyond the current type matching in component integration systems. Additional useful information might be size of data arrays or files, shape, etc. Knowing this information might permit the scheduler to pick the most efficient service for a given invocation context. So the short answer is that good API specifications will be very important both in ensuring correctness and efficiency.

Mladen Vouk

Well defined, open and information rich APIs are extremely important in ensuring interoperability of workflows and understanding of the semantics behind different components and services. Without that we are heading towards another mixed-language programming problem that may create "stove-pipes" and isolation between communities instead of promoting the opposite.

Questioner: Keith Jackson

What role does semantic information play in a component architecture? What kinds of semantic information should a service expose?

Dennis Gannon

Semantic information plays an extremely important role in service composition. It can tell us if two services can truly be composed. Just because they are type compatible, it does not mean that the output of one service is really suitable for the input of another. Semantic information goes well beyond what you can express in standard type theories. For example, it can tell you about the dynamic range of a service, information about its time complexity based on input values, information about resource requirements for a given input.

Ken Kennedy

There are two kinds of semantic information: that which is of use to the developer and that which can be used by the compiler or program integration system to improve performance. From the compiler perspective (my specialty) we need to know when two sequences of component invocations are equivalent in a certain calling context so that we can optimize the program to that context. From that perspective, (asymptotic) running time of the underlying algorithm is important semantic information.

Mladen Vouk

I believe that without appropriate semantic information it will not be possible to move to large scale, diverse, hierarchical and verifiable, as well as fault-tolerant, workflow solutions. There are probably be at least two major categories of semantic information: a) canonical (e.g., that associated with supporting sciences such as mathematics, statistics, computer science, information technology, ...) related to such elements as data and data structures, operations on those structures, related events and behaviors, constraints and assumptions, re-usable functions, process models, etc., etc.;

and b) domain specific (which may cover a wide range of properties, from domain specific data structures and operations to performance, reliability and security requirements, to domain specific process models and dos and don'ts etc.). The trick is to have rich enough and flexible enough models and interface specification options to allow interfaces to automatically exchange, match, and assess mutual semantic and other interface information and provide self-verification and validation.

Questioner: Anne Trefethen

How do we get community agreement on the semantics?

Dennis Gannon

First find a common meta-language to describe the semantics of components. Second, we can work on basic interoperability. One can start with a set of domains where this is a concern, for example, biomedical apps. This is an area where three or four of the major workflow tools are in current use and many of the same services are used. One could convene a meeting to look at interoperability and semantics.

Ken Kennedy

It is very difficult to agree on a language in which to specify semantics, because the language needs to support the reasoning styles that are needed by particular tools. For example, in our work we wanted to be able to substitute a loop around a get of an out-of-core data array element with a get of a whole row or column. There is no way to do that without having deep compiler concepts like dependence built into the language. In other words, different systems will need different languages to support their activities.

I should note that my group is working with a developer who wants to replace much of the functionality of full MPI with a smaller efficient set of primitives that could be combined to provide all the functionality of the current MPI. In other words, they want a compiler that can replace MPI calls with provably equivalent calls to the lower-level library. (Here Gropp comments that this was not done in the original because it was so tightly integrated with the underlying platform). My comment in response: The platform would be an additional (silent) parameter to the component library.

Mladen Vouk

I think that a fairly broad meeting, relatively soon --- probably within a year --- that would involve both open source and closed source workflow communities, developers and stake holders is an essential step in bootstrapping workflow related interoperability, interfaces, protocols, etc.

Bill Gropp

One example was the process that started the MPI Forum. Ken Kennedy called a workshop of many of the developers of message passing systems to answer the question "is it possible to standardize message passing for scientific computing?". The result of this workshop was a commitment by many of those developers to consider a possible standard. Mladen's talk listed many open source workflow system; perhaps a similar workshop would identify, if not one area of standardization, a much smaller number of topics, some of which may be able to develop standards or standard practices. It may also provide a way to develop standards for the interoperation of workflow tools, or standards for sharing representations of workflows.

PART 2

APPLICATION EXPERIENCE

R. Boisvert, Session Chair; B. Einarsson, Discussant

P. Gaffney & T. Hopkins: *Virtual Manufacturing - A Vision for Virtual Paint Operations*

D. Schissel: *Service-oriented Computation in Magnetic Fusion Research* (Abstract)

D. Walker: *Lessons Learned from the GECEM Project*

Panel Discussion

Virtual Manufacturing
A Vision for Virtual Paint Operations

Patrick Gaffney[1], Tim Hopkins[2]
[1] BSSI AS, Post Box 18, Nyborg, Heiane 4, 5879 Bergen, Norway
pat@bssi-tt.com,
WWW home page: http://www.bssi-tt.com
[2] Computing Laboratory, University of Kent
Canterbury, Kent, CT2 7NF, UK
t.r.hopkins@kent.ac.uk,
WWW home page: http://www.cs.kent.ac.uk/people/staff/trh/index.html

Abstract. The present paper deals less with Grid computing than with other aspects of this conference, namely numerical software. The goal of our work is to use mathematical modeling and computer simulation to avoid building non-production prototypes in manufacturing processes. Of particular interest is to eliminate prototypes associated with *painting processes* used in the automotive industry. Since painting processes are difficult to simulate accurately, the numerical software employed in the computational simulation is quite complex and requires substantial computing power to get a decent result within the timeframes of an industrial operational environment. On the other hand, the rewards for getting it right go straight to a company's bottom line: eliminating prototypes leads to tangible savings in terms of paint and materials, man power, energy costs, reduced warrantee costs, improved operational processes, and improved quality of the finished product. Getting it right therefore, is the subject of this paper.

1 Introduction

To most people painting a car conjures up pictures, from Discovery Channel and elsewhere, of robots spray painting cars on an assembly line. Although this is the way most vehicles end up by being painted it is by no means the whole story. For that, one needs to go back and look at the processes that prepare the metal of the car body so that it can become the final shiny product seen on the road.

Please use the following format when citing this chapter:

Gaffney, P., Hopkins, T., 2007, in IFIP International Federation for Information Processing, Volume 239, Grid-Based Problem Solving Environments, eds. Gaffney, P. W., Pool, J.C.T., (Boston: Springer), pp. 71-88.

That shiny product is the reflection of a sequence of processes that prepare the vehicle to sustain the effects from inclement weather - corrosion, while providing a base coating of the metal that enhances the quality of the finished vehicle.

The processes are well known to most people, although they may not connect them to being applied to cars on the road. Broadly speaking the processes consists of cleaning the metal of the vehicle body, preparing the metal to receive paint, applying a protective coating - electrocoating, rinsing, and baking. The protective coating is organic and the baking process is the final act that melts the resin polymer in the coating to provide the required corrosion protection.

It is crucial to get this sequence of painting processes right because errors at any stage have a detrimental impact on the bottom line of the automotive company, and some errors will become apparent to the unhappy owner. Errors will occur for a variety of reasons: maybe the cleaning was not effective enough, maybe some of the protective coating remains in puddles in the vehicle as it enters the oven, maybe the protective coating did not adequately cover all areas of the vehicle so that hard to reach areas do not have enough coating or maybe they do not have any. The list is almost endless, and each one of these items is significantly costly to fix.

In an attempt to understand the causes of errors and identify suitable remedial action, companies have traditionally experimented with physical prototypes of new vehicles by subjecting them to the same painting processes. However, experimentation and testing on physical prototypes is necessarily limited to the number of prototypes that can be built, not to mention the costs incurred in terms of manpower, materials, time, and the fact that the physical operating conditions, i.e. the paint tanks and cure ovens, must be used for the experiments, and therefore the normal manufacturing process must be interrupted, which in itself is an unacceptable cost to bear.

The *hope* of uncovering better ways of ensuring success in the application of the painting processes mentioned above is a vain one if all that is done is to use *physical* trial and error experimentation. On the other hand the *hope* becomes a reality if one can use computers to replace the *physical* nature of the experimentation. To do this requires that the painting processes must be simulated on a computer and this simulation requires detailed and accurate mathematical models of the underlying physics and chemistry of each painting process.

2   Virtual Manufacturing

Virtual manufacturing is the application of computer software to simulate a new product and the processes required to take that product from a design concept through to its actual manufacture using physical materials. Software simulation allows problems to be identified and remedied before the fabrication of the product begins.

Virtual manufacturing is not a new concept; it has been around for several decades, promoted, justifiably, by the use of finite element techniques to model complex geometries thereby expanding the range of products that are susceptible to this process.

The finite element method is a computational method to solve complex three-dimensional partial differential equations, especially those where it is important to know what happens in the *interior* of the solution domain.

Another technique involves recasting the partial differential equations as integral equations and then employing Boundary Integral Methods for their solution. For this recasting to be possible, a fundamental solution of the partial differential equations, a so-called Green's function, must exist. The set of industrial problems for which a Green's function exists is not as large as the set of problems that can be solved by the finite element method. However, for many industrial problems in engineering, it is possible to determine a Green's function and for these cases boundary integral methods are an alternative solution technique to the finite element method. Boundary integral methods are useful when it is important to know what happens on the *boundary* of a closed region as opposed to the *interior*. There are many industrial processes where the solution is only required on the boundary and for these cases, boundary integral methods are often the only practical approach because including the interior of the region makes a solution by the finite element method computationally intractable. Three particular processes where the solution is required on the boundary are:

- Electrochemical processes
- Transient heat flow in an oven
- Crack propagation

Thus, the boundary integral technique further extends the range of problems that can be addressed by virtual manufacturing. There are two main aspects of virtual manufacturing though: the simulation of the new product *and* the simulation of the processes. Finite element and boundary integral techniques extend the range of products that can be simulated but it still remains to simulate the processes themselves and the processes mentioned above are non-trivial.

Recent advances in the mathematical techniques underpinning the boundary integral method combined with advances in computer hardware and software mean that virtual manufacturing can be extended to simulating electrochemical processes especially those involved in the painting processes described in the previous section.

3   Characteristics of Painting Processes

Although painting processes are simple to describe, the resultant three-dimensional mathematical models of them are complex and range from potential theory, through fluid flow and computational fluid dynamics, to elasticity, to name but a few. Nevertheless, the overriding most important consideration of any simulation of these processes is the inclusion of *time*. Steady-state descriptions of these processes are completely inadequate as a basis for *predicting* what will happen in the physical process. Operators need to know what happens at any instant of a process and therefore accurate time-dependent solutions are a necessity for employing computational simulation as a replacement for testing and experimentation using physical prototypes.

Computational simulations of painting processes are time dependent and for operational reasons a true time-stepping solution method must be employed. Solution domains involve complex geometries consisting of automobiles, paint tanks, cleaning tanks, and cure ovens. A *virtual* toolset that replaces *physical* trial-and-error testing thus requires incorporating all of these items and human experience into software that can be used easily by non-computer specialists, at both ends of the manufacturing chain: the upstream users at the design stage and the downstream users at the manufacturing stage. Only when this is done properly, and the software is validated, will users be convinced to switch to virtual tools as part of their everyday work environment.

4 Validation

The previous paragraphs help to characterize the nature of the software that industrial operational environments need. At the heart of the simulation software are methods and techniques that are traditionally described as *numerical software*. It is a long strenuous path to take that numerical software and form a system that commercial users will feel comfortable with. It is not only the look-and-feel of the software that is important it is the confidence that using the software will help them to understand better the physical manufacturing processes that they are really interested in. This means effectively that the users are confident of the results obtained from the simulation, in other words the software has been validated to produce accurate results that can be relied upon. This level of confidence is often not present in what many people regard as *numerical software*.

The testing regime, to which operational software of the functionality and calibre described above is subjected, is rigorous in the extreme. The process begins after the initial software has been written and takes the form of unit testing on geometries that exhibit some of the behavior expected in real automobiles and that can be verified by simple laboratory experiments conducted by the automobile company. Even these tests are more rigorous than those used to verify software published in ACM TOMS for example. As development proceeds, test geometries evolve in complexity until at a certain stage actual vehicle parts and bodies are used to stress test the software. This process is monitored closely by end users who actually reproduce the results by running the software themselves on their own machines and compare results with measurements taken of physical prototypes that have been stripped down and measured after painting.

These testing and validation procedures contribute to confidence building and numerical software developers should take heed and learn from them. For example, in addition to testing on increasingly complex models the process benefits from the active participation of an *independent champion* of the software, namely the automobile user. As development of the software proceeds it is in the interests of the automobile company that the software succeeds and therefore aberrations and errors that come to light from their testing are immediately brought to the attention of the developers. In the course of developing the virtual toolset described in this paper, approximately 80% of the time has been spent on testing, verification, and debugging.

5   Virtual Paint Operations™ (VPO™)

VPO™ is the name of a family of software products and services developed by BSSI over the last 10 years according to the descriptions given in the previous sections, where the champion in this case is Ford Motor Company in North America. The software addresses the simulation of the painting processes: electrocoating, drainage, baking, and the elimination of air pockets. Each simulator in the toolset is a time stepping *predictor* that enables the operator to access the results of the simulation at any moment in time. Thus, for example, it is possible for an operator to monitor the oven baking process and see how the predicted solution behaves at every second the automobile is in the oven. In this way, the company can develop operating strategies that enable them to take account of changes in operations, for example different oven loads, without interrupting daily operations in the actual oven.

To address look-and-feel, the software is operated through a unified interface that provides access to all the simulators from one graphical user interface. The painting processes described previously are not independent of each other. For example, doing a poor job of electrocoating has an affect on the quality that can be expected from the cure oven. Consequently, the emphasis of the interface design is in the inter-operability of the simulators. Being able to simulate different what-if scenarios that *couple* baking, drainage, and electrocoating simulators - by passing data and results backwards and forwards between the different simulators - is an emphasis that stems from watching how users perform their daily tasks. The tasks are not independent and therefore as far as possible it should be possible to use the simulators in a similar way.

Operational environments, especially manufacturing processes that produce millions of items per year, have a strong emphasis on timeliness: operations and decisions need to be taken quickly and in a time that does not hamper the manufacturing process or delay the throughput of items (vehicles in this case). Consequently, it is very important that the simulators produce results quickly – not necessarily the *final* results but intermediate ones. For example, in a simulation of the electrocoating process of a vehicle the VPO™ EPD code can produce output at every $1/1000^{th}$ of a second and this output is available to the user for analysis as soon as it is produced. In this way, the user can take decisions without having to wait for the simulation to finish.

The single most effective way of handling timeliness, and the production of results rapidly, is to use parallel computing, and in today's environments clusters are the preferred architecture.

Of course all of the above – real-time visualization of results, coupling, inter-operability of simulators, and computational steering - assumes that information, in the form of intermediate results from the simulator, is readily available to the user, which it is from the VPO™ System operating in a Grid-like environment, but it is not when the system is constrained to work in batch environments.

Of the painting processes discussed above, the one that is the most complex to simulate and computationally intensive is electrocoating.

6   Electrocoat Simulation – VPO™ EPD

The process to apply rust-preventing coatings to automobiles must ensure that all parts of the vehicle have an adequate minimum build of paint. Currently, the main method used to minimize salt spray induced corrosion involves application of an epoxy-based urethane coating using an electrodeposition technique called electrocoating. Car parts are suspended from a gantry, lowered, and transported through a tank filled with the urethane paint called electrocoat or e-coat. Each part is treated as a cathode and by applying a voltage to the anodes; the paint adheres to the car part.

Basic mathematical model

(a)   The rate that paint is deposited on the cathode is a function of the local current density j:

$$d/dt(L_F(t)) = \beta * j$$

L_F is the thickness of the paint and β is the current efficiency.

(b)   The current density j, as a function of position over the cathode surface, is obtained from the *normal derivative* of the electric potential Φ, which is determined by solving the 3D Laplace equation $\nabla^2\Phi=0$, subject to boundary conditions.

(c)   No boundary values are specified on the cathode but there is a time dependent relationship between surface potential and current density.

Basic numerical methods

Complicated car frame geometry and anode configurations are composed of thin metal and are thus modelled as an infinitely thin crack geometry. In order to treat thin parts, boundary integral equations for surface potential and surface flux are employed. By using the integral equation approach the normal derivative of the electric potential, see (b) above, is calculated directly, i.e., *without numerical differentiation*. The integral equations are approximated using a Galerkin method, which allows for a straightforward and mathematically correct analysis of the hypersingular flux equation essential for treating thin parts as a single surface. Accurate and efficient Galerkin singular integration algorithms based upon analytic integration have been developed by Gray [16]. Finally, a new proprietary time stepping algorithm is used to track the time evolution of the paint distribution (a).

The boundary integral equations are reduced to a finite system of linear equations by approximating the surface in terms of the elements defined by the nodal points of a computational grid, and then interpolating the surface potential and flux in terms of values at these nodes. This results in a matrix system

$$G[Y] = H[\Phi]$$

In this system, H and G are square matrices and [Φ] and [Y] are column vectors of the nodal values of potential and current. Taking into account the known boundary conditions, these linear equations must be solved simultaneously with the relationship between surface potential and current density (see (c) above).

The deployed commercial versions of the VPO™ EPD Simulator implement the above numerical methods in Fortran 90/95 adapted to parallel processing using the message passing interface, MPI.

Basic computational method

The main computational method is parallel processing, and in this paper the discussion focuses on the use the message passing interface (MPI) [3]. The computational problem decomposes into four main steps.

1. **Data distribution**: since each process needs access to the whole geometry the data files are read in and a copy stored on each process. We note here that one of the major users of this software is insisting on staying with MPI-1 [7]; we are developing using mpich2 [9] (but only using the MPI-1 subset). While MPI-2 [8] has facilities to allow each process to access the data files, we use the MPI-1 model where the master node reads the data and broadcasts it to all the other processes.

2. **Construction of the matrices**: The G and H matrices are both of order n where n is dependent on the total number of nodes defining both the car part (cathode) and the anodes and the tank.

   The elements of these arrays require the computation of a large number $(O(n^2))$ of two dimensional numerical integrals. The basic computational loop is of the form

   do $i \in S$
     do $k \in T^k$
       integral (element(i), element(j))

   where S is the set of all elements in the grid and T^k is a subset of these elements that is dependent on the type of integration taking place and the position of the element within the grid. Each element in S is involved in four different types of integral and the execution speed of these types differs by almost two orders of magnitude. All the integrals may be performed independently and each one only affects a maximum of six rows in each array. In addition, the updated rows are generally close together due to the way in which the grid generator assigns node numbers. Finally, the set of elements, T^k, only affects the column indices that are updated although these indices may take on a wide range and, for one type of integral, almost the whole row may be involved.

It therefore seemed sensible to assign contiguous blocks of whole rows to each process and to arrange the processes in a single column.

3. **Solution of the linear system**: This requires the factorization of G followed by the solution of n sets of linear equations where G is a general, dense matrix.

4. **Timestepping**: At this stage the main computational overhead is a sparse matrix / full vector multiply where the order of the sparse matrix is only dependent on the number of cathode (vehicle component) nodes. Generally this is substantially smaller than the order, n, of the original system. The sparsity level is not uniformly high but, given the size of the resultant systems and the large number of time steps required, taking account of sparsity is well worth the effort.

Timeline

Figure 1 shows an approximate timeline of the progression from initial development to full customer deployment. Almost from the beginning of development the testing and validation process began, getting progressively more complex as time passed.

Figure 1. Timeline showing development of VPO™ EPD

Challenges		1999	2000	2001	2002	2003	2004	2005	2006	2007
	Test geometry Flat plates					Mini-Door	Rocker Panel Door frames Full vehicle			
(A)	Implementation			Serial				Parallel		
	Deployment to users									
	Implementing new functionality stemming from users experiences with the software									
	Determining user workflows									
(B)	Incorporating into production									

Testing and validation commenced with simple geometries because those are the ones that can be used for testing and experimenting in actual laboratory conditions, without impacting any manufacturing process. Simple laboratory experiments are the heart and key to the success of the VPO™ EPD simulator.

For a given electrocoat, the parameters used in simulating the electrocoating process can be determined, tested, and verified against laboratory experiments applied to simple geometries. These parameters are then incorporated into the mathematical model that is the core of the VPO™ EPD simulator, which can then be used in simulations using more complex geometries. When the supplied electrocoat changes, the laboratory experiments are repeated and the simulator model adjusted accordingly. This is a crucial aspect because it means that the model does not have to be retooled when it is applied to real vehicles, or when new vehicle models are produced, or when the conditions in the electrocoat tank change for any reason.

The following figures show some of the test geometries and their progression in complexity.

Mini-door

The geometry shown in the picture is extremely simple and is designed to reflect some of the characteristics found in real vehicle parts. The area indicated by the arrow is of particular interest to the thin-surface approach used in VPO™ EPD because at this junction a number of surfaces meet and have to be treated in a mathematically correct manner, proprietary techniques for which have been developed by BSSI.

Rocker panel

The rocker panel can be considered to be among the most problematical vehicle parts when it comes to electrocoating. It is a complicated structure with many interior parts that combine to form inaccessible areas where it is difficult for the e-coat paint to reach. If this happens then, the likelihood of corrosion problems in later life increases dramatically and this is the main reason why the use of VPO™ EPD is so important – to identify strategies that will avoid this situation.

Door Frame

A door-frame is the lion of vehicle parts. It consists of the rocker panel plus the supporting pillars for the vehicle's doors and wheels. It is a supremely majestic, complicated structure and the accurate modeling of electrocoating this vehicle part is a challenge, which when successful is immensely satisfying.

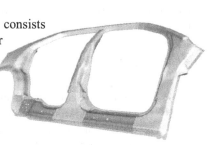

Larger part

The challenge to simulating a realistic operating environment not only comes from the size of the cathode – in this case a full vehicle frame – but also the tank and anodes in which the vehicle is transported. The tank shown in the picture is 35m long and contains 265 anodes, each one of which has to be meshed and placed in the correct position relative to the vehicle.

An indication of the relative sizes between the different geometries mentioned above can be seen in Table 1 where the number of nodes and elements required to model each one using VPO™ EPD are displayed.

Table 1. Example problem sizes for various car parts

	Nodes	**Elements**
Mini-door	2700	2758
Rocker panel	22906	21323
Door frame	34224	31163
Larger part	94156	86420

After running the gauntlet of complex geometry, and producing simulated parameter values to within limits set by the automotive company, the VPO™ EPD simulator can be applied in any vehicle program with confidence. Because of the underlying architecture employed, parallel processing using MPI, any vehicle geometry can be simulated within a time frame that is consistent with the automotive company's operational requirements.

Size and execution time are not the issues for discussion, rather the remainder of this paper addresses the challenges marked (**A**) and (**B**) in Figure 1.

7   (A) Implementation

The serial code mentioned in the timeline above began as a Fortran 77 prototype that was capable of running small geometries, such as flat plates and mini-doors. The code was developed on a 32-bit stand-alone PC using a commercial Fortran compiler [1].

A separate activity to write a commercial standard code began, from scratch, in 2003, and used Fortran 90 [2]. This move allowed a number of improvements, among which were:

1.   The use of allocatable arrays and linked lists to ensure that memory requirements were kept to a problem dependent minimum.
2.   The use of modules to encapsulate parts of the simulation, such as the simulation model. This allowed for easier changing of, and experimentation with, simulation models.
3.   The execution speed decreased by approximately 25%.

The Fortran 90 serial code provided the basis for the commercial parallel code generated using MPI [3] together with associated numerical libraries such as ScaLAPACK [4].

Hardware
A requirement imposed by BSSI is that the parallel architecture used for simulations should, as far as possible, be composed from inexpensive, environmentally friendly, commodity hardware. In other words, if a cluster is to be used then consider one built from PCs that conform to this description. This requirement is not necessarily advocated by industry and in fact as later sections will show not adhering to the requirement imposes a hurdle to the vision for *virtual* paint operations that is the theme of this paper.

The initial implementation of the MPI version of the simulator used a 4-node, 32-bit architecture comprised of Intel Celeron 2.4 GHz machines, each with 2 GB of memory and interconnected with a gigabit network. This provided a great test environment, for a total cost of less than $3000, and enabled experimentation on small to medium sized geometries.

The major drawback with the 32-bit cluster was that it restricted the amount of memory available to 2 GB per processor. To accommodate larger memory requirements in a cost effective manner required the use of larger memory chips as well as an increase in the number of processors. This prompted a move to 64-bit architecture (to allow the addressing of larger amounts of memory) which in turn required a change of compiler technology from Lahey to PGI [15] since, at the time Lahey did not support full 64-bit addressing for individual arrays. The initial configuration for the 64-bit cluster was a 9-node cluster with each node comprising a 64-bit AMD Athlon 3800 processor, rated at 2.4 GHz, each node of which has 3 GB of memory and, as before, the nodes are interconnected by a gigabit network. In 2004, the total cost of this setup was less than $8,000 and has, until recently, been used to simulate the full range of vehicle geometries needed in operations at BSSI.

Source code

For ease of development, it was decided to have a single source code and to use fpp [5] to extract either the sequential or MPI versions of the software.

The decision to use fpp appeared to have several advantages, for example, sharing the majority of the source code between the two versions would mean that, in many cases, a single edit would correct or update both versions of the software. In practice the disadvantages far outweighed the advantages. As the code developed the use of macros increased and it became difficult to update the source with confidence, indeed it was often necessary to extract both versions to check that changes made were as intended. More importantly, it was not possible to use software tools, like the NagWare suite [6], on the master version. These problems contributed to a general downward drift in both the readability and testability of the code until they were finally separated.

MPI

The basic MPI framework is available from Argonne via the MPICH1 and MPICH2 implementations. Other implementations tend to be minor variations on the basic package and most of the time it is difficult to find out exactly what are the variations and what they might be useful for. Therefore, the starting point for our work was MPICH1 and then MPICH2.

Our experiences with MPI, starting out as complete beginners, have been mixed. The MPICH2 [9] implementation is freely available and is first class. The final product is efficient and has been error free. Our only minor gripe is that the installation guide listed a number of configuration options which appeared not to be either implemented or working. However the advice and help we received via email was excellent and we soon had a working installation.

We could have used far more assistance from support tools throughout the implementation and maintenance of the software. Debugging is an order of magnitude more difficult for a distributed code and a good profiler would have enabled the early detection of inefficient parallel code and poor data distribution. As is to be expected a Google search for MPI support tools returns a large number of hits; what is required (and appears to be missing at the moment) is a definitive guide to which tools are (and are not) worth investing time and effort in.

We found the mpiP lightweight profiling library [10] very useful once we had learnt how to interpret the information it presented; we were impressed with both the documentation and the best-efforts support that were on offer. For a debugger TotalView [11] looks good but it is commercial (we were looking for open source) and thus Jumpshot [12] looks potentially useful.

There is also a problem with the migration to MPICH2. One of our industrial partners is staying with MPICH1; they have an efficient implementation and a large software base that still uses the earlier version. Despite the fact that MPICH2 contains all of MPICH1 they will neither upgrade nor make both versions available.

Compiler vendors have not, as yet, entered the specially tuned MPI installation market to any great degree. Few vendors offer pre-compiled versions of MPI itself and all that appears to be on offer are vanilla implementations with no special optimizations.

ScaLAPACK

In an MPI-based parallel environment, the *standard* package for solving dense linear systems using direct methods is ScaLAPACK, [4, 13], the parallel brother of LAPACK. Consequently, the ScaLAPACK routines *dgetrf* and *dgetrs* (see [4] for details) were used to implement step 3 in section 6 above. According to the ScaLAPACK manual [4] these routines for solving dense sets of linear equations work most effectively on a rectangular grid of processes with the data distributed using a block-cyclic distribution. Distributing by row slicing is likely to be inefficient and this is borne out by the execution times on a selection of test geometries. For example, the execution times obtained by solving the linear equations with $n=7178$ are given in Table 2.

Table 2. Execution times for ScaLAPACK routines *dgetrf* and *dgetrs* for solving GY = H with n = 7178

Grid	Time (seconds)
2 x 2	356
4 x 1	626
4 x 2	185
8 x 1	341

These timings clearly show the advantage of using a two dimensional grid even for a very small number of processes. The problem here is that a block cyclic distribution is sub-optimal for the parallel computation of the integral (step 2 in section 6 above). However, as the problem size grows the $O(n^3)$ complexity of the solution of the linear systems of equations dominates the computation and a move to a block cyclic distribution becomes far more appealing.

ScaLAPACK represents a monumental software effort; essentially it provides all the functionality of Lapack in distributed form with MPI forming one of the available base level communication libraries. We suspect that the manual [4], while comprehensive, is now somewhat out-of-date as concerns example hardware and advice on how to tune the routines to deliver maximum throughput; a maintained web based manual would be an advantage here.

The downside of ScaLAPACK is that it is based on a number of layers that have remained unloved for the better part of a decade and the whole package requires considerable effort to install. The installation document is very old as are the Makefiles that are included (many for platforms that only now exist in museums). While some of the system dependent configuration settings can be obtained easily by running a number of small programs provided in the distribution, others are obscure. A mechanism that would allow successful installers to donate their makefiles and/or complete libraries would also be extremely helpful. Finally there is no easy way to extract and build a subset of the ScaLAPACK routines – for example, VPO™ EPD only wanted to call two top-level routines but the building of a call tree and the extraction of the routines in that tree was and is a non-trivial task.

The learning curve for ScaLAPACK is quite steep. Solving some problems was certainly not helped by the opacity of some of the error messages. For example, when using $P \times 1$ grid of processes to solve a general, square linear system of order n, it seems logical to set the size of the local blocks to $mb = \lceil n/P \rceil$ and nb to n (since each process will be holding all the columns). This results in an illegal value for nb error; which could only be resolved by examining the source code where it was discovered that nb needs to be equal to mb.

Finally, there are a number of support routines that act in rather peculiar ways; for example, the subroutine INFOG2L which *computes the starting local row and column indices and process row and column indices of a global element of a block-cyclically distributed matrix*. Put another way, if we wish to find the value of a_{ij} calling INFOG2L with the values i and j will return k, l, r and c such that element a_{ki} on the process in position (r,c) in the grid holds the required value. Now, it would appear safe to assume that, given i and j define a unique element, INFOG2L would return the same result on every process. However, this assumption is wrong because the routine requires the user to state which process is calling the routine so that it can return the wrong answer on all the processes except the one holding the element. It is not clear why this decision was made, especially as it is actually more efficient to compute the correct answer on all processes.

Such quirky behaviour is strange but the problem does not end there. At least one other implementer, IBM [14], has included this routine in their parallel ESSL library and they even provide an example which shows how the wrong answer is computed by all processes except one; consistency at all costs? We need to take care not to spread such peculiar behaviours and this requires some form of active maintenance.

Summary

For those of us who experienced the heyday of numerical software development in the 70s and 80s, it is depressing to discover that many of the hard earned lessons from that era appear to have been forgotten. As an example:

> *One of us (PG) was recently interviewed for over an hour by a very pleasant young man at Intel who turned out to be completely ignorant of the existence of NAG or IMSL, and who had never heard of the work on floating point arithmetic by Kahan and the*

IFIP Working Group on Numerical Software, and who, needless to say, was blissfully unaware of the extent to which that legacy of work is today present in the very good Intel Math Library.

In the world of cluster programming that level of ignorance appears to be very common and one feels cast adrift into a parallel world that seems to exist without any knowledge of, or influence from, the body of numerical software that existed before and after the BLAS; for this is the one piece of software that is peddled by the vendors as the general panacea for all one's numerical problems. When it comes to implementing high quality mathematical software for a parallel environment using MPI, the current situation is woeful. The present state of the open source MPI implementations certainly require some tuning and perhaps this is to be expected – if an out-of-the-box solution is required then some would say that commercial software should be used instead of open-source. This might very well be the case except at this stage it is very difficult to determine the differences between the open-source versions of MPI and those available from commercial vendors, except the price.

The exercise of constructing high quality mathematical software suitable and robust enough for commercial applications using open source / freely available software is possible but requires a great deal of effort and perseverance. The expenditure of this effort is tempered by the thought that many other users have, most likely, already trodden the same path and what a good idea it would be if such duplication of work could be avoided. It really is time that the developers of packages like ScaLAPACK. PBLAS, etc took a lead from the thriving open source community currently producing high quality software using the facilities provided by, for example, SourceForge. Here projects are kept alive and up-to-date either by the original authors or by other interested (and knowledgeable) parties rather than being allowed to languish unloved on the original authors web or ftp site. Sites like SourceForge provide a central, easy to find location where users can download the most recent version of the software, report bugs, donate Makefiles and ask questions; software improves by expanding the user community and gaining feedback.

It is possible with determination, and a strong and encouraging *champion* of the software, to produce quality industrial strength software. Real vehicle parts, including full frame automobiles and trucks, are now straightforward to simulate using the parallel version of VPO™ EPD in an elapsed time that makes experimentation with different designs practical. The end result is a software product that enables significant reduction in costs, enhances good environmental practices, and improves the quality of the end product, namely the vehicles on the road.

7   (B) Incorporating into production

This section describes the most interesting aspect of this work because the *value* of the work depends on how successful it is to engage the workforce in using the new *virtual* toolset. If we fail in this regard then, it doesn't really matter how clever we have been in solving complex simulation problems since end users will not use the tools, for one reason or another. And one lesson we have learned from many years of working with large corporations: it doesn't always follow that it is the fault of the software that is the reason why users do not use it, for they have other influences that may be more powerful than the ones you thought of in designing the software. Those influences boil down to one word: people. People in all levels of the organization will have and will always want a say, justified or not, in the use of the software – and that is the problem that has to be addressed and solved if the software is to be a success. People come and go but the software must remain for the good of the company.

Skills - *engagement*

Complex manufacturing computational problems are rarely solved by the push of a button, and even if they were it would not be sensible to avoid human intervention at some point, if only to examine results and messages stemming from the computation.

Currently, industrial operational environments rely heavily on people with hands-on experience that it is crucial to utilize in the computer simulation of complex processes. This experience needs to be captured and used in order to augment decision making processes encoded in software.

For computer simulations to be more effective than physical prototyping, software must be adapted to the existing skill base rather than the other way around:

(a)   Software should be designed to use the knowledge and experience of users, because the processes being simulated cannot normally be performed effectively without their input and guidance.

(b)   Users should feel comfortable in using the software – as far as possible the graphical controls, labels, and functions of user interfaces should reflect terminology and processes that are familiar to users from their working experience in the plant.

(c)   Users must have confidence in the software – this can only be gained over time and by comparing results from the virtual process with those from the actual events.

(d)   Generating what-if scenarios and experimenting to see the effects of different hypotheses will produce substantial quantities of output that needs to be analyzed, interpreted, and distilled into summaries for management to make the correct decisions. The existing workforce may be equipped to do these tasks but their job will be easier and more effective if the software contains tools to mine the data and extract trends and patterns.

Only when all of these aspects are addressed successfully can the real benefits of virtual processing be obtained: a workforce that is *engaged* in the virtual process and that has the confidence to experiment with the software. Only then will they gain an understanding of what is possible and what will improve the end product and, in the process of achieving this, they will improve their own job satisfaction.

The timeline in section 5 shows that this process for VPO™ EPD began in 2003 and continues as the software evolves - *real* software continues to evolve as feedback and experience are gained from people.

The vision

It has been our experience that even when the workforce is engaged and eager to work with software tools that give them more insight; very often the wherewithal to use the software is not at their disposal because of computer policies that inhibit the true use of computer technology. In this regard, the freedom experienced by the Grid community is definitely lacking in industry – in our opinion to its detriment. Putting this to one side then, the vision that BSSI sees for using *virtual* toolsets in manufacturing processes, not just painting processes, is one where  employees are empowered to run tools like VPO™ at their own workplace rather than through a centralized computing facility. The work conducted by BSSI over the last 10+ years shows that with the advances in computer technology and the consequent drop in prices, it is no longer necessary to use large computing facilities to obtain the benefits from virtual simulations. However, if some find objection to this remark then we can qualify it by saying that the simulation of painting processes described in this paper can definitely be accomplished by inexpensive, environmentally friendly, *personal* workstation clusters. All of the tools in VPO™ run on this type of cluster.

Personal clusters can have far reaching consequences for an industry fully committed to reducing costs by using computational simulation wherever appropriate. One obvious consequence is that a workforce equipped with *personal clusters* is much more likely to collaborate especially when the virtual tools are naturally interrelated as they are in VPO™. Successful collaboration is optimal for the company and therefore, the next stage of VPO™ that is already underway is the distributed environment shown in the picture where each personal cluster uses a combination of message passing and shared memory parallel processing.

Acknowledgments

The *champion* of VPO™ EPD, and the entire VPO™ toolset, is Ford Motor Company, and one individual in particular Jacob Braslaw. Both of them are to be commended for their foresight in starting the work over 10 years ago, which led to VPO™ EPD, and for their determination to see the work through to its present operational state with BSSI.

The experimentation with different workstation clusters and hardware would not have been possible without the willing participation of a hardware supplier with good business and service sense. BSSI is fortunate to have access to such a vendor in Datakjeden, [17], and especially their manager Stein Tore Hansen to whom we are gratefully thankful.

For help with their Fortran compiler above and beyond what normally one experiences, BSSI is very grateful to the support from PGI, [18], and their David Borer.

Finally, we would like to thank Brian Smith, for providing an early version of his Test Harness, [19], which we intend to integrate into our software maintenance cycle to improve and ease both our regression testing and debugging activities.

References

[1] Lahey Computer Systems, Lahey/Fujitsu Fortran 95 User's Guide, Linux Edition, Revision C, 2001.

[2] ISO/IEC, Information Technology -- Programming Languages -- Fortran - Part 1: Base Language (ISO/IEC 1539-1:2004), ISO/IEC Copyright Office, Geneva, 2004.

[3] W. Gropp, E. Lusk and A. Skjellum, Using MPI: Portable Parallel Programming with the Message-Passing Interface, Second Edition, The MIT Press, Cambridge Massachusetts, 1999.

[4] L. S. Blackford , J. Choi, A. Cleary, E. D'Azeuedo, J. Demmel, I. Dhillon, S. Hammarling, G. Henry, A. Petitet, K. Stanley, D. Walker and R. C. Whaley, ScaLAPACK User's Guide, Society for Industrial and Applied Mathematics, Philadelphia, PA, USA, 1997.

[5] Numerical Algorithms Group Ltd., fpp: Fortran language pre-processor for the NAGWare f95 compiler, NAG Ltd, Oxford, UK, 2005.

[6] Numerical Algorithms Group Ltd., NAGWare Fortran Tools (Release 4.1), NAG Ltd, Oxford, UK, 2001.

[7] M. Snir, S. Otto, S. Huss-Lederman, D. Walker and J. Dongarra, MPI – The Complete Reference: Volume 1, The MPI Core, The MIT Press, Cambridge Massachusetts, 1998.

[8] W. Gropp, S. Huss-Lederman, A. Lumsdaine, E. Lusk, B. Nitzberg, W. Saphir and M. Snir, MPI – The Complete Reference: Volume 2, The MPI-2 Extensions, The MIT Press, Cambridge Massachusetts, 1998.

[9] W. Gropp, E. Lusk, D. Ashton, P. Balaji, D. Buntinas, R. Butler, A. Chan, J. Krishna, G. Mercier, R. Ross, R. Thakur and B. Toonen, MPICH2 User's Guide: Version 1.0.3, Argonne National Laboratory, 2006.

[10] J. Vetter and C. Chambreau, mpiP: Lightweight, Scalable MPI Profiling, Version 3, http://mpip.sourceforge.net/, October, 2006.

[11] Etnus, TotalView Debugger, http://www.etnus.com/Documentation/index.php

[12] A. Chan, D. Ashton, R. Lusk and W. Gropp, Jumpshot-4 User's Guide, Argonne National Laboratory, 2005.

[13] Netlib, Scalapack Tools, http://www.netlib.org/scalapack/tools/infog2l.f

[14] IBM Corporation, Parallel Engineering and Scientific Subroutine Library for AIX: Guide and Reference, Version 3, Release 2, 2003.

[15] Portland Group, PGI User's Guide: Parallel Fortran, C and C++ for Scientists and Engineers, Oregon, US, 2006.

[16] L. J. Gray, J. M. Glaeser, T. Kaplan, *Direct Evaluation of Hypersingular Galerkin Surface Integrals*, SIAM Journal on Scientific Computing, volume 25, Number 5, pp. 1534-1556, (2004).

[17] http://www.datakjeden.no/default.asp?bID=1

[18] http://www.pgroup.com/

[19] Brian T. Smith, A Test Harness TH for Numerical applications and Libraries, these proceedings.

Q&A – Patrick Gaffney, Tim Hopkins

Questioner: Ian Reid

Are you using ACML for LAPACK / ScaLAPACK? If not, you should since it will almost certainly be the fastest for AMD processors. It is freely available from the AMD Website and is developed / supported by AMD & NAG.

Tim Hopkins:

Not at the moment. We looked at the download site several months ago and it appeared that Scalapack was no longer supported as it was listed only under their archive section. Given your comments we will look into this again.

Questioner: Boyana Norris

(a) Is the linear system sparse or dense?
(b) Why did you decide to use ScaLAPACK?

Pat Gaffney:

The linear systems are not sparse they are full matrices.

The first implementation of the system uses direct methods and therefore the MPI version is implemented using ScaLAPACK.

Another version of the system uses an acceleration technique, the Fast Spectral method that we have developed and that uses sparse techniques: the coefficient matrix is never assembled, and an iterative solver is required. This reduces the memory requirements significantly.

Questioner: Bill Applebe

Could commercial codes not have been used?

Tim Hopkins:

Certainly for the numerical computation there wasn't any software commercial or otherwise that implemented the methods we are using.

Pat Gaffney:

It is always possible to cobble together existing codes but that would not be as effective as the approach we have taken with VPO. Our customer tried for many years to use just such an approach and found it difficult to obtain necessary functional changes and support from the "one-size-fits-all" commercial code suppliers. For one thing, VPO has a uniform interface where all the VPO modules are accessible in one place. This was an important feature for the end customer and not one shared by disjoint systems.

However, by far the most important advantage of the VPO approach is that all of the modules: electrocoating, baking, drainage, voids, vibration, and future spray models, use the *same* computational grid, which is a definite advantage to the end-customer who already has a plethora of grids to contend with. Minimizing the number of grids by solving a range of problems using one grid is a distinct advantage and one offered by BSSI's VPO.

Questioner: Brian Smith

How do you test the software and how do you validate that the simulations are valid? What role does the customer play in the testing and validation process for the software?

Pat Gaffney:

The end customer has a rigorous sequence of procedures that must be followed before any software is accepted for operations. In the VPO work, testing is a continuous process involving both the end-customer and BSSI working closely together.

Comment: Ian Reid

On debuggers, you might like to look at DDT from Allinea as a cheaper alternative to Totalview.

Tim Hopkins:

Thanks for the information. Looking on their Web site they are also offering an optimization and profiling tool specifically for MPI applications. We will be evaluating these in the near future.

Questioner: Ron Boisvert

You painted a somewhat discouraging picture of the state of existing math software components that you are using to build your system. Given that such software is the underlying engine for technical applications, do you think that component-based grid systems and service oriented computing is realizable in the near term?

Tim Hopkins:

I'm sure that it is realizable in the near term in as much as people will be able to access the same low quality software they are currently familiar with via grid systems. What we are not hearing is how suppliers of grid systems intend to ensure that their users only have access to high quality, reliable and robust software. Perhaps this is a golden opportunity to impose quality on end users!

Service-oriented Computation in Magnetic Fusion Research

David Schissel

General Atomics

Abstract. Fusion science seeks a new power source and is advanced by experiments on fusion devices located worldwide. Fundamental to increasing understanding of fusion is the comparison of theory and experiment; measurements from fusion devices are analyzed and compared with the output of simulations to test the validity of fusion models and to uncover new physical properties. Integrating simulations with experimental data (or with other simulations) is in many cases a labor-intensive task as different codes use different data storage formats. Moreover, the timely comparison of simulation with observations made during an experiment requires rapid turnaround both of analysis codes and simulation runs. Many simulations require extensive input and output processing, further increasing the amount of work necessary to achieve viable scientific results. Workers with the National Fusion Collaboratory are developing, deploying, and evaluating new technologies that facilitate analysis of experimental data and comparison with the results with those of simulations. Complex physics codes are made available on the National Fusion Grid (FusionGrid) as comprehensive computational services. Using the Globus Toolkit", a service-based approach was developed and subsequently combined with the TRANSP transport code to the benefit of fusion scientists. Output from both simulation and experimental codes are stored in MDSplus, the de facto standard for secure data storage of fusion data. Access control for the resources of FusionGrid is greatly simplified_for both users and administrators_through unified authentication and authorization using X.509, a grid-wide certificate management system, and a grid-wide authorization system. Web-based solutions such as the recently developed Elfresco reflectometry code further simplify the process by making simulations available to scientists and providing an alternative to traditional distribution of code. Future work includes the development of parallelized modules to speed up long-running codes along with the extension of MDSplus. These

Please use the following format when citing this chapter:

Schissel, D., 2007, in IFIP International Federation for Information Processing, Volume 239, Grid-Based Problem Solving Environments, eds. Gaffney, P. W., Pool, J.C.T., (Boston: Springer), pp. 91-92.

improvements will help accommodate the continuous data streams that will be found in future fusion devices such as ITER. This paper will present a discussion on specific solutions, examine deployment areas that present a challenge, and highlight areas where further work is required.

Q&A – David Schissel

Questioner: David Walker

Could you comment on the similarities and dissimilarities between how the fusion community is using the grid and how the HEP community is using it; e.g. for analyzing LHC data?

David Schissel

The HEP/LHC community is using grid technology to move huge quantities of data to Tier sites for analysis that occurs after the experiment. For the experimental fusion community the quantity of data is not nearly as large. Thus, our usage of the grid is for more interactive work with data as well as providing computational services. Recent discussions between the fusion and HEP communities have identified areas of commonality between what FusionGrid has accomplished and what is needed by HEP to monitor (not analyze), in real-time ongoing experiments. The communities are examining ways to work together for their mutual benefit. It should be noted that both communities are using the grid for human communication with Access Grid and VRVS/EVO technology.

Questioner: Brian Smith

What is the current reliability levels (of network, computation, experimental /fusion systems)?

David Schissel

Network connectivity for fusion research in the United States is provided by ESnet with a reliability (this is from my memory) of somewhere between three and five 9's. The complex Tokamak systems that include power supplies, heating systems, diagnostics and computers are less reliable than ESnet but this is due to the lack of redundant systems whose cost would be prohibitive.

Questioner: William Gropp

You said a goal was to create a "standard toolset." What does standard mean here? Follow-up: How did you achieve your community standards?

David Schissel

Within the experimental fusion community there is a history of sharing computer codes rather than each individual institution solving the same problem. Most likely the best example of this is the MDSplus data acquisition and management system. My statements regarding a standard toolset were made within this context and were not meant to imply that a standards body would be created for a formal declaration. Our community's standards are created informally but good communication between the major organizations is critical. The history of communication and sharing within our community makes this a rather straightforward exercise.

Questioner: Ronald Boisvert

You explained that security/authentication issues remain a challenge to scaling your system to larger number of users. Are there other middleware type systems that are causing similar problems for you? What are the critical systems and services that need improvements for builders of grids systems to use?

David Schissel

Security issues are by far on the top of our list. Another item we are still working towards is a solution for federated web portals that are relatively easy for scientific users to interact with and to add services to. The other issue that has been a problem for us is network multicast. Although ESnet supports this we find that many local LANs do not.

Comment: Mary Thomas

It is difficult to get Fusion Security people to open port 80 for portals.

Questioner: William Gropp

Security may require more than single authentication (single point of failure). Would your users accept 2 logins or more? At what point do they throw up their hands? Follow-up: A service model that does not require accounts may provide an alternative solution. Would this be a feasible approach?

David Schissel

We always ask the question: what do users gain for what they give up. So the answer to your question, would they accept 2 logins or more, really depends on what they gain. If they perceive the gain to be small they would not be accepting of multiple logins. Our goal in FusionGrid is a onetime login for all of our services.

Questioner: Dennis Gannon

Can DOE learn from TeraGrid on the security issue?

David Schissel

The FusionGrid project has continued to reach out to other projects and other grids to learn and to make progress. Our adoption of MyProxy in the middle of our project I think is a good example of this. So the short answer to your question is yes. The longer answer is that the security requirements dictated by different government bodies (e.g. NSF vs. DOE) can change solutions from one grid to another and so the applicability of particular solutions may vary.

Lessons Learned from the GECEM Project

David W. Walker
School of Computer Science
Cardiff University
5 The Parade, Roath,
Cardiff CF24 3AA, United Kingdom
david@cs.cf.ac.uk
WWW home page: http://users.cs.cf.ac.uk/David.W.Walker/

Abstract. The Grid-Enabled Computational Electromagnetics project (GECEM) has developed a portal for performing electromagnetics simulations. The portal is based on the GridSphere portal framework and uses JSR168-compliant portlets to access remote web services. The GECEM portal supports an execution pipeline that starts with an input geometry which is processed to generate surface and volume computational meshes, which in turn are input to a computational electromagnetics (CEM) simulation. The CEM simulation produces the final output file which consists of a vector of values at each mesh point. A distributed collaborative visualization tool has been integrated into the portal to view the CEM simulation results. This paper discusses how the GECEM portal can be extended into a more general portal for a certain class of scientific computation. A model of a scientific portal will be presented in which abstract workflows are built out of workflow patterns. The resulting workflows are then embedded into the portal for use by end-users. A virtualized data store may be used to support checkpointing and archiving.

1 Introduction

This paper describes the Grid-Enabled Computational Electromagnetics (GECEM) project, and discusses its main research outcomes and the lessons learned from the project. In particular, a model is proposed for the composition and use of distributed service-based applications that addresses the perceived and stated needs of scientific end-users who have little or no expertise in portals and service-oriented infrastructure.

Please use the following format when citing this chapter:

Walker, D., 2007, in IFIP International Federation for Information Processing, Volume 239, Grid-Based Problem Solving Environments, eds. Gaffney, P. W., Pool, J.C.T., (Boston: Springer), pp. 95-111.

The GECEM project was funded mainly by the UK's Department of Trade and Industry as part of its contribution to the e-Science Core Programme[1], with additional contributions coming from the project's industrial partners, BAE SYSTEMS and Hewlett-Packard ([1]-[3]). The other collaborating partners were Cardiff University, the University of Wales Swansea, the Welsh e-Science Centre, and the Singapore Institute of High Performance Computing. The project was completed at the end of 2005, and ran for 27 months. Further details may be found in the project final report[2].

The overarching objective of the GECEM project was to apply Grid technologies to enable large-scale scientific and engineering research across a globally-distributed extended enterprise in which the partners only partially trust each other. Subsidiary project objectives included the exploration of secure code sharing and computation capability; the grid-enablement of legacy codes by exposing them as web services; and, the development of a GECEM portal as an integrated user interface to the underlying GECEM services and tools. Computational electromagnetics was chosen as the target application area because of the particular interests and expertise of the project partners, however, the same approach and techniques used in the GECEM project could be applied equally well to other areas, such as computational fluid dynamics and structural mechanics.

The remainder of this paper is arranged as follows. Section 2 presents an overview of the GECEM application and the Grid infrastructure on which it runs. In Section 3, issues relating to trust and security in the GECEM project are discussed, and the GECEM portal is described in detail in Section 4. In Section 5 the lessons learned from the GECEM project are enumerated, and a model of a scientific portal is presented in which abstract workflows are built out of workflow patterns that can then be embedded into the portal for use by end-users. Related work is discussed in Section 6. Ideas for future work and a summary of the main points of the paper are presented in Section 7.

2 GECEM Grid and Application

The GECEM application can be viewed as a workflow, or execution pipeline, with four main stages (see Fig. 1):

1. Creation of the surface mesh from a specification of the geometry of the object to be modelled. This takes as input a file describing the geometry of the problem, typically generated by a CAD system, and outputs a file describing the resultant surface mesh.
2. Creation of the volume mesh based on the surface mesh file generated in step 1. This outputs a file containing the volume mesh.
3. Solution of the computational electromagnetics (CEM) simulation. This takes as input the surface and volume mesh files generated in steps 1 and 2, and outputs a file representing the solution.
4. Perform collaborative visualization of the output file.

---

[1] http://www.epsrc.ac.uk/ResearchFunding/Programmes/e-Science/default.htm
[2] http://www.wesc.ac.uk/projectsite/gecem/doc/GECEM%20Final%20Report.pdf

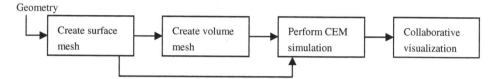

Fig. 1. The GECEM execution pipeline.

In addition to the main dataflows represented by arrows in Fig. 1, each stage in the workflow takes a small number of additional control inputs stored in files. In the GECEM project the objects to be modelled are typically quite complex, such as aircraft and ships.

The first three stages in the workflow perform the three main numerical tasks – the input geometry is converted into surface and volume meshes which are then used to carry out the CEM simulation. Each of these stages is performed by a separate executable legacy code written in Fortran. This code is called from a C wrapper which in turn is wrapped as a Java program using the Java Native Interface (JNI). This is then deployed as a service within an Apache Tomcat container.

A demonstration based on the Globus Toolkit 2, showing the transfer of files between the different stages in the GECEM workflow and the execution of the GECEM services, was given at the UK e-Science All Hands Meeting in September 2003. This showed the basic functionality of the GECEM virtual organisation, and was subsequently developed into the GECEM portal, discussed in Section 4, based on the Globus Toolkit 3.2. The collaborative visualization capability, which is shown as the final stage of the GECEM workflow in Fig. 1, was added in the last few months of the project. This uses the Resource-Aware Visualization Environment (RAVE) which is an infrastructure based on web services for supporting collaborative visualization in a distributed environment.

The first two stages of the GECEM pipeline are performed by the Surface Mesh Generation Service and the Volume Mesh Generation Service, the executable code for which resides permanently on particular hosts. However the CEM simulation step of the pipeline is performed under the control of the CEM Migration Service. Invocation of the CEM Migration Service causes the CEM executable to be migrated to a selected target machine, together with the user-specified input files. The code then executes, its output is sent to a user-specified location, and the code on the target machine is then deleted, along with any associated datasets. The CEM Migration Service is discussed further in Section 3.

Grid infrastructure compatible with the Open Grid Services Architecture (OGSA) was used to establish a virtual organization across the project participants. This infrastructure provided for the authorization and authentication of users, the exchange of data files between sites, and the remote execution of applications. In the GECEM Grid the services for surface and volume mesh generation and CEM migration were located on machines at the University of Wales Swansea (UWS). The services for supporting collaborative visualization using RAVE were hosted at the

Welsh e-Science Centre (WeSC). The CEM Migration Service offered a choice for migrating the simulation code from UWS either to a machine at Cardiff University, or to a machine at the Singapore Institute of High Performance Computing (IHPC).

A typical use case of the GECEM Grid is shown in Fig. 2 in which a geometry file created by designers at BAE SYSTEMS is input to the mesh generation services at UWS. The resulting surface and volume meshes are then passed to the CEM Migration Service (also at UWS) which migrates the executable code and input files to a machine at WeSC. After the CEM simulation code has executed at WeSC the results are then examined in a collaborative visualization session.

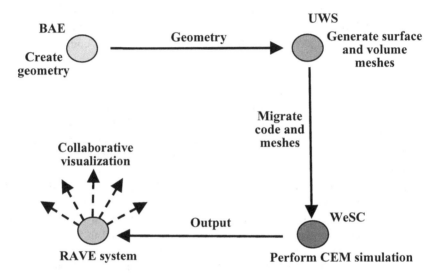

Fig. 2. Typical use case for the GECEM Grid. The dashed arrows emanating from the RAVE system represent the collaborative visualization of the CEM simulation output.

3   Trust and Security in the GECEM Grid

The GECEM Grid represents a type of extended enterprise in which the partners only partially trust each other, which places constraints on how resources are shared. For example, designers at BAE SYSTEMS may be prepared to share geometry files but not the software systems that create these files. UWS may allow authorized users to access their codes as web services, but may not want to permit users to logon to their machines to execute the codes directly from the command line. Similarly, the owners of the high performance machines at WeSC and IHPC may not wish to permanently host the CEM simulation code, but may allow it to reside on their machines on a short-term basis. In many extended enterprises it is this type of partial trust that mandates a distributed solution, since if there were complete trust between all partners all the software and data could be placed at a single location.

Authentication of users of the GECEM Grid is based on e-Science certificates. These are X.509 certificates issued by the UK e-Science certificate authority. Since the services accessed through the GECEM portal are based on GT3.2, the portal makes use of the Grid Security Infrastructure (GSI) for the authentication of users, services, and resources[3]. GSI also provides for "single sign-on" to Grid resources and the delegation of credentials. Single sign-on refers to the ability of a user to perform a single action of authentication (such as entering a password) to access the distributed resources that he or she is authorized to use. Delegation is a mechanism whereby a user or service can delegate a subset of their access rights to another service.

The GECEM portal uses the MyProxy online credential repository [4] managed by the Grid Operations Support Centre of the UK e-Science programme[4]. The MyProxy Upload Tool, developed in the CCLRC DataPortal project, is used to upload a user's proxy credentials to the MyProxy repository. The user can choose how long they wish their credentials to be kept in the repository and how long any proxies generated are valid. The user also needs to choose a username and MyProxy pass phrase, which is subsequently used to log into the portal, effectively giving single sign-on access to the GECEM resources. GridFTP is used to perform secure file transfers between sites in the GECEM Grid.

The GECEM project explored the concept of the secure migration of applications in which an executable code is securely migrated to a remote computer, its execution is initiated and its progress monitored, and then it is deleted on completion, returning the output to the user. The intent is to leave no permanent trace of the application executable or its input and output files on the machine where the application is executed, and to ensure that no third parties (including system administrators) can access or interfere with the application or files during the migrate/execute/return cycle. Current computer architectures and operating systems allow system administrators complete control over the operating system kernel. Hence the system administrator can spy on and interfere with any application. Researchers in the area of secure remote execution are investigating the concept of "platform virtualization" in which a Virtual Machine Monitor (VMM) runs at the lowest level of the software architecture, below the operating system kernel, thereby preventing the operating system from having direct access to the machine hardware [5]. Virtualization allows the same compute hardware to run multiple operating systems simultaneously, with the VMM providing each operating system with an abstraction of the real machine hardware called a Virtual Machine (VM). The VMM ensures that each operating system running on top of a VM is kept separate, and acts as a control point restricting what an operating system can do with the hardware resources of the system. Thus, if a "guest" application is run atop its own VM it will be secure from other general users and from the administrators of any other operating systems running on the system. Some future chipsets will provide support for virtualization and hardware physical protection facilities that will allow the secure migration and remote execution of applications.

---

[3] http://www.globus.org/security/
[4] http://www.grid-support.ac.uk/

In the case of the Surface Mesh Generation Service and Volume Mesh Generation Service the executable code resides permanently on particular hosts. However, the CEM Migration Service differs in that it causes the executable code to be securely migrated to a selected target machine, together with any necessary input data sets. The code then executes, its output is sent to a user-specified location, and the code on the target machine is then deleted, along with any related data sets. This behaviour has many of the features required for the secure migration and remote execution of an application. However, the application code and files are vulnerable while on the remote computer – in fact, as noted above, it is currently impossible to ensure completely secure remote execution (or, indeed, secure local execution). However, the CEM Migration Service does reduce exposure to risk in remote application execution.

4 The GECEM Portal

The GECEM portal is a problem-solving environment (PSE) composed of a collection of JSR168-compliant portlets and services for mesh generation and CEM simulation. A portlet is a pluggable user interface component used with the context of a portal framework. From a user's point of view a portlet is a window in a portal that provides a specific service or function. A portlet processes requests and generates dynamic content, and the content of multiple portlets are typically aggregated together to form a portal web page. A portlet's life cycle is managed by a portlet container. Portlet standards, such as JSR-168 and Web Services for Remote Portlets (WSRP), are helping to make portlet-based portals the most common way of presenting aggregated web content to consumers [6].

The GECEM portal provides the main interface through which services are accessed. The portal supports the composition of applications from service-based components, the execution and monitoring of such applications on remote resources, and collaborative visualization, exploration, and analysis of the application results. In addition, the portal also provides an interface to meshing services and supports the collaborative visualization of meshes.

Two key decisions on the design of the portal were made early in the project. The first was to use the publicly-available open-source GridSphere[5] portal framework as the container of the GECEM portal. The second design decision was to base the GECEM services on Globus Toolkit 3.2, as this was the most recent version of the toolkit available early in the project. GT4 was not available until close to the end of the project, and it was decided not to migrate the services to this version of the toolkit. As discussed in Section 2, the GECEM services are simply wrapped legacy executables.

GridSphere 2.0.4 was used in the GECEM portal [7], together with GridPortlets 1.1 [8]. GridSphere was deployed in the Tomcat 5.0.30 servlet container. The GECEM portal has a three-tier architecture, as shown in Fig. 3. The GridPortlets are a set of portlets, developed by the same research team that developed GridSphere,

---

[5] http://www.gridsphere.org/

and are used for tasks such as credential management, resource browsing, file browsing, and file transfer.

The GECEM portlets in Fig.3 allow a user to set up a job as a sequence of one or more stages in the GECEM pipeline (see Fig. 1), with specified input and output files. Prior to each stage portlets are used to select the input files to be used, and the directory in which to store output files. These files and directories may be on any of the machines that are members of the GECEM virtual organisation. Services are discovered dynamically using a UDDI server at WeSC, and where multiple equivalent services are available for a particular task, perhaps employing different algorithms or numerical methods, the user can select from these. Service discovery and invocation are also controlled through GECEM portlets.

The Resource-Aware Visualization Environment[6] (RAVE) was used to provide a collaborative visualization capability within the GECEM portal. RAVE is a collaborative visualization environment that scales across visualization platforms, ranging from large immersive devices all the way down to hand-held PDAs [9, 10]. RAVE is based on web service technologies, and provides for distributed rendering on remote machines. The data to be rendered may reside on one machine, the rendering may be done on one or more other machines, and the rendered image may be displayed on yet another machine. In the RAVE architecture a Data Service is used to store and distribute the data sets to be rendered. A machine with enough power to render the data may use an Active Client, which reads directly from the Data Service and renders locally. Smaller machines, such as a laptop or PDA may use a Thin Client, which reads rendered frame buffers from an intermediate Render Service hosted on a more powerful machine. Active and Thin clients can join a single visualization session, enabling collaboration between users on vastly differing resources.

A RAVE Portlet was developed and integrated into the GECEM portal. The RAVE Portlet first presents the user with a list of Data Services of choose from. These are discovered dynamically using a UDDI service. The user next initiates a collaborative visualization session, which users at other locations can also join, and then selects a data set to render. Next a Render Service is selected to carry out the rendering – this is selected from a list populated from a UDDI registry. The final step is to indicate whether the local client is an active or thin client – in the former case any render service selected in the previous step is ignored and the data set is rendered on the local client. The data set will then be rendered in the GECEM portal on the local client and on any other machines that have joined the collaborative session. Users can then navigate, and interact with, the data set. Two main modes of collaborative visualization are supported:

1. Each user independently explores the same data set.
2. One user acts as "leader" and all other users view the data set from the same location as the leader.

Users are represented graphically in the visualization by an avatar, which can be seen by other users in the collaborative session.

---

[6] http://www.wesc.ac.uk/projectsite/rave/

Before visualization the output produced by the CEM simulation must be converted to a form that can be handled by RAVE. This is done within the CEM Migration Portlet of the GECEM portal before accessing the RAVE Portlet.

The addition of audio communication between collaborating users was considered, but it was decided that the recent advent of Voice over IP (VoIP) services, such as SKYPE[7], made it unnecessary to develop a custom solution.

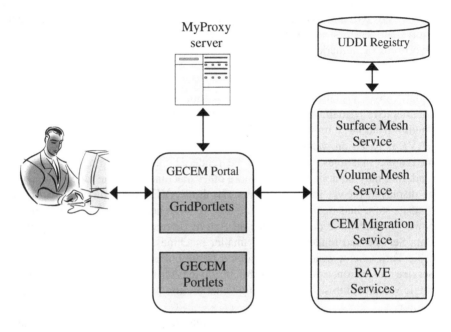

Fig. 3. Three-tier architecture of the GECEM portal.

5 Lessons Learned

The lessons learned from the GECEM project can be divided into two types: technical and non-technical. The non-technical lessons are quite generic and are mainly concerned with the management and conduct of projects with several partners in which there are interdependencies in the software development process and reliance on third-party software. In such cases it is important to avoid single points of failure whereby a particular problem can bring the whole project to a halt. Exposure to risk can be reduced by planning alternative strategies to follow if difficulties arise.

On the technical side, portals were found to be effective in providing a high-level interface for scientific users that shields them from the complexities of using distributed resources via the Grid. Portlets make it easy to integrate heterogeneous resources within a unified interface that can be accessed from any Web browser.

---

[7] http://www.skype.com/

The model of a distributed application model embodied in the GECEM portal consists of a linear workflow structure with a fixed number of nodes. Each node is a placeholder for a particular type of activity which is implemented by a service. Thus, there is a placeholder for surface meshing, a placeholder for volume meshing, and so on. It is the responsibility of the portal user to associate an actual service instance with each placeholder node in the workflow by making a selection from the services discovered by the UDDI portlet. The static nature of the workflow in the GECEM portal was found to be too restrictive by some of the portal's users who expressed an interest in dynamically composing service-based applications. However, even limited changes, such as adding another placeholder node to the linear workflow, require the portal to be reconfigured and new portlets to be developed by hand. This requires a degree of expertise beyond that of most end-users – indeed, it should be the aim of the portal developer that it be easily usable by those with no expertise in portal technologies. The challenge, therefore, is to support some degree of application composition by typical scientific end-users in a portal built out of portlets. There are numerous tools for composing service-based applications – examples include Triana [11], Kepler [12], and Taverna [13]. However, these are all stand-alone systems that may be difficult to embed within a portal, and that would perhaps provide more features than many end-users require. Furthermore, incorporating such composition tools would introduce unnecessary software dependencies into the portal. A better approach is to perform the workflow composition tasks external to the portal as this ensures a clear separation of form (the structure of the workflow) from content (the actual service instances and inputs used), and allows a number of third-party workflow composition tools to be used to create the initial workflow structure.

The approach to workflow composition advocated here is to use a tool that can design workflow structures out of simple workflow patterns [14, 15]. Once the desired workflow structure has been created, it would then be processed to create a new portal with the workflow embedded in it. As in the original GECEM portal, each node in the workflow would be a placeholder with which the user must associate a service instance, and inputs and outputs of the workflow would be files to be identified by the user. As an example, consider the workflow patterns on the left-hand side of Fig. 4. Pattern A, having just one input and one output, can be used to construct linear workflow structures similar to that illustrated in Fig. 1. Pattern B has two inputs and one output and can be used to construct a much more general class of binary tree structures, as shown on the right-hand side of Fig.4.

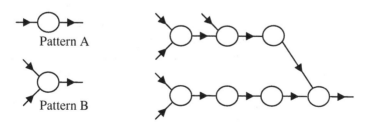

Pattern A

Pattern B

Fig. 4. The right-hand side of the figure shows a workflow structure that can be created from the two workflow patterns on the left of the figure.

The workflow structure on the right-hand side of Fig. 4 has five inputs and one output. Pattern B is a simple merge pattern; one could also consider a split pattern in which a node has one input and two outputs. Indeed, a tool that allows the user to specify the number of inputs and outputs of a node would provide for all the above patterns, and support the design of a large class of data-driven graph-structured workflows. Such abstract workflow structures can be expressed in almost any of the existing workflow description languages.

If services are virtualized and discovered within the portal from a service registry such as UDDI, then there has to be a mechanism for the portal to determine which service implementations match a given placeholder node in a workflow structure. This problem of matching concrete service instances to abstract service specifications is currently a topic of much research (see, for example, [16-18]). The simplest approach is to use a service name to perform the matching, but this works only if all service providers agree to use the same naming scheme. Other approaches make use of metadata and/or ontologies to allow independently-developed services to be discovered and matched to placeholder nodes. Rather than use the metadata and ontology approaches to service matching in end-user tools, it is probably more effective to assume that in the future "spiders" will examine the contents of multiple resource registries, and use the metadata published therein to classify and name services in order to produce meta-registries of services [19]. In a meta-registry all equivalent services will be given the same unique service type which acts as a global name. It is then necessary to distinguish between the local name a service is given in a service registry and the global name it is given in the meta-registry. If a user associates a local name with a placeholder node then the portal would be able to discover all the services with the same type in the meta-registry. These services would then be offered to the portal user who would then select one of them, thereby associating a concrete service instance with the placeholder node. Alternatively the user might browse the meta-registry to find an appropriate service to use.

In the original GECEM portal services are virtualized, but the files that act as input and output to the GECEM services are not. As discussed in Section 7, it would be useful to provide a virtualized file store from which to select input files in the portal. There is then a problem of deciding which files in the virtualized file store are compatible with the inputs of a particular service. The simplest solution is to identify different types of files by a unique file type, and to associate each input and output file of a service with one of these types. As in the problem of matching abstract and concrete services, it is possible to make use of metadata descriptions of files and service inputs/outputs to determine which files are compatible with a particular service input or output. Once again it is possible to use this metadata to associate a unique file type with each service input/output, and to perform this association independently of the workflow design tool proposed here. Thus, it can be assumed that in an abstract workflow it is possible to refer to services by unique service types and to its inputs and outputs by unique file types.

Once a workflow structure has been created, unique service types must be associated with each placeholder node. After this step the unique file type of each nodes inputs and outputs can be determined. Henceforth, the association of unique service and file types with placeholder nodes will be referred to as labeling the workflow. The final step is to embed the labeled workflow into the portal – this will be referred to as compiling the workflow. It should be noted that compiling a workflow does not bind abstract services to specific service instances - this is what the end-user does within the portal. Compiling a workflow automatically generates the portlets corresponding to each node in the labeled workflow. These portlets will be used by the end-user in the portal to specify the specific services to be used (thus, the portlets support discovery and binding). Compiling also configures the portal so these portlets are visible to the user within the portal. The compilation step can also ensure that the workflow is consistently labeled by checking that the unique file type of each node output is the same as that of the node input to which it is connected.

Functionally the design, labeling, and compilation of a workflow, together with the use of the portal itself, are independent tasks that could be performed by distinct tools and interfaces. However, there are a number of ways in which these functions could be combined. For example, the design, labeling, and compilation tasks could be merged into a single tool. In this paper it is assumed that each of these tasks is performed by a separate tool, as shown in Fig. 5. Thus, if the labeling tool accepts as input workflow structures described in a subset of BPEL, this allows existing tools to be used to design the workflow.

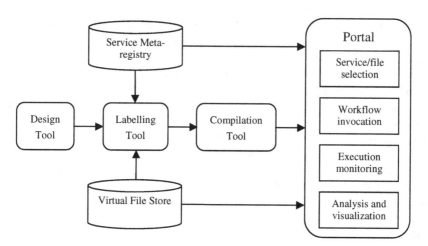

Fig. 5. The relationship between the design, labeling and compilation tools, and the portal. Also shown are some of the functions of the portal.

6 Related Work

The GridSphere portal framework is used across a range of scientific disciplines to create portlet-based portal interfaces[8]. For example, the e-Physics portal developed by researchers at The University of Melbourne has been used to perform parameter sweep studies for a magneto-hydrodynamics astrophysics code, ZeusMP [20]. Unlike the GECEM portal, where the user is responsible for selecting between semantically equivalent services, in the e-Physics portal resource selection is usually done automatically by the Gridbus Broker [21]. This difference arises from the distinct modes of use for which the GECEM and e-Physics portals were designed. The GeneGrid portal [22] is another example of a scientific portal based on GridSphere, and provides access to a virtual bioinformatics laboratory that allows users to construct experiments by either composing new workflows or reusing workflows created previously. The Astrophysics Simulation Collaboratory [23] uses the GridSphere portal framework to manage numerical relativity simulations based on the Cactus Computational Toolkit [24].

The portals mentioned in the previous paragraph all provide end-user interfaces for particular application domains. The P-GRADE portal supports the composition and execution of workflows, and is not tied to any specific application domain [25]. The P-GRADE portal is similar in some respects to the GECEM portal: both portals are based on GridSphere, both represent the input/output of data to/from a workflow node in terms of files, and both make use of certificates, GSI, and MyProxy servers in the authorization and authentication of users and resources. The P-GRADE portal provides a workflow editor that may be used to create new workflows and edit existing ones. For each node in a P-GRADE workflow the end-user must specify the client-side location of the binary executable, and its type (sequential, parallel MPI, or parallel PVM). The end-user must also select the resource that the executable is to run on by first choosing the particular Grid to be used and then the resource on that Grid. These choices are made using dropdown listboxes that are configured by the portal administrator. The P-GRADE portal user must also specify the location of the workflow's input and output files. Thus, the P-GRADE portal differs from the GECEM portal in that the former does not provide access to virtualized services and files. In addition, the distinction between abstract and concrete workflows, discussed in Section 5, is not clearly made in the P-GRADE portal approach. Another distinction is that the P-GRADE portal uses the DAGMan workflow scheduler [26] to perform file transfers required to execute the workflow, and for the submission of jobs (representing workflow nodes) to Grid resources, whereas the GECEM portal handles these tasks directly by itself.

The concept of an abstract workflow underpins the Griphyn Virtual Data System (VDS; formerly known as Chimera) and its portal interface, Chiron [27]. Virtual data is stored in a Virtual Data Catalog (VDC), and is represented and queried by an XML-based Virtual Data Language (VDL). When queried for a data product, the VDC generates an abstract workflow for creating that data. This abstract workflow can then be used to generate a concrete workflow by mapping requests for data and computation onto actual resources – a process often referred to as "planning". The

---

[8] See http://www.gridsphere.org/gridsphere/gridsphere?cid=projects

Chiron portal uses the Pegasus planner [28] to generate a concrete workflow, which is then submitted to DAGMan for execution on the Grid. The Pegasus planner uses a Transformation Catalog to map the logical names of transformations (called a "service type" in Section 5) to physical resources and executable locations, and the Metadata Catalog Service and Replica Location Service for data publication and discovery. Pegasus can also be used independently through its own portal for workflow submission and management.

The Grid Execution Management for Legacy Code Architecture (GEMLCA) provides an easy way to expose legacy application binary codes as OGSA-compatible services [29]. In GECEM this was done by wrapping the original source code, but in GEMLCA a front-end Grid service layer handles parameter passing and contacts a Globus Master Managed Job Factory Service (MMJFS) to submit the legacy application for execution. GEMLCA has been integrated with the P-GRADE portal so that legacy codes and other service components can be used to create application workflows that can then be executed on the Grid [30].

7 Future Work and Conclusions

Based on the work carried out in the GECEM project, Section 5 has introduced a set of tools for building a portal around a particular user-designed workflow structure constructed from simple workflow patterns. To achieve this, an abstract workflow is created by first generating a workflow structure using a design tool and then associating an abstract service (identified by a service type) with each node in the workflow using a labeling tool. The labeling tool also associates a file type with each service input and output. The workflow is then embedded into the portal using a compilation tool, the main task of which is to automatically generate the portlets needed to allow a portal user to select for each node in the workflow a concrete service that is consistent with the abstract service associated with the node, and also to select the input files of the workflow. Service types and file types are essentially names that are unique within the virtual organization using the portal.

The approach described in Section 5 targets end-users who want to perform "what-if" styles of computational investigation in which the particular service that is bound to a node in a workflow may be selected via the portal shortly before workflow execution. For example, this allows a user to experiment with different algorithms for performing a particular task. On a longer timescale the user also wants to create new workflows and to create portals for their execution and management. It is assumed that a user will run many workflows before generating a new one, so it appears sensible to create the abstract workflow external to the portal. This also allows third-party workflow composition tools to be used, provided the compilation tool is able to recognize how they represent abstract workflows. It might be argued that, rather than having a separate portal for each workflow structure, it would be better to manage all the workflows to be used by a Virtual Organization through a single portal interface. This does not appear to raise any technical difficulties, and it would be quite simple to write a portlet for each workflow to integrate them into a single portal.

The portal generated through the design-label-compile process is similar to the GECEM portal in that it provides mechanisms for the user to specify the files to be input to the portal workflow and the services to be invoked. In the current GECEM portal services are virtualized, but not the related input and output data sets. Thus, users currently must identify data sets by specifying a specific file on a specific machine (by using portlets based on the GridPortlets file browser portlet). In future work a virtualized file store will allow authorized users to manage, access, and use data sets without needing to refer to which physical resource they are actually stored on. All input, intermediate, and final data products will be stored in the virtualized file store. This will allow a workflow to be started from any intermediate point for which the necessary input files are held in the virtualized file store. In addition, files will be annotated to support metadata-based searches of the virtualized file store. The metadata would include provenance information (how, why, when, and by whom the file was produced) and other data deemed necessary to provide a description of a file. In particular, the metadata should include sufficient information to distinguish files of different types. The simplest way to do this would be if the files were in XML format – then files conforming to the same XML Schema would be of the same type. The advantage of being able to distinguish files by their type is that it is then possible to match files to the inputs and outputs of services, so when the portal user is deciding what file to select as the input to a service, only those files of the correct type are presented to them.

This paper has shown how end-users, with no expertise in Grid computing or portal development, can make you of simple tools to compose scientific workflows that can then be automatically embedded within a portal. The design, labeling, and compilation tools are used to specify a workflow and generate a portal that supports the end-user in selecting specific services and files for executing an instance of the workflow. The integrated view presented here of scientific workflow composition and portal design addresses concerns raised by end-users of the GECEM portal, and supports a common mode of use of distributed resources based on the input/output of files to/from services. Future work will investigate the use of this approach in other scientific application areas, such as computational fluid dynamics and structural mechanics.

Acknowledgements

The author would like to acknowledge the efforts and assistance of the other members of the GECEM project team, and would particularly like to thank Dr Maria Lin for her work on implementing the GECEM portal, and Dr Yu Chen for supporting the GECEM services. It is also a pleasure to thank Dr Ian Grimstead and Mr Ganesan Subramaniam for their work on developing the RAVE system and the RAVE portlet, Dr. Omer Rana for commenting on a draft of the paper, and Dr Alan Davies for helpful discussions on the GECEM portal.

References

1. D. W. Walker, J. P. Giddy, N. P. Weatherill, J. W. Jones, A. Gould, D. Rowse, and M. Turner, "GECEM: Grid-Enabled Computational Electromagnetics," in Proceedings of the UK e-Science All Hands Meeting, 2003. ISBN 1-904425-11-9. http://www.nesc.ac.uk/events/ahm2003/AHMCD/pdf/105.pdf.

2. M. Lin, D. W. Walker, Y. Chen, and J. W. Jones, "A Grid-Based Problem-Solving Environment for GECEM," in Proceedings of the Fifth International Symposium on Cluster Computing and the Grid, held in Cardiff, UK, 9-12 May 2005. ISBN 0-7803-9075-X. http://users.cs.cf.ac.uk/David.W.Walker/papers/CCGrid2005Final.pdf.

3. M. Lin and D. W. Walker, "A Portlet Interface for Computational Electromagnetics on the Grid," in Proceedings of the 17th IMACS World Congress, held in Paris, France, 11-15 July 2005. ISBN 2-915913-02-1. http://users.cs.cf.ac.uk/David.W.Walker/papers/IMACS2005Final.pdf.

4. J. Novotny, S. Tuecke, and Von Welch, "An Online Credential Repository for the Grid: MyProxy," in Proceedings of the Tenth International Symposium on High Performance Distributed Computing (HPDC-10), IEEE Press, pp. 104-111. August 2001. http://www.globus.org/alliance/publications/papers/myproxy.pdf;

5. P. Barham, B. Dragovic, K. Fraser, S. Hand, T. Harris, A. Ho, R. Neugebauer, I. Pratt, and , Warfield, "Xen and the Art of Virtualization," in Proceedings of the ACM Symposium on Operating Systems, October 2003. http://www.cl.cam.ac.uk/Research/SRG/netos/papers/2003-xensosp.pdf.

6. F. Bellas, "Standards for Second-Generation Portals," IEEE Internet Computing, Vol. 8, No. 2, March 2004.

7. J. Novotny, M. Russell, and O. Wehrens, "GridSphere: A Portal Framework for Building Collaborations," Concurrency and Computation: Practice and Experience, Vol. 16, No. 5, pp. 503-513, April 2004.

8. M. Russell, O. Wehrens, and J. Novotny, "The GridPortlets Web Application: A Grid Portal Framework," in Proceedings of the Sixth International Conference on Parallel Processing and Mathematics, published by Springer as Lecture Notes in Computer Science, Volume 3911, 2006.

9. I. J. Grimstead, N. J. Avis, and D. W. Walker, "RAVE: The Resource-Aware Visualization Environment," accepted for publication in Concurrency and Computation: Practice and Experience, 2006.

10. I. J. Grimstead, N. J. Avis, R. N. Philp, and D. W. Walker, "Resource-Aware Visualization Using Web Services," in Proceedings of the UK e-Science All Hands Meeting, September 2005. http://users.cs.cf.ac.uk/I.J.Grimstead/RAVE/AHM2005-full.pdf.

11. I. Taylor, M. Shields, I. Wang, and A. Harrison, "Visual Grid Workflow in Triana," Journal of Grid Computing, Vol. 3, Nos. 3-4, pp. 153-169, September 2005.

12. B. Ludäscher, I. Altintas, C. Berkley, D. Higgins, E. Jaeger, M. Jones, E. A. Lee, J. Tao, and Y. Zhao, "Scientific Workflow Management and the Kepler System,"

Computation and Concurrency: Practice and Experience, Vol. 18, No. 10, pp. 1039-1065, August 2006.

13. T. Oinn, M. Greenwood, M. Addis, M. N. Alpdemir, J. Ferris, K. Glover, C. Goble, A. Goderis, D. Hull, D. Marvin, P. Li, P. Lord, M. R. Pocock, M. Senger, R. Stevens, A. Wipat, and C. Wroe, "Taverna: Lessons in Creating a Workflow Environment for the Life Sciences," Computation and Concurrency: Practice and Experience, Vol. 18, No. 10, pp. 1067-1100, August 2006.

14. O. F. Rana and D. W. Walker, "Service Design Patterns for Computational Grids," in *Patterns and Skeletons for Parallel and Distributed Computing*, pp. 237-264, published by John Wiley, ISBN: 1-85233-506-8, 2003.

15. E. Gamma, R. Helm, R. Johnson, and J. Vlissides, *Design Patterns: Elements of Reusable Object-Oriented Software*, published by Addison-Wesley, ISBN: 0-201-63361-2, 1995.

16. S. Balzer and T. Liebig, "Bridging the Gap between Abstract and Concrete Services: A Semantic Approach for Grounding OWL-S," in Proceedings of the Third International Semantic Web Conference, published by Springer as Lecture Notes in Computer Science, Volume 3298, 2004.

17. S. Majithia and D. W. Walker, "Automated Composition of Semantic Grid Services," in Proceedings of the UK e-Science All Hands Meeting, September 2004.

18. R. Lara and D. Olmedilla, "Discovery and Contracting of Semantic Web Services", in Proceedings of the W3C Workshop on Frameworks for Semantics in Web Services, Innsbruck, Austria, 9-10 June 2005.

19. T. Goodale, S. A. Ludwig, W. Naylor, J. Padget, and O. F. Rana, "Service-Oriented Matchmaking and Brokerage," in Proceedings of the UK e-Science All Hands Meeting, September 2006.

20. B. Beeson, S. Melnikoff, S. Venugopal, and D. G. Barnes, "A Portal for Grid-Enabled Physics," in Proceedings of the 2005 Australian Workshop on Grid Computing and e-Research, pub. ACM Press, pp. 13-20, 2005.

21. S. Venugopal, R. Buyya, and L. Winton, "A Grid Service Broker for Scheduling Distributed Data-Oriented Applications on Global Grids, " in Proceedings of the Second International Workshop on Middleware in Grid Computing, pub. ACM Proess, pp. 75-80, 2004.

22. N. Kelly, P.V. Jithesh, S. Wasnik, R. McLaughlin, F. Fragoso, P. Donachy, T. Harmer, R. Perrott, M. McCurley, M. Townsley, J. Johnston, and S. McKee, "The GeneGrid Portal: A User Interface for a Virtual Bioinformatics Laboratory," in Proceedings of the UK e-Science All Hands Meeting, September 2005.

23. R. Bondarescu, G. Allen, G. Daues, I. Kelley, M. Russell, E. Seidel, J. Shalf, and M. Tobias, "The Astrophysics Simulation Collaboratory Portal: A Framework for Effective Distributed Research", Future Generation Computer Systems, Vol. 21, No. 2, pp. 259-270, 2005.

24. T. Goodale, G. Allen, G. Lanfermann, J. Masso, T. Radke, E. Seidel, and J. Shalf, "The Cactus Framework and Toolkit: Design and Applications," in Proceedings of the Fifth International Conference on Vector and Parallel Processing," pub. Springer, 2003.

25. P. Kacsuk and G. Sipos, "Multi-Grid, Multi-User Workflows in the P-GRADE Grid Portal," Journal of Grid Computing, Vol. 3, No. 3-4, pp. 231-238, 2005.

26. D. Thain, T. Tannenbaum, and M. Livny, "Distributed Computing in Practice: The Condor Experience," Concurrency and Computation: Practice and Experience, Vol. 17, Nos. 2-4, pp. 323-356, 2005.

27. Y. Zhao, M. Wilde, I. Foster, J. Voeckler, J. Dobson, E. Gilbert, T. Jordan, and E. Quigg, "Virtual Data Grid Middleware Services for Data-Intensive Science," Concurrency and Computation: Practice and Experience Vol. 18, No. 6, pp. 595-608, 2006.

28. G. Singh, E. Deelman, G. Mehta, K. Vahi, and M.-H. Su, "The Pegasus Portal: Web-Based Grid Computing," in Proceedings of the 2005 ACM Symposium on Applied Computing, pub. ACM Press, 2005.

29. T. Delaitre, A. Goyeneche, P. Kacsuk, T. Kiss, G. Z. Terstyanszky, and S. C. Winter, "GEMLCA: Grid Execution Management for Legacy Code Architecture Design," in Proceedings of the 30th Euromicro Conference, pub. IEEE Press, pp. 477-483, 2004.

30. L. Bitoni, T. Kiss, G. Terstyanszky, T. Delaitre, S. Winter, and P. Kacsuk, "Dynamic Testing of Legacy Code Resources on the Grid," in Proceedings of the Third Conference on Computing Frontiers, pub. ACM Press, 2006.

Q&A - David W. Walker

Questioner: Dennis Gannon

What about using Java Webstart applications for launching workflow applications.

David Walker

Webstart is useful in Java-centric applications. It will ensure that the correct JVM and user GUI is installed at the client end, and download the application for execution on the client machine, and initiate execution. In the GECEM portal we want the application to run remotely, not on the client side, so the use of Webstart would not be appropriate. Also Webstart requires the application to be pure Java, whereas the remote applications that GECEM access are Fortran codes called from C which is then wrapped as Java using JNI. Finally, I believe the client GUI also needs to be written in Java to work with Webstart which isn't the case for a portlet-based GUI.

Questioner: Boyana Norris

Are there any tools you are aware of that implement support for workflow templates/patterns that can then be specialized by users or middleware?

David Walker

I am not aware of any such tools – one of my reasons for bringing up this topic at the workshop was the hope that someone here would tell me about them.

Questioner: Gabrielle Allen

What is the advantage of wrapping a legacy application as a Web service, or alternatively, why do we need to expose applications as Web services?

David Walker

I think that the main advantage of using Web services stems from the set of frameworks, tools and supporting software that exists for Web services. Job submission and monitoring, and security are of particular importance. Web services are also becoming widely-used to coordinate interactions between distributed, coupled application components, so exposing a piece of software as a Web service makes it easier for third parties to use it.

Bill Applebe [comment on Gabrielle Allen's question]

There are several toolkits for wrapping legacy applications to make them easier to use in many contexts (e.g., web or batch). For example, Pyre from Caltech (Python wrappers).

Comment: Mladen Vouk

I think templates work provided one can abstract a group of workflows and provide an appropriate data model to which applications can conform.

Anne Trefethen [comment on Boyana Norris' question]

In the context of problem-solving environments such as Iris Explorer, templates and patterns are provided.

Monday PM Panel Discussion

Panel

- Anne Trefethen
- David Schissel
- Patrick Gaffney
- Tim Hopkins
- David Walker

Questioner: Jim Pool

Many applications referenced in the presentations are numerically intensive. Have you encountered issues in incorporating numerical software, for example, handling exceptions due to error messages from subroutines?

David Walker

Web service mechanisms exist for exception handling, but to integrate "dusty deck" subroutines with these would require some work. The error messages would need to be stripped out from the subroutines, and an error code returned. If the subroutine is wrapped in Java then the exception would then have to be caught in the Java wrapper code, and handed off to the web service exception handling mechanism, for example as a SOAP fault. Service specific exception classes can be used to handle exceptions.

David Schissel

With our ASP model, we provide computational services for specific codes, not access to general numerical libraries. We do however have developers who use numerical libraries in the physics services that they provide and we have encountered no difficulty.

Questioner: William Gropp

What can be done to avoid problems caused by making it easy to connect to poor software (we have experience with poor numerical libraries that have been widely used)?

David Walker

A reputation broker could be used to provide information on the trustworthiness of a piece of software, with the aim of discouraging the use of poor software.

Anne Trefethen

Unfortunately researchers are often in the position where they are more likely to choose to use software they can get for "free" than commercially supported software. Of course "free" doesn't always mean of low quality, but it does mean that the quality checks we would like to see are often not in place. If we imagine a service oriented provision of numerical software then we may also see an accumulation of knowledge regarding particular services – be it simply use statistics or mechanisms for user community information tagging – perhaps as in commercial activities such as Amazon or eBay.

David Schissel

In fusion, we push communication. For example in the experimental community you can replace the word software with data and have an equally relevant question. Using a piece of data or software in a complete knowledge vacuum is considered very dangerous as the specialized knowledge that indicates areas of non-applicability typically only gets communicated through human interaction. Could this be more automated? Yes, it most likely could be, but we have not seen a good solution to this problem.

Tim Hopkins

This is part of the much wider problem of the quality control of numerical/scientific software. There is little tool support for software testing especially for Fortran and C that is not commercial and expensive. Software testing for numerical codes is generally quite poor. So we need to make the requirements for integrating scientific software into grid applications more stringent. In particular it should be mandatory that such software comes with some evidence of thorough testing. Preferable this should be performed/confirmed independently of the software authors.

One of the major problems at the moment is that there is far too much flaky software being used by practitioners who are not in a position to recognize when such code might/does deliver poor/incorrect results. These users need protecting.

Questioner: Ron Boisvert

Much numerical software continues to be developed as Fortran 77 subroutines. To what extent is this preventing its adoption in grid applications? For example, would math software based on virtual machine environments, like Java, be more easily integrated into grid applications?

David Walker

I don't think the development of subroutines using Fortran 77 in itself prevents its adoption in grid applications. It is quite easy to wrap such software in Java and hence to expose it as web services – indeed, there are tools that support this.

Pat Gaffney:

Speaking from our experience in working with commercial industrial companies, we do not perceive the Fortran language as an inhibitor in any way, quite the contrary, many engineers and scientists are experienced in Fortran. My own company, BSSI, specializes in multi-programming environments, notably Fortran and Java because Fortran is preferable for the complex numerical simulations that we do. A by-product of this is that the use of Fortran for this purpose makes it easier for our customers to work collaboratively with us. We can share Fortran modules with them for them to modify and plug back into our systems. This promotes collaboration and, since we use Fortran 77, 90, and 95, it is especially easy for a range of experienced scientists and engineers to collaborate with us. In this way, customers and BSSI grow collaboratively together which is necessary for the types of problems we solve.

Bill Applebe

Math software based on languages such as Java has not been very successful (there was an effort called Java Grande to promote scientific Java in 2000 that fizzled out). The reason is simply that Java is not very efficient (whether interpreted or compiled). Fortran and C will continue to be the dominant languages for scientific programming for the foreseeable future. Coupling Fortran and C to the languages used for web applications (Python, Java, .NET) requires wrappers, that unfortunately are not particularly easy to write or maintain.

Tim Hopkins:

My experience of numerical software producers is that they are mainly interested in implementing their algorithms as proof of concept. Much of the code first submitted to ACM TOMS even lacks robust user input checking; so I can't believe that we will be able to convince authors of such software to spend their time creating wrappers to allow integration of their code into grid applications. Nor should we; this is a task for people who possess a different skills set.

Anne Trefethen

There are many efforts at the moment to develop automatic tools for wrapping legacy applications and whether Fortran or C is used there should be no real difficulty.

Comment: Jim Pool

We are not discussing a new problem. Ken Kennedy gave a talk at the "Second Pasadena Workshop on System Software and Tools for High Performance Computing Environments" in January 1995, with an excellent description of a possible approach to transitioning research level codes to near production codes. Subsequently there was a workshop expanding these ideas. However, no US federal agency felt this problem was within its charter.

Gabrielle Allen

In your experience so far, which part of your grid PSE worked best and which were you most disappointed in?

David Walker

The use of portlets to provide access to remote services and to aggregate content worked well in the GECEM portal. The main disappointment was in the incompatibilities between some of the software used to create the portal and provide the services. Debugging and fixing problems was difficult.

David Schissel

From a general standpoint, at the start of the FusionGrid project five years ago, we were most disappointed with the hype of available functionality compared to what could actually be accomplished for scientists on day one. From a technical standpoint, the conflicting requirements between site security and grid security and the lack of LAN multicast support and reliability have been the most disappointing. On the positive side, by working on this project the fusion community has had the pleasure to work with a large number of computer scientists who are eager to make adjustments or even fundamental changes to their software to support our community's needs. We certainly hope that these relationships continue into the future as we see them helping to push our science forward.

Questioner: Brian Smith

The emphasis in the presentations in this session has been on services, particularly those facilitating access to grid facilities. Do you see the focus changing to request technical enhancements or tools rather than services?

David Schissel

We see this as a cyclical development so we feel that both are and will continue to be important.

David Walker

I don't see the provision of services and the use of technical enhancements or tools as being mutually exclusive. Indeed, the portal/service approach provides a way of seamlessly incorporating new capabilities into a grid computing environment.

Anne Trefethen

I think we see both. There are requirements for new service capabilities and technical enhancements and tools. Particularly as different architects are considered this will often lead to further detailed enhancements or adjustment of algorithms.

Pat Gaffney:

Yes, but this is also happening now. Working as closely with the end-customer as we do, we are continually probing the customer to discern new functionality that would make their job easier. Often, the user can be reluctant to come forward with requests and this is probably because many software vendors are disinclined to modify their software. This is not true with BSSI; it is a deliberate commercial policy to have a continual development cycle that improves our commercial software according to user needs.

For a number of reasons, some of which are discussed in our talk, the focus at the moment is primarily on services but not exclusively. Software tools, in the form of finished products, are of interest to the end-customer but their successful adoption depends on the number of inhibitors the organization imposes on the use of the tools and on the allocation of resources for learning and running the tools. I do not see these inhibitors being reduced in the short term.

PART 3

INFRASTRUCTURE: SERVICES

A. Trefethen, Session Chair; M. Mu, Discussant

J. Treadwell: *Open Grid Services Architecture* (Abstract)

B. Norris: *Middleware for Dynamic Adaptation of Component Applications*

T. Jackson: *A Virtual Organization deployed on a Service Orientated Architrecture for Distributed Data Mining Applications*

Panel Discussion

Open Grid Services Architecture

Jem Treadwell
Hewlett-Packard

Abstract. A decade after taking its first steps as a research project, grid computing is on the road to "pervasive adoption" across all types of organization, from the campus to the enterprise data center. While many forms of grid infrastructure exist today, some proprietary and some based on open protocols and software components, the key to continued progress in the evolution of grid computing is standardization. By building grids and applications on standards-based components, architects can meet their organizations' needs with confidence that they are interoperable with other standards-based grids, and that they can grow and adapt as those needs change. The Global Grid Forum's (GGF) Open Grid Services Architecture (OGSA(tm)) describes a service-oriented grid architecture that addresses standardization by defining a set of foundational capabilities for interoperable grids. The OGSA working group publishes the architecture framework and related documents. In this session the speaker will: * Discuss the evolution of grid computing; * Explain how a service-oriented grid fits with other leading-edge enterprise technologies; * Provide details of OGSA and its core capabilities, including progress and plans.

Please use the following format when citing this chapter:

Treadwell, J., 2007, in IFIP International Federation for Information Processing, Volume 239, Grid-Based Problem Solving Environments, eds. Gaffney, P. W., Pool, J.C.T., (Boston: Springer), pp. 123.

Q&A – Jem Treadwell

Questioner: G. Allen

How will scientific applications interact with OGSA?

Jem Treadwell

The question related to an existing application and to the use of the Simple API for Grid Applications (SAGA) being specified by the Open Grid Forum's SAGA Research Group. In some cases, OGSA services such as the Basic Execution Service (BES) will invoke legacy applications without change, other than perhaps the use of simple wrapper scripts. OGSA services will be specified with Web service interfaces, so where direct interaction *is* needed these interfaces will need to be invoked. While it may not be practical for legacy applications to become Web service clients, it does seem reasonable for SAGA or other intermediate APIs to handle the necessary protocol exchanges.

I would strongly encourage SAGA-RG and any group that is concerned with interfacing with OGSA to contact Hiro Kishimoto, the OGSA Working Group co-chair, to arrange a joint meeting.

Questioner: D. Gannon

Great job presenting OGSA! When do you see implementations of OGSA emerging? Will H.P. implement a version of OGSA?

Jem Treadwell

I think it will take another year or so for OGSA to evolve to a point where commercial products are based on it. Although the OGSA WSRF Basic Profile is close to publication, the higher-level service specifications and profiles such as HPC, Data, and Execution Management must be completed before it can be applied in practical applications. The various groups developing these are making good progress, but standards work always takes time.

The specifications and profiles will arrive gradually, and developers will implement them alongside their existing interfaces—so the move to a fully OGSA-compliant infrastructure will be a gradual migration, rather than the sudden appearance of a full OGSA suite.

HP's grid solutions are based on a combination of internally developed components and open-source and partner products. As the various OGSA specifications arrive I'd expect that we'll adopt them in our own products where they make sense and where our customers have a need for them, and we'll encourage our partners to adopt applicable standards as they become available.

Questioner: A. Trefethen

Could you say more about the convergence of the conflicting standards? Do you anticipate further basic profiles?

Jem Treadwell

The WSRF Basic Profile was so named because there was a strong desire within the GGF community that OGSA should not be constrained to a WSRF-based stack, and we were expecting to develop a WS-Management based profile. However, given the recent announcement from Microsoft, HP, IBM & Intel that they are working on a converged stack, there is currently no activity on a WS-Management profile. Once the converged stack is published I would anticipate that we would revise the OGSA Basic Profile, but bear in mind that the convergence path has been designed so that no refactoring will be required for work based on either WSRF or WS-Management.

Questioner: W. Gropp

Experiences with languages show that the best are designed by 1 or 1 1/2 people to give a simple, uniform, consistent vision. OGSA seems to be the opposite. What is or can be done to ensure that the parts of OGSA are consistent?

Jem Treadwell

Standards work is usually the work of a broad-based committee, although sometimes a standard is based on work donated by a small group or something that is already widely adopted, either of which can make the process smoother and faster, and maybe yield a better result. OGSA is far-reaching, but its components – e.g. BES, Data Management, HPC – are being developed by focused working groups, often driven by a core of three or four people. The OGSA group frequently holds joint meetings – both telecons and face-to-face meetings – with those groups, to discuss the integration and ensure that we have consistent goals.

Questioner: A. Trefethen

I am interested to see that one of the first profiles is HPC. Are the follow-on profiles listed as a wish list or have they been identified by specific groups who will drive then?

Jem Treadwell

The HPC profile was proposed by Marvin Themer of Microsoft, to address a specific product need. Marvin is driving the work, and it's making rapid progress. The OGSA Security profiles, which address secure communication, have been developed within the OGSA-WG, and are nearing publication. The other proposed profiles will follow completion of the underlying service specifications, and will be developed by the working groups developing those specifications.

Middleware for Dynamic Adaptation of Component Applications

Boyana Norris[1], Sanjukta Bhowmick[1,2], Dinesh Kaushik[1], and
Lois Curfman McInnes[1]

[1] Mathematics and Computer Science Division, Argonne National Laboratory,
9700 South Cass Ave., Argonne, IL 60439, U.S.A.
[2] Department of Applied Physics and Applied Mathematics, Columbia University,
200 S.W. Mudd Building, 500 W. 120th Street, New York, NY 10027, U.S.A.
[norris,bhowmick,kaushik,mcinnes]@mcs.anl.gov

Abstract. Component- and service-based software engineering approaches have been gaining popularity in high-performance scientific computing, facilitating the creation and management of large multidisciplinary, multideveloper applications, and providing opportunities for improved performance and numerical accuracy. These software engineering approaches enable the development of middleware infrastructure for computational quality of service (CQoS), which provides performance optimizations through dynamic algorithm selection and configuration in a mostly automated fashion. The factors that affect performance are closely tied to a component's parallel implementation, its management of parallel communication and memory, the algorithms executed, the algorithmic parameters employed, and other operational characteristics. We present the design of a component middleware CQoS architecture for automated composition and adaptation of high-performance component- or service-based applications. We describe its initial implementation and corresponding experimental results for parallel simulations involving time-dependent nonlinear partial differential equations.

1 Introduction

As computational science progresses toward ever more realistic multiphysics and multiscale applications, no single research group can effectively develop, select, or tune all of the components in a given application, and no single tool, solver, or solution strategy can seamlessly span the entire spectrum *efficiently*. Component- and service-based software development approaches help manage some of the complexity of developing such large scientific applications. Current component and service specifications, however, provide support only for basic manipulation of components and services, such as repositories, instantiation, connection, and execution. Common component interfaces and service specifications enable easy access to suites of independently developed algorithms and implementations, and dynamic composability facilitates switching among different implementations during runtime. The challenge then becomes how to

Please use the following format when citing this chapter:

Norris, B., Bhowmick, S., Kaushik, D., McInnes, L. C., 2007, in IFIP International Federation for Information Processing, Volume 239, Grid-Based Problem Solving Environments, eds. Gaffney, P. W., Pool, J.C.T., (Boston: Springer), pp. 127-149.

automatically make sound choices from among the available implementations and parameters, with suitable tradeoffs among performance, accuracy, mathematical consistency, and reliability. Such choices are important both for the initial composition and configuration of an application and for adaptive control during runtime.

With the increased availability of solution methods implemented as components or services, a major challenge is to ensure that the choice of one of many implementations of a particular interface produces a result of the desired quality within a reasonable amount of time. One can address this challenge by automating at least some of the process of selecting and configuring components, with the goal of minimizing execution time within a set of quality constraints. In order to provide such support, a specification is needed that describes the quality metrics, i.e., metadata for functional and nonfunctional properties and requirements of components. Furthermore, the performance of components must be monitored and recorded in a nonintrusive fashion. In addition, the performance data must be analyzed in order to construct performance models of individual components and whole applications, which can then be used by heuristics that take into account performance information and quality constraints in order to compose and adapt applications in an optimized fashion.

Computational Quality of Service. We are addressing this challenge by developing a high-level specification and corresponding middleware for *computational quality of service* (CQoS) [49], or the automatic selection and configuration of components to suit a particular computational purpose. CQoS extends the familiar concept of quality of service (QoS) in networking with domain-specific quality metrics and the ability to specify and manage characteristics of the application in a way that adapts to the changing computational environment. Traditional QoS emphasizes system-related performance effects such as CPU or network loads to implement application priority or bandwidth reservation in networking. Although performance is a shared general concern, high efficiency and parallel scalability are more significant requirements for high-performance scientific applications, along with algorithmic or problem-specific qualities, such as the level of solution accuracy achieved by a particular algorithm. This situation has motivated us to define an expanded notion of CQoS that better reflects the characteristics and needs of high-performance component- or service-based scientific applications.

Common Component Architecture. While our goal is a component-neutral or service-model-neutral CQoS architecture, our work to date on implementing CQoS middleware employs the Common Component Architecture (CCA) [4, 7, 17], which is designed specifically for the needs of parallel, scientific high-performance computing (an area where other component approaches are limited). A comprehensive description of the CCA, including a discussion of how it differs from other component models, is available [7]; here we present a brief overview of the CCA environment, focusing on the aspects most relevant to CQoS infrastructure.

The specification of the Common Component Architecture [16] defines the rights, responsibilities, and relationships among the various elements of the model. Briefly, the elements of the CCA model are as follows:

- *Components* are units of software functionality that can be composed together to form applications. Components encapsulate much of the complexity of the software inside a black box and expose only well-defined interfaces.
- *Ports* are the abstract interfaces through which components interact. Specifically, CCA ports provide procedural interfaces that can be thought of as a class or an interface in object-oriented languages, or a collection of subroutines, or a module in a language such as Fortran 90. Components may provide ports, meaning that they implement the functionality expressed in a port (called *provides* ports), or they may use ports, meaning that they make calls on a port provided by another component (called *uses* ports). Components that provide the same port(s) are considered functionally equivalent and can thus be used interchangeably.
- *Frameworks* manage CCA components as they are assembled into applications and executed. The framework is responsible for instantiating components, destroying instances, and connecting *uses* and *provides* ports without exposing the components' implementation details. The framework also provides a small set of standard services that are available to all components. The CCA implementation of the CQoS infrastructure described in this paper relies on the CCA specification and basic services to provide new middleware components for performance monitoring, analysis, and dynamic application adaptation.

Paper Organization. The remainder of this paper introduces our component middleware architecture for CQoS. Section 2 discusses related work, and Section 3 introduces several high-performance scientific applications that motivate this research, with emphasis on simulations involving the parallel solution of time-dependent, nonlinear partial differential equations (PDEs). Section 4 describes our approach and implementation, and Section 5 presents preliminary experimental results. Section 6 discusses conclusions and directions of future work.

2 Related Work

Adaptive software for scientific computing is an area of emerging research, as evidenced by numerous recent projects and related work [14, 18, 21–26, 31, 35, 36, 39, 40, 43, 53, 55, 57, 60, 62–66, 69]. Many approaches to addressing different aspects of adaptive execution are represented in these projects, from compiler-based techniques to development of new numerical adaptive algorithms.

Three approaches of interest for specifying semantic information are models, contracts, and service-level agreements. Furmento et al. [28] as well as Gu and Nahrstedt [30] discuss performance models and their use in overall component application assembly at runtime within the context of distributed environments; Beugnard et al. [8] define a general model of software contracts and discuss approaches for making components contract-aware. Similarly, the SAM-code model of adaptable mobile agents [1] allows the specification of contracts — consisting of one precondition and one postcondition — for each adaptable method. Violations are used to select from different implementations of a method at runtime. The GlueQoS work of Wohlstadter et al. [68] focuses on mediating quality-of-service requirements — specified as assertions — between clients and Web services. Bennett et al. [6] discuss the need for service-level agreements for defining the terms and conditions of use, with agreements providing a minimum of coupling between components. They also emphasize the importance of characterizing relevant component features to ensure both the correct use and provision of services. Raje et al. [50] describe a QoS framework for distributed, heterogeneous components and provide a catalog of QoS metrics [13]. The Software-Implemented Fault Tolerance (SIFT) environment for Adaptive Reconfigurable Mobile Objects of Recovery (ARMOR) processes [67] relies on their model for functional reconfiguration to adjust application behavior to meet dependability requirements. In this case adaptation is accomplished through user-specified assertion checks at critical execution points and the use of microcheckpointing to adjust application state accordingly.

In the area of dynamic adaptation based on monitoring application behavior, Reiner and Pinkerton [52] explore dynamically changing control parameters to improve operating system performance and use experiments to determine improved settings. They develop a methodology for adaptive tuning as well as algorithm, policy, and (fixed) parameter selection. Whisnant et al. [67] rely on human intervention to deal with reconfiguration after a problem is detected at runtime. Feather et al. [27], however, use event monitoring of behavioral deviations and changing environmental conditions to reconcile the intended system behavior with individual requirements at runtime. In these cases, monitoring an application at runtime involves checking control parameters and monitoring events, including application failure.

Unlike these efforts, our approach is specifically targeted at large-scale parallel computations and relies on high-level interface specifications and technologies tailored for scientific computing. In designing our CQoS interfaces and middleware components, we rely on the existing high-performance infrastructure provided by the CCA, in which multiple component implementations conforming to the same external interface standard are interoperable and the runtime system ensures that the overhead of component substitution is negligible.

3 Motivating Applications and Algorithms

As discussed in [45], a variety of high-performance scientific applications motivate the development of infrastructure for computational quality of service,

including mesh partitioning in combustion simulations [58,59], resource management in quantum chemistry [38], and the solution of linear systems that arise in
nonlinear PDE-based simulations in domains such as high-energy accelerators,
computational fluid dynamics, and radiation transport. A common feature of
these large-scale, long-running simulations is the combination of diverse numerical capabilities, such as physics models, discretizations, linear solvers, nonlinear
solvers, and optimization solvers, each having multiple implementations with
varying degrees of fidelity, robustness, efficiency, and scalability. Moreover, it
is not generally known a priori which combination of implementations will be
best suited for a particular problem instance and computational environment.

Before explaining in Section 4 our approach to handling these issues with
CQoS middleware, we briefly introduce two parallel PDE-based applications in
which a significant fraction of overall execution time is devoted to the solution of
large-scale, sparse linear systems. In this context, CQoS focuses on selecting and
configuring linear solvers (typically preconditioners and Krylov methods) based
on the context of the overall simulation. Because the properties of linear systems
in time-dependent or nonlinear applications may significantly change during
the course of a simulation, CQoS-enabled adaptive multimethod solvers have
promise to improve robustness and reduce overall time to solution [10–12, 44].
Section 5 presents experimental results of CQoS-enabled adaptive linear solvers
for these two applications.

Transonic Euler Flow. We consider the solution of the unsteady compressible
three-dimensional Euler equations using PETSc-FUN3D [3], an unstructured
mesh code originally developed by W. K. Anderson [2] and subsequently parallelized using MeTiS [34] for mesh partitioning and the PETSc library [5] for the
preconditioned Newton-Krylov family of implicit solution schemes. This code
uses a finite volume discretization with a variable-order Roe scheme on a tetrahedral, vertex-centered mesh; details of the discretization and parallelization are
discussed in [3]. We explore the standard aerodynamics test case of transonic
flow over an ONERA M6 wing using the frequently studied parameter combination of a freestream Mach number of 0.839 with an angle of attack of 3.06°. The
robustness of solution strategies is particularly important for this model because
of the so-called λ-shock that develops on the upper wing surface, as depicted
in Figure 1. The PDEs are initially discretized by using a first-order scheme;
but once the shock position has settled down, a second-order discretization is
applied.

Radiation Transport. Under the assumptions of isotropic radiation with no
frequency dependence, transport through a material characterized by spatially
varying atomic number (Z) and thermal conductivity (κ) can be modeled by
the following coupled nonlinear equations in radiation energy density (E) and
material temperature (T):

$$\frac{\partial E}{\partial t} - \nabla \cdot (D_E \nabla E) = \sigma_a(T^4 - E), \quad \frac{\partial T}{\partial t} - \nabla \cdot (D_T \nabla T) = -\sigma_a(T^4 - E) \quad (1)$$

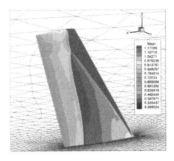

Fig. 1. Mach contours on the ONERA M6 wing at freestream Mach number = 0.839.

with

$$\sigma_a = \frac{Z^3}{T^3}, \quad D_E(E,T) = \frac{1}{3\sigma_a + \frac{|\nabla E|}{|E|}}, \quad \text{and } D_T(T) = \kappa T^{\frac{5}{2}}. \tag{2}$$

In order to restrict the maximum speed of propagation to the speed of light, the above formula for diffusivity D_E includes Wilson's flux limiter $|\nabla E|/|E|$ [29, 46], which makes these governing equations highly nonlinear. The spatial discretization in [29] employs Galerkin finite elements with linear piecewise continuous basis functions over simplices in 2D and 3D. Temporal integration is done by a solution-adaptive implicit Euler method. This code shows excellent scalability on the TeraGrid, Blue-Gene, and System X platforms [29].

The cross section of the computational domain in 3D is the unit square, with a radiation flux incident on the left boundary. The atomic number is location dependent (only in x and y):

$$Z(x,y,z) = \begin{cases} 10 \text{ for } \frac{1}{3} \le x \le \frac{2}{3} \text{ and } \frac{1}{3} \le y \le \frac{2}{3}, \\ 1 \quad \text{elsewhere.} \end{cases} \tag{3}$$

The boundary conditions for Equations (1) are set by imposing a constant radiation field at $x = 0$:

$$\mathbf{n} \cdot D_E \nabla E + \frac{E}{2} = 2 \text{ at } x = 0 \text{ and } \mathbf{n} \cdot D_E \nabla E + \frac{E}{2} = 0 \text{ at } x = 1,$$
$$\text{and } \mathbf{n} \cdot \nabla E = 0 \text{ at } y = 0 \text{ and } y = 1,$$

where $\mathbf{n}$ is the outward unit normal to the boundary, as in [42]. The temperature contours showing the propagation of the thermal front at $t = 1$ and $t = 3$ are given in Figure 2.

Algorithmic Overview. Both of these nonlinear PDE-based applications employ Newton-Krylov methods (see, e.g., [47]) within the PETSc library [5] to solve nonlinear equations of the form $f(u) = 0$, where $f : R^n \to R^n$, at each timestep of the simulation. We use a two-step sequence of (approximately) solving the Newton correction equation

$$(f'(u^{\ell-1}))\, \delta u^\ell = -f(u^{\ell-1}) \tag{4}$$

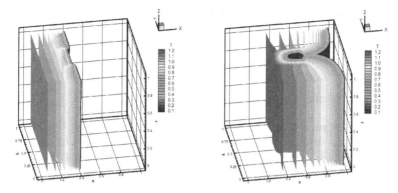

Fig. 2. Evolution of material temperature in time for a 3D example with a tetrahedral mesh of 237,160 vertices and 1,264,086 elements. The left figure shows the temperature contours at $t = 1$, while the right shows temperature at $t = 3$.

and then updating the iterate via $u^\ell = u^{\ell-1} + \delta u^\ell$. If the Jacobian matrix f' is poorly conditioned, the Krylov method will require an unacceptably large number of iterations. The system (4) can be transformed into the equivalent form $B^{-1}f'(u^{\ell-1})\delta u^\ell = -B^{-1}f(u^{\ell-1})$ through the action of a preconditioner, B, whose inverse action approximates that of f', but at smaller cost. We thus consider in Section 5 a variety of different preconditioners and Krylov methods, with a goal of achieving low computational cost and scalable parallelism.

The radiation transport code uses an analytical second-order accurate Jacobian matrix f', where the preconditioner is derived from the same matrix. In contrast, the compressible Euler application employs matrix-free Newton-Krylov methods (see, e.g., [15]), with which we compute the action of the Jacobian on a vector v by directional differencing of the form $f'(u)v \approx \frac{f(u+hv)-f(u)}{h}$, where h is a differencing parameter. We use a first-order analytic discretization to compute the corresponding preconditioning matrix.

For both applications, the time to solve the Newton correction equation (4), is a significant fraction of overall execution time (about 35% for the radiation transport code and about 75% for the compressible Euler code). Moreover, as further discussed in Section 5, changes in the numerical characteristics of the linear systems reflect the changing nature of the simulations. For example, the use of pseudo-transient continuation [37] in the compressible Euler application generates linear systems that become progressively more difficult to solve as the simulation advances (see Figure 5). Likewise, the linear and nonlinear systems become progressively more challenging as the timesteps (based on dynamical scales of the problem) increase in the radiation transport application (see Figure 6). Consequently, both applications provide strong motivation for the development of CQoS middleware to support multimethod adaptive linear solver algorithms.

4 Computational Quality of Service for Components

This section describes in detail our approach to defining and implementing computational quality of service for components, which was introduced in Section 1.

4.1 Approach

We begin by reviewing the main requirements for enabling computational quality of service support in component-based scientific applications. First, we must be able to monitor the performance of individual components without requiring manual code modifications. The performance data must be collected and stored for later access. Performance information alone, however, is not sufficient to enable effective adaptive strategies in numerical software. Thus, we must also identify nonfunctional *quality* metrics, which are problem- or algorithm-specific, and nonintrusively record the resulting metadata corresponding to these metrics along with the performance data. The accumulated runtime information can also be augmented with a priori or source-based analysis of algorithms, whenever such are available. Given this combined database, the application performance can be characterized by means of different approaches, including machine learning and statistics. The results of such analyses would be used to construct performance models for individual components or whole applications. Finally, there must be a mechanism for specifying dynamic adaptation (component reconfiguration or substitution) based on these performance models and additional problem metadata.

Our goal is to address these requirements by providing middleware for component- or service-oriented frameworks, with the CCA as our initial target component model. We rely on the discipline of interface definition, which is at the core of both component- and service-based software engineering approaches, in order to automate the gathering of performance and other data, as well as to enable automated dynamic reconfiguration and substitution of computational units, expressed as either components or services.

The principal purpose of CQoS in the context of high-performance computing is to provide methodology and support for optimizing the time to solution of component- or service-based applications. We have identified two main ways through which this goal can be achieved: (1) by optimizing the selection component instances for the initial composition of an application and (2) by dynamically reconfiguring or substituting component instances.

4.2 Architecture

To support CQoS in scientific applications, we describe a high-level architecture that is not dependent on a particular component or service model (Figure 3). This architecture consists of two main parts: (1) *measurement and analysis* components, which are responsible for monitoring and gathering performance information and other metadata and for operating on and augmenting these data, and (2) *control infrastructure*, which consists of components that implement domain-specific adaptive strategies, along with runtime services for component reconfiguration and substitution. Work that has contributed to the design of this architecture is described in [32, 41, 45, 49, 51, 61].

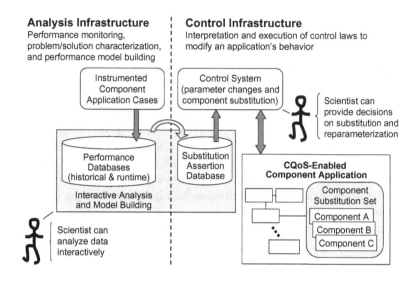

Fig. 3. CQoS middleware architecture overview.

The monitoring portion of the infrastructure deals with collecting performance data, as well as domain-specific metadata that is related to or may impact the performance of an application. The two main requirements for the monitoring and data gathering support are that (1) minimal or no code changes are needed to enable monitoring, and (2) the overhead of the data gathering functionality is negligible with respect to the rest of the computation.

The analysis infrastructure consists of components that operate on any available performance data and associated metadata for individual components or whole applications. Different types of analyses, for example statistical or machine learning, can be incorporated in order to derive a characterization, or model, of the performance of an application or its constituent components. The models generated by analyses or provided by developers are stored in the persistent performance database, along with references to and from the performance data from which they were generated. When performance models of individual components are available, analysis components for generating whole-application models, such as those described in [41], can be employed to derive a performance model for an application composed from these components. Another source of performance models is analytic closed expressions for the execution time provided by users or source code analysis tools. Such models are usually less accurate and are limited by the complexity of the parameterization used. While the accuracy of performance models can vary greatly, the availability of such models is crucial for enabling CQoS support, both for initial application composition and for runtime adaptation.

4.3 Implementation

While the high-level architecture described in Section 4.2 represents our vision of the general structure of middleware for CQoS support, it does not dictate low-level implementation details; thus, specialized implementations can be provided for different computational environments. Our current focus is on tightly coupled high-performance architectures because the majority of our motivating applications are written for such platforms using a single-program multiple-data (SPMD) programming model. This does not preclude implementations targeting more loosely coupled Grid-based environments, which would be able to reuse at least some of the middleware analysis and control infrastructure implementations.

We have implemented portions of the architecture described in Section 4.2; an early prototype is described in [48]. The initial implementation provides automated performance instrumentation of C++ CCA components using the Tuning and Analysis Utilities (TAU) software [54]. In addition to providing portable instrumentation capabilities, TAU provides a database format definition, the Performance Data Management Framework (PerfDMF) [33], for storing performance data and other application metadata. In our initial implementation, we leveraged the performance monitoring approach described in [41], extending it to collect component-specific metadata in addition to performance metrics. For example, in an application involving the solution of a nonlinear PDE using a Newton-based solver, we monitor and record the number of nonlinear iterations. Furthermore, we implemented context-sensitive monitoring of performance and related metadata; for example, within each nonlinear solution, we monitor and record the linear solver algorithm used, the preconditioner type, and the number of linear iterations (for iterative Krylov subspace solvers). In the database, performance and algorithm-specific execution metadata is associated with an application *experiment*, which is defined as an application instance consisting of a set of component instances and their configurations. Including component configuration parameters in the CQoS metadata is crucial because they can significantly change the performance characteristics of an application; different parameter values can result in drastically different performance for the same set of components. For example, in a driven cavity fluid dynamics simulation [19], the lid velocity and Grashof number determine to a large degree the difficulty of the problem instance; in addition, algorithmic parameters, such as the initial CFL number, affect the convergence speed and thus total execution time.

Our initial use case for the CQoS infrastructure focuses on enabling adaptive algorithms for the solution of nonlinear PDEs. In particular, we target multi-method approaches to adaptive linear system solution, such as those described in [10, 11, 44]. While it is possible to define application-independent adaptive strategies based only on general data mining of the historical performance information, our initial approach is based on developing application or domain-specific analysis and corresponding control components, which employ both the performance information and the associated application-specific metadata. The main disadvantage of this approach is that it is not generally applicable in a black-box fashion to arbitrary applications for which we have gathered sufficient performance data. A significant advantage, however, is that by focusing on developing analysis algorithms and adaptive strategies for a particular application domain, we are able to construct much more accurate performance models and more detailed control components, resulting in greater potential performance improvements.

An implementation of a subset of the CQoS infrastructure for adaptive linear solver components in time-dependent nonlinear PDE-based applications is illustrated in Fig. 4. New middleware components for monitoring the performance of nonlinear and linear solver components and for recording algorithm-specific metadata are introduced. An adaptive strategy component serves as a proxy for a linear solver component, presenting the same public interface as a non-adaptive linear solver component. The adaptive strategy can be implemented as one or more components; in this case, it combines the analysis and control portions of the CQoS architecture for selecting among different linear solver algorithms throughout the nonlinear solution process.

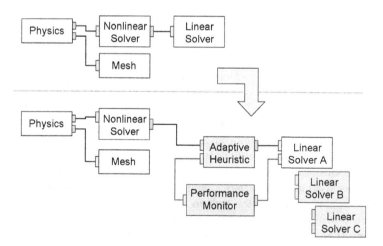

Fig. 4. Adaptive linear solver components in nonlinear PDE applications: a typical component application without adaptivity (top) and the same application with support for performance monitoring and adaptive linear solvers (bottom).

We have developed a number of adaptive heuristics with various degrees of generality. For example, an approach that is generally applicable to Newton-based nonlinear system solution is to monitor the nonlinear rate of convergence and switch linear solvers when a given threshold is reached. Approaches that exploit some domain or application-specific knowledge in addition to the algorithmic metadata can result in more effective adaptive behavior. For example, a change in a physical parameter that is known to affect the characteristics of the linear systems can be used to trigger linear solver component substitution. In general, when designing new adaptive strategies, we exploit both application-specific and algorithmic parameters whenever possible. Initial heuristics for a new application domain may be fully manual, using human insight to guide the adaptation, and gradually evolving into more automated strategies that include more sophisticated analysis components.

5 Experimental Results

We used the Jazz cluster at Argonne National Laboratory to run the simulations for the compressible Euler and radiation transport applications introduced in Section 3. The cluster has a Myrinet 2000 network and 2.4 GHz Pentium Xeon processors with 1-2 GB of RAM. We experimented with one problem instance from each motivating application, both of which required the solution of large-scale linear systems with sparse coefficient matrices. The compressible Euler code generated Jacobian matrices of rank approximately 1.8×10^6 with 1.3×10^8 nonzeros, while the radiation transport code generated matrices of rank 4.5×10^5 with 6.3×10^6 nonzeros. We ran the simulations on four processors using *base solvers* composed of various Krylov methods and subdomain solvers for a block Jacobi preconditioner with one block per processor.

We compare the performance of the simulations using adaptive solvers with that of the base solvers. Use of adaptive solvers can improve the overall performance by dynamically selecting the most appropriate method to match the needs of the current linear system, such as combining more robust (but more costly) methods when needed in particularly challenging phases of solution with faster (though less powerful) methods in other phases. Adaptive solvers can be defined by the heuristic employed for method selection. The efficiency of an adaptive heuristic depends on how appropriately it determines *switching points*, or the iterations at which to change linear solvers. In this paper we employed sequence-based adaptive heuristics, which rely on a predetermined sequence of linear solvers and then "switch up" to a more robust but more costly method or "switch down" to a cheaper but less powerful method as needed during the simulation. The sequence of base solvers is ordered by the *average time per nonlinear iteration* required by each solver. This measurement provides a rough estimate of the strength of the linear solver.

5.1 Transonic Euler Flow

Solver Specifications. We employed the following four base solvers, consisting of a Krylov method and block Jacobi preconditioner with one block per processor with the specified subdomain solver:

1. GMRES with SOR as a subdomain solver, designated as GMRES-SOR
2. Bi-conjugate gradient squared (BCGS) with no-fill incomplete factorization (ILU(0)) as the subdomain solver, called BCGS-ILU0
3. Flexible GMRES (FGMRES) with ILU(0) as the subdomain solver, designated as FGMRES-ILU0
4. GMRES with ILU(1) as a subdomain solver, designated as GMRES-ILU1

Adaptive Heuristics. The compressible Euler code uses pseudo-transient continuation [37] to advance the solution to an assumed steady state. The CFL number [37] provides a good indication of the relative difficulty of the resulting Newton system, with lower CFL numbers indicating systems that are better conditioned and thus easier to solve than those with higher CFL numbers. The left-hand graph of Figure 5 shows that the change in CFL number is inversely reflected by the change in the nonlinear residual norm. Thus, the nonlinear residual norm is a good indicator of the level of difficulty of solving its corresponding Newton correction equation: the lower the residual norm, the more difficult the linear system. Based on trial runs of the application, we divided the simulation into four sections: (a) $||f(u)|| \geq 10^{-2}$, (b) $10^{-4} \leq ||f(u)|| < 10^{-2}$, (c) $10^{-10} \leq ||f(u)|| < 10^{-4}$, and (d) $||f(u)|| < 10^{-10}$. Whenever the simulation crosses from one section to another, the adaptive method switches up or down accordingly.

The relative linear convergence tolerance was 10^{-3}, and the maximum number of iterations for any linear solve was 30. We ordered these methods for use in the adaptive solver as 1, 2, 3, 4, according to the average time taken per nonlinear iteration in the first-order discretization phase of the simulation, which can serve as a rough estimate of the strength of the various linear solvers for this application.

Results. The right-hand graph of Figure 5 show the switching points among these methods in the adaptive polyalgorithmic approach. The simulation starts with method 1, then switches to method 2 at the next iteration. The switch to method 3 occurs at iteration 25. The discretization then shifts to second order at iteration 28, and the initial linear systems become easier to solve. The adaptive method therefore switches down to method 2. From this point onward, the linear systems become progressively more difficult to solve as the CFL number increases; the adaptive method switches up to method 3 in iteration 66 and method 4 in iteration 79. The last change is accompanied by an increase in the time taken for the succeeding nonlinear iteration. This increased time is devoted to setting up the new preconditioner, which in this case changes the block Jacobi subdomain solver from ILU(0) to ILU(1) and consequently requires more time

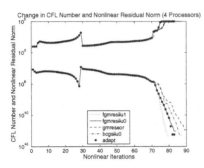 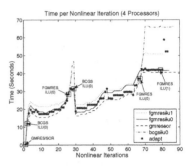

Fig. 5. *Left:* Convergence rate (lower plot) and CFL number (upper plot) for the base and adaptive solvers on 4 processors. *Right:* Time per nonlinear iteration for the base and adaptive solvers on 4 processors. The labeled square markers indicate when linear solvers changed in the adaptive algorithm.

for the factorization phase. The execution time of the adaptive polyalgorithmic scheme is 3% better than the fastest base method (FGMRES-ILU0) and 20% better than the slowest one (BCGS-ILU0).

5.2 Radiation Transport

Solver Specifications. We employed the following four base solvers, consisting of a Krylov method and block Jacobi preconditioner with one block per processor with the specified subdomain solver:

1. GMRES with SOR as a subdomain solver, designated as GMRES-SOR
2. Flexible GMRES (FGMRES) with ILU(0) as a subdomain solver, designated as FGMRES-ILU0
3. GMRES with ILU(0) as a subdomain solver, designated as GMRES-ILU0
4. Bi-conjugate gradient squared (BCGS) with with ILU(0) as a subdomain solver, designated as BCGS-ILU0

The relative linear convergence tolerance was 10^{-3} and the maximum number of iterations for any linear solve was 80.

Adaptive Heuristics. In contrast to the previous application, the radiation transport code completely solves a nonlinear system at *each* time step. The number of nonlinear iterations (4-10) required for convergence of each nonlinear system is quite small, rendering the use of adaptive solvers specific to each nonlinear solution unnecessary. However, the difficulty of the nonlinear systems themselves varies over the timesteps, and this factor can be utilized to generate adaptive solvers. Thus, the linear solvers stay constant during the solution of each nonlinear system but may change as the degree of difficulty in nonlinear equations changes with the timesteps.

The left-hand graph of Figure 6 plots the timestep size with respect to the simulation's progress. We sampled the average time per iteration at time intervals of 1 second. The right-hand graph shows the average time per iteration of the base solvers at these intervals. We note that although solvers 1 and 4 remain in their highest and lowest positions, the relative order of solvers 2 and 3 varies, especially between the time intervals 2 and 3. Thus the sequence of solvers is 1, 2, 3 and 4, except in the interval (2-3 seconds), where the sequence is 1, 3, 2 and 4.

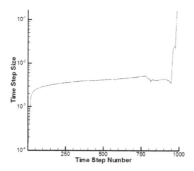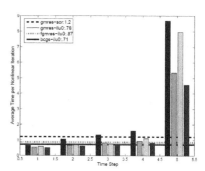

Fig. 6. *Left:* Change in timestep size over the simulation. *Right:* Change of average time per nonlinear iteration as simulation progresses. From left to right the bar indicates average time per iteration of solvers 1, 2, 3, and 4 within the timestep interval given in the x-axis. The legend shows the average time for each solver, over the entire simulation.

In addition to the timestep, a good indicator of the difficulty of the problem is the ratio of the linear iterations to nonlinear iterations. As the relative difficulty of the nonlinear system increases, this ratio increases correspondingly.

Results. We experimented with an automated adaptive solver, where the linear solver changes with change in the ratio of the linear to nonlinear iterations increases by 10%. Generally we switched to a faster solver if the increase was more than 10%; however, the ratio increased significantly in the first few step up to 30%. Therefore we switched from solver 1 to solver 3 skipping the intermediate solver 2. Another aberration to this rule was in the (2-3 second) interval where, since solvers 2 and 4 have nearly the same average time per iteration, we switched from solver 4 to solver 2 when the ratio increased by 10%. Since a switch in solvers can potentially increase the time, chiefly because of data structure manipulations needed when resetting the Krylov method and preconditioner, we kept the solver fixed for a window of at least four timesteps and then switched if necessary.

The solver switches shown in Figure 7 are as follows. The simulation begins with method 1 and switches to method 3 at time step 6, and then to method

4 at timestep 10. The next switch occurs at time step 552 to method 2. Then at timestep 740 the solver is changed to method 3, and finally at step 744 the solver becomes method 4 and this is maintained to the end. The automated adaptive solver is 1.2% better than the fastest base method (BCGS-ILU(0)) and 42.0% better than the slowest method (GMRES-SOR).

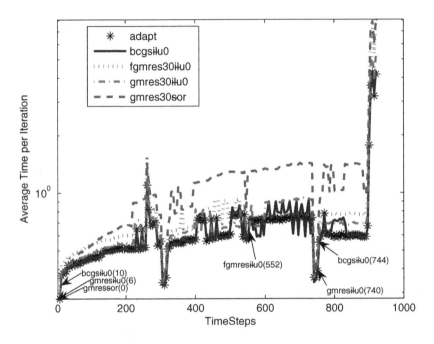

Fig. 7. Time per nonlinear iteration for the base and adaptive solvers on 4 processors. The markers indicate when linear solvers changed in the adaptive algorithm (the time step number is in parenthesis).

These preliminary experiments with the two motivating applications highlight the promise of adaptive solvers in the context of long-running simulations in which a single algorithm may not perform best throughout the entire simulation. These experiments also emphasize that solver performance differs considerably across application domains. For example, while BCGS-ILU(0) performed well for the radiation transport code, it was not the best performer for the transonic Euler code. The experiments also show that heuristics for adaptive multimethod solvers depend on the nature of the application.

Ongoing work includes applying these insights in adaptive strategies to larger problem instances of the radiation transport and transonic Euler applications. We are also working to incorporate scalable solver components [56] under development by the Terascale Optimal PDE Simulations (TOPS) project [20], which define a common interface through which one can provide easy access to a broad range of scalable solvers developed by different groups at different institutions.

6 Conclusions

Motivated by the emerging needs of high-performance component-based scientific applications, we have introduced a general middleware architecture for computational quality of service, which provides support for runtime adaptation of component- or service-based applications with the goal of reducing the overall time to solution. We described an initial implementation of the CQoS architecture for CCA components, which provides support for adaptive algorithms, such as linear system solution. We demonstrated the effectiveness of this adaptive approach on parallel simulations of radiation transport and transonic Euler flow. While our current emphasis is on SPMD component applications, the overall architecture can be implemented in other contexts, such as distributed components and service-based applications.

Our current work focuses on refining the initial implementation to conform more closely to the CQoS overall architecture, including separation of analysis and control middleware components, as well as a robust implementation of the database management components. Future plans include adding more general analysis algorithms for extracting performance characteristics using statistical and machine learning methods [9] and leveraging related work by Eijkhout and Fuentes [26] on matrix characterization and metadata. We also will continue to explore the use of our CQoS approach in new application domains.

Acknowledgments

This work was supported by the U.S. Department of Energy under Contract W-31-109-Eng-38 and by the National Science Foundation award 04-06403. We thank the members of the Common Component Architecture Forum for many stimulating discussions about high-performance software components. We also thank Barry Smith for making some enhancements to the PETSc library to facilitate the development of adaptive solvers.

References

1. Noriki Amano and Takuo Watanabe. A software model for flexible and safe adaptation of mobile code programs. In *Proceedings of the International Workshop on Principles of Software Evolution*, pages 57–61, Orlando, FL, May 2002.
2. W. K. Anderson and D. Bonhaus. An implicit upwind algorithm for computing turbulent flows on unstructured grids. *Computers and Fluids*, 23(1):1–21, 1994.

3. W. K. Anderson, W. D. Gropp, D. K. Kaushik D. E. Keyes, and B. F. Smith. Achieving high sustained performance in an unstructured mesh CFD application. In *Proceedings of Supercomputing 1999*. IEEE Computer Society, 1999. Gordon Bell Prize Award Paper in Special Category.

4. R. Armstrong, D. Gannon, A. Geist, K. Keahey, S. Kohn, L. McInnes, S. Parker, and B. Smolinski. Toward a Common Component Architecture for high-performance scientific computing. In *Proceedings of the Eighth IEEE International Symposium on High Performance Distributed Computing*, 1999.

5. S. Balay, K. Buschelman, W. Gropp, D. Kaushik, M. Knepley, L. McInnes, Barry F. Smith, and H. Zhang. PETSc users manual. Technical Report ANL-95/11 - Revision 2.3.2, Argonne National Laboratory, 2006. `http://www.mcs.anl.gov/petsc`.

6. K. Bennett, P. Layzell, D. Budgen, P. Brereton, L. Macaulay, and M. Munro. Service-based software: The future for flexible software. In *Proceedings of the 7th Asia-Pacific Software Engineering Conference (APSEC 2000)*, pages 214–221, 2000.

7. D. E. Bernholdt, B. A. Allan, R. Armstrong, F. Bertrand, K. Chiu, T. L. Dahlgren, K. Damevski, W. R. Elwasif, T. G. W. Epperly, M. Govindaraju, D. S. Katz, J. A. Kohl, M. Krishnan, G. Kumfert, J. W. Larson, S. Lefantzi, M. J. Lewis, A. D. Malony, L. C. McInnes, J. Nieplocha, B. Norris, S. G. Parker, J. Ray, S. Shende, T. L. Windus, and S. Zhou. A component architecture for high-performance scientific computing. Intl. J. High-Perf. Computing Appl., in press, 2006.

8. Antoine Beugnard, Jean-Marc Jézéquel, Noël Plouzeau, and Damien Watkins. Making components contract aware. *IEEE Computer*, 32(7):38–45, July 1999.

9. S. Bhowmick, V. Eijkhout, Y. Freund, E. Fuentes, and D. Keyes. Application of machine learning to selecting solvers for sparse linear systems. submitted to International Journal of High Performance Computing Applications.

10. S. Bhowmick, D. Kaushik, L. McInnes, B. Norris, and P. Raghavan. Parallel adaptive solvers in compressible PETSc-FUN3D simulations. In *Proceedings of the 17th International Conference on Parallel CFD*, 2005. Also available as Argonne National Laboratory preprint ANL/MCS-P1283-0805.

11. S. Bhowmick, L. C. McInnes, B. Norris, and P. Raghavan. The role of multi-method linear solvers in PDE-based simulations. In *Lecture Notes in Computer Science*, volume 2667, pages 828–839, 2003. Computational Science and Its Applications-ICCSA 2003.

12. S. Bhowmick, P. Raghavan, L. C. McInnes, and B. Norris. *Faster PDE-Based Simulations Using Robust Composite Linear Solvers*, volume 20, pages 373–387. 2004.

13. G. J. Brahnmath, R. R. Raje, A. M. Olson, M. Auguston, B. R. Bryant, and C. C. Burt. A quality of service catalog for software components. In *Proceedings of the Southeastern Software Engineering Conference. http://www.ndiatvc.org/SESEC2002/*, 2002.

14. R. Bramley, D. Gannon, T. Stuckey, J. Villacis, J. Balasubramanian, E. Akman, F. Berg, S. Diwan, and M. Govindaraju. The Linear System Analyzer. In *Enabling Technologies for Computational Science*. Kluwer, 2000.

15. P. N. Brown and Y. Saad. Hybrid Krylov methods for nonlinear systems of equations. *SIAM Journal on Scientific and Statistical Computing*, 11:450–481, 1990.

16. CCA Forum. CCA specification. `http://cca-forum.org/specification/`, 2006.

17. CCA Forum homepage. http://www.cca-forum.org/, 2006.
18. R. Chowdhary, P. Bhandarkar, and M. Parashar. Adaptive QoS management for collaboration in heterogeneous environments. In *Proceedings of the 16th International Parallel and Distributed Computing Symposium (IEEE, ACM), 11th Heterogeneous Computing Workshop*, Fort Lauderdale, FL, 2002.
19. T.S. Coffey, C.T. Kelley, and D.E. Keyes. Pseudo-transient continuation and differential algebraic equations. *SIAM J. Sci. Comp*, 25:553–569, 2003.
20. D. Keyes (PI). Towards Optimal Petascale Simulations (TOPS) Center. http://tops-scidac.org/, 2006.
21. J. D. de St. Germain, John McCorquodale, Steven G. Parker, and Christopher R. Johnson. Uintah: A massively parallel problem solving environment. In *Proceedings of the Ninth IEEE International Symposium on High Performance and Distributed Computing*, August 2000.
22. J. D. de St. Germain, A. Morris, S. G. Parker, A. D. Malony, and S. Shende. Integrating performance analysis in the Uintah software development cycle. In *Fourth International Symposium on High Performance Computing (ISHPC-IV)*, pages 190–206, May 15-17 2002.
23. Jack Dongarra and Victor Eijkhout. Self-adapting numerical software and automatic tuning of heuristics. In *Proceedings of the International Conference on Computational Science*, 2003.
24. Jack Dongarra and Victor Eijkhout. Self-adapting numerical software for next generation applications. *International Journal of High Performance Computing Applications*, 17:125–131, 2003. also LAPACK Working Note 157, ICL-UT-02-07.
25. Thomas Eidson, Jack Dongarra, and Victor Eijkhout. Applying aspect-orient programming concepts to a component-based programming model. In *Proceedings of the 17th International Parallel and Distributed Processing Symposium (IPDPS) April 22–26, 2003, Nice, France*, 2003.
26. V. Eijkhout and E. Fuentes. A proposed standard for matrix metadata. Technical Report ICL-UT 03-02, University of Tennessee, 2003.
27. M. S. Feather, S. Fickas, A. van Lamsweerde, and C. Ponsard. Reconciling system requirements and runtime behavior. In *Proceedings of the 9th International Workshop on Software Specification and Design*, pages 50–59, April 1998.
28. N. Furmento, A. Mayer, S. McGough, S. Newhouse, T. Field, and J. Darlington. Optimisation of component-based applications within a Grid environment. In *Proceedings of SC2001*, 2001.
29. W. D. Gropp, D. K. Kaushik, D. E. Keyes, and B. F. Smith. A parallel implicit solver for diffusion limited radiation transport equations, 2006. Accepted for the Proceedings of the 16th International Conference on Domain Decomposition Methods.
30. X. Gu and K. Nahrstedt. A scalable QoS-aware service aggregation model for peer-to-peer computing Grids. In *Proceedings of HPDC 2002*, 2002.
31. E. N. Houstis, A. C. Catlin, J. R. Rice, V. S. Verykios, N. Ramakrishnan, and C. E. Houstis. A knowledge/database system for managing performance data and recommending scientific software. *ACM Transactions on Mathematical Software*, 26(2):227–253, 2000.
32. P. Hovland, K. Keahey, L. C. McInnes, B. Norris, L. F. Diachin, and P. Raghavan. A quality of service approach for high-performance numerical components. In *Proceedings of Workshop on QoS in Component-Based Software Engineering, Software Technologies Conference*, Toulouse, France, 2003. Also avail-

able as Argonne National Laboratory preprint ANL/MCS-P1028-0203 via `ftp://info.mcs.anl.gov/pub/tech_reports/reports/P1028.pdf`.

33. K. A. Huck, A. D. Malony, R. Bell, and A. Morris. Design and implementation of a parallel performance data management framework. In *Proc. International Conference on Parallel Processing (ICPP 2005)*. IEEE Computer Society, 2005.

34. G. Karypis and V. Kumar. A fast and high quality scheme for partitioning irregular graphs. *SIAM Journal of Scientific Computing*, 20:359–392, 1999.

35. K. Keahey, P. Beckman, and J. Ahrens. Ligature: A component architecture for high-performance applications. *International Journal of High-Performance Computing Applications*, (14):347–358, 2000.

36. Peter J. Keleher, Jeffrey K. Hollingsworth, and Dejan Perkovic. Exploiting application alternatives. In *19th International Conference on Distributed Computing Systems*, 1999.

37. C. T. Kelley and D. E. Keyes. Convergence analysis of pseudo-transient continuation. *SIAM Journal on Numerical Analysis*, 35:508–523, 1998.

38. Joseph P. Kenny, Steven J. Benson, Yuri Alexeev, Jason Sarich, Curtis L. Janssen, Lois Curfman McInnes, Manojkumar Krishnan, Jarek Nieplocha, Elizabeth Jurrus, Carl Fahlstrom, and Theresa L. Windus. Component-based integration of chemistry and optimization software. *Journal of Computational Chemistry*, 24(14):1717–1725, 15 November 2004.

39. Benjamin C. Lee, Richard Vuduc, James Demmel, and Katherine Yelick. Performance models for evaluation and automatic tuning of symmetric sparse matrix-vector multiply. In *Proceedings of the International Conference on Parallel Processing*, Montreal, Quebec, Canada, August 2004.

40. H. Liu and M. Parashar. Enabling self-management of component based high-performance scientific applications. In *Proceedings of the 14th IEEE International Symposium on High Performance Distributed Computing*. IEEE Computer Society Press, July 2005.

41. A. Malony, S. Shende, N. Trebon, J. Ray, R. Armstrong, C. Rasmussen, and M. Sottile. Performance technology for parallel and distributed component software. *Concurrency and Computation: Practice and Experience*, 17:117–141, Feb–Apr 2005.

42. D. J. Mavriplis. Multigrid approaches to non-linear diffusion problems on unstructured meshes. *Numerical Linear Algebra with Applications*, 8:499–512, 2001.

43. Michael O. McCracken, Allan Snavely, and Allen Malony. Performance modeling for dynamic algorithm selection. In *Proceedings of the International Conference on Computational Science (ICCS'03), LNCS*, volume 2660, pages 749–758, Berlin, 2003. Springer.

44. L. C. McInnes, B. Norris, S. Bhowmick, and P. Raghavan. Adaptive sparse linear solvers for implicit CFD using Newton-Krylov algorithms. In *Proceedings of the Second MIT Conference on Computational Fluid and Solid Mechanics, Cambridge, MA*, volume 2, pages 1024–1028. Elsevier, 2003.

45. Lois Curfman McInnes, Jaideep Ray, Rob Armstrong, Tamara L. Dahlgren, Allen Malony, Boyana Norris, Sameer Shende, Joseph P. Kenny, and Johan Steensland. Computational quality of service for scientific CCA applications: Composition, substitution, and reconfiguration. Preprint ANL/MCS-P1326-0206, Argonne National Laboratory, Feb 2006. Available via `ftp://info.mcs.anl.gov/pub/tech_reports/reports/P1326.pdf`.

46. D. Mihalas and B. Weibel-Mihalas. *Foundations of Radiation Hydrodynamics*. Dover Publications, Inc., Mineola, NY, 1999.

47. J. Nocedal and S. J. Wright. *Numerical Optimization.* Springer-Verlag, 1999.

48. B. Norris, L. McInnes, and I. Veljkovic. Computational quality of service in parallel CFD. In *Proceedings of the 17th International Conference on Parallel CFD,* 2005. Also available as Argonne National Laboratory preprint ANL/MCS-P1283-0805 via `ftp://info.mcs.anl.gov/pub/tech_reports/reports/P1283.pdf`.

49. B. Norris, J. Ray, R. Armstrong, L. C. McInnes, D. E. Bernholdt, W. R. Elwasif, A. D. Malony, and S. Shende. Computational quality of service for scientific components. In *Proceedings of the International Symposium on Component-Based Software Engineering (CBSE7), Edinburgh, Scotland,* 2004. Also available as Argonne National Laboratory preprint ANL/MCS-P1131-0204 via `ftp://info.mcs.anl.gov/pub/tech_reports/reports/P1131.pdf`.

50. R. Raje, B. Bryant, A. Olson, M. Augoston, and C. Burt. A quality-of-service-based framework for creating distributed heterogeneous software components. *Concurrency Comput: Pract. Exper.,* (14):1009–1034, 2002.

51. J. Ray, N. Trebon, S. Shende, R. C. Armstrong, and A. Malony. Performance measurement and modeling of component applications in a high performance computing environment : A case study. In *Proceedings of the 18th International Parallel and Distributed Computing Symposium,* April 2003.

52. David Reiner and Tad Pinkerton. A method for adaptive performance improvement of operating systems. In *Proceedings of the 1981 ACM SIGMETRICS Conference on Measurement and Methodology of Computer Systems,* pages 2–10, September 1981.

53. Self-Adapting Large-scale Solver Architecture, see `http://icl.cs.utk.edu/salsa`, 2006.

54. S. Shende and A. D. Malony. The TAU parallel performance system. *International Journal of High Performance Computing Applications,* 20(2):287–331, 2006.

55. Shweta Sinha and Manish Parashar. System sensitive runtime management of adaptive applications. In *Proceedings of the Tenth IEEE Heterogeneous Computing Workshop,* San Francisco, CA, 2001.

56. B. Smith et al. TOPS Solver Components. `http://www.mcs.anl.gov/scidac-tops/solver-components/tops.html`, 2006.

57. M. Sosonkina. Runtime adaptation of an iterative linear system solution to distributed environments. In *Applied Parallel Computing, PARA'2000,* volume 1947 of *Lecture Notes in Computer Science,* pages 132–140, Berlin, 2001. Springer-Verlag.

58. Johan Steensland and Jaideep Ray. A partitioner-centric model for SAMR partitioning trade-off optimization: Part II. In *Proceedings of the 6th International Workshop on High Performance Scientific and Engineering Computing (HPSEC-04),* August 2004. Held in conjunction with The 2004 International Conference On Parallel processing (ICPP-04), in Montreal, Canada.

59. Johan Steensland and Jaideep Ray. A partitioner-centric model for SAMR partitioning trade-off optimization: Part I. *International Journal of High Performance Computing Applications,* 19:1–14, 2005.

60. Cristian Tapus, I-Hsin Chung, and Jeffrey K. Hollingsworth. Active Harmony: Towards automated performance tuning. In *Proceedings of SC02,* 2002.

61. N. Trebon, A. Morris, J. Ray, S. Shende, and A. Malony. Performance modeling of component assemblies with TAU. Presented at Compframe 2005 workshop, Atlanta, June 2005.

62. Jeffrey S. Vetter and Patrick H. Worley. Asserting performance expectations. In *Proceedings of SC02,* 2002.

63. Richard Vuduc, James Demmel, and Jeff Bilmes. Statistical models for empirical search-based performance tuning. *International Journal of High Performance Computing Applications*, 18(1):65–94, February 2004.

64. Richard Vuduc, James W. Demmel, and Katherine A. Yelick. OSKI: A library of automatically tuned sparse matrix kernels. In *Proceedings of SciDAC 2005*, Journal of Physics: Conference Series, San Francisco, CA, June 2005. Institute of Physics Publishing.

65. R. Clint Whaley and Antoine Petitet. Minimizing development and maintenance costs in supporting persistently optimized BLAS. *Software: Practice and Experience*, 35(2):101–121, February 2005. http://www.cs.utsa.edu/~whaley/papers/spercw04.ps.

66. R. Clint Whaley, Antoine Petitet, and Jack J. Dongarra. Automated empirical optimization of software and the ATLAS project. *Parallel Computing*, 27(1–2):3–35, 2001. Also available as University of Tennessee LAPACK Working Note #147, UT-CS-00-448, 2000 (www.netlib.org/lapack/lawns/lawn147.ps).

67. K. Whisnant, Z. Kalbarczyk, and R. K. Iyer. A foundation for adaptive fault tolerance in software. In *Proceedings of the 10th IEEE International Conference and Workshop on the Engineering of Computer-Based Systems*, pages 252–260, April 2003.

68. Eric Wohlstadter, Stefan Tai, Thomas Mikalsen, Isabelle Rouvellou, and Premkumar Devanbu. GlueQoS: Middleware to sweeten quality-of-service policy interactions. In *Proceedings of the 26th International Conference on Software Engineering (ICSE '04)*, pages 189–199, May 2004.

69. K. Zhang, K. Damevski, V. Venkatachalapathy, and S. Parker. SCIRun2: A CCA framework for high performance computing. In *Proceedings of the 9th International Workshop on High-Level Parallel Programming Models and Supportive Environments (HIPS 2004)*, Santa Fe, NM, April 2004. IEEE Press.

Q&A – Boyana Norris

Questioner: M. Thomas

What is the cost of using these components?

Boyana Norris

For single-language components, the cost of a component method invocation is equivalent to a virtual function call. For multi-language components, the cost is equivalent to several function calls, and is usually negligible if the methods being called are not too fine-grained.

Questioner: A. Trefethen

Is the cost of mixed language components part of the decision making in composing a set of components? It may be optional to keep to a single language?

Boyana Norris

Currently the cost of mixed language component calls is not accounted for in the composition because it is normally insignificant. In general, at least measuring and reporting this cost can help application developers make better design choices when creating component interfaces. It is also possible to develop components for use in a single-language environment, currently C++ or C, as well, and the CCA Forum is developing runtime component frameworks for support of additional languages, such as Fortran.

Questioner: W. Enright

If there are two independent components (e.g., mesh-selector and linear solver), the choice of best combination may not be straightforward. How can this be handled?

Boyana Norris

The analysis of arbitrary combinations is too costly to perform at runtime and is thus not well suited to adaptive execution (although some simple heuristics may be possible). Thus, the CQoS infrastructure would decrease the number of good combinations of components by performing offline analyses using any available performance data and models for individual components, and then constructing a performance model for the performance of the whole application with different combinations of component instances. This provides a set of static combinations (one of which will be the initial application configuration), which can then be used by adaptive strategies for deciding on component substitution at runtime.

Questioner: M. Thune

A key concern is the overhead for the actual adaption. How are you addressing this?

Boyana Norris

The adaptive heuristics we have developed so far are very inexpensive; more costly analyses needed are performed offline, prior to executing the application whenever possible and the results are stored in the performance database and loaded for use by dynamic adaptive strategies.

Questioner: Peter Hemker

Is automatic selection of an algorithm (e.g. the selection of a preconditioner) a sufficiently well-defined problem that allows complete automatic treatment? (Shouldn't one provide additional insight about the problem to make a proper decision?)

Boyana Norris

We don't believe that full automation is possible with the current amount of information available in typical numerical libraries and thus additional information is necessary. This type of information is provided by a domain specialist (e.g., an expert in Krylov linear solution methods) and incorporated into the component's metadata.

Questioner: A. Trefethen

Have there been difficulties in agreeing the additional metadata?

Boyana Norris

Yes, there are some disagreements in selecting the format itself, as well as the actual contents, but for now the CQoS group is small and thus able to agree relatively easily.

Questioner: A. Trefethen

Depending on the choice made, xml vs. interface, what will the impact be on the users?

Boyana Norris

Some format choices will have a significant impact on usability, e.g., XML, and thus need additional tools for making creation, editing, and searching easier. Associating the metadata with interfaces has the advantage of being local to the interfaces it applies to, but it can easily become very verbose and obscure the interface definitions themselves.

Questioner: B. Ford

Place of preconditioning as compared with use of multi-method algorithms. Is there not often more to be gained from preconditioning rather than heuristic method selection?

Boyana Norris

Different types of preconditioners are considered "methods" in the multi-method approach, for example a composite solver that consists of using GMRES(30) with SOR preconditioning and then switching to GMRES(30) with ILU(1) preconditioning is considered a 2-solver method.

A Virtual Organisation deployed on a Service Orientated Architecture for Distributed Data Mining applications

Thomas Jackson, Mark Jessop, Martyn Fletcher, Jim Austin
Advanced Computer Architectures Group,
Department of Computer Science,
University of York, UK
{tom.jackson, mark.jessop, fletcher, austin}@cs.york.ac.uk

Abstract. Industrial and scientific research activity increasingly involves the geographically distributed utilisation of multiple tools, services and distributed data. Grid and Service Orientated Architecture concepts are being widely investigated as a means to deploy Virtual Organisations to support the needs for distributed collaboration. A generic Distributed Tool, Service and Data Architecture is described together with its application to the aero-engine domain through the BROADEN project. Two fundamental issues for the design of the VO have been addressed: how to maximise the potential of Grid computing to address the complex data mining challenges in the condition monitoring application; and how to maximise the potential of a SOA to build and deploy a flexible and efficient collaborative workbench that integrates the required tools and services.

1 Introduction

The Grid and Service Orientated Architecture (SOA) paradigm offer significant opportunities for the development and deployment of Virtual Organisations (VO) which can support complex scientific and engineering interactions. This paper describes the development of a VO architecture to support a condition health monitoring application in the aero-engine domain. This VO provides an integrated and Distributed Tool, Service and Data Architecture built on Grid technologies [1] which is driven by the operating requirement to derive commercial and scientific benefit from distributed data assets. The architecture has been developed to support the requirements of the BROADEN project (Business Resource Optimisation for

Please use the following format when citing this chapter:

Jackson, T., Jessop, M., Fletcher, M., Austin, J., 2007, in IFIP International Federation for Information Processing, Volume 239, Grid-Based Problem Solving Environments, eds. Gaffney, P. W., Pool, J.C.T., (Boston: Springer), pp. 155-170.

Aftermarket and Design on Engineering Networks) project. BROADEN is a follow-on to the DAME (Distributed Aircraft Maintenance Environment) Grid pilot project [2].

The basis of the VO in this application context is to provide a geographically distributed set of users with access to tools and distributed data to carry out collaborative fault diagnosis. The characteristics of this specific VO are typical of many collaborative VO domains:

- Geographically distributed data – potentially in vast amounts.
- Geographically distributed users - not necessarily distributed to the same places as the data.
- Diverse system stakeholders with different roles and access rights.
- Legacy tools which are standalone but may need to interoperate with other tools.
- Disparate distributed diagnostic tools and services which must be brought together in a configurable workflow system.
- Security and Quality of Service as essential prerequisites

1.1. The Condition Monitoring Application Domain

Modern aero engines operate in highly demanding operational environments with extremely high reliability. However, Data Systems & Solutions LLC and Rolls-Royce plc have shown that the adoption of advanced engine condition monitoring and diagnosis technology can reduce costs and flight delays through enhanced maintenance planning [3]. Such aspects are increasingly important to aircraft and engine suppliers where business models are based on Fleet Hour Agreements (FHA) and Total Care Packages (TCP). Rolls-Royce has collaborated with Oxford University in the development of an advanced on-wing monitoring system called QUICK [4]. QUICK performs analysis of data derived from continuous monitoring of broadband engine vibration for individual engines. Known conditions and situations can be determined automatically by QUICK and its associated Ground Support System (GSS). Less well-known conditions (e.g. very early manifestations of problems) require the assistance of remote experts (Maintenance Analysts and Domain Experts) to interpret and analyse the data. The remote expert may want to consider and review the current data, search and review historical data in detail and run various tools including simulations and signal processing tools in order to evaluate the situation. Without a supporting diagnostic infrastructure, the process can be problematic because the data, services and experts are usually geographically dispersed and advanced technologies are required to manage, search and use the massive distributed data sets. Each aircraft flight can produce up to 1 Gigabyte of data per engine, which, when scaled to the fleet level, represents a collection rate of the order of Terabytes of data per year. The storage of this data also requires vast data repositories that may be distributed across many geographic and operational boundaries. The aero-engine scenario is also typical of many other domains, for example, many areas of scientific research, healthcare, etc.

2 The VO Requirements

The diagnostic focus of the BROADEN and DAME projects has required investigation into two fundamental issues for the design of the VO:

- How to maximise the potential of Grid computing to address the complex data mining challenges in the condition monitoring application;
- How to maximise the potential of SOA to build and deploy a flexible and efficient collaborative workbench that integrates the required tool and services.

This paper reports on both of these aspects; describing a highly distributed pattern matching architecture for Grid deployment and the use of the emerging Enterprise Service Bus (ESB) framework as a means to integrate and deploy a dynamic workbench for the VO collaboration. The requirements to address both of the above issues will be explored in more detail, and will be followed by a detailed description of the solutions being developed.

2.1. The Data Mining and Pattern Matching Problem

A central challenge of the project has been to develop a data mining and pattern matching architecture within a grid framework that can scale to the terabytes of distributed data inherent within the application domain. A fundamental aim of this work has been to devise a solution that separates the distributed nature of the problem from the searching/pattern matching problem. There has also been a requirement to keep the solution generic so that the solutions can be mapped into other grid applications requiring distributed search. To this end the following broad objectives for the system were identified:

- **Scalable**. The system should be designed to operate on large data sets and utilise many remote resources efficiently.
- **Flexible**. It must be possible to add and remove resources and data assets from the system dynamically.
- **Robust**. The system should have high availability and maintain operational capability where one or more resources fail. As a consequence of this there should not be a central point of failure.
- **Transparent**. The distribution should be hidden from the end user.
- **Efficient**. The architecture should minimise the amount of data that is moved across the network infrastructure in achieving the data mining objectives.
- **Parallel**. Where searching at different locations provides concurrent operations, the architecture must support parallel execution.
- **Storage Format Independent**. It should be independent of the underlying database technology used to store the data repositories, and should operate transparently across a heterogeneous, distributed data archive facility.

The BROADEN system requires an architecture that can address these functional requirements in addition to meeting the operational demands imposed by the data management issues. A central premise of the BROADEN system is that it must operate on geographically distributed data. The scenario is that every time an aircraft lands, vibration and performance data is downloaded to the system from the QUICK monitoring units fitted to each engine. In future deployed systems, the volume of data downloadable from the QUICK system may be up to 1 GB per engine per flight. Given the large volume of data and the rate at which it is produced, there is a need to consider how the data is managed.

In order to illustrate the requirements of the aero-engine application, consider the following scenario. Heathrow, with its two runways, is authorized to handle a maximum of 36 landings per hour. Let us assume that on average half of the aircraft landing at Heathrow have four engines and the remaining half have two engines. In future, if each engine downloads around 1 GB of data per flight, the system at Heathrow must be capable of dealing with a typical throughput of around 100 GB of raw engine data per hour, all of which must be processed and stored. The data storage requirement alone for an operational day is, therefore, around 1 TB, with subsequent processing generating yet more data.

With such a vast amount of data being produced a centralised repository may place unacceptable demands on data bandwidth and will not provide a scaleable solution. Small subsets of the data could be moved for processing and analysis purposes but this would be a solution only in some limited cases, as most services will need the ability to use full data sets. Therefore, it is desirable to store data in distributed nodes and to distribute the services which act on the data actually with the data. The architecture should permit the use of distributed nodes to store data (and services), assuming other issues such as security, etc. are satisfied.

2.2. The Workbench Requirements

One of the challenges, to date, of building and deploying VO's based on SOA, is that of systems integration. Toolkits are available, such as the Globus toolkit [5], for developing and deploying web-services. However, these provide little support for the integration of the end-to-end services at the VO level within workbench or similar collaborative working environments. Within the DAME project a major part of the project effort was expended on the design and integration of the system portal that exposed tools and services to the diverse end-users. Although the final demonstrator was effective, it was a bespoke solution and not easily scaled to the needs of industrial deployment. Some of the challenges that have to be addressed within the BROADEN project lie with the nature of the tools and services that need to be deployed within the diagnostic process. A major issue has been the requirement to allow users to add tools to the system with the minimum of change to the tools. However, the characteristics of the tools being deployed in the domain means that they are often not easily integrated within a VO. For example, in many cases:

- Tools are designed to operate standalone - this is typical of legacy tools;
- Tools not designed to interoperate with other tools - again this is typical of legacy tools;

- Tools have thick desktop clients that are not efficiently deployed as a web-service

Similar diverse issues are found when analysing the nature of the web-services. The services issues can be summarised as:

- Services may be centralised - this is typical in legacy systems;
- Service may be distributed - particularly located near the data sources;
- Services may be autonomous e.g. data input services triggered by data arrival;
- Services will need to be composed as links in a workflow

The VO architecture should accommodate all the above issues, but do so in a way that supports flexibility and reconfiguration. The architecture should allow all the above tool types to interact with one another as necessary, with a minimum of change both to the tools and the system architecture, whilst still addressing the need for virtualisation and supporting many geographically dispersed users. In the following sections the data mining and pattern matching Grid solution is described, followed by an analysis of the use of ESB as the integration framework for the VO.

3 The Pattern-Matching SOA Architecture

This section introduces a service orientated architecture for deploying pattern matching and/or search functionality against data distributed over many geographically separate locations. This is based around three primary web service enabled components:

- A data-management system for handling data arriving from an aircraft or other data asset;
- A distributed query system;
- A virtual data archiving service.

The discussion will focus on a description of the architecture for the distributed query service and the virtual data archiving service. At the heart of the distributed query process are a range of web services that encompass the Pattern Match Controller (PMC), the Pattern Match Service (PMS) and the Storage Request Broker (SRB).

The distributed concepts within BROADEN dictate that the PMC and PMS services are hosted remotely and replicated at the diverse data repositories (e.g. at each potential airport where data is downloaded and stored). These services and the data repository form a 'Data Node' within the architecture. For the purpose of this architecture definition, each node will be treated as a single resource. In practise, it is likely that each node will utilise many resources, for example, high performance clusters, tape archives, desktop PCs and laptops. The key assumption made is that the communication bandwidth available between resources at a single node is significantly higher than that available between the distributed nodes. The role of each service will be outlined in the following sections.

3.1. The Pattern Match Controller and Search Process

The Pattern Match Controller (PMC) is the front-end service for distributed search operations. The PMC controls the search process at each node and provides all communication between nodes. An instance of the PMC resides at each node.

Each PMC:
- Has a catalogue of all other nodes in the system, to ensure that search requests can be sent to all nodes.
- Has access to a local Pattern Matching Service (PMS), which it can instruct to carry out searches.
- Manages results for all 'active' searches at its own node.

Pattern match searches can be initiated either from an end-user or from automatic workflows in the task brokerage system. In both cases, a client service (an example application providing a GUI is detailed in [6]) communicates, via web service protocols, with its nearest PMC service to request a search. The query takes the form of a request to match a region of interest against the stored fleet data at each node. The PMC node that receives the request becomes the 'master' node for that unique search task. All other nodes in the system are referred to as 'slaves' for that search.

A search scenario is shown in Figure 1. Numbered arrows show communication between services. The exact order of some communication is dependent upon when individual pattern matching services complete their search.

1. A client delivers a search request to a PMC. This becomes the master PMC for this search, and returns a unique identifier for this search that the client can use in later communication.
2. The master PMC passes the search request to all available slave PMCs.
3. All PMCs (including the master) pass the search request to their local Pattern Matching Service. At each node searching commences.
4. At each node, as the Pattern Matching Service completes its search and passes the result to its local PMC. Pattern Matching Services then clean up, discarding the search results. At the master node, the result is merged into the overall result set.
5. Slave PMCs pass the results to the master PMC. The slave PMCs can now clean up and discard the search results. The master PMC merges the new results into the overall result set as they arrive.
6. The client makes a request for the results. The master PMC returns the complete results with additional information informing the client that the search is complete.

The client can request the current search results at any time. The master PMC returns the current result set with additional information such as how many nodes have completed their search task. Typically, a client will request results at regular intervals until the search is finished.

One of the stated aims was to build a generic framework for diagnostics. An API has been designed to support this objective; it does not contain any domain specific data types or structures. The API only specifies how components should interact with the pattern match architecture. This means that application specific components can be built and configured as required by particular implementations to work with the PMC. The PMC receives domain specific data as part of a search request, but does not need to understand it, just how to deliver it to the appropriate services. The PMC is a re-usable component appropriate for distributing search requests regardless of the problem domain.

Each node can behave as a completely stand-alone pattern matching entity, capable of matching against data stored at its location. As new nodes are added, each PMC maintains a list (or catalogue) of all the nodes within the system. For each node, the IP address of the PMC at that node is the only information required. If a node fails, its entry is kept in each node list maintained by each PMC. This allows search results to reflect the fact that the entire dataset is not being searched against. If a node is to be permanently removed, a de-registration process is invoked.

These architectural features address the requirements for scalable, efficient and flexible functionality. Any number of nodes can be supported, each operates independently, and searches are carried out asynchronously. The PMC passes search requests to and from other services, without requiring any understanding of the nature of the search request. Any data that can be contained within the search request structure can be supplied as a search request. Achieving, appropriate results depends upon providing PMS implementations that can understand and process the request.

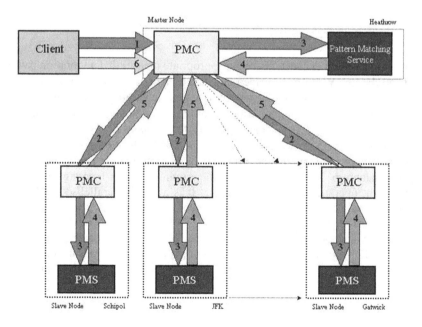

Fig.1. The communication required to complete a typical search process

3.2. Pattern Match Service

The Pattern Matching Service is responsible for performing the search across the data held at a node. This means that the pattern-matching process is handled entirely independently to the search requesting mechanism. This provides for flexibility in the architecture, and does not constrain the query process to any particular pattern-matching algorithm; the PMS can deploy any available pattern matching and/or indexing algorithms as appropriate. It receives search requests from its 'local' PMC and upon completion of the search sends the results back to the PMC. At each node the Pattern Matching Service can access the data stored there without consideration of data stored at other nodes. This feature addresses the requirement for a scalable and concurrent system by permitting the query process to be carried out as an inherently parallel operation across all nodes.

3.3. Example Query Process

To provide an example of the functionality a PMS might perform we describe the search process in the BROADEN system; matching vibration patterns against the historical flight data. The aim is to find vibration patterns that are 'similar' to the anomaly just observed (the 'query' pattern, q). The problem can be stated as finding a set of time series sub-sequences R .

$$ R = \{x \in X | d(x,q) \le \tau\} $$

τ is the maximum distance (using an appropriate metric) that a vibration pattern can be from the query and be considered a match. This is an instance of the 'query by content' or 'query by example' problem, a significant area of data mining research [7, 8, 9]. Where τ is varied to return a set of a fixed number (k) of matches in R , this is referred to as a k-nearest neighbour (k-NN) search.

Within the BROADEN system this search algorithm is implemented using the AURA [10] technology, which provides high performance neural network based pattern matching. AURA is pivotal to the requirements for meeting search requests within tight operational time constraints. It is a highly parallelised and massively scalable search engine that can implement the k-nearest neighbour algorithm extremely efficiently on massive datasets. However, as already stated, the PMS architecture is algorithm independent and the AURA pattern match engine can easily be replaced or accompanied by other pattern matching algorithms as required for the relevant data set. Simple API's allow any algorithm to be made available to the PMS if deployed as a standard web-service.

3.4. PMS Data Transfer

Passing large volumes of data (that may not be required) around the system is likely to increase search times and/or bandwidth requirements. To reduce the volume of network traffic generated, the actual data for each match is not passed between services. Details for each match include an identifier that specifies the location of the data for that result. If a client wishes to examine a result it must fetch the data, which could be located at any node in the system. Clients should be able to access/retrieve result data through a single service, without concern for which node the data is located at, i.e. treating the dataset as a single entity at a single location.

A data management system is required that will provide a single logical view to the distributed dataset and allow clients to access data from the same service, regardless of location. This data management service is responsible for 'looking up' the location of the data and fetching it.

3.5. Storage Resource Broker (SRB)

The Storage Request Broker [11] was selected as the storage mechanism to provide a virtual file indexing system at each node within the system. SRB is a tool for managing distributed storage resources, ranging from large disc arrays to tape backup systems. Files are indexed via SRB and can then be referenced by logical file handles that require no knowledge of where the file physically exists. A Meta-data Catalogue (MCAT) is maintained which maps logical handles to physical file locations. Additional system specified meta-data can be added to each record. This means that the catalogue can be queried in a data centric way, e.g. engine serial number and flight date/number, or via some characteristic of the data, rather than in a location centric fashion. When data is requested from storage, it is delivered via parallel IP streams, to maximise network through-put, using protocols provided by SRB. SRB can operate in heterogeneous environments and in many different configurations from completely stand-alone, such as one disc resource, one SRB server and one MCAT, to completely distributed with many resources, many SRB servers and completely federated MCATs.

The BROADEN system currently utilises a single MCAT but the architecture described here could be deployed with an MCAT at each node. In this configuration a user could query their local SRB system and yet work with files that are hosted remotely in a number of diverse database/file systems. The arrival of aircraft vibration data is simulated at each node; new data is stored directly into SRB on a local resource. Each location stores engine data under a logical file structure based on node location, engine type, engine serial number and flight information. Data may be made visible to any user or client regardless of their location. Pattern Matching Services access local data using SRB, querying the SRB MCAT to locate all data at that node.

The client application can access SRB directly to fetch the data for individual matches as required. This means that the client application does not need to know, or be concerned with where the data is actually located. SRB's logical view allows PMCs and pattern match services to operate on a distributed data set only accessing local data, while other BROADEN services can treat the data as if held at a central repository.

4 The Generic Distributed Tool, Service and Data Architecture

The discussion has presented an architecture that permits data mining and pattern matching queries to be carried out on highly distributed data, and on data that could potentially be managed in a highly heterogeneous range of database technologies. The architecture is generic in that the services are not constrained to any particular search task or any set of search algorithms. Considerable efforts have been expended to make the architecture robust and scalable, and to separate out the mechanisms for requesting and managing the results of queries from the process of pattern matching through the diverse data repositories. It has been demonstrated and deployed in a real-world application domain and found to be highly effective in managing the problems associated with searching distributed data assets. The following sections describe how this architecture is deployed at the heart of the VO system built around an ESB enabled workbench/portal.

The issues relating to the difficulties experienced with integrating services into a SOA to facilitate a Virtual Organisation were described earlier. The lack of tool support for integration was identified. This issue is now being addressed within the developers' community and one of the emerging frameworks for building SOA's is the Enterprise Service Bus [12] concept. The purpose of an ESB is to provide a communications 'bus', based on XML web-service standards, that facilitates application and process integration by providing distributed processing, intelligent routing, security, and dynamic data transformation. All of these services are essential elements of an end-to-end SOA, and by providing them in a standardised way as part of an infrastructure it avoids the overhead of system developers having to implement these in a bespoke manner. The other advantages of an ESB approach, which make it amenable to adoption in the BROADEN VO, are that it is distributed and that it is message based, to provide loose coupling between services. An instance of an ESB may be used within the architecture as a simple messaging and translation mechanism between the tools of the system. Tools are able to register with the ESB providing information about their type of service, their functions and the respective data formats. Translation specifications are provided to the ESB in a standard format and the ESB provides translation facilities on a tool pair basis and even on a function pair basis, if necessary.

The ESB keeps a registry of all connected tools, and routes messages between tools and translator components. Tools, once registered, might become unavailable, move to different locations or change their data formats without informing the ESB. Therefore a method of continuous verification and notification of each service will also be implemented.

Workflow, for use in the Global Workflow Manager, can be expressed in BPEL4WS and in order to make the update of workflows more user-friendly, a GUI will be included in the Workbench.

All of these properties have led to its adoption as the proposed integration framework for the BROADEN Virtual Organisation. This VO provides support to a diverse range of distributed end-users through access to a workbench. This workbench is being developed as a browser-based portal (for ease of deployment) that sits on top of an ESB architecture which orchestrates and integrates the underlying diagnostic tools and services.

Figure 2 provides an overview of the generic architecture that is being developed around the ESB. The elements shown are:

- The Graphics and Visualisation Suites which contain a set of tools at a particular user location.
- The Enterprise Service Bus to enable tool interactions.
- The distributed nodes which encapsulate the data and high performance services (see figure 3).
- The global workflow manager which provides service orchestration on demand from the individual users or as an automatic activity in an event driven mode.

Figure 3 shows the generic overview of the simplified architecture:

- The Pattern Match Controller (PMC) is a distributed component, which manages the distribution of service requests and collection and aggregation of processed results.
- The Processing Services act on local data and provide high performance search, signal extraction facilities, etc.
- Distributed Data Management provides access to local and distributed data through Storage Request Broker abstraction mechanisms.
- The Local Workflow Manager Management provides automatic and requested workflows to be enacted with a single distributed node. A local workflow may also be part of a global workflow controlled by the global workflow manager.
- The Local Resource Broker manages selection of local resources in keeping with specified Service Level Agreements (SLAs).
- Data Loading Services populate the local data stores in each node. These services may also perform other tasks such as data integrity checking, error correction, etc. on input data.
- Databases / Data stores are provided for each type of data resident in the node.

The capabilities of PMC and ESB are complementary; one provides flexibility at the cost of performance, the other reduces the flexibility but gives a gain in performance. An analysis is underway to measure these issues within the BROADEN application. We see the eventual possibility of migrating the functional aspects of ESB that are determined as essential into the PMC, once these have become clear through trial deployment.

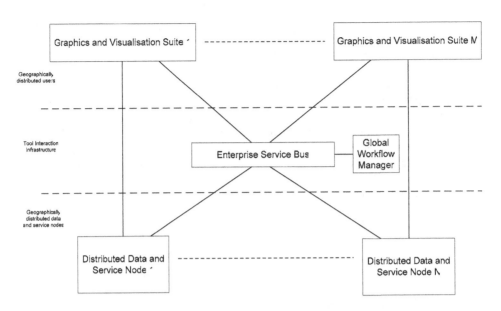

Fig.2. Overview of the Generic Tool, Service and Data Architecture

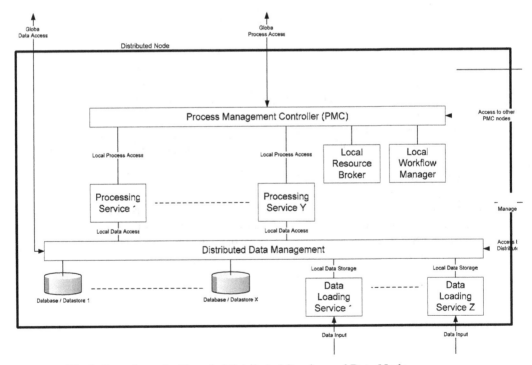

Fig.3. Overview of a Generic Distributed Service and Data Node

Figure 4 shows there are a number of tools that communicate with each other, ranging from visualisation services, data analysis, data management and workflow orchestration. The visualisation tools provided are:

- Case Based Reasoning Viewer [13] including Performance Curve Test (PCT) Viewers.
- Signal Data Explorer (SDE) is a visualisation tool used to view vibration spectral and extracted time series data [6, 14] and performance data. It also acts as the front end to the high performance pattern matching services.
- QUICK Data Viewer is a visualisation tool which allows a user to view spectral data, extracted features and events occurred [4]

The data repository at each node is responsible for storing all raw engine data along with any extracted and AURA encoded data. Each node is populated with:

- The Pattern Match Service (PMS) which is based on Advanced Uncertain Reasoning Architecture technology [10] and provides high performance pattern matching for use with the SDE or in workflows.
- The QUICK Feature Provider service which provides features and events to a client such as the QUICK Data Viewer.
- The XTO (eXtract Tracked Order) service which extract specific time series from the raw spectral vibration data.
- The Data Orchestrator is the Data Loading Service and is responsible for "cleaning" and storing all raw engine data.

Also included in the BROADEN architecture is a centralised CBR Engine and Knowledge Base [13].

The development carried out to date suggests that ESB provides an appropriate framework in which to deploy and develop the VO for the application domain, in that all of the above diverse services can be readily integrated into the architecture. The generic architecture has been developed to be application neutral. It will be implemented for the BROADEN application during the course of the project. This will allow us to assess the strengths and weaknesses of PMC and ESB for the task. Future work will include:

- The testing and demonstration of the generic architecture in the BROADEN application domain.
- The testing and demonstration of the generic architecture in other application domains.
- The introduction of fault tolerance as appropriate (inter and intra node).
- The exploration of fault tolerance techniques within the ESB.

5 Conclusions

The paper has described the development of a VO to support distributed diagnostics for condition health monitoring applications. For this VO domain, as for many other application domains, the issues of distributed data management are central. A distributed SOA architecture has been presented that is being deployed within an industrial pilot study within the BROADEN project. The architecture is generic and will support a diverse range of data analysis methods for VO's. As an example, the methods are being redeployed within the context of a UK wide e-Science project to develop a collaborative working environment and data arching system for neural spike train data (the CARMEN project). Lessons learnt from the DAME project in regard to the development of a workbench to support the VO have been carried forward and have motivated the adoption of the Enterprise Service Bus as an integration framework. This is contributing to the development of an architecture that is flexible, configurable and based on common standards that will encourage reuse.

This work builds on the tools and services developed during the DAME project. A generic architecture has been developed, which integrates:

- Geographically distributed nodes containing data repositories and services.
- Geographically distributed users.
- Legacy Tools.
- Purpose designed tools.

It is a Grid based architecture used to manage the vast, distributed, data repositories of aero-engine health-monitoring data. In this paper we have focused on the use of a generic architecture to enable the general concept to be in other application areas and with varying degrees of legacy systems and designs. The middleware elements are generic in nature and can be widely deployed in any application domain requiring distributed tools and services and data repositories.

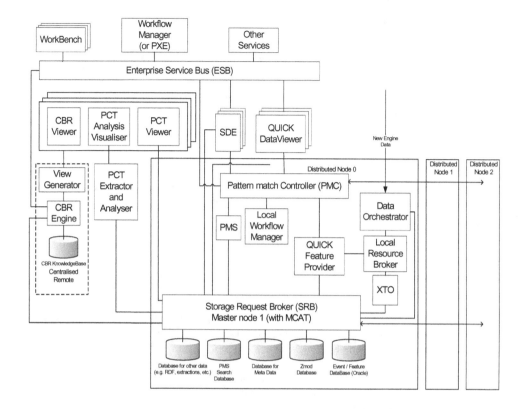

Fig.4. Overview of BROADEN Tool, Service and Data Architecture

6   Acknowledgements

The work reported in this paper was developed and undertaken as part of the BROADEN (Business Resource Optimisation for Aftermarket and Design on Engineering Networks) project, a follow-on project to the DAME project. The BROADEN project is funded via the UK Department of Trade and Industry under its Technology Innovation Programme and the work described was undertaken by teams at the Universities of York, Leeds and Sheffield with industrial partners Rolls-Royce, EDS, Oxford BioSignals and Cybula Ltd.

7 References

[1] I. Foster, C. Kesselman and S. Tuecke, "The Anatomy of the Grid: Enabling Scalable Virtual Organizations", Int. J. Supercomputer Applications, vol. 15, no. 3, 2001.

[2] J. Austin et al., "Predictive maintenance: Distributed aircraft engine diagnostics," in The Grid, 2nd ed, I. Foster and C. Kesselman, Eds. San Mateo, CA: Morgan Kaufmann, 2003, Ch. 5.

[3] Data Systems and Solutions Core Control^{TM} technology. www.ds-s.com/corecontrol.asp

[4] A. Nairac, N. Townsend, R. Carr, S. King, P. Cowley, and L. Tarassenko, "A system for the analysis of jet engine vibration data," Integrated Computer-Aided Eng., vol. 6, pp. 53–65, 1999.

[5] The Globus Toolkit, www.globus.org

[6] Laing, B., Austin, J., A Grid Enabled Visual Tool for Time Series Pattern Match, In: Proceedings of the UK e-Science All Hands Meeting 2004, Nottingham, UK.

[7] R. Agrawal, C. Faloutos, and A. Swami, "Efficient Similarity Search in Sequence Databases", in Proc. 4th Int. Conf. Foundations of Data Organization and Algorithms (FODO), 1993, pp. 69-84.

[8] E. Keogh, K. Chakrabarti, M. Pazzani, and S. Mehrotra, "Dimensionality Reduction for Fast Similarity Search in Large Time-Series Databases", Knowl. Inf. Syst., vol. 3, no. 3, pp. 263-286, 2001.

[9] E. Keogh and S. Kasetty, "On the Need for Time-Series Data Mining Benchmarks: A Survey and Empirical Demonstration", in Proc. 8th ACM SIGKDD Int. Conf. Knowledge Discovery and Data Mining, 2002, pp102-111.

[10] The AURA and AURA-G web site, Advanced Computer Architectures Group, University of York, UK. http://www.cs.york.ac.uk/arch/NeuralNetworks/AURA/aura.html.

[11] SDSC Storage Request Broker [Online]. Available: http://www.sdsc.edu/srb/

[12] David A. Chappell. "Enterprise Service Bus – Theory in Practice". O'Reilly. ISBN 0-596-00675-6.

[13] M. Ong, X. Ren, G. Allan, V. Kadirkamanathan, H. A. Thompson, P. J. Fleming (2004). "Decision support system on the Grid". Proc Int'l Conference on Knowledge-Based Intelligent Information & Engineering Systems, KES 2004.

[14] Martyn Fletcher, Tom Jackson, Mark Jessop, Bojian Liang, and Jim Austin. "The Signal Data Explorer: A High Performance Grid based Signal Search Tool for use in Distributed Diagnostic Applications." CCGrid 2006 – 6th IEEE International Symposium on Cluster Computing and the Grid. 16-19, May 2006, Singapore.

Q&A – Tom Jackson

Questioner: Dennis Gannon

Can the system continuously monitor the data searching for faults and alerting users of possible problems? Is this software accessible? Is it open source?

Tom Jackson

Yes, the system has workflow scripts that automatically scan the data for faults as it arrives at the data repository. If faults are found an alert is sent to a diagnostic engineer.

The PMC middleware stack has been developed within the UK e-Science programme and is open source.

Questioner: Bill Applebe

(Remark: this is very useful for clinical DB's that cannot be copied – only subset queries legal) How is the client side implemented?

Tom Jackson

There is a standardized web-service (SOAP) client side API that can be easily integrated into user application software.

Questioner: Anne Trefethen

1. *How does the evolving OGSA standard affect the infrastructure you are using?*
2. *Security is a major issue for industry use of "grid" – have you solved these issues?*

Tom Jackson

Answer (1): We restrict ourselves to web-service standards for the current implementation, to avoid issues with evolving OGSA standards.

Answer(2): We have addressed them within the context of security measures within the available GT4 toolkits, in that the services can ask for authentication and authorization via X509 certificates.

Questioner: Brian Smith

How do you handle false pattern matches? Are they frequent and how do they impact the acceptance of your approach?

Tom Jackson

False positives need to be avoided as far as possible; they can prove costly within the maintenance process. We are still validating the algorithms to determine how serious or frequent this may be. There is still a relative lack of fault data as the systems do not go live on commercial aircraft until late 2006.

Tuesday AM Panel Discussion

Panel

- Boyana Norris
- Jem Treadwell
- Tom Jackson

Questioner: Brian Smith

Quality of Service (QoS) typically has metrics associated with it. Also interactions back to the requestor after the analyzer discovers what is possible. Do you see these metrics being developed and interaction being supported?

Tom Jackson

Yes, we are working on intelligent QoS systems that permit analysis of operational conditions and dynamic adaptation to fit, where possible, the constraints of the user QoS profile.

Questioner: Brian Smith

Are other areas of aircraft monitoring possible and being investigated?

Tom Jackson

Yes, we have had some talks with other airline company's about the use of the technology for airframe monitoring, as one example.

Questioner: Anne Trefethen

Does the OGSA take quality of service into account?

Tom Jackson

There is a lot of activity within GGF addressing the issues relating to QoS, and it is a high priority issue.

Boyana Norris

In the case of CQoS, continuous close interaction with an ever-expanding number of application domains is a priority and directly affects the design and implementation of the interfaces and middleware component infrastructure.

Jem Treadwell

Yes, QoS is addressed in the Self-Management capability, and the GGF's GRAAP working group is developing the WS-Agreement specification, which can be used to establish service-level agreements. Note that there is no activity on self-management within OGSA at the moment, as we focus on the more basic capabilities.

Questioner: Anne Trefethen

Are we convinced that service architectures of the sort being discussed are going to deliver across a range of applications?

Tom Jackson

The major IT companies, such as IBM and Sun, continue to back the SOA model as the basis for systems integration and deployment. The model is becoming increasingly mature and accepted across a broad range of disciplines. Emerging technologies such as Enterprise Service Bus (ESB) make the SOA approach even more valid as they enhance the integration process.

Jem Treadwell

We (HP) see service-oriented architecture being used by customer and partner organizations in a wide range of markets, both for new applications and in making legacy applications more easily available. As an architectural principle it just makes sense, and its use is not restricted to applications based on Web services.

Questioner: Anne Trefethen

Are the developments of these underlying service architectures sufficiently connected to the applications?

Boyana Norris

As I mentioned in the answer to the previous question, the CQoS effort is considering a broad range of applications in all the stages of the design and implementation of the interfaces and middleware component infrastructure.

Questioner: Brian Ford

As you prepare to commercialize this system, are there particular problems rooted in its grid nature that make the activity more difficult, or even not possible?

Tom Jackson

The system is currently being evaluated for commercial deployment. The academic partners have spin out companies that provide a commercial route for deployment of the software. The fact that it is Grid based does not appear to pose any problems with commercialization at this stage.

Questioner: Brian Ford

How do you establish the effectiveness of this technical approach in commercial environments? How do you establish the value to concerns such as the national health service, oil industry etc? The value-for-money for the organization is not always clear.

Tom Jackson

This is the basis for the current DTI BROADEN project. The project concepts were developed under UK e-Science programme, DAME, but the commercial scalability and deployment issues are being addressed within BROADEN in partnership with Rolls-Royce IT providers, EDS.

Questioner: Mary Thomas

What is the status/progress of speeding up security (GSI) protocols?

Jem Treadwell

While there are a number of groups working on security within GGF (now OGF), I'm not sufficiently involved to comment on what they're doing, or their progress. However, I think this question relates to Globus rather than OGSA or GGF, and we need to be clear that Globus and OGSA are not the same thing: the Globus Toolkit is a grid middleware implementation. [Thanks to Keith Jackson, who supplied a response on behalf of the Globus development team.]

PART 4

INFRASTRUCTURE: NUMERICAL SOFTWARE

W. Enright, Session Chair; T. Hopkins, Discussant

X. Wang: *THCORE: A Parallel Computation Services Model and Runtime System*

K. Jackson: *PythonCLService Tool: A Utility for Wrapping Command-Line Applications for the Grid*

A. YarKhan: *GridSolve: The Evolution of a Network Enabled Server*

B. Smith: *A Test Harness TH For Numerical Applications and Libraries*

Panel Discussion

THCORE: A Parallel Computation Services Model and Runtime System[*]

Qingxuan Yin[1], Xiaoge Wang[1]

1 Department of Computer Science and Technology, Tsinghua University
Beijing 100084, China wangxg@tsinghua.edu.cn,
WWW home page: http://os.riit.tsinghua.edu.cn

Abstract. Wrapping parallel programs or parallel numerical library functions into software components and using them as computation services in service-oriented programming presents a method of delivering powerful computation capabilities of multi-processor supercomputers to the application developers who may only familiar with their desk-top or hand-held computing environment. These parallel computation services on computer clusters are used as ordinary software components on the desktop programming environment with their internal parallel or distributed characteristics hidden from the users. In order to use the parallel scientific computation applications and libraries as the software components conveniently in the development of new applications, a parallel computation service model and the runtime system that support this model on computer clusters are presented and some design and implementation issues are discussed in this article.

1 Introduction

Parallel and distributed computing on computer clusters is an effective way to speed up large-scale scientific computations. However, it is more difficult to build up applications on such environment than that on a sequential machine. A traditional way of developing a large application on such environment usually requires a great deal of tight collaboration between experts in computer architecture, algorithm design and application area and leads to a monolithic program. Although there are many successful sophisticated parallel scientific libraries and packages available such as PETSC [1, 2], SCALAPACK [3] and BLACS [4] for application developers, it still requires the application developers to have certain degree of expertise in programming on such parallel/distributed computing environment. When using these

[*] This work is supported by the National High-Tech Research and Development Plan of China (No.2003AA1Z2090), and by Basic Research Foundation of Tsinghua National Laboratory for Information Science and Technology.

Please use the following format when citing this chapter:

Yin, Q., Wang, X., 2007, in IFIP International Federation for Information Processing, Volume 239, Grid-Based Problem Solving Environments, eds. Gaffney, P. W., Pool, J.C.T., (Boston: Springer), pp. 179-192.

libraries, one usually needs to know how to initiate such environment in the code before using the library functions and know how to compile his/her own code with the libraries on the parallel computer and to start the application using some job and resource management tools. The debugging of parallel program on a computer cluster is even more difficult. For those scientists and engineers who are not familiar with parallel/distributed programming on computer clusters, these difficulties could be a serious obstacle for development of applications requiring high performance computation.

Service-oriented programming is a way to ease the difficulties mentioned. It separates the development of computation services components from the development of applications composed from the services. The development of computation services put the efforts on the design and implementation of algorithms of the services to make them efficient and reliable on their runtime environment, while the development of applications using selected services would focus the efforts on the business logic and the workflow of the applications.

In this paper, THCORE, a component model and its runtime systems are introduced. It unifies the interface of components running on sequential and parallel/distributed computers. The implementation differences between the components on sequential and parallel/distributed machines are encapsulated inside the component and managed by the corresponding component runtime systems. In this model, application developers do not need to have knowledge of parallel programming but still could use the computation power of parallel computers. The parallel computation services implemented as the THCORE components are used to compose the application in the same way as other components. The well developed and frequently used mathematics libraries, legacy packages, and even applications could be wrapped into components to provide computation services for other applications. The detail of the parallel computational service model of THCORE and its runtime system on computer clusters are presented.

The rest of the paper is organized as the following. An overview of THCORE and other related works are presented in section 2. The parallel computing service component model will be introduced in Section 3. The component runtime system for computer clusters is introduced and discussed in Section 4. In Section 5 the performance issues is discussed. Some experiment results that evaluate the overhead of componentization is shown. Related work will be mentioned in Section 6. The last section gives the conclusion and direction of future work.

2   Overview of THCORE and Related Work

THCORE is designed as a lightweight, efficient and reflective component platform for pervasive computing. It is written in C for the best performance and minimum memory footprint. Its component model adopts the component object model of Microsoft's COM/DCOM with some new extensions to suit the pervasive computing environment that includes as well as embedded systems and high performance computer systems. THCORE supports the binary level interoperability protocol, transparent local/remote invocations as in COM/DCOM. It deploys a standard runtime substrate that manages the execution context of components. For example, a component can be instantiated in different running spaces: it can be created in the same process of application for efficiency, or be created outside the application process for system isolation, or it could even be created on remote machine connected via network.

Multi-level reflection is one of the new features brought into THCORE component model. It provides the access to both interface-level and component-level Meta data. Interface-level Meta data contains the definition of interfaces, functions and parameters. It provides the finest grain of self-description information of the system, and it is obtained by using the IMetaInterface interface of THCORE component. With the help of this, middleware can dynamically load components and invoke the method without generating accessing code. Component-level Meta data is used to describe a component's requirement of execution context (such as hardware and OS requirement). The Meta data in this level also contains the information of the reliance of dependency that one component lies on others. Component-level Meta data can be accessed by ICompMetaInterface interface of THCORE component. This reflection feature is very useful in supporting adaptive programming.

Some system services are provided for programming with THCORE model and platform, including event service, cache service and parallel computing service. Some THCORE related research projects have been reported. PURPLE [12, 13] is a component-based reflective middleware for pervasive computing which is built upon THCORE platform. It provides support for adaptive context-aware programming. The structural and functional modules that compose the middleware platform are THCORE components. THAOP [14] is a lightweight and flexible Aspect Oriented Programming Framework based on THCORE component platform. It provides support for component-level AOP. FT_THCORE [15] is a fault tolerant extension of THCORE specification and platform. It implements the easy component replication and voting strategy so that it supports N-Version Programming.

As the applications in pervasive computing usually involve several different computation environments ranging from resource limited mobile/handheld devices to powerful multi-processor supercomputers, THCORE is design to provide the interoperability between computation components (services) on different environments. As it is lightweight, THCORE can be installed on the resource limited devices. The discussion of the extension on COM/DCOM for embedded devices will not be discussed in this paper. But, the model adopted from COM/DCOM may not be viable for the parallel program directly. There are two design issues need to be considered. First, we wish to hide parallel programming from the programming with THCORE. Second, we allow the services components to be implemented by parallel program and executed on parallel/distributed computer systems. The details of the design and implementation for the extension of component model for parallel computation services and the correspondent runtime system on the computer clusters are discussed in section 3 and 4.

It is not a new topic to hide the parallel programming from the development of applications while the computation power from parallel programming is used for the execution of the application. Take Matlab for example. It is well known that Matlab is a convenient tool for engineering computation. It does not introduce explicit parallel computation concept into its programming. But it may need large amount of computation power so much that the parallel computing may become necessary. Researchers have presented many methods to make parallel Matlab. A survey was performed [9] and 27 parallel MATLAB projects, such as MatPar, MatLab*P and so on are found through extensive web searching. The approaches to make MATLAB parallel are different: some compile MATLAB scripts into parallel native code; some provide a parallel backend to MATLAB, using MATLAB as a graphical front-end; and some others coordinate multiple MATLAB processes to work in parallel [10]. Take Matpar [5] for example. Matpar is a software program in C/S model that allows MATLAB users to take advantage of a parallel computer. Some calls to certain built-in MATLAB functions are replaced with calls to Matpar functions on the client side. The code of Matpar function calls in turn initiates a session on a parallel computer. The parallel code uses parallel mathematical libraries to produce a solution that is sent back to the calling program. Because of the limitation of the model, Matpar is difficult to be reused to build other applications. And it is difficult for Matpar to deal with different software and hardware environment. As the compiler is special designed for Matpar and Matpar is based on some parallel mathematics libraries, it is quite difficult to expand the functions that Matpar is supporting.

As a component model designed specifically for high performance computing, CCA (Common Component Architecture) [11] is better known in the HPC community. In CCA, components interact with each other and with a specific framework implementation through standard application programming interfaces (APIs). Each component can define its inputs and outputs by using a scientific interface definition language (SIDL); these definitions can be deposited in and retrieved from a repository by using a CCA Repository API. The goal of CCA is to gain abstractions that capture high-performance concepts in component architectures, which can enable more efficient interactions between SPMD programs. There are also tools associated with CCA to help with decomposition of legacy code into CCA components for reuse. Although the goal of CCA is also to foster the component-oriented programming, there are two main differences from THCORE: the first is the user knowledge requirement. To use CCA, one needs to have certain knowledge in parallel programming. The second is in the way of component composition. CCA allows parallel component to be more tightly connected because the interface contains the information of "parallelism" while THCORE hide parallelism completely from the interface. Therefore, CCA is more suitable for the development of component based parallel applications while THCORE is better for the application deployed on the heterogeneous computing environment such as in pervasive computing scenarios.

3   The Model of the Parallel Computation Services

One of the characteristics of service-oriented programming is the separation of service interface from its implementation. A client requests a computation service by invoking its interface. The implementation of the computation service, whether in sequential or parallel program, is transparent to the user. To the client of the service, interface will take the input from the client and return the results of the computation to the client all through one "port". This matches with the way of human thinking and it is easy for implementation of business logic. On the other hand, single processor may not provide enough power for the computation so that multi-processor computers are introduced into the application. It is a common solution for the fast computation. In such case, we wish a service could be running on multi-processor machine. However, as the execution of a parallel program are quite different from that of a sequential program, the structure of a parallel service on a computer cluster is different from its counterpart on desktop computers and other hand-held devices.

The design of the model for the parallel computation services on computer clusters takes two factors into consideration. First, a parallel program is most likely to have "sequential" entrance though more parameters may be required to start a parallel execution. By "sequential" entrance, we mean that the program has single starting point, and its input and output data are in a whole, rather than in the form of partitioned pieces. Therefore, it is viable to keep the interface of parallel computation services the same as the interface of other sequential computation services with a few extra parameters. In addition, all parallel computation service should have a main process/thread to act as a "driver" and entrance of the parallel program. It is responsible for partition, distribution and aggregation of data structures for parallel computation if necessary. Second, as the services are executed on multiprocessor computer systems, in general, the number of processors to be used should be specified in advance by someone in someway, and the mapping from program's logic process to the physical processors needs to be performed. To run a parallel program, one needs to submit the job via job management tool such as PBS [16]. The number of processors and other execution parameters are submitted to the job manager system and the manager will arrange the resources for the execution.

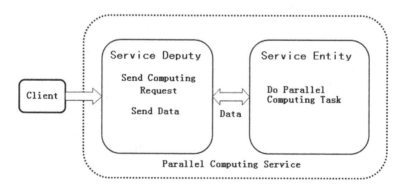

Fig. 1. Parallel Computation Service Model

The model of parallel computation service is shown in Figure 1. A service is made of two parts: service deputy and service entity. The service deputy is a sequential code. It acts as if it is the implementation of the service to the client, but in fact, it is only a "driver" and a "wrapper" of the parallel computation program. The service entity is a parallel code that implements the computation function and will execute on parallel computers or computer clusters in our case. The service deputy receives the request from the clients and analyses the request to generate the information for the creation of the parallel tasks of the computation function including the task partition, data partition and distribution, synchronization mechanism of the algorithm, etc. The service deputy itself does not implement any parallel computing. The service entity receives the information from the service deputy and implements the parallel computation function. The input data sent from the client is received by the service deputy and then forwarded to the service entity accordingly. On return, the output data of the service moves on the same path from opposite direction to the client.

The course of making a parallel computation service is similar to that of making a normal component in THCORE except that the code of the parallel computation function has to be separated from the interface. It starts with the description of interface using IDL (interface definition language). The compiler of IDL will then generate the code of the interface. The interface provides an abstraction of its implementation and serves as the connection point between its client and the service it provides. In developing normal component, one could insert the code of the component function into the interface code. But in the parallel computation service case, the parallel computation function has to be separated. As the service deputy is actually only a "driver" and a "wrapper" of the parallel program, what contained in it is the information regarding the function identifiers, the code of creating multiple tasks and transferring data. Therefore, it can be generated by IDL compiler automatically as part of the interface code. Some sequential part of the parallel computation function, such as the pre/post processing steps, can be inserted into the interface code as the part of the service deputy if it is desired. The development of the service entity is similar to the development of a parallel program. The only difference is that the implementation of the parallel computation function has to be registered with the component runtime system as the interface. This is the result of the separation of sequential and parallel part of implementation.

The limitation of this model is that it does not provide the parallel interface for the composition of parallel computation services. It can be seen that the data in and out from the service component are packed into one single stream while the internal presentation is distributed for the parallel/distributed computation. If two parallel computation services are requested consecutively, the output data of the first service will be redistributed when it is used as the input data of the second services even though both services have the same internal distribution of the data. The time spent in the data movement would cause a serious problem in performance. The performance issues will be discussed in section 5.

4   The Service Runtime on Computer Clusters

For supporting the execution of the parallel computation service on computer clusters described in the previous section, a service runtime system is designed and implemented. This runtime system should have the following functions:

- **Service activation:** As the same as the function of THCORE runtimes on desktop computers and handheld devices, it should provide runtime support for the service. When a service interface is invoked by a client, the runtime system should be able to activate the code, including both service deputy and service entity, to run on the cluster. It serves as a service container and connects the deputy and entity parts of the service.

● **Resource management:** As the amount of computation in a service may vary with the input parameters, such as the problem size and accuracy of the solution, the resource of the cluster, such as the number of processors, may vary from execution to execution. As an advanced function, the system should have the capability to allocate and manage the resource efficiently. It should dispatch the computation task to the processors appropriately in order to make good use of all the processors in the cluster for load-balance and better efficiency. In some sense, the runtime system performs the function of job manager like PBS and bears more responsibility for the success of execution of a parallel computation service than the operating system of the machine.

4.1   Architecture Overview

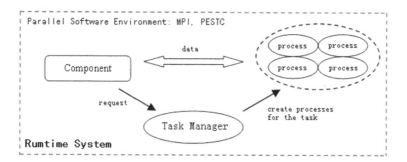

Fig. 2. Architecture of the service runtime system on computer clusters

The architecture of the runtime system for computer clusters is shown in Figure 2. In addition to the function of service activation, as THCORE runtime on desktops and handheld devices, it has a task manager module that performs the function of resource manager. It takes the information regarding the parallel computation characteristics of the service entity, such as the number of tasks to be created, from the service deputy, and then creates tasks and allocates the processors for the parallel tasks accordingly. When a client requests a parallel computation service by invokes its interface, the runtime system activated the interface code and the service deputy, a message of parallel computation task request is sent by the deputy to the task manager module of the runtime. The task manager parses and analyses the request, determines whether to accept this request or not, determines the number of processor to run the parallel tasks when the request is accepted, assigns processors to the tasks, and create a set of MPI [6, 7] processes on the processors for the execution of the parallel program of the service entity. The task manager is implemented as a MPI process. It calls MPI library functions to create the MPI processes. The processes of the task receive the input data from the service entity directly, and send the computation result data back to the service deputy after the completion of the task. The processes of the parallel tasks will end themselves when the tasks are finished.

Service runtime system is running on a computer cluster. All the communication and data transfer on it are implemented through socket provided by the operating system. The location of the service deputy, the parallel processes of the service entity and the task manager of the runtime on cluster nodes is flexible. They are not necessarily located on the same node of the cluster. In general, each node of the cluster would host only one process of the tasks because running more than one processes on a node may reduce the efficiency of the execution.

4.2   Task Manager

The task manager is the core of the runtime system. It is consisted of five parts: the message queue of parallel task request/completion, the interface manager, the task dispatcher, the task scheduler and a queue of the tasks to be schedules,. The interface manager takes the message of task request from the message queue, analyzes the message, and creates the task for the request accordingly. The task dispatcher determines the number of processes that should be created for the task and dispatches the task to appropriately selected processors. The task scheduler schedules of the tasks in the waiting task queue. The flow chart of the task manager is shown in Figure 3.

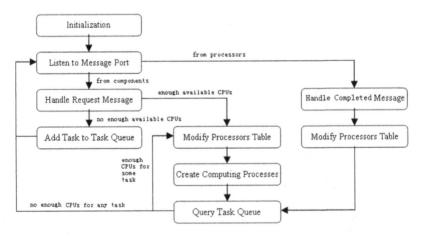

Fig.3. Flow Chart of the Task Manager

During the course of initialization, the message queue is set and a socket port associated with it is established to receive the message of task request from the service deputy and the message of task completion from task processes, a processor table is created for the task dispatcher to record the status of the processors, and the task queue is created for the task scheduler.

After initialization, the task manager takes a message from the queue if there is any. If the message is a task request from the service deputy, the interface manager is called to analyze the request. Then the task dispatcher is called to determines how many processors are wanted for this task according to the available information such as the computational complexity of the task, the total number of the processors in the cluster, the number of the available processors in the cluster, the length of the task queue and possibly some other information. If the number of the processors wanted for the task is less than the number of the currently available processors in the cluster, the execution of the task could start. The task dispatcher is called to start the task. Otherwise, the task will be inserted into the task queue. In the situation that the number of the processors wanted by is greater than the total number of processors in the cluster, such as when the problem size is too large, the task request would be refused and the rejection message will be send to the service deputy.

The task dispatcher updates the processor table before it starts a computation task. Then it creates a set of processes to execute the parallel computation task. After the creation, the processes will communicate with the corresponding service deputy directly for the input data and start the computation. The task queue is handled by the task scheduler. A task in the task queue could be scheduled if there is enough number of processors available according to the processor table. If a task is scheduled, the task dispatcher is called to start it. The task will then be deleted from the queue. When a computation task is completed, a task completion message is sent to the task manager. On receiving the message, the task dispatcher updates the processor table. The task is finally accomplished at this point.

4.3   The Processor Management Strategy

The management of the computation and resources is the main concern of the runtime system design. The processors are the most important resource in the cluster. How to make the best use of the available processors is a question that designers of the runtime system must answer. Improving the efficiency of the processors and increasing the task throughput are the goal of the design of the resource management policy of the system.

The design of the processor management strategy is different for the traditional batch job management tools on clusters. For the transparency of parallel implementation of a parallel computation service, the number of physical/logical processors wanted to run the service is determined by the runtime system at runtime, while in most batch job manager tools, the number of processors needed to run a program is usually set by the owner of the program at the time when the job is submitted. The number of the processors assigned for the task is determined by the system at runtime according to the size of the task and the capacity of the cluster. The size of a task is measured by the computation complexity provided by the service provider in the interface description and the size of the computation input/output data available when the service is requested. The capacity of the cluster is measured by rate of the number of the total processors and the number of the available processors in the cluster. Generally the number of processors wanted by a task is determined at the time when the task request is generated. We allow it to be changed later when necessary. For example, when a node of the cluster is down, the previously determined number of processors wanted for some tasks has to be reduced. Meanwhile, when a computer node is added into the cluster, the number of processors determined for some tasks may be increased appropriately.

When the number of available processors is large enough for more than one task in the queue, the selection of the task to be scheduled may influence the efficiency of the processors in the cluster. The policy for the scheduling is designed as the following:

- A. Priority scheduling is applied. The task priority is the most important factor for determining the execution order of tasks. No tasks with lower priority could be executed unless there is no tasks with higher priority could be scheduled. Each task has its priority set when created. The priority could be determined according to several factors, such as the client's user ID, size of the task, even the time of task creation.
- B. When several tasks are of the same priority and number of available processors is large enough for any of them, the task that needs more processors should be scheduled prior to those tasks that need fewer processors. The goal of this policy is to make more processors busy and schedule the large sized task as early as possible. In this way, the possibility of large sized tasks staying in the queue for a long time waiting for available processors could be reduced.
- C. If several tasks have the same priority and need the same number of processors, the order them are scheduled to run is the same as the order they enter the queue. The task that is inserted into the queue earliest should be scheduled to run first.
- D. Dynamic priority is introduced into task scheduling. A task, which has been waiting for certain period of time, should have its priority increased. Otherwise, a large sized task with lower priority may be waiting for too long to be acceptable.

The implementation of the design is currently undergoing. A prototype of the runtime for clusters is realized. On this prototype, some parallel computation services are developed for experiments. As the parallel libraries/packages are valuable legacies, we also developed some services by wrapping parallel mathematic library functions of PETSC. It is clear that the client of the parallel computation services does not need the knowledge of parallel programming. On the opposite, the developer of the services would appreciate greatly the knowledge and experiences of parallel programming. This is exactly one of the objectives of THCORE.

5   Performance Issues and Experiments

The performance of service runtime is important to the practices of service oriented software development. Compare to the monolithic program, the overhead of service oriented software comes from two main sources: additional code and data movement. Additional code is consisted of the code of service wrapper and the "glue code" that connects the service and its client. In our model of parallel computation service, the code that connects the service deputy and service entity is considered as glue code as well. Data movement includes the movement between client and services and the movement inside the service between its deputy and entity. To evaluate the overhead of the proposed model and its runtime system, a simple experiment is conducted.

A parallel computation service is implemented to offer the service of solving linear systems. A client program requests the service by invoking the parallel computation service. Timers are installed inside the program to measure the time that spent by different portions of the program. The experiment is carried out on a small cluster of 2 nodes. Each node has a 2.4G CPU and 512M memory. The nodes are connected by 100M LAN. The OS is linux-2.6.16 and the parallel programming environment is LAM-MPI 7.1.2. The parallel computation service is implemented using PETSC version 2.3.1.

Following quantities are measured and the results are collected:

1. Service invocation time (T1): The time cost by invoking a non-parallel component of THCORE. This time could vary by the location of the service execution. When the service is executed in the same process as its client, this time will be the smallest. It is about 0.0015 seconds in the experiment. This quantity shows the minimum overhead when connecting service and client in THCORE.

2. Parallel service invocation time (T2): The time cost by invoking a parallel computation service only without data transferring and computation. It is about 0.4158 seconds. This quantity shows the minimum overhead when connecting a parallel computation service with its client. The big gap between T1 and T2 is from the additional work in activating additional processes and establishing the communication channels among the processors.

3. Data movement time (T3): The time cost by invoking a parallel computing component with data transferring but no computing. When the input data is of the size of 16400 double precision numbers and the output data is of the size of 4000 double precision numbers, it is about 8.660 seconds. The quantity T3-T2 tells the overhead of data movement for this test problem. It is determined mainly by the speed (latency and bandwidth) of the interconnection network between the nodes of the cluster.

4. Total overhead: We measure the total time of solving linear systems by invoking a parallel computation service (T4). It is about 59.020 seconds when using 2 nodes. It is about 104.625 seconds when using one node. As the comparison, we also measure the total time of solving the same problem using the same parallel functions from the library in a monolithic style of programming (T5). It is about 49.905 seconds when using 2 nodes and about 96.625 seconds using one node. The quantity T4-T5 gives the total overhead of service oriented programming in THCORE.

From the experiment results, we know that the overhead is mainly consisted of the data transferring. As the scientific computation often has a large size of input/output data, the cost of transferring data may become dominant. We should reduce the time cost by transferring data to make better efficiency. Besides the improvement of interconnection network, to increase the service granularity is a way to reduce the data traffic. It should also be pointed out that the increase in the granularity of a service may reduce the reusability of the service.

During an invocation of a parallel computation service, the input data is sent from client to the service via interface and then distributed internally from the service deputy to the service entity and the output data is sent in the opposite direction back to the client. If all three parties could be located as close as possible, the efficiency could be increased. Considering the client is not located on the cluster, the possible location plans of the three parties are:

1. The service deputy is located together with the client in the same process and the client invokes the service in the way as a local component. The data transferring between the client and the service deputy could be ignored and only the remote data transferring between the service deputy and the entity remains.

2. The service deputy is located in a cluster node and the client invokes the service as a remote component. The data transfer will be the sum of the remote data transfer between the client and the service deputy and the remote data transfer among the nodes of the cluster.

3. The service deputy is neither located with the client nor with the entity in the cluster. Although this is not practical, it is valid in THCORE. In this case, the data transferring is consisted of the remote data transfer between the client and the entity and the remote data transferring between the deputy and the entity using the external network, which cost the most.

The first location plan is the most efficient. A mechanism to arrange the location of the parties may reduce the cost of data movement. To further reduce the data movement cost is an important issue of performance for the future work.

6   Conclusion and Future Work

This paper presents a parallel computation model for computer clusters and the design of its runtime system for supporting service-oriented programming on clusters. This model will bring the great convenience to the scientists and engineers who have to deal with large scientific computations but may not have enough experiences of parallel/distributed programming. A simplified prototype of the runtime system on cluster is realized for experiments. The preliminary experiments are conducted. The analysis of the results shows that the overhead of the service-based program comparing to the conventional parallel program is mainly from to the data movement. The strategy of overhead reduction includes the trade-off between the granularity of services and their reusability and the proper arrangement of the location of the parties associated in the data movement.

More study and further research efforts will be put in the investigation for efficient methods and tools to wrap the popular parallel libraries/packages into parallel computation services and the optimization of the performance of the runtime system. The future work will also include the study in the algorithms of resource management and the improvement of the quality of service of the runtime system. The coordination of the runtime system with the operating system of the cluster and the batch job management software, such as PBS [16], to improve the performance of the applications and the throughput of the computer systems will be an interesting subject of the future research as well.

Acknowledgement

Authors are very grateful to all the members of the THCORE project team for their contribution to make this paper possible. They are Yu Chen, Xing Fang, Kuo Zhang, Yanni Wu, Du Zhao, Zhenkun Zheng and Gang Feng besides the two authors of this paper. Thanks also go to Professor Craig C. Douglas for his encouragement and helpful suggestions towards the research in this direction.

References

1. S. Balay, W.D. Gropp, L.C. McInnes, and B.F. Smith, PETSc home page. http://www.mcs.anl.gov/petsc, July 1997.
2. S. Balay, W.D. Gropp, L.C. McInnes, and B.F. Smith. PETSc 2.0 Users Manual, Tech.Rep. ANL-95/11 – Revision 2.0.22, Argonne National Laboratory, Apr 1998.
3. J. Dongarra and L.S. Blackford, ScaLAPACK tutorial, Proc. of Applied Parallel Computing, Industrial Computation and Optimization, Third International Workshop, PARA '96, Aug. 1996.
4. J. Dongarra and R. C. Whaley, A User's Guide to the BLACS v1.1 , Technical Report CS-95-281, University of Tennessee, Knoxville, Tennessee, 1997.
5. NASA Jet Propulsion Laboratory, Matpar; http://www-hpc.jpl.nasa.gov/PS/MATPAR
6. Message Passing Interface Forum. MPI: A Message-Passing Interface Standard. University of Tennessee, Knoxville, Version 1.1, June 1995.
7. Message Passing Interface Forum. MPI-2: Extensions to the Message-Passing Interface. University of Tennessee 1997; http://www.mpi-forum.org/docs/docs.html
8. X.G. Wang, X. Fang. THCORE home page; http://os.riit.tsinghua.edu.cn
9. R. Choy. Parallel MATLAB survey, 2001; http://www.interactivesupercomputing.com/reference/ParallelMatlabsurvey.htm
10. M.D. Barnell, B.J. Rahn. Migrating modeling and simulation applications on to high performance computers. SPIE Vol. 6227, p. 198-205
11. R. Armstrong, D. Gannon, A. Geist, K. Keahey, S. Kohn, L. McInnes, S. Parker and, B. Smolinski, Toward a Common Component Architecture for High-Performance Scientific Computing, Proceedings of the 8th IEEE International Symposium on High-Performance Scientific Distributed Computing, August 1999
12. K. Zhang, X.G Wang, Y.N. Wu, Z.K. Zheng, PURPLE: a reflective middleware for pervasive computing, ICITA 2005: the third Information Technology and Applications 2005, vol.1, p. 64- 69, Tsinghua University, July 2005
13. K. Zhang, Y.N. Wu, Z.K. Zheng, X.G Wang, Y. Chen, A component-based reflective middleware approach to context-aware adaptive systems, ICWE2005: the fifth International Conference on Web Engineering, vol. 3579, p. 429-434, Tsinghua University, July 2005

14. G. Feng, Q.X. Yin, X.G. Wang, THAOP: An Aspect Oriented Programming Framework, SPCA 2006: the first International Symposium on Pervasive Computing and Applications Proceedings, p. 127-132, Tsinghua University, August 2006

15. Q.X. Yin, G. Feng, X.G. Wang, Y. Chen, Increase Reliability of Pervasice Oriented Component Platform via N-Version, SPCA 2006: the first International Symposium on Pervasive Computing and Applications Proceedings, p. 95-98, Tsinghua University, August 2006

16. Veridian Systems, OpenPBS v2.3: The Portable Batch System Software, Veridian Systems, Inc., Mountain View, CA, September 2000. http://www.openpbs.org/scheduler.html

Q&A – Xiaoge Wang

Questioner: William Gropp

What sort of efficiency measurements are you considering (from the slide on challenges)?

Xiaoge Wang

One of the objectives of Grid technology is to make resources more available. Many people are using Grid to reduce the computation time. We have been looking at the total execution time as well. But according to our experiences, the overhead of service and data distribution over the infrastructure could be high. If it is not carefully considered, we may lower the resource efficiency when we try to reduce the execution time using Grid resources. So, certain measurements should be taken into consideration in doing resources management. But we have not yet make it clear what sort of measurements we will consider.

Questioner: Mary Thomas

Are there future plans to work with other user interfaces such as Matlab, portals, etc?

Xiaoge Wang

We have done some work on wrapping the THCORE components into Web services automatically using the information of the interface described in the IDL file. For work with other user interfaces, we have not yet done anything. Yes, it will be very interesting to see how it works with Matlab or other portals.

Questioner: Masaaki Shimasaki

You mentioned virtualization for security as a future challenge. Do you have any specific ideas or plans for it?

Xiaoge Wang

Isolating the users' working space from the system or the infrastructure is a way of providing a certain type of security. THCORE currently only provides isolation at the process level and at the physical machine level. In other words, we can now invoke the components in the same process, or in a different process or in a separate physical machine.

Another way of isolation that we would like to investigate is to invoke the component on a virtual machine which could actually be running on the same physical machine. In this way, we may reduce the data transfer time and still maintain the same degree of isolation. In addition, we tried to use the cache to improve the performance of remote invocation, but it changed the degree of isolation of remote invocation of a component. Using virtualization such as

Xen (http://www.cl.cam.ac.uk/research/srg/netos/xen/) may maintain the same degree of isolation but reach the goal of component cache.

Questioner: Asim YarKhan

Does THCORE need a client side stub for the services? How about static languages like C and Fortran?

Xiaoge Wang

Answer is Yes and No. If a client invokes a component to execute in the same process, then a stub is not required. It links to the component similar as using a dynamic link library or shared object. But if the client would like to invoke the component to run in a separate process or in a remote machine, then it will need a stub. In the case that client is a script, then the stub is dynamically generated using metadata.

Questioner: Dennis Gannon

How does your component architecture differ from CCA? How does your IDL differ from CCA's SIDL?

Xiaoge Wang

First of all, I do not have deep knowledge about CCA. I only read some tutorials and publications. So the comparison here is far from accurate or complete. At the design phase, we did look at CCA as I listed in the related work, and found that CCA is a model that takes care of all sorts of issues in parallel programming but it is not exactly what we need. I need to point out that, THCORE is a component model that was originally designed for component based software running on resource limited systems. It aims at independent development of components and an efficient way of putting components together through the interface to make an application. This mode allows the individual component to change its internal implementation without affecting the application. CCA considers more issues in putting parallel components together.

Based of the above arguments, I may guess that there is quite a difference between these two IDLs in detail. But I do not have enough knowledge to make a fair complete comparison.

PythonCLServiceTool: A Utility for Wrapping Command-Line Applications for The Grid

David E. Konerding and Keith R. Jackson

Distributed Systems Department

Lawrence Berkeley National Laboratory,

Berkeley, CA 94720

California, USA

[dekonerding,krjackson]@lbl.gov

WWW project page: http://dsd.lbl.gov/gtg/projects/PythonCLServiceTool/

Abstract.

The international science community has invested large amounts of money in developing numerical and computational codes for everything from basic math to application specific codes. These codes are now a vital part of the scientific process. However, running these codes can be challenging. Many require a highly specialized environment, and may only run in a few locations. To maximize the usage of these codes, it is necessary to enable network access to them. We discuss our recent work in developing automated tools to enable network access to command line applications using Grid[1] tools.

Please use the following format when citing this chapter:

Konerding, D. E., Jackson, K. R., 2007, in IFIP International Federation for Information Processing, Volume 239, Grid-Based Problem Solving Environments, eds. Gaffney, P. W., Pool, J.C.T., (Boston: Springer), pp. 195-211.

1. Introduction

The international science community has invested large amounts of money to develop numerical and computational codes for everything from basic math libraries to application specific codes. These codes are now a vital part of the scientific process. However, their usage often requires a specialized environment, and may only run in a small number of locations. To maximize the usage of these codes, it is necessary to enable remote network access to them. In this paper we will discuss our work to use Grid technologies to expose numerical/computational codes as Grid services. A Grid service is simply a network accessible service that uses standard protocols to describe its interface and for access. Typically today these protocols are based on industry standard Web Services[2].

We will begin the paper by looking at related work in the Web Service area. We will then look at the architecture of our system, PyCLST (Python Command Line Service Tool). After examining the overall architecture, we will look at a concrete example of PyCLST usage. Following a brief look at performance, we will discuss our future plans and conclusions.

2. Related Work

There are several existing software products which provide similar functionality to PyCLST. SOAP::Clean[3] (written in Perl) and O'SOAP[4] (written in O'CAML) served as the initial inspiration for PyCLST and provide a limited set of the functionality in PyCLST. The primary difference between PyCLST and SOAP::Clean/O'SOAP is that PyCLST is architected around Grid standards rather than plain SOAP[5]. This has a number of implications including:

1. Grid services enhance the security support in SOAP. SOAP lacks a standard authorization mechanism. Many Grids use a standard authorization mechanism based on a *gridmap* file. Grid security[6] also provides single-sign-on to reduce the number of times a user must enter their password. Another important feature Grid services offer is *delegation*. Delegation allows a user to grant some sub-set of her rights to a third-party. For example, after a computational job has run, output files might need to be moved to tertiary storage. While the user could manually move the files, it would be easier to have the computational service move them for her. Delegation allows the user to grant the service the right to interact with the tertiary storage system on her behalf.

2. SOAP has limited support for data transport. Binary data must be base-64 encoded which adds a 33% overhead, and large files must be broken into chunks for efficient transfer. Grid services provide efficient, high-performance, and secure data transport. We will use the standard GridFTP[7] protocol to transfer large input and output files between clients and services.

3. SOAP has no standard support for building stateful web services. Each SOAP service typically does this in an ad-hoc manner. Some use cookies,

others pass session identifiers with each SOAP message, but there is no standard way to manage state in Web Services. Grid services adopt the WS-Resource Framework[8] set of standards to provide state management. In particular, the Resource Context subset of WS-RF provides a unique "handle" shared between the service and client that refers to a particular request stream. The WS-Lifetime subset is used to manage the lifecycle of the service (create and destroy a resource context) and WS-ResourceProperty is used to manipulate meta-data associated with the service and provide a substrate for state change notification.

4. SOAP has no support for asynchronous notifications, so the command line client needs to periodically poll the server for result data or keep a request open for a long time. Grid services adopt the WS-Notification[9] to provide asynchronous notifications.

Each of these features is used by PythonCLServiceTool to provide enhanced functionality relative to SOAP::Clean and O'SOAP. Further, because client computers commonly have firewalls that prevent WS-Notification data being retrieved, we include code that detects and works around firewalls using a polling-based, rather than callback-based, response mechanism.

Kepler[10], an open source workflow execution tool built on the Ptolemy Framework[11], has a Web Service Harvester. The Harvester inspects WSDL[12] files and builds workflow actors which are capable of accessing the service defined by the WSDL file. This allows users to easily interface Kepler with existing web services without having to write code for new actors. Many other systems provide similar functionality, however, unlike PythonCLServiceTool, these tools are only used to generate client bindings to an existing service. Because PythonCLServiceTool exposes command-line applications using a standard web service interface and provides a WSDL file describing the service, tools like the Web Service Harvester can be used to generate their own clients to the wrapped service.

3. Architecture

3.1 Overview of general architecture

Developers configure PythonCLServiceTool clients and servers using a simple user-written configuration file containing named sections populated by key/value pairs. Because all PythonCLServiceTool clients and servers have a great deal of common functionality with just a small amount of command-specific generated code, a collection of template files are interpolated at client/server generation time. The command line parsing code is generated programmatically.

PythonCLServiceTool uses several existing Python frameworks rather than duplicating existing functionality. PythonCLServiceTool uses an asynchronous I/O framework called Twisted[13] for grid and web service communications, as well as external process management. Because the service can handle multiple simultaneous requests without delay, we needed an asynchronous I/O library. Without this functionality, the service would block on data send/receive operations and on process launching/management.

PythonCLServiceTool co-opts an existing standard Python framework used for packaging and distributing software called setuptools[14] for generating clients and servers. Setuptools provides an extensive plug-in framework normally intended for package installation, but we also use it for template substitution and service configuration and deployment. Optionally, the runtime and configuration files for the server can be packaged into a single executable file for easy server deployment. PythonCLServiceTool uses the setuptools *bdist_egg* and *bdist_wininst* features to build a self-contained installer containing the entire service or client runtimes.

The PythonCLServiceTool server generation process creates a Twisted server, the server configuration file, and the necessary runtime code for running the server. The PythonCLServiceTool client generation process creates a Twisted client, a client configuration file, and the necessary runtime code for running the client. Optionally the runtime and configuration files for the client can be packaged into a single executable file for easy client distribution. The client interface is intended to be exactly like the command line interface. It uses the same flags, and ideally should be a direct replacement for the command line application. However, because the client and server processes run in different file system contexts, and users will want to run jobs on files stored on the client computer, PyCLST adds a special syntax to the command-line shell that indicates that the referred-to file should be transferred to the server before job execution.

To ensure that only valid users may access deployed services, PyCLST supports the standard grid-map-file format which is used by the Globus Toolkit®[15] to authorize users based on the subject name contained in their X.509[16] certificate. Also, if the PyCLST server is run with super-user privileges, it will change identity to run the application as the local user specified in the map-file.

3.2 Configuration file format.

The configuration file is based on the Windows INI file format as interpreted by the Python ConfigParser module. A sample configuration file that wraps the *blast* command is seen in Figure 1. As you can see, it is a simple set of name value pairs separated out into different sections.

The user specifies the name of the executable to be run on the server side. The executable name should be specified as an absolute path to ensure that other executables earlier in the server container's PATH are not executed.

The developer specifies the name of the service, which is normally the same as the suffix of the executable pathname (the name of the binary). The service name is incorporated into the service in a number of ways: it is used to form a unique name for the server configuration files, the name of the generated SOAP parsing and encoding scripts, and the WSDL file.

The developer specifies all of the arguments that the executable is capable of accepting. There are two main types of arguments that command line applications are capable of taking:

- Positional arguments derive their meaning from their position in the command line. Developers indicate the position of an argument through the prefix name of the argument, for example, all position argument definitions starting with "arg1" refer to the argument in the first (left-most) position. The Unix *cat* command outputs the contents of files in left-to-right positional order on the command line. In this example, the configuration file specifies that the cat command can take up to three positional arguments (technically, the *cat* command can take many more but we left that out for brevity). All the positional arguments are specified as 'optional' because the cat command can be invoked without any positional arguments, in which case cat will read from standard input.

- Option arguments start with one or two dashes and may be followed by a value. "Option" in this context is taken from the Python *optparse* module, and does not mean that it is optional whether the argument is required. It merely indicates that this type of argument is typically used to indicate an optional different behavior. The developer indicates whether an option argument has a value associated with it and whether it is "optional". Option arguments with no value look like "-X" while arguments with a value look like "-X something". In this example, we specify two of cat's option arguments, -n and --version. The -n option to cat causes it to print line numbers at the beginning of each line. The "—version" option causes cat to output its version number.

There are a number of complex issues associated with argument parsing. Although the vast majority of applications follow simple conventions of allowing a mix of positional and option command line arguments, several perverse applications have much more complex rules. A comprehensive review of all applications (or even just standard Unix commands) is far beyond the scope of this document. Nevertheless, there are commands such as *tar*, *dd*, and *find*, each of which violates some of the conventions supported by PythonCLServiceTool. Tar allows multiple options to be coalesced into a single option (such as -xvf, which means extract verbosely from a file). PythonCLServiceTool has no configuration file syntax to support expressing when variables can be coalesced, and would interpret this as a single option called "xvf", which would not be recognized. The user can work around this restriction by specifying the options separately, "-x -v -f". dd is an odd Unix command which does not prepend its option arguments with dashes, so options look like "count=BLOCKS" instead of "-count BLOCKS". The developer can simply define these as positional arguments, losing some of the power of option arguments. The find command has a complex, stateful command line in which order matters. There is no support for checking for valid ordering at the client-side in PythonCLServiceTool; in this case, the find command run on the server will report an error. We reasoned that the *tar*, *dd*, and *find* behaviors are relatively rare and did not justify additional configuration file syntax or option parsing code. Ideally, all applications would conform to the GNU standard for command line options, and we would support exactly that standard, but our support covers the vast majority of cases without being unduly complex. Fortunately the scientific applications we are targeting typically follow the GNU standard anyway.

3.3 Grid Toolkit Support

PythonCLServiceTool uses the pyGridWare[17] toolkit to support all of its grid- and web-services functionality. The pyGridWare toolkit includes code to generate Python grid services from WSDL files, as well as runtime libraries for constructing and running grid services and clients. PyGridWare provides support for the WS-Resource Framework collection of standards used by grid services, as well as WS-Notification. When building a grid service, pyGridWare generates a text file that contains all the configuration details for the service (such as encryption, authorization, and authentication, as well as logging and other common service functionality), a script containing all the code to start the service on a deployment host, and the generated code for a specific grid service.

The code generated by PythonCLServiceTool follows standard WSRF practices in using a standard web service to manage multiple stateful instances. This ensures a deployed service can handle multiple simultaneous requests, each with its own "context" that ensures individual results are delivered to the correct user.

3.4 Template files and Code generation.

When the developer requests server or client code generation, a collection of template files which contain all the generally required common functionality are string interpolated using the configuration file substitution values for *name* and *executable*. The command line client stub, pyGridWare server container startup scripts, client and server runtime libraries, server configuration file, WSDL[12], and XML schema[18] corresponding to the interface of the service are generated. These WSDL and XML schema files can be re-used by other applications that can re-implement either the client or service sides of a PythonCLServiceTool instance. Users are not tied to using our Python clients. The usage of standard web service protocols means that new clients can be generated in any language that supports the WSRF/WS-N protocols suites. The output filenames from the template substitution are based on the input filenames, but are string interpolated to customize them to the service instance. This allows co-installation of the runtime code for several services in the same directory.

Some Python code specific to a PythonCLServiceTool instance is generated automatically (not from template files). The command-line parser and encoding and decoding routines are generated automatically from the argument definitions in the configuration file, because this generated code is highly dependent on the specific details of the command line application arguments.

PythonCLServiceTool utilizes nearly all the basic features of a WSRF based Grid client and service. It has been carefully documented to make it clear how basic Grid functionality (such as web service code generation, notifications, security, and deployment) can be used from Python. Developers are welcome to use and adapt the template file and code generation features of PythonCLServiceTool to develop their own grid applications.

3.5 Tool Usage and Deployment

PythonCLServiceTool leverages an existing Python project-building installation framework known as setuptools. It uses setuptools to string interpolate the template files, build deployable service instances, and build distributable clients. We chose to use setuptools because Python users are familiar with the standard setuptools commands; a simple

```
% python setup.py install
```

will generate the code, configure the service, and deploy it.

The PythonCLServiceTool generated service is typically deployed as a collection of files: the server configuration file, server startup script, and server runtime implementation code. The service configuration file is a simple text file with the same syntax as the PythonCLServiceTool configuration file used to generate the client and service. It defines logging, SSL security, authorization, the server port and interface, URLs to the grid services and the name of the executable. The startup script is either a shell script (on Unix-like platforms) or a DOS batch file (on Windows). The server runtime contains all the string-interpolated template files

PythonCLServiceTool uses the Twisted framework and pyGridWare toolkits to provide a web server that hosts the specific service instance. Multiple service instances (corresponding to different command-line applications) can be co-located into a single web server directory; this simplifies using a single machine to host multiple services (it is also possible to have multiple separate servers each using a different port).

When a client requests the service to run the command line, the service parses the SOAP-encoded command line, and uses the Twisted Framework to fork an external process that executes the command line. Twisted's internal asynchronous reactor support provides standard output, standard error and process return code to the service instance without blocking the service container. As bits of standard output and error become available from the process, the service instance pushes that data to the client via notifications. If firewall or other considerations disallow client notification support the client will detect it and poll the server.

The client side script is designed to be easily distributed to users. It uses the setuptools feature *bdist_rpm* to produce an RPM on RPM-based Linux systems. It can build self-contained executables for DOS- and Unix-like systems which include the client scripts, runtime libraries, and, configuration file. From the perspective of a user, the client script operates identically to the original command line (insofar as the configuration file is an accurate representation of the original command line's arguments).

3.6 File staging

Because users frequently have files stored locally that they need to process remotely, PythonCLServiceTool provides the ability to specify input files that are to be staged onto the server. PyCLST allows the user to specify local files, which are to be transferred to the server, through a special command-line syntax. The filename of the local file is enclosed in an '{' and '}'. For example:

```
% cat.sh {/tmp/localInputFile}
```

will transfer the file */tmp/localInputFile* from the client machine to a temporary directory on the server, and when the job runs on the service, it will have the temporary file name substituted into the command line.

Files are currently staged by base64 encoding by default but the staging mechanism could also be implemented using GridFTP, RFT, or other file movement mechanisms. This support is necessary for moving large data files. In the future PyCLST will optionally create a server working directory for each job instance and transfer all the files created in the directory during job execution back to the client.

4. Example Usage of PythonCLServiceTool

4.1 Wrapping the NCBI BLAST application *blastpgp*

We now demonstrate a concrete example of using PythonCLServiceTool: wrapping a very popular bioinformatics tool called BLAST[19]. Specifically, we will demonstrate wrapping the *blastpgp* command distributed with NCBI BLAST. *blastpgp* searches a protein sequence database against a protein query sequence, permitting gaps in the alignments between query and database sequences. Biologists use this application to identify novel genes based on their similarity to existing, well-characterized genes. BLAST is significantly faster than other sequence-search algorithms, although it is not as accurate as methods such as Hidden Markov Models.

In this example we will assume that the host on which the service is deployed already has the BLAST databases installed and properly formatted, while the query sequence is stored on the client machine.

A minimal blastpgp command line looks like the following:

```
% blastpgp -i query.fa -d database
```

The –i option lists a local filename which contains the query sequence, while the –d options lists the name of a database which is located using the BLASTDB variable. Because this option does not refer to an actual full path name but rather a collection of files in the BLASTDB directory which are prefixed by the database name, PythonCLServiceTool is not currently able to stage BLAST database files. This is generally not a problem because normally users would use a database preinstalled and formatted at the service. Blastpgp takes a number of options that affect its behavior, although except for –i and –d, all of these are optional. It takes no positional arguments.

The blastpgp wrapper config file is given in Figure 1. We have wrapped the two required options, -i and –d, and also wrapped several other commonly used options: -o, which allows the output to be redirect to a local (local to the service) file, -e which defines a different statistical cutoff threshold than the default, and –m which allows the output file format to be adjusted. Each of the options takes a value, and other than –i and –d are optional (not required). To create the service and client, enter
```
% python setup.py install.
```

In this example, running *python setup.py install* deploys both the service and the client to the local Python installation.

4.2 Running the Example

After the service and client have been deployed, start the service container. The name of the service container startup script on Unix-like systems is *start-container_blastpgp.sh* and on Windows is *start-container_blastpgp.bat*. The server can be started in any directory; that directory will act as the "current directory of the server", meaning executable files will be run from that location and relative file path references will be computed from that location. Create a protein sequence query file in the current directory. Call it *test.fa* and have it contain the following query sequence:

```
>gi|33357914|pdb|1P85|M
MDKKSARIRRATRARRKLQELGATRLVVHRTPRHIYA
QVIAPNGSEVLVAASTVEKAIAEQLKYTGNKDAAAAV
GKAVAEALEKGIKDVSFDRSGFQYHGRVQALADAARE
AGLQF
```

Download the sample database pdbaa from
```
ftp://ftp.ncbi.nlm.nih.gov/blast/db/FASTA/pdbaa.gz
```

and decompress it in this directory. Next run the blastpgp command
```
% formatdb -o T -I pdbaa
```
to create the BLAST index file.

Run the client command, which is called blastpgp.sh on Unix-like systems and blastpgp.bat on Windows, with the following options: *-d pdbaa –I test.fa*. If it is successful, *blastpgp* will print many lines of useful information including which sequences in the database match the query, the alignments of those sequences to the query, and statistical scores.

Finally, test the client with a local file. Move the test.fa file created in the service deployment directory to /tmp or some other folder, and run the following command (if your shell (most Unix shells do) has its own use for { and }, quote those characters with \):
```
% blastpgp.sh -d pdbaa -I {test.fa}.
```

5. Performance

A natural question arises when exposing numerical/computational codes as Grid services. Is the performance adequate? Despite the obvious benefits of exposing your codes over the network, if the performance is not sufficient it will not be used. Because PyCLST is based on the Python WSRF toolkit, pyGridWare, we will focus on examining the performance of pyGridWare. We will discuss the basic XML parsing performance and the additional overhead of various security options.

In pyGridWare the overwhelming majority of the overhead is in XML parsing. Messages must be serialized into an XML format before crossing the wire, and then de-serialized back into Python on the receiving end. Clearly the choice of an underlying XML parser is very important. We were able to gain a factor of 20 performance gain by switching to a C based XML parser with a Python interface from a pure Python XML parser.

We recently tested pyGridWare using a 2.0GHz dual opteron Linux machine. When running both client and server on the same machine to avoid network round trip time, we see that basic WSRF operations take a little less then 10ms per operation. Over 90% of this time is XML parsing. This is the baseline for what is possible, but in a real-world application security will become important.

While security is essential to running production level Grid services, it does add significant overhead. Using the same testing environment as before, we examined two different authentication mechanisms. The first is based on the widely used IETF standard TLS[20] protocol. This is the same protocol used on the WWW to interact with your bank, or place an order on Amazon. The second authentication mechanism uses XML security primitives to sign the SOAP messages being exchanged. In both cases, a Python binding to the open-source OpenSSL[21] toolkit provides the cryptographic primitives. Tests using the TLS protocol take approximately 25ms per operation. By using the support in the TLS protocol to re-use a security context, it is possible to amortize this overhead over a number of calls. Message level security based on XML security is significantly slower. Operations take approximately 65ms per round-trip.

While there are many applications where introducing a 10ms overhead would be unacceptable, we have found that for the applications we are targeting the performance of PyCLST is acceptable. For example, a typical BLAST query may run for 30 seconds. When you amortize the 25ms overhead over the entire 30 second run, the PyCLST overhead is negligible.

6. Future Work

6.1 Wrapping Command Line Applications for Grid Workflows

We anticipate that PythonCLServiceTool will be used to wrap command lines that are integrated into workflows. When multiple grid services are orchestrated together as a workflow, it is desirable for the user running the workflow to be able to delegate their credentials to services which carry out work on their behalf. This is an important feature for enabling an important optimization, which is that services will communicate in a third-party manner without sending the results of jobs back to the client, and also eliminates the need for users to type their passwords for each individual operation in the workflow. For example, BLAST output is frequently parsed by a secondary program to produce a compacted representation. It would be inefficient for a workflow to run an external BLAST program, collect the standard output, then forward it on to the standard input of the parsing program; instead, it is much more efficient for the standard output of the BLAST program to be connected directly to the standard input of the parsing program. This sort of third-party communication requires that the two services have the appropriate permissions, which is enabled through credential delegation. Credential delegation is also essential for access to other grid services such as WS-GRAM and RFT, support for which will be included in a future version of PythonCLServiceTool. These features will allow PythonCLServiceTool to add important functionality, including the ability to run jobs through an external scheduler, and reliably manage transfers of collections of large input/output files.

6.2 Authentication and Authorization

Currently, PythonCLServiceTool does not carry out any special checks to ensure that a client request is from an authorized user. This could lead to denial of service and other attacks on the service. PythonCLServiceTool will adopt an authorization model analogous to Globus based on the *gridmap* file. This model uses public-key cryptography combined with a file that maps user certificates into user names. When the client connects to the server, the server requires it to provide a certificate which states the identity of the user. The server validates the certificate, ensuring that it comes from a trusted source, and then uses the user name in the certificate to map to a local user. If a client request is presented without a valid certificate, the server will immediately terminate the request. This file adopts the same format as the Globus gridmap file and performs effectively the same functionality. For example, this line in the gridmap file:

"/DC=org/DC=doegrids/OU=People/CN=David E. Konerding 692119" dek

indicates that a client who presents a certificate with the distinguished name in quotes will be mapped to the local user dek. Multiple certificates can be mapped to a single user on the system which is convenient if it is desired not to add any "extra" user accounts on the system.

In addition to supporting grid-map-file based authorization, we will also implement a standard authorization interface. This will allow others to plug in other more flexible means of authorization, i.e., SAML[22], VOMS[23], etc.

6.3 Advanced File and Job Support

Many applications output collections of files in the run directory of the service, and these files will need to be available to the client. Therefore, PythonCLServiceTool will be enhanced to support several higher-level data transfer mechanisms to facilitate high-performance, reliable file transfer as implemented by RFT and access to storage resource managers and brokers including SRM[24] and SRB[25].

The current PythonCLServiceTool model is to execute an application on the service host. However, in many situations the service host is not the most applicable location to execute the application. Therefore, PythonCLServiceTool will be enhanced to include submission to external batch schedulers using the standard WS-GRAM interface.

6.3 Fault tolerance

There are a number of aspects which could cause a job to fail while running on the service. Further, there are events which could cause the service container to crash. To ensure that the service container is reliable, and outstanding requests persist beyond a crash, the service will store its internal state in a durable disk file using a lightweight but powerful embedded RDBMS, "sqlite"[26].

Another aspect of maintaining a reliable service is to instrument the service with logging functions. This logging is invaluable when, inevitably, something goes wrong with the service. We will integrate support for the NetLogger[27] library, a lightweight but high-performance network logging toolkit designed for use in distributed systems like a Grid. NetLogger integration will enable service developers to get fine-grained views of their service's operation, which is invaluable both during debugging and when diagnosing server failures.

6.4 Programmatic interfaces to legacy programs.

As we stated earlier, PythonCLServiceTool was initially targeted at wrapping command line applications, exposing the standard input, standard output/error, and return code of an application. However, some legacy applications expose their functionality at a library rather than application level. We will enhance PythonCLServiceTool so that it can be used to wrap libraries in addition to applications. These libraries will be accessed through a small command-line client stub which can be used to create service library instances, create instances of data structures defined by the library, invoke functions in the instance, and ultimately destroy the library instance.

Many Fortran applications can be automatically wrapped using the f2py[28] application. This application parses Fortran source code for a library and generates Python modules that can call the Fortran functions in the library directly.
C and C++ applications can be wrapped using SWIG[29]. SWIG parses C and C++ source code for a library and generates Python modules that can call the C/C++ functions in the library directly.

6.5 Config file format

We have identified a number of problems which cannot be addressed using our existing configuration file format. The format, while simple, is cumbersome for applications with large numbers of option arguments, unbounded number of positional parameters, and complex command line parameters that interact with each other. Future versions of PythonCLServiecTool will switch to an XML-based file format that will allow for much more extensive specification of command line behavior and will expose many more implementation details in PythonCLServiceTool to the developer. Since the existing format is useful for many simple applications, a translator from the existing format to the XML format will be provided.

The new XML file format will add support for more complex/varied command line formats (such as better support for /option formats used on Windows), including mechanisms for overriding the default file transfer behavior, redirection of I/O via third party interactions, interactions between command line options, and detection of invalid command lines on the client side.

6.6 Better self-contained deployment

We are investigating the use of py2exe[30] on Windows and freeze on UNIX to create a more self-contained deployment including the Python runtime. The current single-executable deployment contains only the service or client runtime libraries and startup script, thus it requires a valid Python installation on the target machine. We will use Py2exe and freeze to take the generated PythonCLServiceTool package, and combine it with a full Python installation and the required runtime libraries to provide a single executable that can be easily deployed to a service or client host.

7. Conclusion

PythonCLServiceTool addresses two existing problems facing the community: how to make applications available to scientists without distributing the entire software package, and how to make legacy application available on the grid without extensive retrofitting.

As shown in the Performance section, PythonCLServiceTool adds marginal overhead compared to typical long-running scientific applications. Although there is some cost to XML parsing and security, these represent only a tiny fraction of the overall time spent running the application.

There are still several remaining features which must be implemented before PythonCLServiceTool can be used in production environments. The authorization functionality needs to be implemented so that only authorized users can invoke the service. Command-line syntax and back-end support for high-performance file transfers is required before large files and standard input/output can be used. Fault-tolerance, recovery and logging must be implemented for the service to be useful in long-running production environments. Finally, the configuration file syntax needs to be significantly enhanced to support these features and to allow for more sophisticated command line support. Nevertheless, PyCLST has shown the value of simple automated tools to help expose legacy applications as Grid services.

8. Figures

Figure 1

```
[main]
name=blastpgp
executable=/home/portnoy/u5/dek/sw/i386/blast-2.2.13/bin/blastpgp

[optionarguments]

arg1option=-i
arg1desc= Query [File In]
arg1hasvalue=True
arg1optional=False

arg2option=-d
arg2desc= Database [String]
arg2hasvalue=True
arg2optional=False

arg3option=-o
arg3desc= Output File For Alignment [File out]
arg3hasvalue=True
arg3optional=True

arg4options=-e
arg4desc=Expectation value (E) [Real]
arg4hasvalue=True
arg4optional=True


arg5option=-m
arg5desc=alignment view options
arg5hasvalue=True
arg5optional=True

## BLAST does not have any position arguments.
[positionarguments]
```

9. Bibliography

1.   Foster, I., C. Kesselman, and S. Tuecke, *The Anatomy of the Grid: Enabling Scalable Virtual Organizations*. Intl. J. Supercomputer Applications, 2001.
2.   Kreger, H., *Web Services Conceptual Architecture*. 2001, IBM.
3.   Cornell.edu. *SOAP::Clean*. 2006   [cited; Available   from: http://www.asp.cornell.edu/SOAP-Clean/.
4.   Cornell.edu. *O'SOAP*. 2006   [cited; Available   from: http://www.asp.cornell.edu/osoap/.
5.   *Simple Object Access Protocol (SOAP) 1.1*. 2000, W3C.
6.   Globus Project, *Grid Security Infrastructure (GSI)*. 2002.
7.   Globus Project, *The GridFTP Protocol and Software*. 2002.
8.   *Web Services Resource Framework (WSRF) - Primer v1.2*. 2006, OASIS.
9.   *Web Services Base Notification 1.3 (WS-BaseNotification)*. 2006, OASIS.
10.   Ludascher, B., et al., *Scientific Workflow Management and the Kepler System*. Concurrency and Computation: Practice & Experience, 2005(Special Issue on Scientific Workflows).
11.   *Ptolemy*. 2006   [cited; Available   from: http://ptolemy.eecs.berkeley.edu/ptolemyII/.
12.   Christensen, E., et al., *Web Services Description Language (WSDL) 1.1*. 2001.
13.   *Twisted*. 2006 [cited; Available from: http://twistedmatrix.com/trac/.
14.   *Setuptools*. 2006   [cited; Available   from: http://peak.telecommunity.com/DevCenter/setuptools.
15.   Foster, I., C. Kesselman, and S. Tuecke, *The Globus Toolkit and Grid Architecture*. 2001, In preparation.
16.   Adams, C. and S. Farrell, *Internet X.509 Public Key Infrastructure Certificate*. Mar 1999(2510).
17.   Jackson, K.R. *pyGridWare*. 2006   [cited; Available   from: http://dsd.lbl.gov/gtg/projects/pyGridWare/.
18.   Fallside, D.C., *XML Schema Part 0: Primer*. 2001, W3C.
19.   *BLAST*. 2006   [cited; Available   from: http://www.ncbi.nlm.nih.gov/BLAST/.
20.   Dierks, T. and C. Allen, *The TLS Protocol Version 1.0*. 1999, IETF.
21.   *OpenSSL*. 2002 [cited; Available from: http://www.openssl.org/.
22.   *Security Association Markup Language (SAML) Specification v.1.0*. 2002, OASIS.
23.   EU DataGrid, *VOMS Architecture v1.1*. 2003.
24.   Gu, J., A. Sim, and A. Shoshani, *The Storage Resource Manager Interface Specification, version 2.1*. 2003.
25.   Baru, C., et al. *The SDSC Storage Resource Broker*. in *8th Annual IBM Centers for Advanced Studies Conference*. 1998. Toronto, Canada.
26.   *Sqlite*. 2006 [cited; Available from: http://www.sqlite.org/.
27.   Gunter, D., et al. *NetLogger: A Toolkit for Distributed System Performance Analysis*. In *IEEE Mascots 2000: Eighth International Symposium on*

Modeling, Analysis and Simulation of Computer and Telecommunication Systems. 2000.

28.   *F2py*. 2006.

29.   Beazley, D.M. *SWIG : An Easy to Use Tool for Integrating Scripting Languages with C and C++*. in *Proceedings of the 4th USENIX Tcl/Tk Workshop*. 1996.

30.   *Py2exe*. 2006 [cited; Available from: http://www.py2exe.org/.

Q&A – Keith Jackson

Questioner: Brian Smith

Numerical applications often are made up of multiple numeric components. These components frequently pass large amounts of data between components and other applications, the data is returned as part of the service. Are the service tools and techniques able to support such scenarios in a reasonable way?

Keith Jackson

Currently tools are available to support these scenarios, but only in an ad-hoc manner. It is an ongoing area of research to understand what functionality and interfaces services should support to make linking them together into larger applications easier. Today too much of this process must be done manually as part of the workflow. For example, today I would submit a job to a numerical service, and then have my workflow script use GridFTP to move the data to the next service. In the future, it should be possible to tell the first service that it should send its output data to the second service and have it all happen without manually coding the data transfers.

Questioner: Craig Douglas

Where are examples of automated tools in Python that actually generate real, non-trivial services?

Keith Jackson

Currently *SWIG* is the most popular tool to generate Python bindings to C or C++ code. *F2py* is probably the most popular tool for generating Python bindings to Fortran codes. Both have been used extensively to provide interfaces to numerical codes. A good example is the data analysis pipeline for the Hubble telescope. All of the images run through a pipeline that is written in Python, but invokes a large number of services written in C, C++, and Fortran. For more information on wrapping numerical codes in Python, see: http://www.scipy.org/Cookbook.

Comment: Craig Douglas

Visual C 1.0 (circa 1998) compiled and linked 90,000 lines of code to put a window up that said "Hello". Automated tools that generate an enormous number of lines of Grid/Globus code similarly emphasize that Grid services programming is obscenely over-complicated.

Keith Jackson

Indeed Grid service programming can be very complicated. Finding ways to hide as much of that complexity as possible while still providing useful tools to the scientists is an ongoing research problem.

Questioner: Gabrielle Allen

Can you explain more about how services are deployed. Is there one service for each application on the machine? How do you track changes in the application location?

Keith Jackson

Currently there is one factory service for each application on the machine. Each running instance of that service would also have a unique service that encapsulates the running code. Service deployment is still done manually. We plan on leveraging some of the work of Kate Keahey at ANL on automated service deployment. She has been investigating what information you need, and how it should be presented, so that a system can decide where to deploy services in real time.

Comment: Dennis Gannon

We use an application service factory to generate service instances on the fly. This solves the problem of "too many services".

Questioner: Dennis Gannon

How do you handle programs with complex input and output files?

Keith Jackson

Currently the user has to ensure that the proper files are in place before running the service, and then move the output files after the service has completed. Typically this is done using GridFTP. In our visual workflow tool we encapsulate this into a hyper-graph node that uses GridFTP to move the input files in, runs the service, and moves the output files. To the scientist this looks like an atomic operation.

GridSolve: The Evolution of A Network Enabled Solver

Asim YarKhan, Jack Dongarra, and Keith Seymour

Innovative Computing Laboratory,
Department of Computer Science,
University of Tennessee, Knoxville, TN, USA
{yarkhan,dongarra,seymour}@cs.utk.edu

Abstract. GridSolve is a stubless RPC-based client-agent-server system for remotely accessing hardware and software resources. GridSolve emphasizes ease-of-use for the user and includes resource monitoring, scheduling and service-level fault-tolerance. In addition to providing Fortran and C clients, GridSolve enables scientific computing environments (such as Matlab) to be used as clients, so domain scientists can use Grid resources from within their preferred environments. GridSolve is a more highly evolved version of the earlier NetSolve project, and it is based on the emerging GridRPC standard. This paper will discuss the changes and improvements involved in the evolution from NetSolve to GridSolve.

1 Introduction: The Grid and Network Enabled Solvers

The adoption of Grid infrastructures as a major platform for supercomputing holds great promise for accelerating scientific discovery. However, the use of Grid infrastructures has, for the most part, been restricted to the largest and most resource intensive projects. For Grid computing to become a true success story, it must become an infrastructure that can be easily used by the *general* community of scientists and engineers. Within this community of practitioners, the use of scientific computing environments (SCEs) such as Matlab or Mathematica is pervasive. These domain specialists are accustomed to the flexible computing environment provided by an SCE, which gives them the tools and libraries they need to be productive and enables them to go from computation to visualization in a natural fashion.

Network enabled solvers can be used to extend the power of SCEs so that they reach beyond the users desk, and into the network of resources available on the Grid. End users are not required to install and maintain local software and libraries, and can simply use the libraries that have been installed at a remote location. Since the libraries and remote services can be maintained by experts, they can be highly tuned and provide the optimized execution on the remote platform.

The purpose of GridSolve is to create the middleware necessary to provide a seamless bridge between the simple, standard programming interfaces and

Please use the following format when citing this chapter:

YarKhan, A., Dongarra J., Seymour K., 2007, in IFIP International Federation for Information Processing, Volume 239, Grid-Based Problem Solving Environments, eds. Gaffney, P. W., Pool, J.C.T., (Boston: Springer), pp. 215-224.

desktop systems that dominate the work of computational scientists and the rich supply of services supported by the emerging Grid architecture, so that the users of the former can easily access and reap the benefits (shared processing, storage, software, data resources, etc.) of using the latter. The vision of the broad community of scientists, engineers, research professionals and students, working with the powerful and flexible tool set provided by their familiar scientific computing environments, and yet able to easily draw on the vast, shared resources of the Grid for unique or exceptional resource needs, or to collaborate intensively with colleagues in other organizations and locations, is the vision that GridSolve is designed to realize.

2 Foundations of GridSolve: GridRPC and NetSolve

GridSolve is based on the RPC paradigm for distributed computing, but it is an entire environment which provides stubless clients, resource discovery, load balancing, fault tolerance, asynchronous calls, disconnected operation and security. A primary goal for GridSolve is ease-of-use, providing transparent access to resources. GridSolve employs two primary enabling technologies, the NetSolve solver [2] and the GridRPC API [11].

2.1 GridRPC: An API for Grid Remote Procedure Calls

The GridRPC API represents ongoing work to standardize and implement a portable and simple remote procedure call (RPC) mechanism for Grid computing. This standardization effort is being pursued through the Grid Remote Procedure Call Working Group within the Open Grid Forum (formerly Global Grid Forum). GridRPC provides a common setting within which users can develop RPC programs, so that these programs are source code compatible. GridSolve has recently passed a GridRPC compliance test, along with two other GridRPC implementations, Ninf-G [12] and DIET [4].

2.2 NetSolve: A Precursor to GridSolve

NetSolve is a client-agent-server system which provides remote access to hardware and software resources through a variety of client interfaces. A NetSolve system consists of three entities, as illustrated in Figure 1.

- The **Client**, which needs to execute some remote procedure call. NetSolve client interfaces have been implemented in Matlab, Mathematica, Octave, C, Fortran and Java. Client-side stubs are not required to access remote services, the client-side service bindings are looked up from the server as needed.
- The **Server** executes services on behalf of the clients. The server hardware can range in complexity from a uniprocessor to a MPP system and the functions executed by the server can be arbitrarily complex. Server administrators

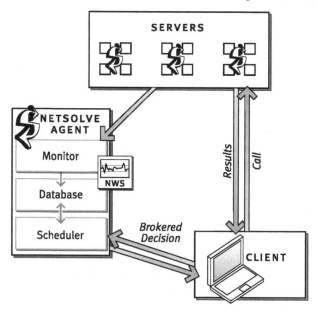

Fig. 1. NetSolve client-agent-server architecture. The agent *monitors* the servers on the Grid and records available service and server status in a *database*. The agent can also record network status using NWS (Network Weather Service). The agent *schedules* the client request to be executed on an appropriate server. The GridSolve system uses the same architectural model.

can write service definitions and add their own services without affecting the rest of the NetSolve system. Since there are no client side stubs, any client can become immediately aware of any services that are added.

– The **Agent** is the focal point of the NetSolve system. It maintains a list of all available servers and services, and performs resource selection and scheduling for client requests as well as ensuring load balancing of the servers.

The system is designed to be easy to use from the perspective of an end-user. The user executes code containing a call to NetSolve similar to netsl('myfunction',parameters, ..). The rest of the remote execution happens transparently from the point of view of the client. The GridSolve client library contacts the agent which finds servers that can satisfy the request, and ranks these servers. The client receives the list of servers and submits the request to the highest ranked server. If the request fails for some reason (e.g. network problems, server down), the client can automatically resubmit to the next server in the list, providing service level fault tolerance. The server executes the requested service and returns the output to the client. In this way, the end user can access Grid resources without having to be aware of all the details involved in finding, allocating and monitoring the resources and managing the software and libraries.

In addition to providing the middleware necessary to perform the brokered remote procedure call, NetSolve provides mechanisms to interface with other existing Grid services. NetSolve can use server-proxies to communicate with several back-end resource and execution managers, such as batch queue managers, the Condor [9] high throughput computing system, and MPI runtime systems. A server-proxy is specific to a back-end system, and accepts requests from the client using the same protocols as a standard NetSolve server. The primary benefit is that the client-to-server communication protocol is identical so the client does not need to be aware of every possible back-end service. The actual resources that execute a service may be a serial machine or a parallel machine, with the same service being implemented using different algorithms on different servers.

NetSolve has several specialized execution mechanisms which support common computing models. There is a task-farming API within NetSolve that supports parameter-sweep or master-worker style applications. A task sequencing API enables workflow type applications where the input data or intermediate outputs are to be retained at the remote server, and to be used in further computation.

NetSolve is distributed with service wrappers for many numerical libraries, such as LAPACK, ScaLAPACK, SuperLU, ARPACK and PETSc. If these libraries are available at the servers, they can be enabled within NetSolve. Some numerical libraries (e.g., BLAS, LAPACK, SuperLU) are even included in the NetSolve distribution, enabling a NetSolve server to provide useful services immediately upon installation.

2.3 Shortcomings of NetSolve

Network design, hardware architectures, and software methodologies have changed substantially since the beginning of the NetSolve project in 1996 [5]. More and more sites are using NATs (Network Address Translators) as a method of extending IP usage within a private subnet and as a security tool. NetSolve was designed before the widespread use of NATs, and it includes a server initiated call-back to the client as part of the communication protocol. This cannot take place if the client is behind a NAT, requiring a complete rewrite of the Net-Solve system. Additionally, NetSolve keeps track of components by IP addresses, which are not globally unique in the presence of private subnets managed by NATs.

NetSolve also uses a wide range of ports for its communications. In this current era of increased network security and omnipresent firewalls, this requirement was awkward to meet. Many sites with strong firewall policies are not setup to unblock and allow network traffic on a wide range of ports.

From the beginning, NetSolve was designed to make it possible for users to add additional services to their servers, to allow them to turn their custom applications into services that can be executed on powerful remote platform and can be accessed easily from desktop clients. However, experience has shown that this process was too complicated for many users, since adding services to NetSolve requires preparing a fairly idiosyncratic service description file, which uses mnemonic fields to describe data types and structure.

When a service is added to NetSolve, a measure of the computational complexity of the service needs to be provided to make it possible for the NetSolve agent to estimate the execution time of that service on various servers and thus rank the servers. This computational complexity was described using a minimal model, which makes it difficult to implement more complex and accurate scheduling algorithms.

3 GridSolve: A Network Enabled Solver

The GridSolve project is an evolution of NetSolve, architected to overcome the shortcomings of NetSolve and to provide a platform for additional development and experimentation. The system architecture of GridSolve is the same as that of NetSolve shown in Figure 1, where a client-agent-server system interact to provide transparent Grid based services to an end-user.

The overall goal of the GridSolve project is to address three general problems: ease of use, interoperability, and extensibility. Improving ease of use refers to improving the process by which libraries and services are added into a GridSolve server. Interoperability encompasses several facets, including better handling of different network topologies, and better interaction with other Grid computing projects. Extensibility in this context means easy extension to new parallel libraries and architectures, support for large datasets, and better resource scheduling to take advantage of growing set of servers and services.

3.1 Ease of use

IDL improvements One of the original design goals was to eliminate the need for client-side stubs for each procedure in a remote procedure call (RPC) environment. However, this design decision tends to push the complexity to the servers. Integrating new software into NetSolve required writing a complex server side interface definition (Problem Description File), which specifies the parameters, data types, and calling sequence. Despite several attempts to create a user-friendly tool to generate the Problem Description Files, it can still be a difficult and error-prone process.

Therefore, we have implemented a simple technique for adding additional services to a running GridSolve server. The interface definition format itself has been greatly simplified and the services are compiled as external executables with interfaces to the server described in a standard format. The server re-examines its own configuration and installed services periodically or when it receives the appropriate signal. In this way it becomes aware of any additional services that are installed without re-compilation or restarting. The server reports the new service to the agent, and thereafter it can be used by any GridSolve client.

3.2 Interoperability

Handling NATs A Network Address Translator [8] presents the same external IP address for all machines within a private subnet, reducing the overall need for unique IP addresses. NATs are often used by end-users as a way of providing multiple machines with network access without requiring that they all be assigned unique global IP addresses. They are also sometimes used a security measure since it is difficult to make inbound connectivity to a machine behind a NAT. However, this causes problems for services such as GridSolve such as: IP addresses may not be unique, IP address-to-host bindings may not be stable, and hosts behind the NAT may not be contactable from outside. To address these issues we have developed a new communications framework for GridSolve. To avoid problems related to potential duplication of IP addresses, the GridSolve components are identified by a globally unique identifier specified by the user or generated randomly. To allow inbound connectivity to GridSolve servers behind a NAT, a GridSolve *proxy* executable is distributed with the software. If enabled, a GridSolve server will use the proxy to channel all communications, keeping a connection to the proxy open at all times. This makes the server usable by clients that would not have been able to connect to the server otherwise.

Firewall concerns To handle firewalls in a more adaptive manner, GridSolve now restricts itself to specific ports for communication. The ports can be specified in the execution environment, allowing communication over any port, including the default HTTP port if necessary, since this port is almost always setup to allow traffic through a firewall.

GridRPC API The GridRPC API was made the core API for GridSolve, enabling compatibility with other Grid programming efforts such as Ninf-G or DIET. Additional capabilities such as the Matlab API are built on top of the GridRPC API. The older NetSolve API is also build on top of the GridRPC API to allow backward compatibility for users that did development using NetSolve.

3.3 Extensibility

Supporting backend resource managers In the older NetSolve system, backend resource and execution managers such as Condor and OpenPBS were supported by creating a specialized server for that environment and compiling it into the server. Though effective, this method was cumbersome and required knowledge of the internals of the code. In GridSolve, supporting different backends has been made easier by defining a interface that requires three scripts for service initiation, probing and cancellation. These scripts are specified within the service description, easily allowing any library routine to be run either on a backend or directly on a GridSolve server.

Disconnected Operation Since some of the backend resource managers (e.g., batch queues) may take a substantial time to execute an application, GridSolve has been extended to support disconnected operations. After a GridSolve service request has been submitted asynchronously, the user can request a serialized representation of the service request. This can be saved, and then used to return to the service at a later time.

Scheduling enhancements GridSolve will retain the familiar agent-based scheduling of resources [13], but in some cases the client has additional knowledge about the appropriate set of resources. Therefore we are implementing an infrastructure that allows resource filtering to be optionally performed by the client. In the older NetSolve system, the only user-provided filter that affects the selection of resources is the problem name. Given the problem name, the agent filters the available servers to select the those that can solve that problem, and then ranks the servers. In the newer GridSolve system, the user can provide additional constraints on the filtering process, for example, a minimum memory requirement or the availability of a database. Also, the client will have access to the complete list of resources and their characteristics so that the user can implement comprehensive scheduling algorithms in addition to enhanced filtering. To enable this functionality, a GridSolve server should provide as much information as possible to the agent as free-form resource attributes. The agent then uses the resource attributes to match the filtering request of the client.

Distributed Storage Infrastructure GridSolve supports a Distributed Storage Infrastructure (DSI) API, allowing it to deal with large data in an efficient manner. Using DSI, a client can deploy large data items, such as a vector or matrix, into high speed network storage. Then, when calling a service, a handle to the data can be transparently provided instead of the data item itself. This allows the service to access the data quickly, and the service can reuse the data from the network storage rather than fetching it from the client on each use. This style of deployment could also allow the user to handle data that is too large to fit into the memory of their local computer. Currently, DSI is implemented on top of the Internet Backplane Protocol (IBP) [3] which provides middleware for managing and using remote storage.

4 Related Work

Several Network Enabled Servers (NES) provide mechanisms for transparent access to remote resources and software. Ninf-G [12] is a reference implementation of the GridRPC API [11] built on top of the Globus Toolkit. Ninf-G provides an interface definition language that allows services to be easily added, and client binding are available in C and Java. Security, scheduling and resource management are left up to Globus.

The DIET (Distributed Interactive Engineering Toolbox) project [4] is a client-agent-server RPC architecture which uses the GridRPC API as its primary interface. A CORBA Naming Service handles the resource registration and lookup, and a hierarchy of agents handles the scheduling of services on the resources. An API is provided for generating service profiles and adding new services, and a C client API exists.

NEOS [7] is a network-enabled problem-solving environment designed as a generic application service provider (ASP). Any application that can be changed to read its inputs from files, and write its output to a single file can be integrated into NEOS. The NEOS Server acts as an intermediary for all communication. The client data files go to the NEOS server, which sends the data to the solver resources, collects the results and then returns the results to the client. Clients can use email, web, sockets based tools and CORBA interfaces.

Other projects are related to various aspects of GridSolve. For example, task farming style computation is provided by the Apples Parameter Sweep Template (APST) project [6], the Condor Master Worker (MW) project [10], and the Nimrod-G project [1]. Request sequencing is handled by projects like Condor DAGman [9].

However, GridSolve provides a complete solution for easy access to remote resources and software. It differs from the other NES implementations by including a tight, simple integration with client PSEs such as Matlab. Interface descriptions for a variety of standard mathematical libraries are distributed with GridSolve, and it is easy for additional services to be added. The ability to use server-proxies to make it possible to leverage additional resource management and scheduling environments also adds to GridSolve's strengths.

5 Ongoing Work and Conclusion

GridSolve is still in an early release phase, as it has not yet implemented all the functionality of its predecessor NetSolve. Some of the ongoing work in the GridSolve project is described below.

- Currently the Matlab client bindings are available, and there is some work done on generating client bindings for IDL (Interactive Data Language). Additional languages such as Mathematica, Octave and Java still need to be added.
- A small set of library bindings is currently distributed with GridSolve (i.e., a subset of LAPACK and SuperLU). A more complete set of libraries bindings (LAPACK, ScaLAPACK, SuperLU, ARPACK and PETSc) will be added.
- There is a Kerberos based security mechanism in the current GridSolve distribution. We are investigating other possibilities to enable better integration with additional security infrastructures.

– Ongoing research is investigating ways to use the history of service executions to build an execution model for the services. These models are then used in a more accurate scheduling of the services on servers.

– Since the GridSolve agent currently maintains information about all resources in the entire system, it may be a scalability bottleneck as the number of resources increases. We are investigating the use of multiple cooperating agents to allow the GridSolve system to be scalable.

The GridSolve project has been designed to fit the needs of the general community of scientists and engineers, to provide an easy to use interface to Grid hardware and software resources. A GridSolve user is relieved of many of the details that make using Grid resources awkward: finding the appropriate resources, ensuring that the needed libraries are installed, submitting the application to the resources, monitoring the execution of the application and transferring results back to their SCE for further viewing and analysis.

The current version GridSolve incorporates major enhancements that are based on real world experience and user feedback. These enhancements include tolerance for NATs, accelerated performance, disconnected operation, improved service setup and deployment, resource filtering and improved scheduling.

References

1. David Abramson, Rajkumar Buyya, and Jonathan Giddy. A computational economy for Grid Computing and its implementation in the Nimrod-G resource broker. *Future Generation Computer Systems*, 18(8):1061–1074, October 2002.
2. D. Arnold, S. Agrawal, S. Blackford, J. Dongarra, M. Miller, K. Seymour, K. Sagi, Z. Shi, and S. Vadhiyar. Users' Guide to NetSolve V1.4.1. Innovative Computing Laboratory. Technical Report ICL-UT-02-05, University of Tennessee, Knoxville, TN, June 2002.
3. A. Bassi, M. Beck, T. Moore, J. Plank, M. Swany, R. Wolski, and G. Fagg. The Internet Backplane Protocol: A Study in Resource Sharing. In *Future Generation Computing Systems*, volume 19, pages 551–561.
4. E. Caron, F. Desprez, F. Lombard, J.-M. Nicod, L. Philippe, M. Quinson, and F. Suter. A scalable approach to network enabled servers (research note). *Lecture Notes in Computer Science*, 2400, 2002.
5. Henri Casanova and Jack Dongarra. NetSolve: A Network-Enabled Server for Solving Computational Science Problems. *The International Journal of Supercomputer Applications and High Performance Computing*, 11(3):212–223, Fall 1997.
6. Henri Casanova, Graziano Obertelli, Berman Berman, and Rich Wolski. The AppLeS Parameter Sweep Template: User-Level Middleware for the Grid. In *Proceedings of Supercomputing'2000 (CD-ROM)*, Dallas, TX, Nov 2000. IEEE and ACM SIGARCH.
7. E. Dolan, R. Fourer, J. J. Moré, and Munson Munson. The NEOS server for optimization: Version 4 and beyond. Technical Report ANL/MCS-P947-0202, Mathematics and Computer Science Division, Argonne National Laboratory, Argonne, IL, February 2002.

8. K. Egevang and P. Francis. The IP Network Address Translator (NAT). RFC 1631, May 1994.

9. James Frey, Todd Tannenbaum, Ian Foster, Miron Livny, and Steve Tuecke. Condor-G: A computation management agent for multi-institutional grids. *Cluster Computing*, 5:237–246, 2002.

10. Jeff Linderoth, Sanjeev Kulkarni, Jean-Pierre Goux, and Michael Yoder. An Enabling Framework for Master-Worker Applications on the Computational Grid. In *Proceedings of the Ninth IEEE Symposium on High Performance Distributed Computing (HPDC9)*, pages 43–50, Pittsburgh, PA, August 2000.

11. K. Seymour, N. Hakada, S. Matsuoka, J. Dongarra, C. Lee, and H. Casanova. Overview of GridRPC: A Remote Procedure Call API for Grid Computing. In M. Parashar, editor, *GRID 2002*, pages 274–278, 2002.

12. Y. Tanaka, H. Nakada, S. Sekiguchi, Suzumura Suzumura, and S. Matsuoka. Ninf-G: A reference implementation of RPC-based programming middleware for Grid computing. *Journal of Grid Computing*, 1(1):41–51, 2003.

13. Asim YarKhan, Keith Seymour, Kiran Sagi, Zhiao Shi, and Jack Dongarra. Recent Developments in Gridsolve. *International Journal of High Performance Computing Applications (IJHPCA)*, 20(1):131–141, 2006.

Q&A – Asim YarKhan

Questioner: William Gropp

What extensions did you need for GridRPC?

Asim YarKhan

GridRPC needed certain extensions to allow the fault tolerance and resource scheduling that GridSolve/NetSolve presents to its users. Currently, in GridRPC, resource binding is done when a function handle is created. However, the data to be submitted is only presented later at call time, which means that if the basic GridRPC API is used we cannot use data information (e.g. size) in making scheduling decisions. Similarly, for transparent fault tolerance, we may want to change the resource used within a call.

Comment: William Gropp

These seem like significant flaws in GridRPC spec -- and an excellent example of the perils of premature standardization.

Questioner: Bill Applebe

In Vgrads how is the issue of "versions" of an application being dealt with, where different compute environments support different versions or configurations of an application?

How does the user specify the version and how are local libraries used by the application located?

Asim YarKhan

Currently VGrADS does not provide internal support for the automatic deployment of a compute environment needed for services. An end user must deploy the services and required libraries as needed. VGrADS provides hooks to Gridftp to make it easier to deploy software onto the virtual grid after the physical resources have been allocated.

Questioner: Anne Trefethen

What types of applications are running using Gridsolve?

Asim YarKhan

GridSolve/NetSolve provide access to a large collection of numerical libraries including LAPACK, ARPACK and ScaLAPACK, and these routines can be used directly by an end-user. However, most of the larger applications created by external users fall into the class of task-farming services. These range from diesel engine design using genetic algorithms to statistical methods for working with MRI data. A more complete list can be found on the GridSolve website.

Questioner: Anne Trefethen

Does the latest version run on MSCCS?

Asim YarKhan

The latest version of GridSolve does not run on the Microsoft Compute Cluster, however, completing the port to the Microsoft Compute Cluster is our next goal.

Questioner: William Gropp

Do you validate data to ensure safety from buffer overflow problems (e.g., sparse data structures)?

Asim YarKhan

GridSolve does not currently validate the data.

Questioner: Marc Garbey

Has there been any experience with distance teaching using the system?

Asim YarKhan

There has been some work using NetSolve as a teaching tool (see the Active Netlib project http://icl.cs.utk.edu/active-netlib/), however this is an area that needs to be further explored.

A Test Harness TH for Numerical Applications and Libraries

Brian T. Smith

Numerica 21 Incorporated

Angel Fire, New Mexico, USA, carbess@swcp.com,

Abstract. TH is a test harness to facilitate the development of scientific software. The operational model is the comparison of the results from running two versions of an application code to ensure the results are equivalent. First, TH is installed into an existing application code that runs to completion on a set of data. Installation tools provide a readily-modified default initial configuration. The application code with TH installed is run in generate mode to create a monitored data file. A second version of the application with TH installed is run in check mode, comparing the current results with the original results. Features include specifiable criterion for data comparison, and a design that facilitates the installation of TH into codes written in any programming language and in parallel SPMD codes. Once installed, TH can be deactivated, permitting the same code to be maintained with and without the test harness in use.

1 Introduction

TH is a test harness to facilitate the development of scientific software, currently in Fortran. The test harness is based on the operational principle that the coder wants to ensure the software is producing the "same" results before and after some changes were made to the software, or between the software running on two different platforms. The test harness is used by taking an existing scientific application code that runs to completion on a set of data, inserting "include" lines by hand or by script for large application codes. The instrumented application code, with an input file specifying the variables that are to be monitored, is analyzed by a software tool called the `builder`. The builder tool creates from provided template files the application-specific "include" files needed to run the application software with the test harness installed. The application code with the test harness installed is then run in generate mode to create a data file against which modified versions of the software or versions on different platforms are run to detect any significant changes in the results.

Please use the following format when citing this chapter:

Smith, B. T., 2007, in IFIP International Federation for Information Processing, Volume 239, Grid-Based Problem Solving Environments, eds. Gaffney, P. W., Pool, J.C.T., (Boston: Springer), pp. 227-241.

The various runs of the software might use different versions of the application code with the test harness installed into them in the same way. Typically scientific applications may be enhanced to improve efficiency, to improve capability, to verify the correct porting to a different platform, to modernize the code, or to check the results with different compiler options, typically optimization flags. The test harness compares current values of data variables with previously obtained values and reports only those that are "significantly" different. The coder only specifies the variables whose data values are to be recorded and compared, and the criterion and tolerances for the comparison; writing and reading the past values and all comparisons are implemented by the test harness, and the test harness reports significant differences that violate the comparison criteria.

In contrast, comparisons by hand of results before and after comparable runs are tedious, error-prone, very difficult, or often impractical because of the different impacts of rounding errors. The test harness addresses this issue by providing data comparators that under programmer specifications check for near-identity rather than identity, comparing results based on relative or absolute tolerances, or both. Comparisons for arrays are facilitated by array comparator routines provided by the test harness. When differences are detected, the diagnostic information printed indicates what the tolerances should be to pass the checking procedures and the first element in array element order that is significantly different. In addition, as needed, the comparators can be made to ignore any differences.

The paper describes the test harness, its operation, its testing, and experience with it in testing various application codes. In section 2, more detail is provided on how the test harness is to be used; in section 3, the tools as well as the input to these tools that build the test harness into the application are described. Section 4.0 describes the tests that have been used to evaluate the test harness; Section 5.0 describes the plans for future enhancements to the test harness and Section 6.0 provides a summary and conclusion.

2.0   The Problem and the Test Harness Concept

A problem encountered by many code developers and code maintainers is to determine whether a large code continues to operate correctly or in the same way as it did in the past after modifying or enhancing it. The modifications or enhancements might be, for example, to improve the code's efficiency, add new features, compile it with different optimization flags, or make modifications that permit it to run on a different architecture. In such scenarios, the code developer has a collection of test to rerun and wants to ensure that the code behaves the same way where the changes should have no effects on the numerical results.

The test harness is a tool to aid in this testing process. Often even modest changes such as rearranging computations or performing them in a different order will change the results numerically. Comparing numerical results by hand is a tedious and error-prone process in which in many cases all the results are different but only by a amount consist with the stability of the numerical computation. The test harness is a tool that permits the comparison of two sets of results using error tolerances specified by the user. The current version of the test harness permits the comparisons of pairs of variables (scalars, arrays, or structured objects), one from a version of the application code run in "generate" mode and the corresponding variables from a version of the code run in "check" mode. The comparisons to be performed are specified by giving the variable by name, the subprogram or program the variable is in, the location of the comparison (for example, on entry to a procedure, exit from a procedure, or at any arbitrary point in a procedure), and the tolerance used for the comparison.

Control of the comparisons and what is compared is specified by input to the harness tool `builder`. The tool creates modifiable application-specific "include" files and a module with module procedures containing the comparator code. The comparator code is in a separate module that can be readily modified by the coder to handle special cases but the typical ordinary cases are provided by default in this separate module. In this way, unusual comparisons, say for combinations of specific elements of arrays or non-intrinsic derived types can be coded into this separate module and references to them can be placed in specific "include" files as needed.

2.1   The Approach in Detail

Figure 1 illustrates the modes of operation of the application code with the test harness installed. The figure assumes the test harness has been installed in two versions of the application code. The flow on the left shows the application code

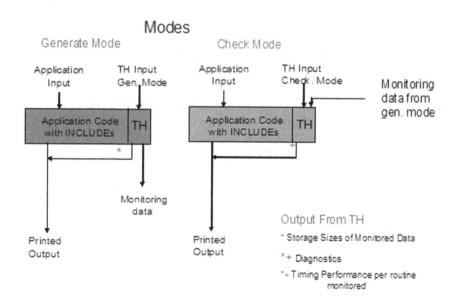

Figure 1: Operation of the Test Harness

with the test harness installed into it where the test harness is run in "generate" mode. The application code reads its input and performs all of its computation as usual, producing its usual output. The test harness records the values of the variables that it is monitoring in an unformatted sequential file. The recorded data includes both application code values and data from the test harness, representing the execution sequence of the monitored procedures. The test harness performs certain consistency tests, providing diagnostics when it detects errors. In addition, it accumulates and prints the frequency counts, execution times, and data sizes written by each monitored application procedure (these are indicated in Figure 1 with an asterisk on the printed output line from the test harness). This latter computation and output can be turned off by input to the test harness.

The flow on the right shows the application code run in check mode. The diagram is essentially the same except that the test harness reads the monitored data generated from the unformatted file created from the test harness code run in generate mode. However, the test harness runs in a different way; this time, it compares the values of the monitored variables with the data from the unformatted file. The comparisons are performed as specified to the builder tool and any variance from the specified tolerances are analyzed and diagnosed on a separate output error unit, specified to the test harness. The analysis process prints the value that the tolerances must be to pass the comparison tests and recommends whether the comparison should use a relative or absolute tolerance criterion. In addition, the test harness again generates frequency counts and execution times, providing an indication of the cost of the monitoring and evaluation, particularly when compared with the similar data generated by the test harness in generate mode (this output is indicated by a plus on the printed output line from the test harness icon in Figure 1).

The operation of the application with the test harness installed implies a relationship between the flow in generate and check mode. This relationship is that the two runs (likely with different versions of the application) must visit the same monitored procedures in the same order. Consequently, the monitoring must be with variables and procedures that are not expected to be vastly different in structure. This is often the case for changes that involve differences of optimization, code modification for efficiency improvements, and a whole host of other practical reasons why the codes are different.

To detect only differences in code flow, the test harness can installed in both versions so that it monitors no application data but monitors only code flow through the monitored procedures; this is sometimes very useful to know in diagnosing the cause of different results in two codes that are supposed to produce the same results.

Figure 2 shows the kinds of "include" lines added to a main program; these "include" lines are required in the main program but are only needed in procedures whose data or operation is being monitored. The "include" lines are similar for any subprogram unit selected for monitoring. An "include" line is required for each additional probe point and each exit from a procedure being monitored. No application-code data need be monitored, in which case the TH is recording and/or comparing an execution trace of the application code through the monitored application subprograms.

Currently, the "include" lines are inserted by hand. The particular "include" lines depend on whether the procedure is an internal procedure, module procedure, and external procedure. Also, the "include" line insertions are different for F compliant code [1] versus Fortran 90/95/2003 [2] compliant code. The "include" line insertions are specified in detail in the User's Guide [3] for the test harness; a future tool, currently designed and partially implemented, will perform the required insertions in all procedures of an application and will monitor all eligible variables that are potentially referenced by the procedure and potentially defined by the procedure at entry points to and exit points from the procedure. As shown in Figure 2, the "include" lines are spelled with the keyword "binclude", in order to distinguish them from Fortran include lines; whether they are spelled "binclude" or "include" or some other way is specified in the input to the builder tool.

Once the procedures for monitoring are selected, the variables in these procedures are determined. The "include" lines are inserted, and the builder tool builds the application specific "include" files. Then an includer tool is run in one of two ways; one way builds the application with active version of the "include" files illustrated in Figure 1; a second way builds the application with the test harness disabled or inactive, thus providing a production version of the application code where there is no interference from the test harness. These alternative ways of generating executable code permit one version of the code to be maintained and at application build time, the user has the choice of building the application for testing or production.

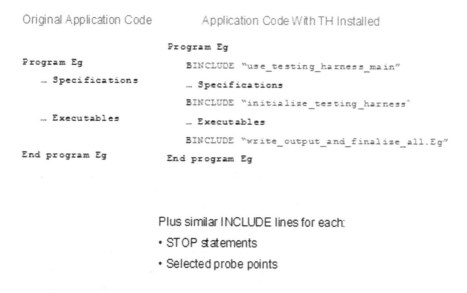

Figure 2: Installing the Test Harness in the main program - an example

2.2   The Usage Scenario

Figure 3 illustrates the use of the test harness over time, with time progressing from the left side of the figure to the right side; also the code is being developed and enhanced as time progresses. The figure actually depicts the development of the builder tool itself. Initially, an earlier version of the application code has the test harness installed into it; this is depicted at the left of the figure. A test suite is obtained or developed for this early version and the application code with the test installed and activated is run in generate mode for all the test cases. With the test harness in the application code, the application code is modified, being improved in efficiency or capability, or just ported to a different machine. The code is then run in check mode with the same test cases and the new results are compared with the previous results. When corrections are made, the code is rerun and the results compared again until the results are acceptable.

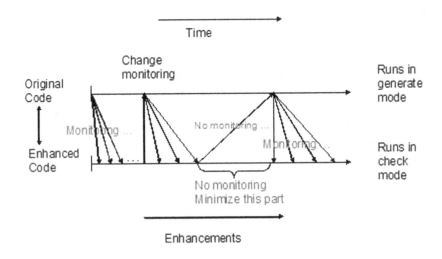

Figure 3: Test Harness Usage Scenario

At some point, what is monitored may be changed (as indicated in the left middle of the figure) and maybe new test cases are developed; at such a time, the application with the test harness installed is rerun in generate mode, creating a new collection of recorded results, which are then compared to evaluate the effect of the further changes and enhancements. Occasionally, changes will be made that cannot be monitored with the test harness (for example, changes that cause monitored execution flow to be different between the code run in generate mode and check mode) unless what is monitored is changed; this is depicted in the figure just left of the middle of the figure. Finally, the code reaches a state where its performance is satisfactory (extreme right of the figure) and it is put into production. The test harness can remain installed in the code but made inactive ready for future activation and further evaluation when investigating new test cases.

The above scenario was followed in the development of the builder tool itself. An early version of the test harness was installed in the initial version of the builder tool code. The builder tool uses floating point computations sparingly but the test harness allows comparisons of data values of all intrinsic types; comparisons for identity of integer, logical, and character values immediately indicated unexpected in parts of the code that used to work before certain enhancements were made.

Once the test harness is installed in an application, it measures and displays the execution times and counts of the monitored subprograms, and the sizes of the check data created by each monitoring probe. This information is useful in controlling the size of the check data files. This becomes a problem either because the place where the data is monitored is executed too frequently or the data monitored is too voluminous. Although the test harness has been successfully used to monitor data where the check data file became as large as 10 gigabytes, the monitoring process may be timing consuming and may need to be curtailed.

To curtail the size of the monitored data, the frequency that each probe generates or check its data may be decreased. Also, for arrays, the elements that are monitored may be specified so that an entire array is not monitored. For each of these changes, the test harness has to be reinstalled into the application using the builder tool to implement the changes.

In addition, the comparison routines can be replaced by comparators that compare norms of matrices or compute condition numbers and compare them, or evaluate the differences in the result in any desired way. Such replacement comparators may be motivated to reduce the monitored data sizes but may also be motivated to focus on the comparisons of significant aspects of the computation that are particularly meaningful to the application. In each of these cases, the test harness has to be rebuilt into the application code by rerunning the builder tool.

3.0   Installation of the Test Harness in an Application Code

The installation of the test harness into an application code requires three steps. First, the "include" lines are inserted into the application code as per the instructions given in [3] and exemplified in Figure 2. Typically, three or four "include" lines are inserted per procedure monitored; the text of the "include" files USE statements, CALL statements, testing harness initialization code, and test harness cleanup code. In addition, an "include" line is needed for each probe that is additional to those at each entry and exit point from each procedure monitored. Any number of additional probes can be inserted at any desired points.

The second step is to prepare the input to the builder tool. It is typically one input file (the builder can be run on parts of the application code but each run of the builder tool requires an input file). This input file specifies the following:
- The input file containing the application code with inserted "include" lines.
- The output file containing the application code modified appropriately to use the test harness.
- The input directory containing the template "include" files
- The output directory containing the specific "include" files activating the test harness.
- The output directory containing the specific "include" files for an inactive test harness.
- The "include" line keyword used in addition to BINCLUDE processed by the builder tool; if it is spelled "include", it will process Fortran INCLUDE lines and if blank or spelled some other way, it ignores the contents of the Fortran INCLUDE files.
- "code" blocks specifying
  o the name of the procedure to monitor
  o the variables monitored on input to the procedure

o the variables monitored on exit from the procedure

o the variables monitored at each specific named probe point

For each variable monitored, the relative error tolerance (relative to machine epsilon) and the absolute error tolerances can be specified; if not specified, the tolerances are zero, requiring identity to pass the comparison tests. There are a collection of other properties that can be specified, such as lower bounds for arrays and selected ranges of elements of arrays to check (required for assumed-size arrays).

The third step is to run first the builder tool with its input and then the includer tool with its modest input (location of directories, input file, output file, and logical unit specifications to avoid portability problems with the tools specifying input/output units not supported in the same way the default units are assumed to be used). The result of running both tools is either the application code with an activated test harness installed in it or an inactivated test harness. In the first case, the application can then be run using the scenario exemplified by Figures 1 and 3. Code enhancements should be implemented in the version of the code after the first step above so that the enhancements can be installed without repeating the building steps unnecessarily.

3.1   Code Insertion into the Application Code

The code lines inserted by hand are "include" lines. However, there is a minor difficulty in this process when the insertion point is prior to any labeled statement, like a RETURN, END, or STOP. In addition, there is no place to insert a probe after an IF statement test but before the object of the IF statement is executed. The problem is that the insertions are essentially INCLUDE lines referring to files containing executable code and must be on a separate line, as required by the Fortran language. To make code insertions in these case, the code has to be restructured using block IF constructs or labeled CONTINUE statements.

As mentioned in 5.0, an additional tool is under development that will insert the required lines in specified places, avoiding such changes by hand. This tool is rather complex because it also is creating default variables to monitor. Refer to 5.0 for a complete description of this and other tools being planned.

In all cases, the source form of the inserted code satisfies both the requirements of fixed form Fortran source or free form Fortran source. Thus, the application code can be written in either free or fixed source form and in Fortran 77, Fortran 90, Fortran 95, Fortran 2003, or F compliant code. The compiler used to compile the application code with the test harness installed must be either a Fortran 90/95/2003 or F compliant compiler.

3.2   Building the Test Harness from Templates

The builder tool builds the test harness into the application by processing template "include". Typically, the builder creates a large number of such specific include files and places them in a separate directory, called the active directory. A second directory of "include" files is created by this tool, which is referred to as the empty or inactive "include" files. A second tool, called the includer, is then run which builds the complete application from the directories of files created by the builder tool. The input to the includer tool specifies which directory of specific "include" files are to be used, building the application using either the active test harness or the inactive test harness.

The template files are in detail in [4].

3.3   Test Harness Input

The test harness input is read from standard input by default and specifies the following items:

- The test harness mode; the mode is either generate, check_and_continue, or check_but_terminate. The mode check_and_continue continues to the completion of the application code no matter what violations of the comparison tolerances are detected. The mode check_but_terminate terminates after the completion of the checking for a probe when the first difference violating the comparison tolerances is found.
- Print performance execution times or not. The execution time for each monitored procedure is printed.
- Print storage information in generate mode. This information includes the size of the data in the unformatted file generated per procedure; the unit size is processor-dependent but on most systems is either a byte or single precision or default real word.

A named input file can be provided to override the input/output units used by the test harness and avoid conflicts with those units used by the application. If not provided, default units are selected. These units specify the test harness input described above, the unit for debugging output, the unit for the unformatted check data file, and error diagnostic unit.

3.4   Performance Of the Test Harness Tools and the Harness Itself

The builder and includer tools perform their builds very quickly, typically in considerably less time than it takes to compile the code, with or without the test harness installed.

The test harness itself does impact the performance of the application code but that depends very directly on the amount of data monitored and the speed of the input/output system. For modest data sizes, say less than a few megabytes, the performance penalty is at most a few seconds; in generate mode, it is hardly noticeable; in check mode, it is typically less than 3 seconds. It is more in check mode because reading unformatted files takes longer and the comparison checks, especially for large arrays, can take some time. As another measure of performance, the test harness added approximately 30 seconds to an application run when creating a 10 gigabyte test file while the application code ran for approximately 10 minutes with and without the test harness code activated.

As suggested above, performance is very dependent on how much data is being monitored. To see how much data is being generated and how long it is taking, the test harness should be run, specifying in its input, "performance" and "storage" in generate mode and "performance" in check mode. Analyzing the tables of storage sizes and performance per procedure will provide an understanding of where the large data and costly performance is coming from. As mentioned above, decreasing the recording and checking frequency, decreasing data monitored per procedure, or decreasing the number of procedures monitored can address performance issues, if and when, costly performance issues are encountered.

Performance timing is always an issue and is very system dependent. The test harness code uses one of three alternative timers; a Fortran 90 timer, and two alternative timers that are available on many Unix/Linux systems. The timing performance procedures are in a visible separate module and are selected by commenting out Fortran lines. In addition, your own reliable timer can be substituted for any of them, provided the module procedure returns time in units of seconds. The Fortran intrinsic procedure CPU_TIME is used by default.

4.0   Experiences with Testing the Test Harness

The tests performed to date have been of varying sorts. First, five serial codes taken from a tutorial for PARAWISE from Parallel Software Products Inc [2]. The tutorial involved the use of test codes implementing a simple 1-D Jacobi algorithm, a 2-D heat conduction and diffusion problem, a 2-D steady state flow prediction code, a simple unstructured mesh algorithm, and the serial version of the NAS-PAR benchmark APPLU. All five application codes were written Fortran 77 using fixed source forms. Each code was then rewritten completely using Fortran 90/95 constructs to the fullest extent, and in particular arrays and modules, including the conversion of block data subprograms to modules. In addition, the source code of the Fortran 90/95 versions is written in free source form. The tests involved running the original Fortran 77 code in generate mode and the Fortran 90/95 code in check mode, comparing the results. In all cases, after fixing various errors in the initial conversion process, the two versions create consistent or comparable results as measured by the test harness.

In two of these codes, the results were most interesting. In the NAS-PAR benchmark, the initial results showed a drastic difference after fixing the conversion errors detected by the test harness. The cause of the final differences was the use of intrinsic function SUM to perform sums rather than use of loops to perform the summations. After several runs using the test harness, the cause of the difference was quickly rectified by using the loop form of the computation rather than the SUM intrinsic in the sense that the differences were reduced to small numbers of rounding errors.

Using the test harness with the 2-D steady state flow prediction code represented a second interesting test case. The input data set used, if run for a large enough number of iterations, shows numerical instability. The original Fortran 77 and the converted Fortran 90 versions display the instability at different numbers of iterations. Using the test harness, one is able to monitor the instability and see how the two versions exhibit the instability at different points in the run. The differences are again attributed to the use of intrinsic functions rather than code loops and can be exposed in the comparative runs using the test harness.

These five test cases are interesting from another aspect. Although the Fortran 90 codes are drastically different than the original Fortran 77 codes, the computation order remained the same using the same input test file. This was partially accomplished by not monitoring data in places and procedures where the execution sequences were different between the two versions of the code. But it also illustrates that major changes in code structure can be performed without distributing the execution sequences in a way that matters to the monitoring.

Initially, a parallel SPMD code was used in developing the design of the test harness. Quickly, it became apparent that a solid serial version was needed first and a version for parallel SPMD code would readily follow. However, the parallel code test harness code has not been tested with the latest version of the test harness, desiring to complete the various needed tools for serial code before addressing in detail the parallel code issues.

4.1   Installation Tests

The test harness is distributed with five installation tests. The simplest one is manufactured test code (that is, constructed to test a few difficult corners of the testing process) but it otherwise is performing silly computations. In particular, the test uses external procedures with entry procedures, both functions and subroutines, including recursive procedures. It is written in two forms, fixed and free source form.

A second set of manufactured installation tests is a collection of 32 programs, one of which is the above test. These additional tests include internal procedures, module procedures, modules, internal and entry procedures in module procedures, and recursive procedures, both functions and subroutines. Also, several of the tests use test code that is F compliant where the "include" lines, to remain F compliant, are required to be different.

Several of these 32 tests check a rather nasty implementation issue with the test harness. The test harness operates by creating internal procedures within the application procedures that perform the generation of the check data files and comparison of the check data files with data from the application when in check mode. This approach is used so that the scope of application procedure is inherited by the harness procedure and thus has access to application data environment without the use of common blocks or long lists of arguments. But because Fortran does not permit internal procedures within internals procedures, this approach had to be replaced by generating code in line to create and read the check data files. In both cases but particularly in the latter case, there is the possibility that variables created for use exclusively by the test harness clash with (have the same names as) application variables. To avoid this conflict and consequent limitation, the generated variable names may be prefixed by a user-specified letter string that is specified by the user to avoid name conflicts. Several of the test cases test this capability.

As a final point, these manufactured test cases can be used as tutorial examples; they illustrate the locations and forms of the inserted "include" lines that are inserted into the codes depending on the procedures and modules, including entry procedures, used in the application code.

4.2   Installation Application Tests

Three of the five application codes are also provided as installation tests. They include the simple 1-D Jacobian code which consists only of a main program and can again be used as an example to follow and study. The other two application installation tests are the APPLU NAS-PAR code and the 2-D steady state flow prediction code that shows the instability with the test input file provided. It is valuable and informative to look at how the tolerances where specified and had to be relaxed so that the test harness would allow the Fortran 90 version to complete execution.

4.3   Documentation

The documentation consists of an overview description [4] of the test harness and a User's Guide [3]. This overview describes the motivation and objectives of the test harness tool, its input, its default output, and its debugging output. It describes the tests in detail that were used to develop the test harness and the role and purpose of each of the "include" files inserted into the application code. Finally, it lists the planned enhancements to the test harness for the next year or so.

The User's Guide gives detailed instructions on where and what include lines need to be inserted into the application code. The User Guide also describes the builder tool's input, which specifies the procedures to be monitored, the variables in those procedures to be monitored, and the particular probes monitoring those variables. Along with the variables are specified their type, kind, rank, and dimension information, how much of an array is to be monitored, the tolerances for performing the comparisons (an absolute tolerance, a relative tolerance, a combination of both, and for arrays, whether the comparison is element-wise or with respect to a norm). In addition, the builder input specifies the frequency each particular probe is executed and debugging information printed (the compared data can be printed but is not recommended in general).

5.0   Future Developments and Plans

Finally, the following planned enhancements of the test harness are in design and partially implemented: 1) an additional tool to automate the insertion of the "include" lines into arbitrary Fortran code and generation of two builder input files; one that monitors no variables but provides builder input for all procedures in the application, and secondly one that monitors all input and output variables to all procedures of the application; 2) portable data formats for all checked data; 3) a C implementation of the template files, permitting C or mixed Fortran/C applications to be monitored, and 4) support for parallel SPMD MPI codes.

5.1   Portable Numeric Formats

There are currently two candidate libraries of procedures being investigated to support portable numeric formats; HDF5[6] and netCDF[7]. The plan is to select one of these and provide the libraries with the distribution to support one of these portable formats. With these formats, comparisons of results between different platforms will be facilitated; currently one has to use with formatted input/output which is not very satisfactory; unformatted input/output is processor-dependent and does not port in general between platforms.

5.2   Enhancements to the Support Tools

The very tedious and error prone aspect of installing the test harness in a large application is the insertion of the "include" lines and the preparation of the builder input files, specifying the variables is to be monitored, their properties (rank, shape), and the error tolerances. This represents a problem for two reasons; the first is it involves the preparation of many lines of files, and secondly, when they are wrong, the diagnostics by the builder tool, the compiler, or test harness itself are obscure and vague, because the errors can only be detected long after reading the input files where the error is present. To overcome this problem, a third tool has been designed and is partially implemented at the time of writing this paper. The tool will insert the correct "include" lines, modify the application source code to avoid the problems with labeled STOP, RETURN, and END statements, and IF statements. Secondly, it will create sample builder input files that can be readily modified by the user but will supply a list of all input and output variables for all procedures in the application. Thus, the new tool performs a sufficiently complete analysis of the application software to generate the need code and avoid the need to have redundant specifications from the user. Future versions of the tool will limit the building of these files to selected procedures specified by the user.

This tool will be written in portable Fortran 95 and available in all distributions. It essentially has to create a complete symbol table for the application, including the attributes of the variables needed to insert the test harness in the application code. However, this implementation is viewed as a reference version that will specify the functionality of the tool; efficient, compiler-specific implementations will likely follow that use the symbol tables generated by the compiler. The tool will be written using an API that will permit the development of symbol-table access procedures to any particular compiler, thereby taking advantage of the efficiency, robustness, and reliability of compiler-generated symbol tables that the reference version is unlikely to ever exhibit.

Once the design and reference implementation is complete, consideration of an implementation that uses a graphics-user interface and menus integrated into a Photran[6] environment will be considered. Such an implementation would then take advantage of the existing and upcoming tools supported by the Photran environment, permitting the development of an integrated maintenance environment for large application codes.

5.3   A C Version of the Test Harness

In its current form without the new tool described in 5.2, the dependence on Fortran is limited mainly to the template file used to create the application specific "include" files. The builder and includer tools restrict their knowledge of Fortran to its line continuation rules in the main. Thus, to create a version of the test harness for C and mixed Fortran/C codes, the template files need to be rewritten in C.

5.4   A SPMD Parallel Version of the Test Harness

The original idea for the test harness came from trying to debug a parallel SPMD code. The test harness's design was to support such code but has not been implemented on such code because the serial capabilities at the time were missing and were also needed for an SPMD implementation. Consequently, the plan is to revisit the development of code for such applications; the main issue is that each processor must create its own check data file and be able to read it in check mode. As with the serial version, the easiest and most frequently needed case is that each processor executes the code in the same execution sequence between the original and modified codes. Many codes behave this way and for these cases, a parallel version of the test harness is planned.

6.0   Implementations

Version 0.6 of the test harness has been installed and tested on the following platforms:
- Linux X86 using the NAG f95, GNU g95, and PGI pgf90 compilers
- Linux EM64T systems using the NAG f95 and GNU g95
- SUSE Linux and AIX using the IBM xlf95
- Cygwin using the NAG f95, GNU g95, CVF and Lahey Fortran compilers
- Windows XP using the CVF, Lahey, and Intel Fortran compilers

Version 0.6 of the test harness with documentation and installation tests is available on CD from the author.

7.0   Summary

A test harness for comparing versions of scientific computational software has been developed. Its main features including the comparison of floating point data by comparators that report only significant differences in the computed data. The criterion used to measure differences is based on relative and absolute tolerances specified by the user. The test harness is very effective at determining that modifications and enhancements to versions of application code maintain the same results as with previous test cases without performing tedious hand comparisons on pages of data.

References

[1] Brainerd, W. S., The F programming language, http://www.fortran.com/F, 2005

[2] Metcalf, M, Reid, J. K, and Cohen, M. Fortran 95/2003 Explained, Numerical Mathematics and Scientific Computation, 2004

[3] Smith, B. T., Creating a test data environment to detect errors in the code conversion process -- an overview, Version 0.6, Nov. 2005

[4] Smith, B. T., The test harness user's guide, Version 0.6, Nov. 2005

[5] PARAWISE, The Computer Aided Parallelization Toolkit, Tutorial Guide, Version 2.4, June 2004, http://www.parallelsp.com

[6] HDF5, http://www.hdfgroup.org/HDF5/, 2006

[7] NetCDF, http://www.unidata.ucar.edu/software/netcdf, 2006

[8] Photran, http://www.eclipse.org/photran, 2006

Q&A – Brian Smith

Questioner: William Gropp

Why did you choose HDF5 instead of another library such as netCDF??

Brian Smith

I had the HDF5 library recommended to me by various colleagues at UNM and NCSA and was not aware of the netCDF library. I was attracted to HDF5 by the fact that the source is available for creating implementations on essentially arbitrary combinations of compilers and operating systems on which the test harness is to be used. The most effective compiler I use for diagnosing non-standard Fortran is the NAG f95 compiler. Unfortunately, the NAG compiler diagnosed the use of several non-standard features which I have not had the opportunity to correct and for the time being I have given up trying to use HDF5. My understanding from discussions after my presentation is that other people have experienced the same problems and recently a revised source of HDF5 is available that avoids these difficulties. Also, during the discussions, I became aware that netCDF is simpler than HDF5 and in addition is not as comprehensive as HDF5 but has the capabilities I need for the test harness. I will now look into both systems.

Questioner: Ian Reid

Can this tool be sensibly used during porting as well as during development?

Brian Smith

Yes. The test harness was designed with porting in mind and is straightforward to use to evaluate the correctness of a port. First, the source code is written in portable Fortran -- a Fortran 90, Fortran 95, and an F (a restricted subset of Fortran 95 that encourages the use of safe Fortran constructs) compliant versions. The source code has been tested currently on over 10 platforms. Secondly, the code created by the tools to install the test harness in the application code is Fortran 90 and F compliant, and is written in a manner to simultaneously be both fixed and free source form compliant, assuming very modest free source form requirements such as lines no longer than 72 characters.

But there is one caveat. Clearly, the tool is only as effective in this role as the test cases are comprehensive in testing the code for a correct port. The effectiveness of the test harness relies on the coverage of the test cases; if the test cases cover the areas that evaluate the portability of the code, the test harness will perform the tests and compare the results, indicating whether the original results are the "same" as the results on the machine to which the code is being ported.

Questioner: Jim Pool

Are any of the five test cases you mentioned library programs we might recognize?

Brian Smith

Yes and no. The application tests are five standard numerical applications: a simple 1-D Jacobi algorithm, a 2-D heat conduction and diffusion problem, a 2-D steady state flow prediction code, a simple unstructured mesh algorithm, and the serial version of the NAS-PAR benchmark APPLU. The first three test application codes are distributed with the test harness software and are used as installation tests. In addition, there is a simple test case on the distribution disk that tests the installation of the test harness in external procedures with entry procedures and a second set of 32 test cases that test the use of the test harness with various other Fortran 90/95 constructs such as internal procedures, and module procedures with entry procedures in various configurations. Finally, I am currently evaluating the test harness using a commercial code of over forty thousand lines of Fortran 77 code. This code is large enough that installing the test harness in the code and creating the input files for the builder tool is tedious and error prone. To overcome this problem, I have designed and begun the implementation of a tool which analyzes the application code, creates the needed input files for the builder tool, and with the builder tool installs with test harness in the application code without requiring hand modifications.

Questioner: Boyana Norris

Have you considered using tools such as the Program Database Toolkit (PDT) for generating a language independent program representation?

Brian Smith

No. But as a consequence of your question, I will look into this toolkit and see how I can use it.

Questioner: Boyana Norris

Are there plans to add support for languages other than Fortran?

Brian Smith

Yes. Certainly C. For the builder and includer tools, a C version of the test harness is straightforward, I believe. It includes rewriting the template files in C and involves rather modest modifications to these two tools, mainly to impose C line continuation rules rather than Fortran rules. For the new tool which installs the test harness into code, a completely new implementation is required because it is essentially a lexer and parser. However, the current version of this new tool is designed to use access procedures to a symbol table generated by a compiler. Re-implementing this new tool for C code implies the access procedures need to be rewritten; hopefully, the design of the rest of the tool is such that very little of it depends on the details of the programming language.

Questioner: Marc Garbey

When code is run on different architectures the difference in numerical results may be the result of ill-conditioning; is there a quantitative test for this problem?

Brian Smith

Yes and no. Such quantitative tests depend on the application. For example, such tests are known for many linear equation and matrix eigensystem computations. Such tests depend on the existence of sensitivity analysis for the application. For the linear equation problem, for example, condition numbers provide the crucial mechanism. Other application areas have similar sensitivity analysis available. The point, though, for the test harness, is that the evaluation/comparison procedures used by default by the test harness are replaceable with code using the same interface. Alternatively, because the test harness code that calls the evaluation/comparison procedures is accessible (embedded in the application code), the user can replace calls to these evaluation routines to calls of procedures of his/her own so that codes using sensitivity analysis, such as condition number generators, can be called and used to evaluate the numerical results with respect to ill-conditioning.

Questioner: Wayne Enright

You used the terms "numerically indistinguishable" and "equivalent" when comparing solutions from different versions of a code. How do these differ and how hard is it to decide if they apply?

Brian Smith

I use these terms to distinguish between two situations which unfortunately are very similar. I reserve the word "equivalent" to mean two results are considered the "same" because they differ by only a few units in the last place and typically I have no error or sensitivity analysis that would suggest that large differences are expected. I reserve the word "indistinguishable" for cases where, because of an error analysis or sensitivity analysis, I can predict expected differences and the observed differences are less than the predicted differences. Thus, the differences are related to whether I can back up observed differences with analysis. The difficulty thus in deciding which applies is easy, but often the required analysis is hard or nonexistent.

Tuesday PM Panel Discussion

Panel

- Asim YarKhan
- Brian Smith
- Keith Jackson
- Xiaoge Wang

Questioner: Ron Boisvert

What do you think will ultimately be the "sweet spot" for scientific/numeric grid services, not only from a technical point-of-view, but more importantly from a business viability point-of-view? For example, will services only provide access to monolithic applications, or would individual lower-level numerical library routines ever make a viable service?

Keith Jackson and Asim YarKhan

It is hard to specify such a "sweet spot". It might be that when the online services provide some additional value, beyond the direct answer to a user request, then end users will be drawn to it; for example, if the numerical routines can embed additional expert knowledge, or can provide accuracy analysis.

Brian Smith

Personally, I cannot see how a business supplying just low-level numerical routines and a service that supports them can be commercial success. The main reasons are that the market for such an activity is not large enough (the market is mainly the vendors that manufacture central processing units and there are not a lot of them) and many people believe that such low-level routines can be created from following algorithms published in the literature and can be obtained from open source repositories. The vendors thus hire experts in the field to develop their own low-level libraries and maintain them over the lifetime of their particular computational architectures.

Where I think there is a potential "sweet spot" for scientific/numeric grid services is in the evaluation of solutions provided by the grid services. The solution sought by the application users are typically a solution to an equation or model of some kind. Software that uses the grid to evaluate a solution against a set of properties the solution must satisfy and provides some sensitivity rating for the solution would be very valuable. Such evaluations could be done a priori and with cycles that are potentially abundant over the grid. However, the creation of software to perform such evaluations on demand is not available now and needs research by our community to develop such software.

Comment: Brian Ford

The sweet-spot may be providing mathematical support to the grid users who come knowing they themselves do not have the necessary mathematics background -- providing that support for them and enabling them to introduce "the solutions" in their environment.

Asim YarKhan

There are some projects to recommend the appropriate algorithm based on the input data sets. For example, the SALSA (Self-Adapting Large-scale Solver Architecture) project analyzes the input sparse matrix and uses statistical knowledge and heuristics to recommend the appropriate solver for the data. GridSolve will add libraries such as this to its remote solving, thus pushing the expert knowledge into the solver rather than expecting the end-user to provide it.

Brian Smith

Yes. I agree but again new initiatives are needed to develop the software that can support applications in this way. It is not clear to me how to do it but is that not want research initiatives are supposed to answer for us?

Comment and Question: Jim Pool

What Brian Ford has suggested requires the numerical software to return more than a simple solution as in current libraries. In GridSolve and using Python wrappers have you had to modify routines or would you have preferred modified routines?

Keith Jackson and Asim YarKhan

GridSolve has generally not modified the numerical routines for its use. However, at the University of Tennessee, we have various projects to provide added value to numerical libraries by embedding some expert knowledge or self-adapting algorithms (see the SALSA and SANS efforts at http://icl.cs.utk.edu/iclprojects/).

Brian Smith

I have had no experience with modifying software for this purpose or using such software.

Comment and Question: Patrick Gaffney

Allowing a user to specify their problem in the language of their own problem domain opens up for the possibility that the specification is numerically unwise; for example "I want to invert a matrix." How do you propose to address this issue with Web services?

Keith Jackson

I believe the service writers are going to have to become smarter. The service itself should check for situations like inverting a matrix and inform the user that what they are doing is unwise. Currently numerical codes are written assuming a high degree of sophistication on the part of the users. As we move more towards a service based architecture, that assumption is no longer going to hold. This will be a large adjustment for the people who write numerical codes, but it will also open their usage to a much broader community.

Brian Smith

We have long had to deal with this problem and in general try to either warn the user that such computations are numerically unwise or not make it easy for the user to perform such computations. Possibly, in the environment where the numerical software is reporting back to the user how sensitive the computed solution is to rounding errors or changes in the input data, such unwise numerical computations will become more apparent to the user.

Comment: Ian Reid

The sweet-spot is likely to be solving widely applicable problems not wrapping sub problems (for example, BLAS routines). This, I think, stems from what Brian Ford mentioned.

Comment: Jim Pool

It was a decade between the development of AMDLIB (Applied Mathematics Division Library) at ANL and the emergence of NAG and IMSL. It requires a long time to transition from demonstration to acceptance and then commercialization.

Questioner: Wayne Enright

Do you feel that the type of verification checks on condition estimates we can determine for a particular data-set/problem can be automatically returned (at a cost) on available as a post-processing step?

Brian Smith

I do not think we have the algorithms and software to do it today, but I think given the need for such condition estimates and the computational resources now readily available to compute such estimates, we need to perform the research to investigate how to do this for a wide variety of problems. The issue in the past, in my opinion, is the scarcity of resources to perform such evaluations made doing so unattractive; computational resources are more plentiful now and in addition the need for solutions you can stand behind and vouch for is now becoming an issue for software producers.

Questioner: Bill Applebe

Can numerical software design make use of experience in commercial software verification and validation?

Brian Smith

I find this difficult to answer. From my experience, verification and validation for most commercial software means extensive testing and evaluation, often using regression tests extensively. Numerical software, if carefully prepared, does the same verification and validation. But where numerical software is backed by sound mathematical analysis, more can often be done. In addition, such testing for numerical software can be enhanced by the using identities and mathematical relationships that must be satisfied by the computed solution. As mentioned earlier, the Grid computational environment gives us an opportunity to do more of that kind of testing, providing our users with more robust and reliable software and solutions.

Questioner: Brian Ford

Is the separation between the group pressing for final digit accuracy in their answers and the group likely to use the grid who are perceived to be looking for reliable and solved problems a distinction recognized in the computer solution market? Can this be marketed?

Brian Smith

Is the separation between the group pressing for final digit accuracy in their answers and the group likely to use the grid who are perceived to be looking for reliable and solved problems a distinction recognized in the computer solution market? Can this be marketed?

Comment: Marc Garbey

Solution verification is becoming a serious issue since Mechanical Engineering is often taught using software only. Important design decisions are set with no serious verification. The Grid gives an additional opportunity to solve this problem.

Comment: Craig Douglas

The educational system has failed. Students do not know enough about math or computer science to do computational science or Grid computing. They know XML, but have no knowledge of C, C++, Fortran or any historical programming language or model.

How can they be expected to know even how to get an answer, much less know if it is wrong, correct, or inconclusive?

Comment: Bill Applebe

Verifying package codes is somewhat easier as techniques such as "grid independence" (runs on multiple grid scales) or a comparison on two different commercial packages can be used.

Questioner: William Gropp

Debugging was mentioned by several of the speakers

What can be done to aid in the debugging of web services and grid components? Should support for debugging be part of the design?

Xiaoge Wang

It would certainly be very helpful if there is something that can help with debugging. But on the other hand, using a provided service may not always match the thing in the user's mind. There is more or less different between custom-made and off-the-shelf things. So, it may need the application developers to be more "tolerant" or flexible in the application design. In the real world, a feature in someone's opinion may be thinking of as a bug by someone else. It will be very difficult in debug when using services.

Brian Smith

Yes. Debugging should be part of the design. Mainly, I think the web services and grid components should have a mode, like a verbose mode, that returns information to the user about the progress of the service or component. The user, after gaining some experience with situations where the services and components are behaving both correctly and incorrectly, can adjust what services he/she uses when and how he/she uses the services. In return, it would enhance the information back to the developers when the user complains about a service or component not working properly. Secondly, the verbose mode should be designed to report on user requests that are incorrect, can not be fulfilled with the resources available in a reasonable time, or tax the system in ways that will cause the requests to be delayed or take considerable time. Such information is useful to the user so that he/she can tailor their use of the services and components in the most effective way.

Questioner: William Gropp

To Brian Smith:
Based on your experience with TH, what features would aid in providing debugging services?

Brian Smith

In terms of debugging over a grid, the biggest single debugging problem is an old serial (and parallel) code problem -- uninitialized memory. Grid computing exacerbates the problem because the resulting code does not port and it is extremely difficult to detect that this is the cause of incorrect results. Most systems have special local techniques to detect uninitialized memory but a uniform, across-the-grid, methodology to address this issue would be a great help.

Comment: Bill Applebe

What is needed is the ability to easily instrument the code without modifying the source to log/profile data and generate visualizations (St Germain has it).

Comment: Boyana Norris

Automated debugging support in SIDL-based CCA components is being developed (allowing the component application execution to be "replayed") -- similar approaches should be possible for services or other component systems.

Comment: Keith Jackson

The NetLogger project I mentioned earlier has some simple tools that will automatically add logging information at each function entrance and exit. This currently supports, C, C++, Fortran, and Python.

PART 5

EVENT DRIVEN APPLICATIONS

D. Gannon, Session Chair; W. Enright, Discussant

C. Douglas: *Dynamic Data-Driven Application Systems for Empty Houses, Contaminant Tracking, and Wildfire Fireline Prediction*

G. Allen: *Designing a Dynamic Data Driven Application System for Coastal and Environmental Modeling*

S. Nadella: *SPRUCE: A System for Supporting Urgent High Performance Computing*

B. Plale: *Data Mangement in Dynamic Environment Driven Computational Science*

Dynamic Data-Driven Application Systems for Empty Houses, Contaminat Tracking, and Wildland Fireline Prediction

Craig C. Douglas[1,2], Divya Bansal[1], Jonathan D. Beezley[3], Lynn S. Bennethum[3], Soham Chakraborty[1], Janice L. Coen[4], Yalchin Efendiev[5], Richard E. Ewing[5], Jay Hatcher[1], Mohamed Iskandarani[6], Christopher R. Johnson[7], Deng Li[1], Minjeong Kim[3], Robert A. Lodder[8], Jan Mandel[3], Guan Qin[5], and Anthony Vodacek[9]

1 University of Kentucky, Department of Computer Science, 773 Anderson Hall, Lexington, KY 40506-0046, USA.

2 Yale University, Department of Computer Science, P.O. Box 208285, New Haven, CT 06520-8285, USA.

3 University of Colorado at Denver and Health Sciences Center, Department of Mathematical Sciences, P.O. Box 173364, Denver, CO 80217-3364, USA.

4 National Center for Atmospheric Research, P.O. Box 3000, Boulder, CO 80307-3000, USA.

5 Texas A&M University, Institute for Scientific Computation, 612 Blocker, 3404 TAMU, College Station, TX, 77843-3404, USA.

6 University of Miami, Rosenstiel School, of Marine and Atmospheric Science, 4600 Rickenbacker Causeway, Miami, FL 33149-1098, USA.

7 University of Utah, Scientific Computing and Imaging Institute, Salt Lake City, UT 84112, USA.

8 University of Kentucky, Department of Chemistry, Lexington, KY, 40506 USA.

9 Rochester Institute of Technology, Center for Imaging Science, Rochester, NY 14623 USA.

Abstract. We describe three different dynamic data-driven applications systems (DDDAS): an empty house, a contaminant identification and tracking, and a wildland fire. Each has something in common with all of the rest and can use some common tools. Each DDDAS is quite complicated in comparison to a traditional static input simulation that is run with large numbers of inputs instead of one longer run that is self-correcting.

Please use the following format when citing this chapter:

Douglas, C. C., Bansal, D., Beezley, J. D., Bennethum, L. S., Chakraborty, S., Coen, J. L., Efendiev, Y., Ewing, R. E., Hatcher J. Iskandarani, M., Johnson, C. R., Li, D., Kim, M., Lodder, R., Mandel, J., Qin, G., Vodacek, A., 2007, in IFIP International Federation for Information Processing, Volume 239, Grid-Based Problem Solving Environments, eds. Gaffney, P. W., Pool, J.C.T., (Boston: Springer), pp. 255-272.

1   Introduction

We quote from the 2005 dynamic data-driven application systems (DDDAS) National Science Foundation solicitation [1], "DDDAS is a paradigm whereby application (or simulations) and measurements become a symbiotic feedback control system. DDDAS entails the ability to dynamically incorporate additional data into an executing application, and in reverse, the ability of an application to dynamically steer the measurement process. Such capabilities promise more accurate analysis and prediction, more precise controls, and more reliable outcomes. The ability of an application to control and guide the measurement process and determine when, where, and how it is best to gather additional data has itself the potential of enabling more effective measurement methodologies. Furthermore, the incorporation of dynamic inputs into an executing application invokes new system modalities and helps create application software systems that can more accurately describe real world, complex systems. This enables the development of applications that intelligently adapt to evolving conditions and that infer new knowledge in ways that are not predetermined by the initialization parameters and initial static data. The need for such dynamic applications is already emerging in business, engineering and scientific processes, analysis, and design. Manufacturing process controls, resource management, weather and climate prediction, traffic management, systems engineering, civil engineering, geological exploration, social and behavioral modeling, cognitive measurement, and bio-sensing are examples of areas likely to benefit from DDDAS." See also [2] for numerous examples and clear definitions of what makes a system a DDDAS.

As small groups, we are working on three kinds of DDDAS critical infrastructure projects funded by the NSF:

- *ITR/NGS: Collaborative Research: DDDAS: Data Dynamic Simulation for Disaster Management*. The emphasis is on wildland fire modeling, simulation, prediction, and a major milestone is to provide real-time information to people fighting actual fires. The final test of the project will be to do a full scale test with a prescribed burn of a mountainside in 2008-2009.
- *ITR: Collaborative Research: Predictive Contaminant Tracking Using Dynamic Data Driven Application Simulation (DDDAS) Techniques*. Multiscale data-driven algorithms and software to easily move data from sensors to computers potentially far away has been developed.
- *DDDAS-TMRP: Collaborative Research: Adaptive Data-Driven Sensor Configuration, Modeling, and Deployment for Oil, Chemical, and Biological Contamination near Coastal Facilities*. Consider a networked drone operating off a coast that recognizes oil in water. Upon detection and alerting the simulation, by dynamically loading into the drone sensor a chemical library specific to hydrocarbon pollution, the sensor can search for chemicals that will identify the source of the hydrocarbons. For example, a diesel-driven ship may have sunk nearby, or a fishing boat may simply be

leaking fuel. 100LL would indicate a small downed aircraft. Depending on the sensor result, very different computations can be done: trace where the ship or aircraft sank and alert rescue, or trace where the boat sailed and what its travel route was to identify the boat and mitigate the problem.

The remainder of this paper is organized as follows. In §2, we describe features that are common in DDDAS. In §3, we describe a whimsical DDDAS that would make a good commercial product for the modern American home. In §4, we describe a contaminant tracking DDDAS based on a set of movable drones in water bodies. In §5, we describe a wildland fire DDDAS. Finally, in §6, we offer some concluding remarks.

2   What Is in a Typical DDDAS

DDDAS environments require new software capabilities for application modeling and composition, dynamic runtime, resource management, data management, and measurement control aspects, as well software architecture drilling across all layers and end-to-end software infrastructure. The DDDAS program solicitation includes a comprehensive list of challenges and has inspired the scientific community, as exemplified by DDDAS projects that have started to address these and other related challenges. In our own DDDAS projects, we have identified several relatively diverse areas that have common issues that must be addressed by DDDAS: computer science, informational, and computational sciences that lead to significant impact for addressing important problems. These include:

1. Effectively *assimilating* continuous streams of data into running simulations. These data streams most often will be...
   a. Noisy but with known statistics, and must be incorporated into the model using stochastic methods, such as filters and smoothers.
   b. Received from a large number of scattered remote locations and must therefore be injected into a usable computational grid.
   c. Missing bits or transmission packets, as for example is the case in wireless transmissions.
   d. Injecting dynamic and unexpected data input into the model.
   e. Limited to providing information only at specific scales, specific to each sensor type.
2. *Warm restarting* simulations by incorporation of the new data into parallel or distributed computations, which require the data but are sensitive to communication speeds and data quality.
3. *Tracking and steering* (control of measurements, models, reporting results, and visualization) of remote distributed simulations to efficiently interact with the computations and to collaborate with other researchers.
4. *Translation components* to rectify when simulation output does not directly match observational data.

5. *Interpretation and analysis components* to assist researchers with collections of simulations.
6. *Application program interface and lightweight middleware components* for designing and creating a DDDAS or DDDAS problem solving environment.
7. Better *scheduling of computational and network resources* so that multiple models, possibly running at different locations, can be coordinated and data can be exchanged in a timely manner.
8. *Virtualization* and *sandbox* implementations for testing purposes and security.

DDDAS assumes that application components, resource requirements, application mapping, interfaces and control of the measurement system can be modified during the course of the application simulation. The diagram in Figure 1 shows how a number of elements might dynamically interact with each other: Any of the components may change without resorting to a new simulation as the computation progresses. Many DDDAS applications are multiscale in nature. As the scale changes, models change, which in turn, changes which numerical algorithms must be used and possibly the discretization methods. DDDAS applications involve a complicated time dependent, nonlinear set of coupled partial differential equations, stochastic or agent-based simulation methods, which add to the complexity of dynamically changing models and numeric algorithms. It also causes computational requirements to change, particularly if dynamic adaptive grid refinement or coarsening methods are used, in response to the dynamically streamed data into the executing model.

To support data management needs in our DDDAS projects, data acquisition, data accessing, and data dissemination tools are typically used. Data acquisition tools are responsible for retrieving of the real-time or near real-time data, processing, and storing them into a common internal data store. Data accessing tools provide common data manipulation support, e.g., querying, storing, and searching, to upper level models. Data dissemination tools read data from the data store, format them based on requests from data consumers and deliver the formatted data to the data consumers. Figure 2 illustrates a simplified view of the software framework of the DDAS system we are developing. In our implementation, the data used to drive a DDDAS system are retrieved periodically by a data retrieval service, extracted, converted, quality controlled, and then staged as dynamic inputs to our simulation models. The extraction process reads the retrieved data based on the meta data associated with them and feeds the extracted values to the conversion model whose major purpose is unit conversion, e.g., from inches to millimeters. The converted data are then analyzed for potential errors and missing values by the quality control model. This control process will ensure the correctness of the data, which is of great importance for the model simulation accuracy. The quality controlled data are then fed to the data storage model, which either saves the data to a central file system or loads them to a central database (this depends on project requirements). The data store model may also need to register the data in a metadata database so that other models can query it later.

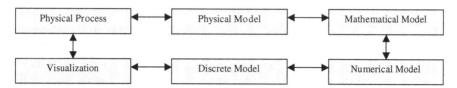

Fig. 1. DDDAS processing [3]

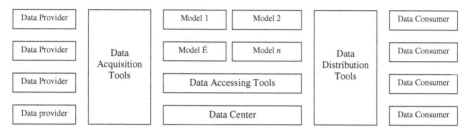

Fig. 2. Data acquisition, accessing, and dissemination software layout in a typical DDDAS project with *n* models

DDDAS research projects have brought together multidisciplinary expertise, involving researchers from a number of fields to synergistically pursue research on creating DDDAS capabilities and environments. There is a learning curve that is nontrivial. DDDAS applications are usually complicated, getting data is usually difficult, and there is already large scale research ongoing using traditional, take initial data and just run a simulation some period of time, and look at the results.

A community web site, http://www.dddas.org [4], has been developed by Prof. Douglas with help from about 50 other DDDAS-related projects. The site currently has a complete funded project list (from 2000 to 2006), virtual proceedings from workshops from 2000 through 2006 [5-8], a number of talks on topics that range from disaster management to transportation to homeland security to how a bat flies, news items, pointers to working DDDAS codes, and the January 2006 NSF DDDAS workshop report [9]. Most of the projects listed are from the United States, though a number of the projects have international partners and interest in DDDAS overseas has been increasing.

3   An Empty House DDDAS

In the United States, it is quite common for homes to be devoid of people for a significant number of hours per day (i.e., "My two cats really own the house."). However, it is advantageous to have the home appear to be lived in and constantly occupied. A *smart home* is able to communicate with the owners and for sensors to be adjusted to the immediate situation, inside or outside.

We need sensors that can detect motion and identify individuals (pictorially and verbally). Depending on the first results from the DDDAS, the sensors will have to detect much more complicated data. Face recognition and some indication of the emotional state is one of the highly successful DDDAS projects [10].

We need to distinguish between animals, vehicles, regular visitors (wanted and unwanted), and irregular visitors. Each category requires its own computational model. Frequently, more than one model must be used in parallel. In fact, the way to implement an empty house DDDAS is two tiered: (1) object detection and identification, and (2) receiving information about a detected object (recognized friendly, recognized undesirable or unrecognized) and chooses an appropriate response. The two tiered approach reduces the load on the second tier so that resources are available for decision making and communicating with the owner and makes it easy to add extra (or new) models later.

Animals can usually be ignored unless individuals are regular nuisances. Ones that live in the house and need to be let in (or out) are a special case and must be recognized as well as the animal's intent. When the occupants are away for an extended period of time, the animals need to be fed and given water on a regular basis.

Vehicles on a driveway are the first point of identification of individual people. For example, recognizing the license plate or corporate identity (e.g., UPS) leads to running a model for acceptable visitors. A moving van might indicate house robbers and a call to the police might be warranted depending on what the people inside it do after getting out of the van. Smoke detection in or near the house obviously needs a call to the fire department.

People walking up to a door (or window) provides a different recognition problem. Examples of walkers include the mailman or other deliver people, product sellers, house robbers, arsonists, and religious nuts. The former is welcome, but the rest are unwelcome and/or a serious threat to the integrity of the house. Being able to identify unwanted visitors and determine which ones will go away with a polite, but firm, "No," is essential and nontrivial to model. A database has to be developed over time as the DDDAS is trained.

For deliveries, a voice greeting needs to be generated, answers to common polite questions (e.g., how are you?), signing for a box or envelope, and directions given to what to do with a delivery. If the delivery is put into a secure box, the contents need to be transferred into the house either immediately or on a regular basis. The house occupants need to be notified of a delivery and who delivered it (using pictures or audio). If a delivery person cannot be answered by the DDDAS, the occupants should have the option of seeing, hearing, and talking to the delivery person in real time. Hence the DDDAS needs to be able to track the occupants seamlessly. Thus, two way, secure communications is required.

Clearly the Household DDDAS is nontrivial, yet much of what is needed to produce a working one has been developed over the past few years in NSF supported DDDAS grants [4]. To make it work requires a set of sensors (motion detectors, microphones, and webcams), mechanical devices to move or rotate the sensors, face and vehicle recognition software, voice decoding, networking (at the house and with the occupants, wherever they might be), and parallel processing to run multiple models simultaneously. Yet the total cost of such a system is not very high thanks to most of the devices and software being either commonplace or already existing. It is a matter of assembling the pieces correctly and devising the DDDAS. This would make an interesting commercial product for installing in new homes where the cost would be dwarfed by construction and land expenses.

4   Contaminant Tracking DDDAS

The most infamous oil spill was the Exxon Valdez oil spill. It was the largest oil spill ever when it occurred, but is no longer ranks among the top 50 largest oil spills globally. Oil spills remain one of the largest threats to coastal water regions and water supplies. Yet even small oil spills can indicate different things, as noted in the DDDAS-TRMP project summary in §1.

The DDDAS contaminant tracking system consists of sensors, a hydrodynamic and contaminant transport models, a data assimilation system, as well as computers, networks, and software to integrate the capabilities of the various components into a unified system for disaster management and mitigation.

Our sensor is a Solid-State Spectral Imager (SSSI) designed to gather hydrological and geological data and then to perform chemical analyses. The sensor is small and light enough to be mounted on various roving platforms so it can be used in remote-sensing situations and can scan ranges of 10-100 meters in distance. Using a laser-diode array, photodetectors, and on-board processing, the SSSI combines spectroscopic integrated sensing and processing with a hyperspace data analysis algorithm.

The SSSI detects and identifies contaminants in water using near-infrared (IR), visible, and ultraviolet light. Absorption, fluorescence, and even Raman spectrometry can be implemented, but absorption spectrometry is the most common. Virtually every organic compound (e.g., polycyclic aromatic hydrocarbons, paraffins, carboxylic acids, and sulfonic acids) has a near-IR spectrum that can be measured, including two classes of terrestrial biomarkers, lipids, and amino acids. Near-infrared spectra consist of overtones and combinations of fundamental mid-infrared bands, giving near-infrared spectra a powerful ability to identify organic compounds while still permitting some penetration of light into samples.

The SSSI has a modest amount of memory and computing capacity on board. The SSSI is reprogrammable in the field. When an interesting chemical trace is discovered, the reaction from the application overseeing the SSSI is two-fold: (a) invoke an appropriate application, and (b) request that the SSSI look for specific other chemical traces using other specific pulse sequences. There is a symbiotic relationship between the sensor network and the application simulation that is typical in a DDDAS.

The SSSI uses Walsh-Hadamard or Complementary Randomized Integrated Sensing and Processing (CRISP) encoding sequences of light pulses to further increase the signal-to-noise (S/N) ratio. In a Walsh-Hadamard sequence multiple laser diodes illuminate the target at the same time, increasing the number of photons received at the photodetector and the S/N. The Walsh-Hadamard sequence can be demultiplexed to individual wavelength responses with a matrix-vector multiply operation. CRISP encoding uses orthogonal pseudorandom codes with unequal numbers of on and off states. The duty cycle of each code is different and the codes are selected to deliver the highest duty cycles at the wavelengths where the most light is needed and lowest duty cycle where the least light is needed to make the sum of all of the transmitted (or reflected) light from the samples proportional to the analyte concentration of interest.

The hydrodynamic model consists of the Spectral Element Ocean Model (SEOM) in its two dimensional shallow water version. The spatial discretization relies on the spectral element method, an h-p type finite element discretization, which relies on relatively high degree (5-8th) polynomials to approximate the solution within each element. The main features of the spectral element method are: geometric flexibility due to its unstructured grids, dual paths to convergence: exponential by increasing polynomial degree or algebraic via increasing the number of elements, dense computational kernels with sparse inter-element synchronization, and excellent scalability on parallel machines. The model can be forced through winds, tides, and lateral injection of mass at inflow boundaries (e.g., river input). The model is supplemented with an advection-diffusion equation to simulate the trajectory of contaminants as they are carried along by the simulated flow.

Using multiple linear regression the Bootstrap Error-adjusted Single-sample Technique (BEST) classification algorithm can be performed in situ, allowing a rover to classify many samples, only notifying the simulation when an interesting substance is found. Once the spectrum of a sample has been collected, it must be classified to determine the substance present. Spectra recorded at n wavelengths are represented as single points in a n-dimensional hyperspace. In this scheme, similar samples produce similar spectra that project as probability orbitals or clusters into similar regions of hyperspace. The BEST metric is a clustering technique for exploring these distributions of spectra in hyperspace.

An initial library can be computed based on substances likely to be found in the target environment. When a substance unknown to the BEST library is found, the sensor can sample nearby points with similar spectra to create a new library entry for the new substance. Scientists can determine the type of substance present by further analyzing raw spectra of the substance provided by SSSI and by using data from their other instruments, apply these data to update the simulation. The SSSI chemical library will comprise substances expected to be in the environment in which the SSSI operates.

The initial deployment of the sensor and model focuses on estuarine regions where water quality monitoring is critical for human health and environmental monitoring. A sample tidal calculation will be performed using a grid that encompasses a bay or set of bays regions and possibly a river region. The model is forced with tidal elevation obtained from tide gauges. Runs without data assimilation have shown good comparison with observation and previous modeling results.

However, for DDDAS the use of data assimilation is imperative to inject observational data in the model while accounting for model and observational errors.

The data assimilation reduces the computational errors associated with initial data, essentially the solution at previous time step, and improves the prediction. Using the first set of measurements, the approximation of the initial data is recovered. As new data are incorporated into the simulator, the initial data are updated using an objective function. We note that the formulated problem is ill posed because there are fewer sensors than the finite dimensional space describing the initial data. The objective function is set up based on both a measurement error as well as a penalization term that depends on the prior knowledge about the solution at previous time steps (or initial data). The prior information is refreshed using the updated initial data. The penalization constants depend on time of update and can be associated with the relative difference between simulated and measured values. In the simulations, both the prior and penalization constants change in time.

To account for the errors (uncertainties) associated with sensor measurements, we consider an initial data update within a Bayesian framework. The posterior distribution is set up based on measurement errors and prior information. This posterior distribution is complicated and involves the solutions of partial differential equations. We could use a Metropolis-Hasting Markov chain Monte Carlo (MCMC) method to generate samples from the posterior distributions. However, a sampling with MCMC is expensive since it requires iterative steps and the acceptance rate is typically low. We developed an approach that combines least squares with a Bayesian approach that gives a high acceptance rate. In particular, we can prove that rigorous sampling can be achieved by sampling the sensor data from the known distribution, thus obtaining various realizations of the initial data. Our approach has similarities with the Ensemble Kalman Filter approach, which can also be adapted to an initial data update.

Consider finding hydrocarbon fuel in a body of water. Gasoline can simply be a sign of pollution from a small boat. Heavier fuel oils could be an indication that a larger boat has a leak or sank recently nearby. Jet fuel could come from a downed aircraft. The SSSI needs to be reprogrammed in the sunken vehicle case and a search and locate application must be invoked to find the accident and rescue any people that may be in danger. Emergency services, the coast guard, and the news media may need to be automatically informed of progress.

Oil droplets can travel nearly anywhere in the ocean. The droplet size exerts a major effect on droplet motion. The rise velocity of oil droplets extends from about 2.5×10^{-7} m/s for a diameter of 2μ m to 4.3×10^{-3} m/s for a diameter of 260μ m. Droplets traveling at 2.5×10^{-7} m/s will ascend only 0.001 m and 0.02 m, over periods of 1 hour and 24 hours, respectively. However, droplets ascending at 4.3×10^{-3} m/s will climb 15 m and 370 m over equivalent periods. A vertical diffusivity of 51 cm^2/s will distribute oil droplets (equally upward and downward) about 6 m and 30 m over the same time. Therefore, the smallest oil droplets act as though they are neutrally buoyant, i.e., transported only by diffusion. However, buoyancy primarily advects the largest droplets.

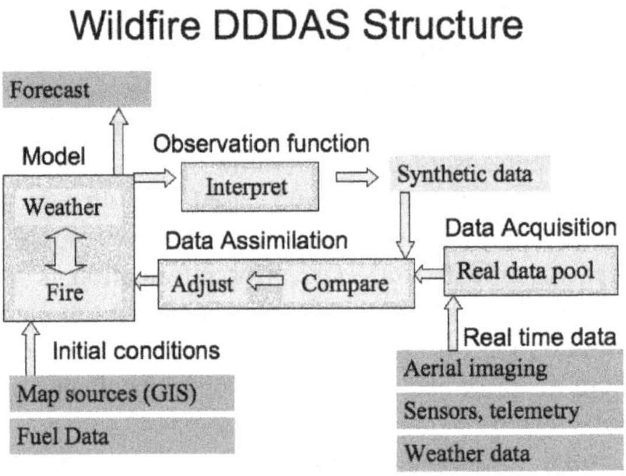

Wildfire DDDAS Structure

Fig. 3. Schematic diagram of a wildland fire dynamic data-driven application system.: blue blocks are functional units and purple are data inputs and outputs

5   Wildland Fireline Predictive DDDAS

Our wildland fire DDDAS is built upon a previously existing coupled atmosphere-wildfire model. Components have been developed and added which (1) save, modify, and restore the state of the atmosphere-wildfire model, (2) apply ensemble data assimilation algorithms to modify ensemble member states by comparing the data with synthetic data of the same kind created from the simulation state, (3) retrieve, process, and ingest data from both novel ground-based sensors and airborne platforms in the near vicinity of a fire, and (4) provide computational results visualized in several ways adaptable to user needs. Fig. 3 presents the actual software structure. The observation function interprets the model variables in terms of observable quantities and produces synthetic data from the model state. The data assimilation compares the synthetic data and the real data, and adjusts the model state accordingly.

The original modeling system is composed of two parts: (1) a numerical weather prediction model and (2) a fire behavior model that models the growth of a wildfire in response to weather, fuel conditions, and terrain. Both models are two way coupled so that heat and water vapor fluxes from the fire feed back to the atmosphere to produce fire winds, while the atmospheric winds and changes in humidity in turn drive the fire propagation. This wildfire simulation model can thus represent the complex interactions between a fire and the atmosphere.

The meteorological model is a three dimensional non-hydrostatic numerical model based on the Navier-Stokes equations of motion, a thermodynamic equation, and conservation of mass equations using the anelastic approximation. Vertically stretched terrain following coordinates allow the user to simulate in detail the airflow over complex terrain. Forecasted changes in the larger scale atmospheric environment are used to initialize the outer of several nested domains and update lateral boundary conditions. Two way interactive nested grids capture the outer forcing domain scale of the synoptic scale environment while allowing the user to telescope down to tens of meters near the fireline through horizontal and vertical grid refinement. Weather processes such as the production of cloud droplets, rain, and ice are parameterized using standard treatments.

Local fire spread rates depend on the modeled wind components through an application of the Rothermel fire spread formula [11]. The heat release rate is based on [12] which characterizes how the fire consumes fuels of different sizes with time after ignition, distinguishing between rapidly consumed grasses and slowly burned logs. Within each atmospheric grid cell, the land surface is further divided into fuel cells, with fuel characteristics corresponding to the 13 standard fuel types [13]. Each fuel cell has four tracers, which identify burning areas of fuel cells and define the fire front. Fire spread rates are calculated locally along the fire as a function of fuels, wind speed and direction from the atmospheric model (which includes the effects of the fire), and terrain slope while a local contour advection scheme assures consistency along the fireline. The canopy may be dried and ignited by the surface fire, so a simple radiation treatment distributes the sensible and latent heat into the lowest atmospheric grid levels.

The empirical fire model uses a submesh representation of the fire region. Within each cell on the fire model grid, a quadrilateral defines the burning region. The burning area in each grid cell is defined by the position of four moving points, called tracers. This representation makes the fire area hard to adjust in data assimilation. As a result, we have developed a translation of the tracers into a level function. The level function is given by values at nodes of the fire grid. The fire region is where the level function is positive. The absolute value of the level function is approximately equal to the Euclidean distance from the fireline. In data assimilation, the level function can be increased or decreased just like the physical quantities in the model and greatly simplifies the assimilation process.

Ensemble filters work by advancing in time a collection of simulations started from randomly perturbed initial conditions. When the data is injected, the *forecast ensemble* is updated to get a new *analysis ensemble* to achieve a least squares fit using two conditions: change in the ensemble members should be minimized, and the data d should fit the ensemble members state u, $h(u) \approx d$, where h is called the observation function. The weights in the least squares are obtained from the covariances of the ensemble and of the data error. For comprehensive surveys of Ensemble Kalman Filters (*EnKF*) techniques, see [14-16]. In general, an EnKF works by forming the analysis ensemble as linear combinations of the forecast ensemble. This raises two concerns, especially in highly nonlinear models: if the change of state in the update is large there may not be suitable forecast members to make linear combinations of in order to match the data. Hence, a linear combination of realizable states may not itself be a realizable state. This results in the need for large ensembles, frequent small updates, and has the potential to break down due to nonphysical states being introduced.

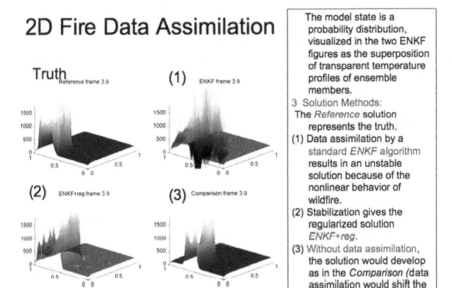

Fig. 4. Comparison of the results of 4 methods of simulating 2-D growth of a fire using an ensemble of solutions where the vertical axis is temperature and the 2 horizontal axes represent x- and y- spatial dimensions

We were using filters based on the EnKF with data perturbation. The data assimilation always produced an ensemble with nonphysical solutions and so that the simulation always broke down numerically. Therefore, we have developed a regularization by adding a term involving the change in the spatial gradient of ensemble members to the least squares procedure [17].

Consider Fig. 4 [18]. The exact solution is shown in the upper left. The ensemble solution with a standard EnkF algorithm is shown in the upper right, which creates unstable and nonphysical solutions. An EnkF solution with stabilization with the Johns and Mandel (2004) method is shown in the lower left, which produces the best, physically realistic solution. The solution of the ensemble without any data assimilation is shown in the lower right, in which the solution of the ensemble drifts away from the solution.

Existing ensemble filter formulas assume that the observation function is linear and then compute with the observation matrix H. To simplify the software, we have derived a mathematically equivalent ensemble filter that only needs to evaluate $h(u)$ for each ensemble member. The ensemble update involves computation with extremely large, dense matrices.

There is clearly a need to adjust the simulation state by distorting the simulation state in space rather than employing an additive correction to the state. Also, while the position of the feature may have error distribution that is approximately gaussian, this is not necessarily the case for the value of the state at a given point. For this reason, alternative error models including the position of features were considered in the literature [19] and a number of works emerged that achieve more efficient movement of features by using a spatial transformation as the field to which additive corrections are made: a transformation of the space by a global low order polynomial mapping to achieve alignment [20], and two-step models to use alignment as preprocessing to an additive correction [21, 22]. We have proposed [23] a new method, a Morphing Ensemble that combines alignment and additive correction into a single step, using ideas borrowed from registration and morphing in image processing [24].

Data comes from fixed sensors that measure temperature, radiation, and local weather conditions. The fixed sensors, positioned so as to provide weather conditions near a fire, are mounted at various heights above the ground on a pole with a tripod base. The data logging and transmission electronics are buried in the soil in a protective box. Wiring to the sensors and antennae is insulated. This type of system will survive burn overs by low intensity fires. These sensors supplement other sources of weather data derived from permanent and portable automated weather stations. The temperature and radiation measurements provide the direct indication of the fire front passage and the radiation measurement can also be used to determine the intensity of the fire. The raw data is logged and transmitted as comma delimited ASCII text for easy use in spreadsheets.

Data also comes from images taken by sensors on either satellites or airplanes. Camera calibration, an inertial measurement unit, GPS, and digital elevation data are used in a processing system to convert raw images to a map product with a latitude and longitude associated with each pixel. The three wavelength infrared images can then be processed using a variety of algorithm approaches to extract which pixels contain a signal from fire and to determine the energy radiated by the fire. The original pixel values, the derived probability of fire in each pixel, and the latitude and longitude information are stored in a Data Center as GeoTIFF images.

Data from previous fires are stored in a data center in GeoTIFF (images), Excel spreadsheet files, or text files (sensors). The Excel data is made more accessible by converting it to a comma separated value (CSV) format. GPS information is stored about each fixed-location sensor. Each sensor's data is time stamped to identify when the data was collected or received (if it comes without a time stamp). For mobile sensors, both the time stamp and GPS information is available.

Data that comes into the data center must go through a process consisting of up to six steps:

- *Retrieval*: Get the data from sensors. This may mean receiving data directly from a sensor or indirectly through another computer or storage device (e.g., a disk drive).
- *Extraction*: The data may be quite messy in raw form, thus the relevant data may have to be extracted from the transmitted information.
- *Conversion*: The units of the data may not be appropriate for our application.

- *Quality control*: Bad data should be removed or repaired if possible. Missing data (e.g., in a composite satellite photo) must be repaired.
- *Store*: The data must be archived to the right medium (or media). This might mean a disk, tape, or computer memory, or no storage device at all if data is not being archived permanently or only temporarily.
- *Notification*: If a simulation is using the data as it comes into the data center, the application must be informed of the existence of new data.

The data is related to the model by the observation equation $h(u) \approx d$. The observation function h maps the system state u to synthetic data, which are the values the data would be in the absence of modeling and measurement errors. Knowledge of the observation function, the data, and an estimate of the data error covariance is enough to find the correct linear combinations of ensemble members in the ensemble filter. The data assimilation code also requires an approximate inverse g of the observation function. For a system state u and data d, is the direction in which the system state can change to decrease a norm of the data residual. For an observation function that is simply the value of a variable in the system state, the natural choice of approximate inverse can be just the corresponding term of the data residual, embedded in a zero vector.

Building the observation function and its approximate inverse requires conversion of physical units between the model and data, and conversion and interpolation of physical coordinates. In addition, synthetic data at instants of time between the simulation time of ensemble members need to be interpolated to the data time. Data is injected into the ensemble to minimize both a weighted sum of the data residual and the change in the ensemble.

The data items enter in a pool maintained by the data acquisition module. The assimilation code can query the data acquisition module to see if there are any new data items available, request their quantitative and numerical properties, and delete them from the pool after they are no longer of use. The properties of the data items include

- a time stamp,
- encoding of the type and parameter values of the observation function and its approximate inverse,
- estimate of the error of the data, and
- the numerical values of the data itself.

From the point of view of the assimilation code, all information about physical units, etc., is encoded in the observation function.

Visualization of the model output as an image is accomplished by brightness, color encoding, and transparency for a visual indication of the location and intensity of the fire, and of the probability distribution of the forecast. 3-D visualization of the fire is more complex and complexity increases if high spatial resolution of the output is desired. 3-D visualization uses model output from the fire propagation code for the flame region and from the atmospheric code for visualization of smoke. Ensemble statistics are used for visualization of probability.

The geographic output of the fire model in 2-D or 3-D is visualized in a number of ways:

- For computer based mapping, manipulation, and visualization of the model output, file formats compatible with the geographic information system (GIS) products are generated.
- A PDF file: the output is a map generated for potential output as hardcopy view of the fire at a set point in time.
- A MPEG-4 (or similar format) file: the time varying output for both 2-D and 3-D is also used to generate a movie.
- A file appropriate for viewing as a layer on top of Google Earth [25].

Our Google Earth Fire visualization system (see Fig. 5) greatly simplifies map and image visualization. The user can control the viewing perspective, zooming into specific sites, and selecting the time frame of the visualization within the parameters of the current available simulation.

6   Concluding Remarks

DDDAS is an interesting field that is trying to abstract into a science a number of previously treated areas. Data assimilation, control engineering, process control, cyber physical systems, and other buzzwords describe special cases of DDDAS (unless you are a researcher in these fields, in which case DDDAS is a special case of your own field).

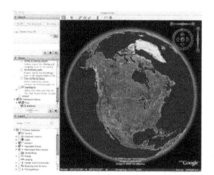
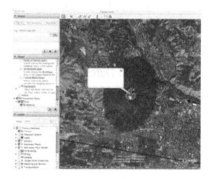

Fig. 5. Google Earth Fire Layering software tool: top left picture is what you get when clicking on Wildfires, top right picture is what you get by clicking on one of the fire symbols on the top left, and the bottom picture shows how the 3D layering appears

There are many application areas in which data can be injected into a running process. Doing it right leads to applications that can run forever instead of simulating short periods of time using static, initial data. While long range predictions can be achieved (e.g., weather prediction) using many runs with different sets of initial data from slightly different initial times, it is not the same as running just one simulation.

Making one traditional application starting from the static, initial data into an application that uses dynamic data to run a long time is good engineering. Abstracting what makes many different applications run as a DDDAS is good science, which is completely different. The purpose of the DDDAS program at the NSF is to do good science that is also good engineering. However, the list of DDDAS projects on http://www.dddas.org goes far beyond traditional engineering topics.

Acknowledgements

This material is based upon work supported in part by the National Science Foundation under grants CNS 0325314, CNS-0324988, CNS-0324989, CNS-0324876, CNS-0324910, ACI-0305466, EIA-0219627, CNS-0540178, CNS-0540153, CNS-0540155, CNS-0540136, and OISE-0405349.

See [26-28] for further information.

References

1. F. Darema et al, DDDAS: Dynamic Data Driven Applications Systems, program solicitation 05-570, National Science Foundation, Arlington, VA, 2005; Site http://www.nsf.gov/pubs/2005/nsf05570/nsf05570.htm visited 10/28/2006.

2. F. Darema, Introduction to the ICCS2006 Workshop on Dynamic Data Driven Applications Systems, in Computational Science – ICCS 2006: 6th International Conference, Reading, UK, May 28-31, 2006, Proceedings, Part III, edited by V.N. Alexandrov, G.D. van Albada, P.M.A. Sloot, and J.J. Dongarra, Lecture Notes in Computer Science 3993, Springer-Verlag Heidelberg, 2006, pp. 375-383.

3. R.E. Ewing, Interactive Control of Large scale Simulations, Workshop on Dynamic Data-Driven Application Systems, National Science Foundation, Arlington, VA, March 8-10, 2000. Site http://www.dddas.org/NSFworkshop2000.html visited 10/28/2006.

4. C.C. Douglas, DDDAS.org. Includes project descriptions, many DDDAS workshop virtual proceedings, and links to DDDAS software. Site http://www.dddas.org visited 10/28/2006.

5. 2003 Dynamic Data-Driven Application Workshop, F. Darema, ed., in Computational Science - ICCS 2003: 3rd International Conference, Melbourne, Australia and St. Petersburg, Russia, June 2-4, 2003, Proceedings, Part IV, P.M.A. Sloot, D. Abramson, A.V. Bogdanov, J.J.

Dongarra, A.Y. Zomaya, Y.E. Gorbachev (Eds.), Lecture Notes in Computer Science, Vol. 2660, Springer-Verlag Heidelberg, 2003, pp. 279-384.

6. 2004 Dynamic Data-Driven Application Workshop, F. Darema, ed., in Computational Science - ICCS 2004: 4th International Conference, Kraków, Poland, June 6-9, 2004, Proceedings, Part III, Marian Bubak, Geert Dick van Albada, Peter M. A. Sloot, and J.J. Dongarra (eds.), Lecture Notes in Computer Science series, vol. 3038, Springer-Verlag Heidelberg, 2004, pp. 662-834.

7. 2005 Dynamic Data-Driven Application Workshop, F. Darema, ed., in Computational Science - ICCS 2005: 5th International Conference, Atlanta, Georgia, USA, May 22-25, 2005, Proceedings, Part II, Vaidy S. Sunderam, Geert Dick van Albada, Peter M.A. Sloot, Jack J. Dongarra (eds.), Lecture Notes in Computer Science series, vol. 3515, Springer-Verlag Heidelberg, 2005, pp. 610-745.

8. 2006 Dynamic Data-Driven Application Workshop, F. Darema, ed., in Computational Science – ICCS 2006: 6th International Conference, Reading, UK, May 28-31, 2006, Proceedings, Part III, edited by V.N. Alexandrov, G.D. van Albada, P.M.A. Sloot, and J.J. Dongarra, Lecture Notes in Computer Science 3993, Springer-Verlag Heidelberg, 2006, pp. 375-607.

9. K. Baldridge, G. Biros, A. Chaturvedi, C.C. Douglas, M. Parashar, J. How, J. Saltz, E. Seidel, A. Sussman, January 2006 DDDAS Workshop Report, National Science Foundation, 2006. Site http://www.dddas.org/nsf-workshop-2006/wkshp_report.pdf visited 10/28/2006.

10. D. Metaxas and G. Tsechpenakis, Dynamic Data Driven Coupling of Continuous and Discrete Methods in 3D Tracking, in Computational Science - ICCS 2005: 5th International Conference, Atlanta, Georgia, USA, May 22-25, 2005, Proceedings, Part II, Vaidy S. Sunderam, Geert Dick van Albada, Peter M.A. Sloot, Jack J. Dongarra (eds.), Lecture Notes in Computer Science series, vol. 3515, Springer-Verlag Heidelberg, 2005, pp. 712-720.

11. R.C. Rothermel, A mathematical model for predicting fire spread in wildland fires. USDA Forest Service Research Paper INT-115, 1972.

12. F.A. Albini, PROGRAM BURNUP, A simulation model of the burning of large woody natural fuels, Final Report on Research Grant INT-92754-GR by U.S.F.S. to Montana State University, Mechanical Engineering Dept., 1994.

13. H. Anderson, Aids to determining fuel models for estimating fire behavior. USDA Forest Service, Intermountain Forest and Range Experiment Station, INT-122, 1982.

14. G. Evensen, The ensemble Kalman filter: Theoretical formulation and practical implementation, *Ocean Dynamics*, 53 (2003), pp. 343–367.

15. G. Evensen, Sampling strategies and square root analysis schemes for the EnKF. *Ocean Dynamics*, 54 (2004), pp. 539–560.

16. M.K. Tippett, J. L. Anderson, C.H. Bishop, T.M Hamill, J.S. Whitaker, Ensemble square root filters, *Monthly Weather Review*, 131 (2003), pp. 1485–1490.

17. C.J. Johns and J. Mandel, A two-stage ensemble Kalman filter for smooth data assimilation, to appear in Environmental and Ecological Statistics, Conference on New Developments of Statistical Analysis in Wildlife, Fisheries, and Ecological Research, Oct 13-16, 2004, Columbia, MI, 2006.

18. J. Mandel, L.S. Bennethum, J.D. Beezley, J.L. Coen, C.C. Douglas, L.P. Franca, M. Kim, and A. Vodacek, A wildland fire model with data assimilation, CCM Report 233, 2006. Site http://www.math.cudenver.edu/~jmandel/papers/rep233.pdf visited 10/28/2006.

19. R.N. Hoffman, Z. Liu, J.-F. Louis, and C. Grassoti, Distortion representation of forecast errors, *Monthly Weather Review*, 123 (1995), pp. 2758–2770.

20. G.D. Alexander, J.A. Weinman, and J.L. Schols, The use of digital warping of microwave integrated water vapor imagery to improve forecasts of marine extratropical cyclones, *Monthly Weather Review*, 126 (1998), pp. 1469–1496.

21. W.G. Lawson and J.A. Hansen, Alignment error models and ensemble-based data assimilation, *Monthly Weather Review*, 133 (2005), pp. 1687–1709.

22. S. Ravela, K.A. Emanuel, and D. McLaughlin, Data assimilation by field alignment. *Physica D*, to appear, 2006.

23. J. Mandel and J.D. Beezley, Predictor-corrector and morphing ensemble filters for the assimilation of sparse data into high dimensional nonlinear systems, to appear, 11th Symposium on Integrated Observing and Assimilation Systems for the Atmosphere, Oceans, and Land Surface (IOAS-AOLS), CD-ROM, Paper 3.12, 87th American Meterological Society Annual Meeting, San Antonio, TX, January 2007.

24. L.G. Brown, A survey of image registration techniques, *ACM Computing Surveys*, 24 (1992), pp. 325–376.

25. S. Chakraborty, J. Hatcher, D. Bansal, and C.C. Douglas, Google Earth Fire Layering Tool, in preparation, 2006.

26. C.C. Douglas, ML-DDDAS research group web site and reports, site http://www.mgnet.org/~douglas/ml-dddas.html visited 10/28/2006.

27. C.R. Johnson, Scientific Computing and Imaging Institute at the University of Utah, site http://www.sci.utah.edu visited 10/28/2006.

28. J. Mandel, NSF funded wildfire project public web site, site http://www-math.cudenver.edu/~jmandel/fires visited 10/28/2006.

Q&A – Craig Douglas

Questioner: Gabrielle Allen

Can you explain more about what information you need about your application to apply the filters?

Craig Douglas

We need to know the physical and chemical properties that we are modeling as well as their error distributions. These are obviously highly problem dependent.

Questioner: Brian Smith

What do you do when you recognize the raw data is false? Do you adjust the algorithm (in the dynamic sense) to ameliorate the present data?

Craig Douglas

In our application, we throw completely bad data out. For data that is borderline, we are still trying to develop general techniques.

In some applications, a human needs to be notified immediately. For example, in Afghanistan, if a Predator drone recognizes a high level human target, a person is notified at a military site to decide whether to allow a missile to take the target out in the next few seconds.

In some applications, bad data means that a different model needs to be loaded and used. For instance, in a water body if we observe certain hydrocarbons, we can check for other chemicals to determine if the we are near a leaking tank of a floating boat or a sunken one. Different models need to be run to trace each case.

Questioner: Marc Garbey

Can you comment on the time scale in the coupling between sensors and simulation code?

Craig Douglas

An airplane flies over and takes pictures. Currently the plane has to land at an airport, have the disk drives moved to a computer connected to the Internet, and upload the pictures (hopefully preprocessed so that only 10-15 KB is transferred per picture) to a data center. Data here is 1+ hour out of date.

A satellite takes pictures and takes 12 hours to download a composite jpeg file. Usually only part of the whole picture gets to Earth before the next set of pictures starts downloading. Data here is 12+ hours out of date.

Ground sensors may be radioed in immediately to a local place at the fire. It might also record information and have to be retrieved by a person. It is hard to say how quickly the data will arrive (instantly to real soon now).

Ideally, an airplane will have sufficient processing power to preprocess data in flight. Due to electromagnetic interference from the fire, the plane needs to fly away from the fire in order to reliably transfer data using a satellite transport system. Then the plane could return for more data collection with requests from the DDDAS for the actual locations of data collection.

Questioner: Dennis Gannon

Please explain the source of the "out of order" data problems?

Craig Douglas

Data comes in out of order due to the transmission methods. See 3 (M. Garbey).

Questioner: Ron Boisvert

Does the need to register aerial images of the forest fires pose any technical difficulties and uncertainty into the process?

Craig Douglas

No. This issue was dealt with over a number of years by the imaging science community. There is both open source and commercial software to handle this aspect of the project. We use open source codes based on GeoTIFF format pictures.

Questioner: Bo Einarsson

Is your system intended to assist the firefighters during the actual work of putting out the fire, or only to be used at a later evaluation?

Both. Part of the proposal to the NSF was an offer to burn a mountain. We hope to do this, with help from the U.S. Forest Service, in either 2007 or 2008.

Designing a Dynamic Data Driven Application System for Coastal and Environmental Modeling

Gabrielle Allen[1], Philip Bogden[2], Richard A. Luettich, Jr.[3], Edward Seidel[4], and Robert Twilley[5]

[1] Center for Computation & Technology and Department of Computer Science, Louisiana State University gallen@cct.lsu.edu
[2] Gulf of Maine Ocean Observing System bogden@gomoos.org
[3] University of North Carolina at Chapel Hill, Institute of Marine Sciences rick_luettich@unc.edu
[4] Center for Computation & Technology and Department of Physics, Louisiana State University eseidel@cct.lsu.edu
[5] Department of Oceanography and Coastal Science, Louisiana State University rtwilley@lsu.edu

1 Abstract

The economically important Louisiana Coastal Area (LCA) is susceptible to hurricane activity which is increasingly aggravated by the continuing erosion of wetlands. Various programs are aimed at building sophisticated models of meteorological, coastal, and ecological processes. The emerging paradigm of Dynamic Data Driven Application Systems (DDDAS) can be applied to these models leading to new scenarios for integrated, real-time simulations that include feedback control with sensors and simulations. This paper describes the motivation and components for a comprehensive DDDAS for coastal and environmental modeling and the implications this has for scientific libraries and high performance computing.

2 Introduction

The Louisiana Coastal Area (LCA) is one of the world's most environmentally damaged ecosystems. In the past century nearly one-third of the wetlands in the LCA, approximately 4500 km^2, has been lost. In its current state of decay, it is expected that by 2050 only one-third of the wetlands in this region will remain. Further erosion of the wetlands will be not only a massive environmental catastrophe, but also adversely affect the livelihoods of millions of people.

The economic importance of the LCA is substantial, containing 25% of U.S. coastal wetlands; 40% of contiguous U.S. salt marshes; 30% of U.S. total fish catch; 17% of U.S. oil. Further, 25% of U.S. national natural gas supplies come from Gulf coast waters. LCA ports handle more tonnage than any port worldwide, and LCA is home to the only "superport" in the contiguous U.S.

Please use the following format when citing this chapter:

Allen, G., Bogden, P., Luettich, R. A., Jr., Seidel, E., Twilley, R., 2007, in IFIP International Federation for Information Processing, Volume 239, Grid-Based Problem Solving Environments, eds. Gaffney, P. W., Pool, J.C.T., (Boston: Springer), pp. 275-293.

Beyond economic loss, LCA erosion has devastating effects on inhabitants of the coastal region, especially in New Orleans. This culture-rich city and its surroundings includes over one million people, and lies in a basin 6 meters under sea level, making it extremely vulnerable to hurricanes and tropical storms. On 29th August 2005 Hurricane Katrina (Figure 1) hit New Orleans, with storm surge and flooding resulting in a tragic loss of life and destruction of property and infrastructure. Soon after, Hurricane Rita caused similar devastation in the much less populated area of southwest Louisiana, and once again parts of New Orleans were under water. In both cases entire communities were destroyed.

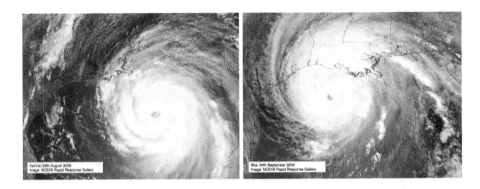

Fig. 1. From left to right, satellite images of Hurricanes Katrina and Rita which made dramatic landfall on the southeast US coast in 2005. Katrina resulted in the loss of nearly 2000 lives and caused some $120 billion of property damage. The storm size at landfall was 460 miles, with 145mph winds (Category 3), and storm surges of up to 22 feet. [Image credits: MODIS Rapid Response Gallery]

The entire LCA is very amenable to comprehensive computer modeling. Today there exist many sophisticated models for this area with processes ranging from ocean circulation and wave propagation to sediment transport and salinity in wetlands. Typically these are isolated models, and currently there is no established standard for tools that forecast an ecosystem response to restoration projects. A generic approach that encompasses the entirety of a restoration project's goals, capable of simulating all relevant interacting processes from erosion to storm surge to biodiversity in the ecosystem, is needed. This framework would need the capability to integrate data from observation and sensor systems and a complete set of detailed computer models, With such a system, more sophisticated decisions for short and long term planning and policy, as well as for immediate emergency response can be made. Decision making would be improved by using algorithms based on both data and detailed, realistic models that can dynamically adapt to real-life scenarios.

An emerging paradigm in computational science that seeks to integrate data streams and computational models, adapting them as needed to control or provide critical information about the behavior of complex systems is called Dynamic, Data-Driven, Application Systems, or DDDAS [1]. DDDAS is finding use in a vast range of complex problems, such as manufacturing supply chains in business, forest fire control [2], or combustion in engines. All these problems have complex systems that can in principle be simulated, and whose response to inputs can be predicted. These responses can then be used to make decisions that may affect or control the behavior of the system itself, or of other systems that depend on it.

The LCA makes an ideal case-study for DDDAS capabilities, as coastal properties change on relatively rapid time-scales. Unlike most ecosystems, due to extensive levee, dam, channel, and controllable water diversion projects over the last century, it is possible to regard the LCA as an *experimental* system. The ecosystem can be, and is regularly, changed and regulated on time scales of hours and days, providing unique opportunities for real-time data acquisition, simulation, monitoring, and control.

To effectively model the LCA region, a much more comprehensive and dynamic approach than currently available is needed. This includes the ability to couple models, invoke dynamic algorithms based on streams of sensor and satellite data, locate appropriate data and computational resources, and create necessary workflows on demand, all in real-time. Such an environment could help better plan restoration strategies, improve ecological forecasting, placement of future sensors, control of water diversion for salinity control, or predict/control harmful algal blooms, and support sea rescue, oil spill response, and shipping forecasts. In extreme situations, such as approaching hurricanes, results from multiple coupled ensemble models, compared with observations, can be used for greatly improved emergency warnings. Input from sensors and control of dams can be optimized to both improve the forecasts and actually reduce flooding. The comprehensive modeling system must be able to handle multiple time and length scales, from hours (storms) to years (restoration) and from meters (estuaries) to kilometers (Gulf of Mexico).

This paper describes the motivation and components for a comprehensive DDDAS for coastal and environmental modeling. Section 3 provides an overview of DDDAS including two detailed application scenarios, Section 4 describes different application communities that provide the scientific and operational background for DDDAS systems, and Section 5 details requirements and needs for the framework.

3 Dynamic Data Driven Application Systems

Simulation codes used today, across the physical and engineering sciences, typically allow only static workflows. Input data and parameter files must be created in advance, and are read by the simulation code at start up, and after this point the user can no longer interact with the running code, except to terminate a run. Integration with observing systems, data archives, and experiments is usually done manually if at all, through static, simplified input files, derived from data archives.

DDDAS describes new complex, and inherently multidisciplinary, application scenarios where simulations can dynamically ingest and respond to real-time data from measuring devices, experimental equipment, or other simulations. In these scenarios, simulation codes are in turn also able to control these varied inputs, providing for advanced control loops integrated with simulation codes. Implementing these scenarios requires advances in simulation codes, algorithms, computer systems and measuring devices.

In 2000 the National Science Foundation held a DDDAS Workshop [3], which included numerous application scenarios which could advance both science and society by incorporating these ideas. Application areas described at the workshop included control of forest fires, predicting the spread of contaminants, improving transportation systems and supply chains, and enabling oil exploration. Recent developments in cyberinfrastructure, including data archives, information systems, metaschedulers, etc, have helped provide surrounding infrastructure needed to implement some of these ideas in practice, which were further developed in another NSF DDDAS workshop in 2006 [4].

In the remainder of this section we describe how DDDAS ideas can be developed and applied to specific problems in storm surge prediction for emergency response and controlled water diversion for ecological purposes. From these application scenarios, we derive a set of requirements on the computational infrastructure, apply them to these and related problems, and suggest new algorithms that need to be developed to advance DDDAS applications generally. While motivated by these problems, many of the basic ideas and requirements are common to other disciplines requiring DDDAS techniques, motivating the need to develop a general DDDAS toolkit.

3.1 Event Driven Hurricane Predictions

When advisories from the National Hurricane Center indicate that a storm in the Atlantic or Gulf of Mexico may make landfall in a region impacting Louisiana, government officials, based on information provided by model predictions (Figure 2) and balancing a number of economic and social factors, must decide whether to evacuate New Orleans and surrounding towns and areas. Such advisories are provided every six hours, starting from some five days before the storm is predicted to make landfall. Evacuation notices for large cities like New Orleans need to be given 72 hours in advance. Here we outline a high level description of a complex DDDAS scenario, illustrated in Figure 3, which provides hurricane predictions using ensemble modeling.

A suddenly strengthening tropical depression tracked by satellite changes direction, worrying officials. The Louisiana Hurricane Center issues an alert to state researchers and an advanced autonomic modeling system begins the complex process of predicting and validating the hurri-

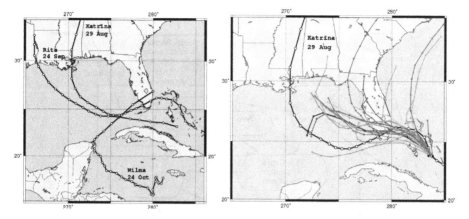

Fig. 2. Forecasting the effects of hurricanes and tropical storms in a timely manner is imperative for emergency planning. The paths and intensity of the devastating hurricanes Katrina, Rita and Wilma [left] during 2005, as with other storms, are forecast from five days before expected landfall using a number of different numerical and statistical models [right]. The validity of model predictions depend on many factors such as the storm properties, location and environment.

cane path. Realtime data from sensor networks on buoys, drilling platforms, and aircraft, across the Gulf of Mexico, together with satellite imagery, provide varied resolution data on ocean temperature, current, wave height, wind direction and temperature. This data is fed continuously into a ensemble modeling tool which, using various optimization techniques from a standard toolkit and taking into account resource information, automatically and dynamically task farms dozens of simulations, monitored in real-time. Each simulation represents a complex workflow, with closely coupled models for atmospheric winds, ocean currents, surface waves and storm surges. The different models and algorithms within them, are dynamically chosen depending on physical conditions (e.g., mud or sand bottoms) and required output sensitivity. Data assimilation methods are applied to observational data for boundary conditions and improved input data. Validation methods are used to compare data between different ensemble runs and live monitoring data, with tracking of data as it flows through the different solvers providing more information for dynamic decisions. Studying ensemble data from remotely monitored simulations, researchers help steer computations to ignore faulty or missing input data. Known sensitivity to uncertain sensor data is propagated through the coupled ensemble models quantifying uncertainty. Sophisticated comparison with current satellite data is made with synthesized data from ensemble models to determine in real-time which models/components are most reliable, and a final high resolution model is run to predict 72 hours in advance the detailed loca-

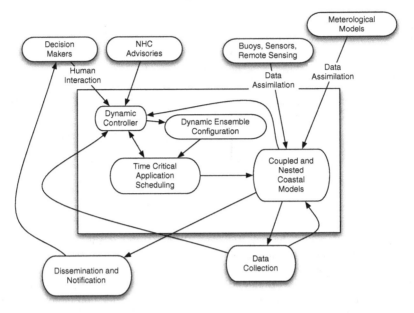

Fig. 3. Predictions of the coastal response to hurricanes, including storm surge and wave height, motivate a control system involving various data sources, human interaction, and time limited scheduling.

tion and severity of the storm surge. Louisiana's Office of Emergency Preparedness disseminates interactive maps of the projected storm surge and initiates contingency plans including impending evacuations and road closures.

3.2 Ecological Scenario

A different DDDAS scenario, involving ecological processes, builds on unique features of the Louisiana ecosystem, which is dynamically controllable via gates in the *Breton Sound diversion*. When opened, this control diversion structure allows the Mississippi River to flow into a wide area of threatened coastal wetland. Currently human intuition is the primary control factor for the gates, targeted at controlling salinity, but this $150M diversion could be scientifically controlled, through automated infrastructure linked to sophisticated models and the increasing array of sensors and satellite images (Figure 4, ultimately treating the whole wetland environment in Louisiana as a steerable DDDAS optimization system.

High-resolution models, coupling hydrodynamic, geomorphic, ecological and water quality components, are dynamically configured through uniform interfaces in a cascade of hydrodynamic models. Runtime toolkits enable dynamic injection of basin sensor data, at runtime, as it becomes available. Results from ensembles of different model cascade combinations, run across regional and national grids, are compared with actual data, allowing optimal validity calibration, choosing the best model cascade combination. Improved results from the hydrodynamic models initiate coupled high-resolution ecological models. These models generate 3-day forecasts for ecological conditions pertaining to chlorophyll content, nutrient concentration, salinity, and turbidity in the basin. These biogeochemical attributes can be used to provide an index of potential eutrophication under specific control diversion structure operations; given the set of real-time boundary conditions of the landscape (especially wind fields). Measurements obtained from the sensors in the basin and complementary satellite data in combination with model-model comparisons could be used to assess and improve the efficiency of the models.

Forecasts from such a framework will help engineers provide ecologically compatible flow conditions to enhance restoration while minimizing eutrophication problems. This is a step towards an automated control scenario, which taken further, determines the optimal flow control variables to achieve desired effects on different ecological parameters. This requires close interaction between the sensors, operational structures and the dynamic modeling framework. More complex scenarios such as effects of opening of multiple structures and their combined effect on the ecosystem could be determined beforehand, thus preventing unintended damages. An intelligent decision making system could then mine results obtained by various permutations and combinations at all possible levels and construct the optimal set of structure control parameters. Decisions could be made based on results generated by such DDDAS frameworks to efficiently control the diversion structures.

Numerous control diversion systems are planned, each costing of order $150M. DDDAS capabilities could play an important role in optimizing the

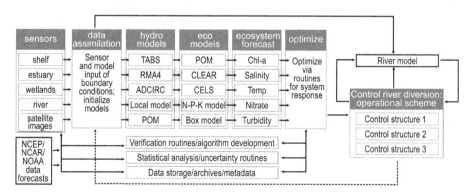

Fig. 4. *A complex ecological modeling DDDAS scenario designed for controlling river diversions.*

operation, design and placement of future structures. An extensive monitoring system is already in place, but is not yet linked to a modeling system. When the DDDAS systems are in place, they will be able to optimize dynamic placement of mobile sensors.

4 Synergistic Realtime Programs

We next describe three ongoing research and development programs (LPFS, CLEAR, and SCOOP) which are active in developing coastal modeling, assessment, and restoration projects in the Louisiana region. These programs form the foundation for the DDDAS research we describe in Section 5 below, which is aimed at advancing these and other programs that can benefit from these techniques.

4.1 Lake Pontchartrain Forecast System

During Hurricane Katrina storm surge water from Lake Pontchartrain flooded the city of New Orleans via breaches in outfall canals whose usual function is to drain rain water out of the city. To ensure this does not happen during future storms, the Army Corp of Engineers has developed a plan to close Interim Gated Structures at the mouths of three canals (17th Street, Orleans, and London, see Figure 5). However, closing these interim gates requires several hours and cannot be undertaken when storm force winds are present. Further, closing the gates should be delayed as long as possible, to allow the storm rain water to be drained from the city.

The Lake Pontchartrain Forecast System (LPFS) [5] has been developed by UNC, LSU and collaborators to provide timely information to the Army Corp to enable their decision making for closing the canal gates. LPFS provides an automated modeling system which is activated if an advisory from the National Hurricane Center (which are disseminated every 6 hours during storm activity) places the track of a storm within 271 nautical miles of the canal mouths (Figure 6). The system then deploys an ensemble of ADCIRC [6] runs (currently five runs are used which are forced by different winds corresponding to the consensus storm and 4 perturbations to this storm) on the compute resources of the Louisiana Optical Network Initiative (LONI) [7] where mechanisms are in place to ensure they have sufficient priority to complete within two hours. The results from the ensemble are integrated together and disseminated via protected web pages.

The operational, distributed LPFS system is providing an application use case for developing new technologies and policies for priority driven and deadline based computing including a general notification mechanism, preemptive scheduling on LONI, and dynamic application set threat levels to prescribe the priority of model runs (Figure 9).

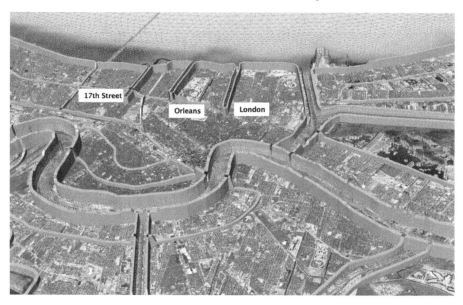

Fig. 5. Visualization of New Orleans superimposed with levees and computational mesh from the LPFS ADCIRC model. The three targeted canals (17th Street, Orleans, and London) are shown leading into Lake Pontchartrain on the north side of New Orleans. [Image credits: CCT Scientific Visualization group, Amanda Long, Werner Benger, Ana Buleu, Shalini Venkataraman, Steve Beck].

4.2 Louisiana CLEAR Program

The Coastal Louisiana Ecosystem Assessment and Restoration (CLEAR) program [8, 9] is developing ecological and predictive models to connect ecosystem needs and opportunity with engineering design. CLEAR is concentrating on a linked set of physical and ecological models. The physical models forecast endpoints of salinity, hydroperiod, and sediment distribution. From this geophysical footprint, predictions are then made of geomorphic features and shifts in land to water distribution. Ecological forecasts then simulate changes in habitat type, habitat use and conditions of water quality. This set of linked models provides the basis for an ecosystem forecasting system (geophysical processes, geomorphic features, water quality conditions, and ecological succession) which is used to evaluate alternative designs of engineering projects based on the projected response of the ecosystem.

The development and application of the models supports a strong adaptive management approach of existing and future projects, defining a body of knowledge by which hypotheses and assumptions can be continuously evaluated to incrementally reduce uncertainty in the model codes and thus improve the accuracy of the ecosystem response.

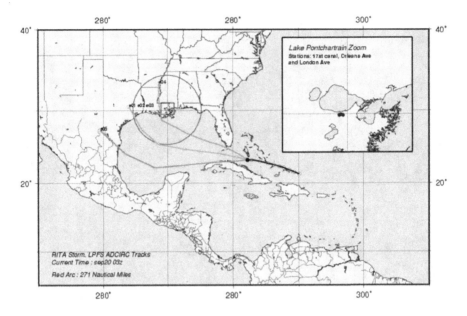

Fig. 6. The Lake Pontchartrain Forecast System deploys an ensemble of models to provide predictions for water level and wind speed at the mouths of three New Orleans Canals. The system is activated automatically if any of the ensemble tracks generated from an advisory from the National Hurricane Center places the hurricane track within 271 nautical miles from the canal mouths (inside the red circle in this image), and provides forecasts within two hours.

CLEAR has developed a modeling tool to evaluate restoration alternatives along with environmental benefits using a combination of modules that predict physical processes, geomorphic features, and ecological succession. The CLEAR program is now continuing to develop conceptual and simulation models to further develop an ecosystem forecasting system that integrates the elements of a comprehensive monitoring and adaptive management program within the LCA to evaluate environmental benefits in the coastal ecosystems of the Mississippi Delta. This system will help answer such questions as what will happen to the Mississippi River Deltaic Plain under different scenarios of restoration alternatives, and what will be the benefits to society?

4.3 SURA Coastal Ocean Observing and Prediction

SURA is a consortium of 62 universities whose mission is to "nurture scientific discovery and grow the scientific capacity of our region and the nation." The SCOOP Program [10, 11] is a SURA initiative in Coastal Research that involves a diverse collaboration of coastal modelers and computer scientists working with government agencies to create an open integrated network of distributed sensors, data and computer models. The SCOOP architecture will serve the needs of the nation for a broad array of services oriented toward applications and research involving coastal environmental prediction. The SCOOP program implements the SURA mission to foster collaboration among its member institutions and to encourage new ideas for collaboration. Thus, by developing this broad community-oriented cyberinfrastructure, the SCOOP program will facilitate the implementation and coordination of projects such as CLEAR and LPFS, and also provide a rich environment for research projects in computer science such as DDDAS. The SCOOP program aims to go one step farther. When aligned with the mission goals of operational agencies focussed on practical applications, the SCOOP cyberinfrastructure should enable transformational collaborations with the research community for use-inspired research that has a fast track to provide tangible benefits for the nation.

SCOOP activities are driven by the need for improved forecasts and real-time information for severe storm events, such as tropical storms and hurricanes. The recent catastrophes in the southeast US following the triad of hurricanes Katrina, Rita and Wilma have highlighted the pressing need for timely and accurate forecasts as well as improved coordination and information transfer between domain experts, policy makers and emergency responders.

SCOOP covers a wide range of activities with the central aim of providing a service-oriented cyberinfrastructure for the community, to be achieved by modularizing critical components, providing standard interfaces and data descriptions, and leveraging new Grid technologies. This cyberinfrastructure will include components for data archiving, integration, translation and transport, model coupling and workflow, event notification and resource brokering. Rather than developing a single community model or toolkit, using framework approaches such as the Earth System Modeling Framework (ESMF) [12] or the Cactus Code [13, 14], SCOOP is building interfaces to allow existing models to communicate with each other with coarse-grained connectivity.

The SCOOP community currently engages in distributed coastal modeling across the southeastern US, including both the Atlantic and Gulf of Mexico coasts. Various coastal hydrodynamic models are run on an operational (24/7/365) basis to study physical phenomena such as wave dynamics, storm surge and current flow. The computational models, include[1] Wave Watch 3 (WW3), Wave Model (WAM), Simulating Waves Nearshore (SWAN), ADvanced CIRCulation (ADCIRC) model, ElCIRC, and CH3D. Atmospheric model results from models such as NAM, NOGAPS, COAMPS, and analytical models provide the wind forcing which feed into the coastal hydrodynamical models. Most SCOOP models are run on an operational basis at least once

---

[1] Wave Watch 3 (WW3): http://polar.ncep.noaa.gov/waves/wavewatch/wavewatch.html, Wave Model (WAM): https://www.fnmoc.navy.mil/PUBLIC/WAM/wam det.html, Simulating Waves Nearshore (SWAN): http://www.wldelft.nl/soft/swan/, ADvanced CIRCulation (ADCIRC) model: http://www.adcirc.org, ELCIRC: http://www.ccalmr.ogi.edu/CORIE/modeling/elcirc/, CH3D: http://users.coastal.ufl.edu/ pete/CH3D/ch3d.html.

Model	Description	Domains	Mesh
ADCIRC: Advanced Circulation Model	2D surge and current	Entire SE	
CH3D: Curvilinear grid Hydrodynamics model in 3D	3D velocities, temperature, salinity, surge	Western Florida	
ElCIRC: Eulerian-Lagrangian Circulation Model	3D baroclinic circulation across rivers to oceans	Chesapeake Bay	
WW3: Wave Watch III	Water depth & wave propagation	Entire SE, parts of Gulf of Mexico	
WAM: Wave Model	Water depth & wave propagation	Gulf of Mexico	
SWAN: Simulating Waves Nearshore	Water depth & wave propagation	Coastal Louisiana	

Table 1. Primary coastal models used in the SCOOP project and the large scale and regional domains on which they are deployed. These models use a variety of meshes and numerical algorithms to simulate different physical properties.

a day and generate 72 hour forecasts. The models are currently run at specific sites with existing local expertise, although the project is implementing a Grid-based infrastructure for future coordinated distributed deployment.

In addition to operational modeling, extreme events such as hurricanes or tropical storms initiate additional automated model workflows. Advisories from the National Hurricane Center (NHC) about impending tropical storms or hurricanes are used to trigger automated workflows that start with the generation of high resolution wind fields around the center of the energetic event. These wind fields then initiate hydrodynamic models at different sites. The current scenario involves the running of ADCIRC (at University of North Carolina), CH3D (at University of Florida), and ELCIRC (at Virginia Institute of Marine Sciences), WW3 (at Bedford Institute of Oceanography and Louisiana State University). Figure 7 shows the different regions for which the SCOOP models provide forecasts.

The resulting data fields obtained from both the operational and storm event scenarios are distributed to the SCOOP partners for local visualization and further analysis, and are also archived for further use in a high available archive [15].

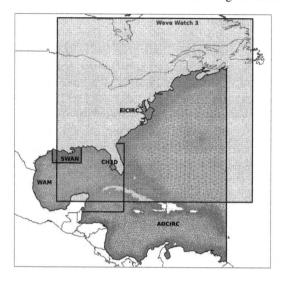

Fig. 7. Illustration of the different geographical regions over which the SCOOP ensemble of coastal models are currently deployed.

5 Components

Implementing the dynamic scenarios described in this paper will require technical advances across the areas of simulation codes, algorithms, computer systems and measuring devices. In this section, we focus on technical issues related to the various components that are needed for these scenarios. From these components, one can build many DDDAS applications, such as those described here, and others.

5.1 Varied Data Sources

Data from many sources needs to be integrated with the various models for accurate simulations of the complex physical systems under study. For example, wind fields are crucial for these applications, and can be provided both from different observational sources and computer models. Each wind field will have different uncertainties; improving the quality/resolution of input data, on demand, can lower uncertainty in forecasts. Implementing these scenarios requires the ability to dynamically create a customized ensemble of both analytic and model wind fields, validated and improved with available sensor data, for specified regions, complete with uncertainty functions that can be propagated through models for sensitivity analysis.

Data from sensors, typically collected by regional observing systems such as WAVCIS in Louisiana or GoMOOS across the Gulf of Maine, needs to be quickly available for real-time verification and data assimilation.

5.2 Data Management

Services for finding, transporting, and potentially translating data are needed to enable current ensemble scenarios and then to scale to complex workflows of coupled interacting models. To support emergency and real-time computing scenrios, data sources need to be highly available, while data transport needs to be fault tolerant with guaranteed quality of service. With new optical networks in place, which can transport 10 Gigabits per second on a single "lambda", we need mechanisms for dynamically reserving and provisioning networks as part of workflows, as well as data scheduling capabilities which ensure that data is in the right place at the right time.

Metadata describing the huge amounts of data, distributed across multiple sources, is also crucial. This should fully describe the data and its history, including information about the models which created it, or the systems which observed it, to provide complete provenance information which can be used to verify and understand results.

5.3 Model-Model Coupling

In both scenarios, cascades of coupled models are used, at different levels; e.g. circulation models, wave models, transport models, etc. Beyond simply defining interfaces between these, one must develop techniques to track uncertainties throughout entire cascades of models, create and optimize workflows on Grids as storms approach or as dams are manipulated, and invoke models or model components preferentially, based on algorithm performance and features for conditions indicated by input data.

5.4 Ensembles

Cascades of models, coupled with multiple components at each stage of the cascade, give rise to potentially hundreds of combinations. One may not know *a priori* which combinations give the best results. Automated and configurable ensemble modeling across grid resources, with continuous validation of results against observations and model-model comparisons, will be critical to dynamically refining predictions on the fly. It will also be necessary to develop algorithms for dynamic configuration and creation of ensembles to provide predictions with a specifiable, required accuracy. In designing these ensembles, the system should also take into account the availability and "cost" of computational resources, noting that the available resources may also depend on the seriousness and urgency of the situation being modeled. For the hurricane scenario, the system should also react to the potential threat of the storm, for example a Category 5 Hurricane could require a highly level of accuracy and quality of services than a Category 3 Hurricane.

5.5 Steering

The scenarios described above both involve automated steering (at both the component and workflow levels) to adjust models to physical properties and the system being modeled. In the hurricane scenario, one could steer sensor inputs for improved accuracy. For the ecological scenario, it would allow one to steer the "experiment"– the active river diversions–which can be controlled by the models to improve water quality, reduce salinity, control algal blooms, etc. The remote steering of model codes, for example to change output parameters to provide verification data, or to initiating the reading of new improved data, will require advances to the model software. Beyond introducing the technical capabilities for steering parameters (which often requires the involvement of domain experts), the mechanism for steering should require authentication for security, and changes need to be properly logged to ensure reproducibility.

5.6 Visualization and Notification

Visualization will be used for different purposes. Detailed visualizations, integrating multiple data and simulation sources showing the predicted effect of a storm (see Figure 8) will be important both for scientific understanding and analysis and for public awareness. For example, the visualization in Figure 8, which is scientifically accurate, would be very effective in impressing on the public the urgency of evacuation on the general population. Interactive and collaborative 3-D visualization for scientific insight will stress high speed networks, real-time algorithms and advanced clients. Visualizations including verification analysis and real-time sensor information will be crucially important.

Notification mechanisms which can automatically inform scientist, system administrators and emergency responders need to be robust and configurable sending the relevant information for a particular device e.g. cell phone, instant message client, email. The automated systems we envisage will require human intervention and confirmation at different points, and here it is important that the system include mechanisms which require authenticated response and have intelligent fallback mechanisms.

5.7 Priority and Deadline Based Scheduling:

Events such as hurricanes cannot be planned, and must be responded to at a time of their choosing. This type of scenario, and the need to run multiple models, concurrently with data streams and analysis tools, leads to new types of requirements on scheduling and reservation systems: priority, deadline-based, and co-scheduling. Not only must computational resources be made available on demand, with a specific deadline and guarantee for results, multiple resources must be scheduled simultaneously and/or in sequence. Furthermore, these resources go beyond traditional computing resources, and now need to include archival data, file systems, networks, visualization systems, and so on.

Fig. 8. Combined visualization of Hurricane Katrina approaching New Orleans, showing the water surge as predicted by the ADCIRC simulation model, cloud density as observed in infrared by the GOES-12 satellite, terrain height information obtained from high-resolution LIDAR measurements (green: above sea level, magenta: below sea level, blue: sea level) with the levee information of the ADCIRC model, overlaid on aereal photography and GIS terrain information. [Image credits: CCT Scientific Visualization group, Amanda Long, Werner Benger, Ana Buleu, Shalini Venkataraman, Steve Beck].

6 Conclusion

We have described some of the new technology components and capabilities which will be needed to enable the DDDAS scenarios outlined in Section 3. However, it is important to recognize that along with these advances, several concurrent developments are needed for these applications to be developed by communities, and actually run on computational environments. For example, the relevant scientific communities need to embrace a model of sharing data, code components, as well as computational resources. As this sociological change

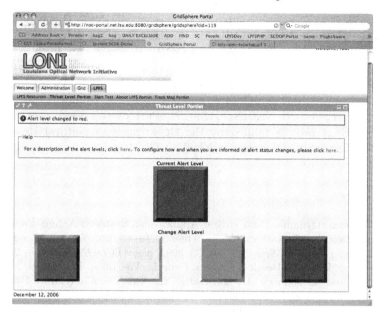

Fig. 9. The LPFS system has been augmented by a threat level system. The threat level can be changed by trusted applications or scientists, and is then used to both notify system administrators, customers and scientists of changing circumstances and to set policies on compute resources for running on demand jobs. This diagram shows a portal interface to the threat level system.

occurs, the communities will also need to adopt more modern software engineering practices and cyberinfrastructure in order ultimately to take advantage of the kinds of components we are developing. At the same time, it will be crucial for component and scientific library developers to adopt practices and interfaces that allow them to be used in this portable, dynamic environment. Finally, and just as importantly, it will be critical for policies to be adopted at computing centers that enable this kind of event-driven computing and data streaming, so that the real-time scenarios we describe can actually be carried out in practice; computational resources of various kinds will have to be available on demand, with policies that take into account the priority of certain jobs, such as hurricane storm surge computations.

Acknowledgements

We would like to acknowledge our colleagues in the SCOOP, CLEAR and LPFS projects who have carried out some of the work described here and contributed to ideas for a DDDAS system for coastal and environmental modeling.

This work has been carried out as part of the NSF DynaCode project (0540374). Funding for this work has also been provided by SURA Coastal Ocean Observing and Prediction (SCOOP) Program, an initiative of the Southeastern Universities Research Association (SURA). Funding support for SCOOP has been provided by the Office of Naval Research, Award N00014-04-1-0721 and by the National Oceanic and Atmospheric Administration's NOAA Ocean Service, Award NA04NOS4730254. Part of this work was supported by the CLEAR project funded by the Department of Natural Resources of Louisiana, Interagency Agreement No. 2511-02-24.

References

1. F. Darema. Dynamic Data Driven Applications Systems: A New Paradigm for Application Simulations and Measurements. In *Lecture Notes in Computer Science, Computational Science — ICCS 2004*, pages 662–669. Springer, 2004.
2. C. C. Douglas, J. D. Beezley, J. Coen, Deng Li, Wei Li, A. K. Mandel, J. Mandel, G. Qin, and A. Vodacek. Demonstrating the Validity of a Wildfire DDDAS. In *Lecture Notes in Computer Science, Computational Science — ICCS 2006*, pages 522–529. Springer-Verlag, 2004.
3. Report from NSF DDDAS Workshop, March 2000, Washington. http://www.nsf.gov/cise/cns//dddas/dd_das_work_shop_rprt.pdf.
4. Report from NSF DDDAS Workshop, January 2006, Washington. http://www.nsf.gov/cise/cns/dddas/2006Workshop/wkshpreport.pdf.
5. Lake Pontchartrain Forecast System (LPFS). http://www.cct.lsu.edu/projects/LPFS.
6. The ADvanced CIRCulation model (ADCIRC): http://www.adcirc.org/.
7. Louisiana Optical Network Initiative (LONI) : . http://www.loni.org.
8. Coastal Louisiana Ecosystem Assessment and Restoration (CLEAR): Building a coastal ecosystem forecasting system. http://www.clear.lsu.edu.
9. Louisiana coastal area. louisiana — ecosystem restoration study — november 2004. volume 4. appendix c — hydrodynamic and ecological modeling. Technical report, 2004. http://www.lca.gov/appc.aspx.
10. SURA Coastal Ocean Observing Program (SCOOP) : http://scoop.sura.org.
11. Bogden, P., Allen, G., Stone, G., Bintz, J., Graber, H., Graves, S., Luettich, R., Reed, D., Sheng, P., Wang, H., Zhao, W. The Southeastern University Research Association Coastal Ocean Observing and Prediction Program: Integrating Marine Science and Information Technology. In *Proceedings of the OCEANS 2005 MTS/IEEE Conference, Sept 18-23, 2005, Washington, D.C.*, 2005. http://scoop.sura.org/documents/050301-04.pdf.
12. Earth System Modeling Framework. http://www.esmf.ucar.edu.
13. Tom Goodale, Gabrielle Allen, Gerd Lanfermann, Joan Massó, Thomas Radke, Edward Seidel, and John Shalf. The Cactus framework and toolkit: Design and applications. In *High Performance Computing for Computational Science - VECPAR 2002, 5th International Conference, Porto, Portugal, June 26-28, 2002*, pages 197–227, Berlin, 2003. Springer.
14. Fokke Dijkstra and Aad van der Steen. Integration of Two Ocean Models. In *Special Issue of Concurrency and Computation, Practice & Experience*, volume 18, pages 193–202. Wiley, 2005.

15. Jon MacLaren, Gabrielle Allen, Chirag Dekate, Dayong Huang, Andrei Hutanu, and Chongjie Zhang. Shelter from the Storm: Building a Safe Archive in a Hostile World. In *Proceedings of the The Second International Workshop on Grid Computing and its Application to Data Analysis (GADA'05)*, Agia Napa, Cyprus, 2005. Springer Verlag.

SPRUCE: A System for Supporting Urgent High-Performance Computing

Pete Beckman[1], Suman Nadella[2], Nick Trebon[2], and Ivan Beschastnikh[3]

Mathematics and Computer Science Division, Argonne National Laboratory
9700 S. Cass Avenue, Argonne, IL 60439 beckman@mcs.anl.gov
Computation Institute, The University of Chicago/ Argonne National Laboratory
5801 S. Ellis Avenue, Chicago, IL 60637 snadella,ntrebon@uchicago.edu
Computer Science Dept, The University of Washington
Seattle, WA 98195 ivan@cs.washington.edu

Modeling and simulation using high-performance computing are playing an increasingly important role in decision making and prediction. For time-critical emergency decision support applications, such as influenza modeling and severe weather prediction, late results may be useless. A specialized infrastructure is needed to provide computational resources quickly. This paper describes the architecture and implementation of SPRUCE, a system for supporting urgent computing on both traditional supercomputers and distributed computing Grids. Currently deployed on the TeraGrid, SPRUCE provides users with "right-of-way tokens" that can be activated from a Web-based portal or Web service invocation in the event of an urgent computing need. Tokens are transferrable and can be restricted to specific resource sets and priority levels. Once a session is activated, job submissions may request elevated priority. Based on local policy, computing resources can respond, for example, by preempting active jobs or raising the job's priority in the queue. This paper also explores the strengths and weaknesses of the SPRUCE architecture and token-based activation for urgent computing applications.

1 Introduction

Scientific computing is playing an ever-increasing role in making critical decisions. For example, global climate modeling played a key role in influencing the Kyoto Protocol for the reduction of greenhouse gas emissions [1]. Likewise, computer models have helped large metropolitan areas plan for new highways and congestion relief [2]. While decision makers would like simulation results as soon as possible, there is often little urgency or a deadline to complete the computation. Developing public policy is rarely fast. There are, however, growing sets of problem domains where key decisions must be made quickly with the aid of large-scale computation. In these domains, "urgent computing" is essential, and late results are useless. A computer model capable of determining where tornadoes will form must provide early warning to local residents. A computation to predict the flow of airborne contaminants from a ruptured

Please use the following format when citing this chapter:

Beckman, P., Nadella, S., Trebon, N., Beschastnikh, I., 2007, in IFIP International Federation for Information Processing, Volume 239, Grid-Based Problem Solving Environments, eds. Gaffney, P. W., Pool, J.C.T., (Boston: Springer), pp. 295-311.

railcar must guide evacuation while there is still time. These on-demand large-scale computations cannot wait in a job queue for Grid resources to become available. However, neither can the scientific community afford to keep multi-million dollar infrastructures idle until required by an emergency. Instead, we must develop technologies that can support urgent computation. Scientists need mechanisms to find, evaluate, select, and launch elevated-priority applications on high-performance computing (HPC) resources. Those computations might re-order, preempt, or terminate existing jobs to provide the needed cycles in time. SPRUCE, the *S*pecial *PR*iority and *U*rgent *C*omputing *E*nvironment, is a system for providing resources quickly and efficiently to high-priority applications that must get computational power without delay. This paper makes two contributions: it presents and analyzes an architecture for supporting urgent computing across large production Grids, and it provides implementation experiences from the TeraGrid [3] deployment.

1.1 Requirements for Supporting Urgent Computing

Urgent computing can be supported in many ways. Priority queues, administrative intervention, and emergency stand-by resources could all be used to provide compute cycles quickly. While these methods may be effective for some usage scenarios, however, they cannot provide a feature-rich architecture capable of supporting large, distributed Grids. A Grid-based architecture for urgent computing must meet the following design requirements:

- Urgent computing jobs must occur within a clearly defined "session." System administrators are notified when sessions begin, permitting periods of increased attentiveness and, if needed, human intervention to provide the resources required.
- The system must support possibly different urgent computing policy frameworks among Grid resource providers and coexist with ongoing operations. For example, some HPC centers may support preemption for certain applications or priorities, while other HPC centers may provide only "run-next" priority following the normal completion of existing jobs.
- Permission to initiate an urgent computing session must be easily transferrable so team leaders, managers, and senior personnel can respond quickly to emergency situations.
- Application team leaders must be able to quickly assemble and authorize sets of users to submit priority jobs across a Grid that spans multiple sites and administration domains.

1.2 SPRUCE Architecture

Our architecture for urgent computing uses a token-based system to address these requirements. Tokens can have various levels of priority and different sets of resources applicable to them. Initiating an urgent computing session begins with the initialization, or "activation," of a token via a Web portal or command line. Tokens are simple authorization codes and therefore completely transferrable either electronically or on a printed card. This design is based on existing emergency response systems proven in the field, such as the priority telephone access system supported by the U.S. Government Emergency Telecommunications Service within the Department of Homeland Security [4]. Users of the priority telephone access system, such as key managers at hospitals, fire departments, government offices, and 911 centers, carry a wallet-sized card with an authorization number. Cardholders can use the code to place high-priority phone calls that jump to the top of the queue for both land- and cell-based traffic. Even if circuits are completely jammed because of a disaster, important traffic can get the priority needed. Since tokens are transferrable, users benefit from tremendous flexibility during critical-response situations.

To support token-based access to elevated-priority resources, the SPRUCE architecture has three main components: user workflow and client-side job submission tools, a Web service-based user interface to manage tokens, and local resource provider agents that can respond to the request for priority access. The remainder of this paper presents the design and implementation of each of these components, an analysis of the architecture, and our experiences deploying the system on the TeraGrid.

2 SPRUCE User Workflow

The SPRUCE workflow is designed for the application teams that can provide computer-aided decision support. Each application team is organized by its principal investigator (PI). The PI selects the computational "first responders," senior staff who can evaluate the request, initiate a SPRUCE session, and engage the other team members. The first responders hold the right-of-way tokens and decide when they should be used based on the best available information and the policies of the Grid system. The PI also selects an "interpreter" to translate the raw data and simulation output into advice for decision makers. For example, imagine an application that models airflow across a city and can be used to evaluate contamination scenarios. The results of that simulation may have many subtle details that need interpretation and presentation to city managers as they formulate response scenarios.

Figure 1 illustrates how the SPRUCE workflow is initiated. A trigger causes the computational first responders to spring into action. The trigger may be automatic, such as an automated warning message from a tsunami alarm buoy, or human generated, for example by a phone call to the PI. For many applications, the computing request may include a deadline. If the results cannot be provided before the deadline, the window for effective decision-support will have passed. The scientists must choose an appropriate priority level for the situation based on the importance of the job to be submitted. SPRUCE right-of-way token holders must adhere to the policies concerning activation and must use

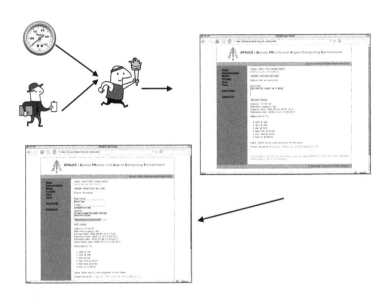

Fig. 1. SPRUCE workflow and token activation

discretion, in the same way that citizens are expected to use good judgment before dialing 911. Users must be aware that misuse can result in the revocation of their tokens.

Interaction with the SPRUCE system starts by activating a right-of-way token. A Web-based portal built on Web services is provided, where the token manipulations can be performed. Additionally, the Web service functionality may be incorporated into automated work-flows, thereby avoiding human intervention in managing tokens. Activation is described in greater detail in Section 3. Often, running a large simulation involves numerous scientists who are responsible for tasks ranging from acquiring the most recent data set to producing a visualization for analysis. The initiator of the SPRUCE session can indicate which scientist or set of scientists will be able to request elevated priority while submitting urgent jobs.

2.1 Choosing Resources

When a scientist wants to choose a resource to run on, two factors must be considered. The application needs to be fine tuned to suit the resource environment, and the policy pertaining to priority access should be functioning correctly.

With the token activated and the application team specified, scientists can organize their computation and submit jobs. Naturally, there is no time to port the application to new platforms or architectures or to try a new compiler.

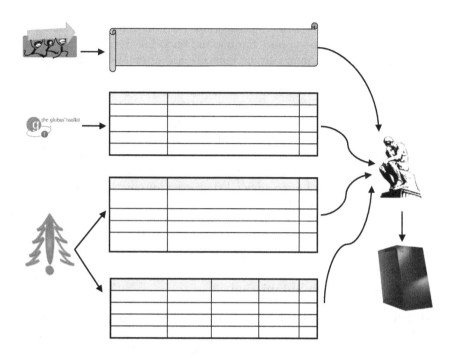

Fig. 2. The SPRUCE advisor helps choose the best resource

Applications must be prepared for immediate use—they must be in "warm standby." All of the application development, testing, and tuning must be complete before freezing the code and marking it ready for urgent computation. Grids such as the TeraGrid have dozens of large-scale computational resources. The SPRUCE architecture supports large, diverse Grids; but ultimately the science teams must select the best resources for their application. Maintaining and validating the accuracy of a simulation require programmer resources, and often application teams narrow their efforts to a handful of favorite platforms and sites. Additionally, these sites should have their priority policy in place and all the hooks needed to implement it immediately when needed. In the same way that emergency equipment, personnel, and procedures are periodically tested for preparedness and flawless operation, SPRUCE proposes to have applications and policies in warm standby mode, being periodically tested and their date of last validation recorded.

From this pool of Grid resources where the validated application awaits in warm standby, the team must select where to submit their jobs. This process can be challenging. In a distributed Grid linking resources provided by independent resource providers, different urgent computing policies will exist. One site may provide only a slightly increased priority to SPRUCE jobs, while another site may kill running jobs and hand the entire supercomputer to extremely urgent computations. On resources where existing jobs are not killed or preempted, current job load will affect resource selection. Data movement may also constrain resource selection. To support finding and choosing resources, SPRUCE users may select resources manually or may use an automated SPRUCE "advisor" (see Figure 2).

The proposed SPRUCE advisor needs four pieces of data to recommend where jobs should be submitted: the deadline for results, the estimated running time of the job, each site's urgent computing policy expressed as a scheduling algorithm for SPRUCE jobs, and the current status of job queues at the resource sites, which can be provided via MDS4 [5] on the TeraGrid. By combining these parameters with the application validation histories for each resource, several resources can be recommended or even automatically selected. If manual selection of the resource is preferred, the user may analyze the job queue status reports from MDS4 and examine previous warm standby results from the SPRUCE database to make a decision. Once the resource is selected, the user submits the job with a designated urgency.

2.2 Prioritized Job Submission

SPRUCE provides support for both Globus-based urgent submissions and direct submission to local job-queuing systems. Currently all the major resource managers such as Torque, LoadLeveler, and LSF and schedulers such as Moab, Maui, PBS Pro, and Catalina are supported. The system can be extended to any scheduler with little effort. Authorized users who have active tokens need only to specify an additional "urgency" parameter when submitting their jobs.

The Globus Toolkit [6] for Grid computing provides the TeraGrid with uniform tools for authentication, job submission, file transfer, and resource description. Users can submit remote jobs to any of the TeraGrid platforms. By extending the Resource Specification Language (RSL) [7], which is used by Globus to identify user-specific resource requests, we give the user the ability to indicate a level of urgency for jobs. A new "urgency" parameter is defined for three levels: *critical* (red), *high* (orange), and *important* (yellow). Urgency levels are used in two places. Gridwide policies and guidelines can help scientists organize and differentiate potentially competing jobs by urgency. On the back end, the resource provider can enable site-local response protocols according to urgency.

The urgency can be specified within a Globus submission job script. Figure 3 shows an example. The site-local job manager agents check for validity of the request based on the token attributes applicable to that particular user and respond accordingly.

Unlike the Globus RSL, local job queue submission interfaces, such as the PBS command *qsub* [8], are often not trivially extended to accept new parameters. To specify the urgency level when submitting directly to a computer's

```
            _test.rsl
+
(&
(resourceManagerContact =
site-contact.teragrid.org/jobmanager-spruce)
(rsl_substitution =
(HOMEDIR "/soft/spruce/examples"))
(executable = $(HOMEDIR)/mpihello)
(jobType = mpi)
(host_types = ia64-compute)
(host_xcount = 4)
(urgency = red)
(stdout = $(HOMEDIR)/globus_stdout)
(stderr = $(HOMEDIR)/globus_stderr)
)
> globusrun -o f globus_test.rsl
Jobnumber.resource.teragrid.org
```

Fig. 3. *globusrun* usage with additional job submission parameters

local job queue usually requires a modified job submission command or a wrapper script. SPRUCE provides a *spruce_sub* script that accepts the additional command line parameter, which can be yellow, orange, or red depending on the required priority.

From the user's perspective, with the job submitted, the final step to the workflow is waiting for the job to be run and the data analyzed. If the resource does not launch the job as expected or if there are run-time errors, the job can be killed or dequeued by using the normally supported tools for the system. Behind the scenes, during the submission process the job is also checked against activated right-of-way tokens. Jobs for users without valid session tokens or unauthorized urgency levels will not be queued. They are rejected immediately. The authorization mechanism is described in the next section.

3 SPRUCE Portal

The SPRUCE portal provides a single-point of administration and authorization for urgent computing across an entire Grid. It consists of three parts:

- The Web-based administrative interface lets privileged users use a standard Web browser to create, issue, monitor, and deactivate right-of-way tokens. It also allows SPRUCE administrators to manage the portal, including adding other administrators, registering new resources, and changing notification email addresses.
- The Web service-based user interface permits token holders to activate an urgent computing session and manage user permissions. Additional features include monitoring session and user information.

– The authentication service verifies jobs. Local site job manager agents ask the remote SPRUCE portal to validate urgent computing jobs. Provided that the user is associated with an active urgent computing session for the local resource and the requested level is within bounds, the portal approves the request.

3.1 Right-of-Way Tokens

Many possible implementations exist for authorizing an emergency computation, ranging from digital certificates, signed files, and proxy authentication servers to shared-secret passwords. In emergency situations, however, simpler is better. Relying on complex digital authentication and authorization schemes could easily become a stumbling block to timely response. Instead, SPRUCE uses simple, transferrable right-of-way tokens (see Figure 4). Tokens are unique 16-character strings that are issued to scientists who have permission to request urgent priority. When a token is created, several important attributes are set: the resource list of included machines, maximum allowable priority, lifetime (period for which elevated priority jobs may be submitted), and expiration date of the token.

Sites can enforce their own policies for each of the allowed priorities. The intent is to have jobs with higher priority displace lower-priority jobs if resources are limited during instances of simultaneous requests. By carefully selecting the attributes of tokens when they are created, local site administrators can make decisions regarding the relative importance of projects and the resources they may use for urgent computation. SPRUCE can support distributed computation in the form of "cross-site" tokens for which resources at multiple sites, or even all resources in the Grid, can be utilized. After a token's lifetime has run out, another token must be activated if additional priority computation is required.

Fig. 4. SPRUCE "right-of-way" token

We emphasize that the right-of-way token is not related to machine access or authentication. Users must already have an account and be able to log on and authenticate in the traditional manner. The token allows the user only to request elevated priority for job submission. Without the token, requests for elevated job priority are simply logged and then ignored. Moreover, after activating the token, only jobs submitted with special, elevated-priority job parameters, described in Section 2.2, will receive unique treatment.

3.2 Administration Interface

Distributed Grids have multiple administration domains. Some Gridwide policies and procedures can be set for all participating resource providers. For the TeraGrid, the Grid Infrastructure Group (GIG) coordinates the software infrastructure, allocation and usage reporting, user support, and Grid security. While each resource provider, such as the San Diego Supercomputer Center, the University of Chicago, or the Texas Advanced Computing Center, has a loosely defined "service level agreement" for participation in the TeraGrid, they are nevertheless independent organizations. To support multiple administration domains and virtual organizations across multiple overlapping Grid systems, SPRUCE maintains a hierarchical Web-based administration interface, which is organized into three levels, each granted powers within its respective domain. Ordered by increasing privileges, these are the site (Grid resource provider), virtual organization, and root administrative domains. Figure 5 illustrates the hierarchical nature of the admin interface.

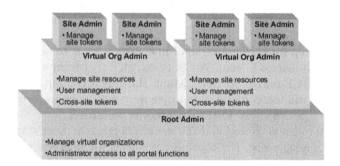

Fig. 5. SPRUCE portal hierarchy of functionality

To permit possibly differing resource and management policies at each site, SPRUCE supports multiple sites under a virtual organization. A token created by a site administrator may be used only for resources present at that site. This strategy enables the site administrator to use SPRUCE in the wider context of a large multisite Grid as well as privately, for local machines and users. The administrator may create and distribute tokens that are limited in scope to the computers the site operates. For example, a local earthquake-modeling team working with an HPC center can be presented tokens that are valid only on the specific supercomputer designated for that research. The local administrator is also responsible for managing the identities of local users as well as the list of machine hosts supporting SPRUCE.

The next level of administration is for the virtual organization spanning several sites, such as the TeraGrid. The administrator for the TeraGrid GIG may issue tokens for resources at multiple sites, in accordance with the policies and service level agreement and management structure of the Grid system. Activating a cross-site token provides users a large collection of machines spread across multiple sites for their jobs. At this level the administrator for the virtual organization can also add new sites.

Administrators also have access to the logging and status information maintained by the portal. Included among this data are the token activation statistics and monitoring of failed attempts to use elevated privilege.

3.3 User Interface

The users of the SPRUCE user interface are the scientists responsible for organizing the application team. Their tasks include monitoring the status of tokens, activating sessions, and organizing the team that may participate in an urgent computing session. The interface for this user community must be simple, fast, and modeled after the workflow described earlier in Section 2. The user services are specifically designed as Web services in order to enable incorporation into existing scientific Web portals and work flows. Users who prefer to use a Web-based interface, can do so at the SPRUCE user portal, which is built on top of these services.

The first step for a computational first responder is to activate a token by entering its 16-digit code via a Web service call either from a local workflow or from the SPRUCE portal. At that instant, the urgent computing session begins. We expect typical token lifetimes to range from 4 to 24 hours, during which the submission of priority jobs to the resources is permitted.

With the token activated and the session begun, the next step in the workflow is user management. For convenience during an emergency, the users who will be running the jobs can be "preloaded" onto a token, if known prior. If not, the participants of the session can be added after token activation. Changes to the user associations of a token are propagated without delay. After a participant is associated with an active token, urgent computing jobs will authenticate correctly. Token holders can also remove participants as needed. All SPRUCE users may monitor basic statistics such as the remaining lifetime of the token.

Since SPRUCE supports urgent computing for Grid users as well as traditional supercomputing users, the portal maintains two methods for specifying the participants in an active session. For those users with Grid credentials, the Distinguished Name (DN) for the user is appropriate. Sites without Grid support can use the Unix username of the participant for the resource.

3.4 Job Authentication

At the core of the SPRUCE architecture is the notion that only while a right-of-way token is active may urgent jobs be submitted. In order to support this notion across a distributed Grid system, a remote authentication step must be inserted into the job submission toolchain for each resource supporting urgent computation. Since the SPRUCE portal contains the updated information regarding active sessions and users permitted to submit urgent jobs, it is also the natural point for authentication.

When an urgent computing job is submitted via Globus or the local queue system, the urgent priority parameters triggers authentication. Remember, this authentication is not for the user, which has already been handled by the traditional Grid certificate or by logging into the Unix-based resource, but is really a "Mother, may I" request for permission to enqueue a high-priority job. That request is sent via the network to the SPRUCE portal, where it is checked against active tokens, resource names, maximum priority, and associated users. If a right-of-way token has already been activated and the other parameters for the job request are within the constraints of the token, permission is granted. All transactions, successful and unsuccessful, are logged.

4 Resource Providers

To support urgent computing for supercomputers via the SPRUCE system, the resource provider must take three actions: register with the SPRUCE portal, formulate a resource specific policy for responding to urgent computing requests, and install SPRUCE components that interface with the job manager and queuing system.

4.1 Portal Registration

Sites participating in SPRUCE need an administrative account on the SPRUCE portal. From that account, administrators can provide the details for each of the computational resources that will support urgent jobs. The site administrator will also provide important contact information that can be used for emergency notification, for example when tokens are activated or critical errors occur. Once that preliminary information has been set up, the administrator may begin generating and issuing right-of-way tokens. If the site is a member of a larger distributed Grid system that is already a part of SPRUCE, it may be merged with the corresponding virtual organization.

4.2 Responding to Urgent Computation

The SPRUCE architecture does not define or assume any particular policy for how sites must respond to urgent computing requests. This approach complicates the architecture and usage scenarios, but it is unavoidable given the current state of systems software for supercomputers. When small-memory vector computers were the standard for HPC computing, preempting jobs was natively supported. Long-running jobs were routinely suspended, not to support urgent decision calculations, but simply to permit shorter jobs to achieve fast turnaround times during compile or debug sessions. Unfortunately, almost all modern supercomputers have lost this once key feature, and therefore the SPRUCE architecture cannot simply standardize the strategy for responding to urgent computation as immediate preemption. Instead, we are left with many possible choices for supporting urgent computation depending on the systems software and middleware as well as on constraints based on accounting for CPU cycles, machine usability, and user acceptance. Given the current technology for Linux clusters and more tightly integrated systems such as the Cray XT3 and the IBM Blue Gene, the following responses to an urgent computing request are some of the possibilities:

- Scheduling the urgent job as "next to run" in a priority queue. This approach is simple and is highly recommended as a possible response for all resource providers. All modern queuing and job management systems support priority queues that will used for selecting the next job to run. No existing computation is killed; and from the perspective of the user community, the impact on normal use is low. The urgent job will begin when all of the existing jobs complete for a given set of CPUs.
- Suspending existing jobs and immediately launching the urgent job. Some systems allow jobs to be suspended but remain resident in memory (sig STOP). Running the urgent job will then force some memory paging, but the suspended job could be restarted later. Some applications that use external data sources and network connections may fail (connections time out and reset) if they are suspended. If a node crashes, the suspended and the urgent job will be lost. The urgent computation will begin almost immediately, making this option very attractive in some cases.
- Forcing a checkpoint/restart of running jobs and enqueueing the urgent job as the next to run. This response is similar to the previous response. Some architectures support system-based checkpoint/restart. Where it is reliable, it could be used to support urgent jobs. Jobs will begin when the checkpoint completes. For large-memory systems, it could be 30 minutes or more depending on I/O and disk rates.
- Killing all running jobs and enqueuing the urgent job as next to run. Clearly this response is drastic and frustrating to users, who will lose their computation. Nevertheless, for extremely urgent computation, what user would demand a black-hole simulation complete before launching an emergency hurricane flood modeling scenario? Urgent jobs could begin immediately after existing jobs are killed.

Another factor in choosing the policy for response is accounting and stakeholder accountability. Certain machines are funded for specific activities, and only small amounts of discretionary time are permitted. In some cases, there may be no specific "charge code" for urgent computing cycles. Furthermore, in order to improve fairness, some form of compensation could be provided to jobs that are killed to make room for an urgent one. For example, users could be refunded their CPU hours, given extra time for their trouble, and rescheduled with higher priority. They could then get back on the machine quickly after the urgent job completes, rather than being relegated to the back of the job queue.

Another idea is to provide discounted CPU cycles for jobs that are willing to be terminated to make room for urgent computation. Some users have extremely robust and well-integrated problem solving environments that can perform checkpoint/restart easily. Some users design their software so only one or two hours of work are lost should a CPU fail or the entire system go down. Such users should be rewarded. A discounted rate would allow them to regain their lost work and run more inexpensively.

The calculation of "maximum time to begin" may play an important role in choosing a response strategy. For machines that support checkpoint/restart or simply killing existing jobs, the maximum time to begin can be bounded, possibly on the order of a few minutes to tens of minutes. If it is easy to calculate or determine, it can be used in conjunction with the computation deadline for selecting resources. Unfortunately, jobs with next-to-run priority could wait hours or days before existing jobs complete. In any case, resource providers are encouraged to map all three levels of urgency—critical, high, and important—to clearly defined responses.

Once the resource provider has decided on a policy and has installed SPRUCE, token holders can activate tokens and associate users, who will then submit urgent priority jobs in one of two ways. Jobs can request priority access by specifying urgency parameters either in Globus job submissions or by using a stand-alone command line *spruce _sub* as described in Section 2.2. These requests are processed by the SPRUCE Job Manager component, which verifies the job request and implements the local policy.

Figure 6 gives an overview of how the job requests are handled at the resource provider.

4.3 Handling Urgent Job Submissions

In the Globus architecture, incoming jobs are routed to a job manager. A job manager tailored to support SPRUCE handles the additional job parameters. When an urgent SPRUCE job is submitted, a job script is dynamically assembled and passed to the native resource manager such as PBS Pro or Torque. It then authenticates the request against the portal (see Section 3.4). This filter makes sure that all job scripts were prepared by the job manager rather than a user attempting to sneak a job into the high-priority queue without SPRUCE validation. In the case of the Torque scheduler, a submit-filter [9] script specific to SPRUCE is run every time a job is submitted. If the user does not have sufficient permission, the request is rejected. If the request passes the verification

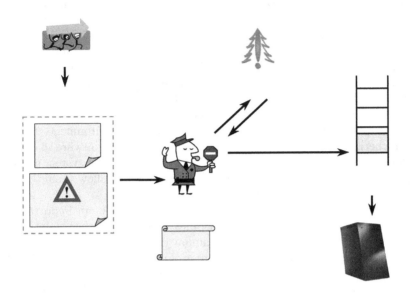

Fig. 6. Resource provider architecture

stage, the actions needed to grant urgent access are performed based on the local site policy and the requested priority level. After verification, the native job scheduler sends the job ID back to Globus, and when the requested resources become available, the queued job is launched.

Local sites can also support the command line version of the urgency job submission mechanism in the form of *spruce_sub*. Submission requests of this type are also routed through the SPRUCE job manager; hence the implementation mechanism remains the same. The only difference between these two submission methods is in the interface.

5 Experiences and Analysis

Currently, SPRUCE is deployed on University of Chicago/Argonne National Laboratory (UC/ANL), Purdue University, Texas Advanced Computing Center (TACC), San Diego Supercomputing Center (SDSC), National Center for Supercomputing Applications (NCSA) TeraGrid resource providers and is in the process of being deployed at Indiana University. Louisiana State University is one of our early non-TeraGrid adopters to use the system for the coastal modeling project SCOOP [10]. We are working with the LEAD Project [11] as they gear up to run severe weather simulations in response to real-time weather data. Tokens are distributed to key members who will act as test users of the system. Efforts are ongoing to configure the applications for periodic warm-standby tests.

The existing implementation of the system encapsulates all the basic framework necessary to allow urgent job submissions. Team first responders can activate and associate user identities with tokens. Team members can then submit jobs with next-to-run priority. The hierarchical administrative domains described in Section 3.2 allow site administrators to manage local tokens.

At the moment, Globus submissions are restricted to the use of the *globusrun* command, and the direct submissions tool *spruce sub* does not handle command line PBS options. All three priority levels map to the next-to-run policy implemented as a priority queue. There are customized distributions to work with most of the popular resource managers and schedulers, as mentioned in Section 2.2. All of them are compatible with pre-Web services versions of the Globus Toolkit. Work is under way to extend the flexibility of the submission tools, enable multisite submissions, and provide extended policy support.

The SPRUCE architecture is designed to work independently or as a part of the Globus installation. The biggest strength of the design is its flexibility: the ability to adapt to any environment it might be interfaced with. The user functionality is implemented completely as Web services using Apache AXIS 2 [12]. External portals and workflows can simply use the Web service interfaces from within their applications. The portal is implemented in PHP and MySQL, uses the underlying Web services, and runs on the Apache Web server. Using a simple Web browser, SPRUCE users can interact with the system. Only minimal additional training is needed, making SPRUCE appropriate for emergency situations. Likewise, administrators will find the interface easy to navigate and use regardless of their environment.

One drawback of the current design of the architecture is that there exists a single point of failure in the form of the portal. If the SPRUCE portal goes down or the user cannot access it, there is no way other way to route the urgent jobs. In order to counteract this weakness, the portal will require redundancy and remote fail-over locations. The existing version of the portal is also subject to the same variety of attacks as other Internet Web servers, including denial of service, spoofing, and abuse of software vulnerabilities. These and other exploits are current research topics and have received considerable attention; we hope to take advantage of these efforts in our future work.

Another challenge is to allow local sites to establish their own policies while keeping SPRUCE installation as simple as possible. Each site needs a customized version of the job manager depending on site policy and scheduler, which cannot be bundled into a common distribution. Hence, site administrators must make minor modifications to the distributed SPRUCE job manager to work with their systems.

6 Future Work

Two of the most attractive and challenging components of the architecture remain to be implemented: the advisor and automated warm-standby testing. SPRUCE jobs are emergency codes that require active maintenance and have certain dependencies that must be taken into account by the SPRUCE advisor before suggesting possible scheduling scenarios to the user. Job-specific information such as running time, data dependencies, and other possible computer-specific characterizations must be collected periodically to ensure that the most recent information is used by the advisor. Warm standby will automate what many users currently do by hand and will ensure the reliability of the monitored emergency codes. It will also help us validate the policy enforcement from time to time. Work is in progress to implement both features by using the INCA monitoring system [13] and MDS4 of the Globus Toolkit. Warm-standby applications require substantial programmer effort, CPU time dedicated to periodic test runs, and fast data transfer. Since the user applications can best be tested for their readiness in the actual environment of the person who will be submitting the job, INCA needs to be customized to submit jobs as the user or collect the data on behalf of the user.

We also plan to incorporate more flexibility to job submissions. Token holders should be able to aggregate tokens and submit jobs from the portal directly. Such flexibility will make SPRUCE a one-stop place to get priority access, select a resource, and submit urgent jobs.

The presented SPRUCE architecture doesn't deal with data movement, which is crucial for most high-performance computations. The advisor will need to take into account transfer delays associated with data movement before advising on the best set of resources. Warm-standby jobs will also have data dependencies that must be resolved automatically. Existing data movement strategies and tools such as the GridFTP project [14] will facilitate SPRUCE. Token-based network authorization would also be a good fit for network provisioning [15].

7 Conclusions

In this paper we have presented the architecture of SPRUCE, a token-based service for providing urgent access to high-performance computing resources modeled after the U.S high-priority telephone system in wide deployment today. The use of tokens allows urgent access to be physically transferrable, and the tokens have restricted access that is encoded prior to their issue. Tokens have expiration dates and lifetimes and may be redeemed only on resources that have been previously encoded into the token. A Web service-based user interface lets scientists manage their tokens easily and efficiently. Moreover, tokens are thoroughly tracked, and all user actions may be monitored by a three-tier hierarchy of administrative domains allowing site, virtual organization, and SPRUCE administrators to enforce policies relevant to their administrative domain.

We have also shown our initial results and an analysis of the architecture for our first TeraGrid customers at the University of Chicago, TACC, SDSC, Purdue University, and NCSA. Currently, we are working on integrating into LEAD portal so scientists can use SPRUCE within their infrastructure. We anticipate significant new developments as more TeraGrid sites and user communities bring SPRUCE support online, including an advanced warm-standby system for periodic testing of emergency codes and policies, a resource selection advisor, and extensions to provide an urgent data movement capability.

References

1. C. D. Keeling, R. B. Bacastow, and T. P. Whorf, "Measurements of the concentration of carbon dioxide at Mauna Loa Observatory, Hawaii," *Carbon Dioxide Review*, pp. 377 – 385, 1982.
2. K. Nagel, R. Beckman, and C. Barrett, "Transmins for transportation planning," in *6th Int. Conf. on Computers in Urban Planning and Urban Management*, 1999.
3. "TeraGrid Project," http://www.teragrid.org.
4. "Telecommunications Service Priority (TSP) program," http://tsp.ncs.gov.
5. J. Schopf, M. D'Arcy, N. Miller, L. Pearlman, I. Foster, and C. Kesselman, "Monitoring and discovery in a Web services framework: Functionality and performance of the Globus Toolkit's MDS4," Argonne National Laboratory, Tech. Rep., 2005.
6. I. Foster, "Globus toolkit version 4: Software for service-oriented systems," in *IFIP International Conference on Network and Parallel Computing*, 2005, pp. 2–13.
7. "Globus Resource Specification Language," http://www.globus.org/toolkit/docs/2.4/gram/rsl spec1.html.
8. "PBS 'qsub' Job Submission Tool," http://www.clusterresources.com/products/torque/docs20/commands/qsub.shtml.
9. "Torque Submit Filter," http://www.clusterresources.com/products/torque/docs20/a.jqsubwrapper.shtml.
10. "Sura Coastal Ocean Observing and Prediction," http://www.scoop.lsu.edu/gridsphere/gridsphere.
11. "Linked Environments for Atmospheric Discovery (LEAD)," http://lead.ou.edu/.
12. "Apache AXIS 2," http://ws.apache.org/axis/.
13. "Test Harness and Reporting Framework (INCA)," http://inca.sdsc.edu.
14. "GridFTP Project," http://www.globus.org/grid software/data/gridftp.php.
15. L. Gommans, F. Travostino, John, Vollbrecht, C. de Laat, and R. Meijer, "Token-based authorization of connection oriented network resources," in *GRIDNETS Conference Proceedings*, October 2004.

Q&A – Suman Nadella

Comment: Craig Douglas

This is highly dangerous from an abuse and political viewpoint. The right approach is to get a fundamental piece of operating systems (checkpoint/restart) implemented universally.

Suman Nadella

Clearly, having system-based checkpoint/restart (CPR) will greatly help the implementation of SPRUCE. For years, CPR was available on many systems, and it permitted very flexible scheduling. However, with the community's move toward clusters with advanced compute node features, system-based CPR is a long way off. There are many Grid applications where compute nodes run TCP/IP services, making automatic system-level check pointing without application code cooperation impossible. While we certainly would benefit from a good CPR system, it is nevertheless important that the framework for supporting Urgent Computing proceed as rapidly as possible, using whatever capabilities exist on each machine. We do not believe, in general, that Urgent Computing poses a significant abuse risk. Scientists who use national supercomputing resources understand how their behavior affects their funding, reputation, and career. Given clear guidelines, we do not believe Urgent Computing will be misused, and should it be misused, the remedy is fast, simple, and effective -- revoke all tokens and kill the Urgent Computing job.

Comment: Gabrielle Allen

I think there are ways to set policies that can be used with on-demand computing, for example, charging less for use of preempt queues.

Suman Nadella

Yes, we believe that with a bit more planning, it may be possible to use a system of rewards and discounts to encourage good behavior and flexible scheduling.

Questioner: Sebastian Goasguen

Why not use standard ACL on a high priority queue?

Suman Nadella

SPRUCE can use whatever means are available to restrict usage on the high priority queue. Some systems provide ACLs. On such machines, SPRUCE can certainly use ACLs to further restrict submissions to only select users. However, we feel it is important to use a token-based system because of the inherent flexibility for Grid and multiple-resource computing as well as the very clear act of "activating a token". Activating a token is meant to signal an

Urgent Condition and alert people even before any ACL or queue is touched. After that happens, ACLs can indeed limit access.

Questioner: Sebastian Goasguen

Why not use the attribute authorization systems like gridshib to 'push' tokens to the resource, i.e., how different is SPRUCE from attribute authorization based system?

Suman Nadella

SPRUCE only uses the tokens to elevate priority, not authorize logins, accounts, or shells. We have specifically stayed clear of all authorization and authentication since each site manages those issues quite differently, and with different tools. Instead, SPRUCE assumes that accounts and the ability to submit jobs are already in place, and the only thing SPRUCE can do is request elevated priority after a token has been activated.

Comment: Brian Ford

This gives us an opportunity to take a responsible position as members of society, to show as scientists we understand the order of issues and have a sense of responsibility and order. It can help us to reposition the evaluation of scientists in the mind of the community. We are not just white coats, bringing doom and gloom from our science. We are responsible individuals who understand the prior need of community for urgent address of immediate emergencies.

Suman Nadella

Yes, thank you for the comment. We too believe that the science community should step forward and offer assistance in several areas where ongoing research can help, such as wildfire and storm prediction. If we begin to work out some of the mechanisms and ideas now, over the next 5 years we will be able to slowly move some of the science apps that could benefit society into a position to actually help.

Comment: Brian Ford

Second point - It is good to think and talk about these issues. We have to start at the beginning and think through the issues. This is what this talk and our reactions are about. Perhaps Nobel Prize winners need to recognize (if they don't already) that there are activities - particularly at specific moments and in special circumstances - that are more important than their individual research (valuable as that may be). There is an order in which computing resources should be used in an emergency. We need to consider and seek to derive that order. Pat Gaffney has a counter view.

Comment: Pat Gaffney

Utilities like water, electricity, and railways should NOT be privatized. They are the responsibility of the Government. Emergencies/ response / analysis etc are the responsibility of Government. Therefore, they should have dedicated resources for this purpose.

Suman Nadella

We understand your concern, but think that the issue is largely about cost, not privatization. Currently, the government uses existing commercial radio stations to broadcast alerts to the public concerning severe weather and abducted children. The US government could maintain a completely independent set of broadcast towers and infrastructure that could then saturate the airwaves with warnings in the event of an emergency. However, everyone realizes that the cost of maintaining completely duplicate infrastructure, only to be used once or twice a month is not cost effective. What SPRUCE does is simply permit supercomputer resources to be used for Urgent Computation. Could the US build a supercomputer center specifically designed for Urgent Computation? Yes. Would it be the best way to use government money? That's a policy question that machine stakeholders need to address. We believe that the responsible use of large-scale resources can be a community service.

Questioner: Mary Thomas

What are your plans to adopt this system to sensor networks or FPGA's?

Suman Nadella

We currently have no plans for integrating sensor networks or FPGA except as they may trigger Urgent Computing jobs. For example, the tornado modeling folks have radar data that can be used to trigger a full-scale Urgent Computing job. Sensor networks may also play an important role in triggering a large computation. FPGAs may be a place where specialized computation can run, but we have not explored that area yet.

Data Management in Dynamic Environment-driven Computational Science

Yogesh L. Simmhan, Sangmi Lee Pallickara, Nithya N. Vijayakumar, and Beth Plale

Computer Science Department, Indiana University, Bloomington IN 47405 USA
{ysimmhan,leesangm,nvijayak,plale}@cs.indiana.edu

Abstract. Advances in numerical modeling, computational hardware, and problem solving environments have driven the growth of computational science over the past decades. Science gateways, based on service oriented architectures and scientific workflows, provide yet another step in democratizing access to advanced numerical and scientific tools, computational resource and massive data storage, and fostering collaborations. Dynamic, data-driven applications, such as those found in weather forecasting, present interesting challenges to Science Gateways, which are being addressed as part of the LEAD Cyberinfrastructure project. In this article, we discuss three important data related problems faced by such adaptive data-driven environments: managing a user's personal workspace and metadata on the Grid, tracking the provenance of scientific workflows and data products, and continuous data mining over observational weather data.

Key words: LEAD, science gateways, cyberinfrastructure, data & metadata management, provenance, data quality, data mining, streams

1 Introduction

Science has evolved over the past several decades, from an empirical and theoretical approach to one that includes simulations and modeling [4]. Additionally, scientific discoveries are increasingly propelled by large, inter-disciplinary groups working across geographical boundaries [40]. For instance, projects such as the Large Hadron Collider aim to solve grand-challenges in science through a collaboration of over 4000 scientists from 40 countries and having access to a central particle accelerator facility costing over US$2 billion [32].

Several advancements in scientific application and computer science have contributed to this evolution. Numerical techniques and algorithms have improved, allowing the real world to be modeled more accurately than ever before [16]. Weather forecasting models such as WRF, short for Weather Research and Forecasting, can now accurately predict regional mesoscale weather at resolutions of 1 Km grid spacing, with an accuracy of over 80%, 5 days in advance of

Please use the following format when citing this chapter:

Simmhan, Y., L., Pallickara, S. L., Vijayakumar, N. N., Pale, B., 2007, in IFIP International Federation for Information Processing, Volume 239, Grid-Based Problem Solving Environments, eds. Gaffney, P. W., Pool, J.C.T., (Boston: Springer), pp. 317-333.

the weather, by integrating data streams across dozens of physical dimensions [20].

Similar advances in computational hardware can now be leveraged transparently through *Science Gateways* [12] that are built on top of standards such as the Common Component Architecture [3] and the *Open Grid Services Architecture (OGSA)* [10]. Science Gateways, also known as *Grids* or *Cyberinfrastructure*, have democratized access to advanced numerical tools, computational cycles, and data resources, that can be uniformly and conveniently accessed by the average scientist through online *Portal* interfaces [21].

However, environmental sciences such as mesoscale meteorology pose special challenges to these Science Gateways since they are largely triggered by events occurring in the external environment. A common requirement that exemplifies this is when a coarse-resolution regional weather forecasting simulation detects a precursor signature of a tornado in a certain region, it should spawn off another fine-resolution simulation in that specific geographical location to see if a tornado is indeed going to form. There are three key implications of such scientific applications that need to be addressed. One, scientific simulations have to be designed such that their structure is dynamic. Secondly, compute and data resources provisioned for the scientific experiments need to adapt to such external events. And lastly, there should be the ability to manage large volumes of data and associated metadata that are generated by various sensors and instruments deployed globally and from the experiments themselves.

In the subsequent section, we delve deeper into the challenges posed by the adaptive and dynamic needs of environmental sciences, and use mesoscale meteorology forecasting in the context of the *Linked Environments for Atmospheric Discovery (LEAD)* [9] project as an example to motivate the problems. In Section 3, we discuss the LEAD Cyberinfrastructure that we are building and the various enabling technologies in it. In Sections 4, 5, and 6, we will look more closely at the data management problems when dealing with terascale data, and successively look at the *myLEAD* personal metadata catalog to describe and manage user's data, the *Karma* provenance framework to track scientific data products and execution of experiments, and the *Calder* data mining tool used with streaming data. Finally, in Section 7, we summarize and present our conclusions.

2 Motivation: Mesoscale Weather Forecasting

Weather forecasting is a static process. Models ingest data generated from sensors like radars, mobile meso-nets, upper-air balloons, geostationary and polar orbiting satellites, commercial aircrafts, and surface observations, for a certain temporal and spatial range required by the forecast model. Then, analysis and assimilation of these data sources take place by performing quality control checks, extrapolating missing data points, and creating a 3D model grid of the forecast region at the given resolution. This is followed by running the actual prediction algorithms using weather models configured by the scientists, and mining of the data to detect abnormal weather patterns. The final step generates 2D/3D images and animations of the forecast that can be disseminated to the scientists and end users. A typical regional prediction of this nature takes about 4 hours to complete, depending on the size of the region and resolution of the forecast.

The key problem with such a model is that it is completely static and the forecast is pre-scheduled to run at certain intervals. Even if a hurricane signature is detected during the data-mining part of the experiment, no action can be taken till the experiment completes, the weather researcher reviews the results, and manually configures and starts another forecast for that particular region. The LEAD project aims to take this well-oiled static computational science mesoscale meteorology forecasting process and tear it apart to be dynamic in response to the environment. There are several benefits to doing this and are supported by recent advancements in weather research.

Firstly, *regional observational models* have better forecast accuracy for a region than do continental models because the resolution of the latter has to be coarser in order to even run on today's computer systems. The solution is to selectively nest regional forecasts within a larger continental model. Secondly, *steerable radars*, notably the CASA Radars, are now being deployed. These allow the focus and collection of high-resolution data on narrow regions, instead of performing 360° swathes all the time. These dynamically steered instruments can be leveraged to increase the forecasting accuracy. And lastly, democratization of scientific resources is now possible through *community resources* such as Teragrid [6] and the availability of well established standards for accessing them. High-schools students can now get access to and learn about the same tools and resources used by weather researchers.

These advances require concomitant advances in fundamental ways in which computational science is done, before they can be leveraged to the fullest extent. These advancements include:

1. Adaptivity in computational models, allowing them to react to external events,
2. Adaptive detection and response to weather, through continuous data mining and instrument steering,
3. Adaptive use of available resources to respond to current computational and data load, and priorities of tasks, and
4. Ability for the underlying data subsystem to mine, record, track, and annotate data products in real time.

In the next section, we give an overview of the overall LEAD architecture. An appreciation of the portal interface to the system and the experiment execution tool is useful for the understanding of the remainder of the paper; so we provide that as well.

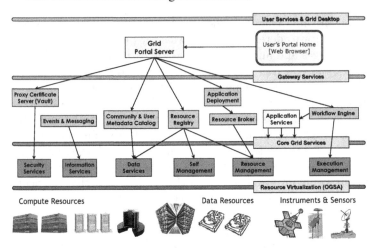

Fig. 1. The LEAD infrastructure is assembled as a set of services that interact with compute, data, and sensor resources, and accessed by a user through a portal.

3 The LEAD Cyberinfrastructure

The LEAD vision is to effect a paradigm shift in the way computation science in mesoscale meteorology is performed, brought about by a service framework for data search and model execution, for weather researchers, and students and teachers at K-12 levels and beyond. The LEAD Cyberinfrastructure builds upon a *Service Oriented Architecture (SOA)* to provide a uniform and secure interface to access resources of common interest to a distributed community of users [12]. Figure 1 illustrates this architecture. At the bottom are physical resources, such as computational clusters, mass-storage, instruments, and sensors. The service architecture virtualizes these resources so that they can be accessed using standard protocols and interfaces, without worrying about the underlying architecture or implementation. The OGSA standard [10] is commonly used as the foundation for resource virtualization in many Grid systems. These resources can be grouped as a set of core services that include security services for authentication and identity mapping, data services for moving, storing, replicating, searching, and accessing data, resource management services to schedule and monitor resources, and execution management services to plan, schedule, and manage the lifecycle of jobs run on the Grid.

On top of these core services are gateway services that provide value-added functionality and are directly exposed to the user community. These include certificate services for identity management and single sign-on capability, metadata catalogs, resource registries, notification services, workflow engines, and application services. The LEAD Portal acts as an online desktop for the users of the gateway, and provides visual interfaces to interact with the various gateway services.

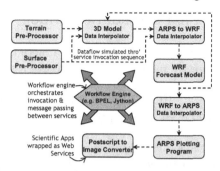

Fig. 2. Typical weather forecasting workflow in LEAD. It goes through stages of ingesting and preprocessing observational data, assimilating it into a 3D grid, running the prediction model on it, and disseminating the forecast as graphics and animations. Each box is a service and their execution is orchestrated by the workflow engine in the center.

Scientists compose experiments, such as complex data searches or model runs, as *workflows*, which consist of domain and middleware services connected as a graph. Domain applications are wrapped as web-services using the Application Factory Toolkit [19]. These application services can be graphically connected together to represent the dataflow between them using the XBaya workflow composer GUI [33], which then compiles the workflow into a Jython or BPEL [1] script that can be executed. A typical weather forecasting workflow is shown in Figure 2. The rectangular boxes represent scientific applications exposed as web-services using the Application Factory. The dotted lines signify dataflow, in the form of files consumed, transformed, and produced by the applications. A workflow engine [39] acts as a central service that orchestrates the invocation of each service in the workflow according to the execution logic.

The adaptivity requirements posited in the previous section are addressed by the LEAD Cyberinfrastructure. The workflow engine is capable of receiving notifications about external weather events that take place, and dynamically alter the execution logic for experiments. This allows for the adaptation of the computational model at runtime. Data mining applications constantly monitor data streams from various sensors looking for abnormal weather signatures. Based on the type of weather activity, these applications can configure and launch an appropriate workflow for the specific geographical region. Resource brokers, self-management services, and monitoring services detect and adapt to failures in the hardware and service substrate, and also provision available services to the required tasks at hand. Provenance services recording workflow execution help workflows resume from points of failure. Personal catalogs tracking a user's experiment assist in reconfiguring and restarting workflows, as also in providing the current status of workflows to the user. These data management tools that enable adaptivity are described in the sections below.

4 myLEAD: Personal Metadata Catalog

The *myLEAD personal workspace* comprises of a metadata catalog service and a separate back end storage manager. The notion of a separate DBMS hosted catalog for metadata is gaining a foothold in computational science through tools such as myGrid [14], MCS [38], and SRB [31], in distributed computing through Lustre [15], and even in enterprise networks through the Acopia ARX [26].

The myLEAD metadata catalog accepts data product descriptions on a wide range of data products including text, binary, images, workflow scripts, and input parameters. Data product descriptions arrive at the catalog as XML documents coded according to the LEAD Metadata Schema (LMS) [30]. A thin service layer provides atomic inserts into the catalog and back end, and performs other duties in cooperation with the workflow system [13]. Early inspiration for the metadata catalog is the Globus MCS metadata catalog [38], and it utilizes the service interfaces provided by the UK e-Science OGSA-DAI tool [2]. It is a distributed service with an instance located at each site in the LEAD Cyberinfrastructure [9]. A user's personal workspace resides at one LEAD Grid site, and is backed up to a master site. Metadata descriptions reside in the metadata catalog, as do smaller data products. Larger products are stored to a storage service, currently the Distributed Replica Service (DRS) [7].

An early estimate of usage of myLEAD is 500 users, where, at any one moment, 25 users are executing a large-scale ensemble computational model. Such ensemble workflows are capable of having up to 1,200 functional applications, and consume and produce up to 10,000 data products [28].

4.1 Data Model

The logical data model for a personal workspace consists of *projects*, *experiments*, *collections*, *logical files*, and *attributes*. Users can store one or more projects in their workspace. Under the projects, one or more experiments, which can themselves contain several collections, can be included. Logical files can belong to one or more collections, experiments, or projects. The structure of a personal workspace can vary based on the user's preference or the design of the applications that cooperate with the metadata catalog. These logical data model objects can be described by attributes associated with them. Attributes can be keywords, or simple or complex name-value pairs that are added during the creation of the objects and enhanced during future accesses to it.

The relational schema we have developed for the data model is highly generalized. Figure 3 shows the UML diagram for a slightly simplified version of the database schema. The database maintains most of the components of the data model in a single table. For instance, experiments, projects, and collections for all user spaces are stored in a single table. Logical files are kept in a separate table. The term *Attribute* is used in the general sense to mean a descriptive feature of a data object. Hereafter, we capitalize it to distinguish it from the

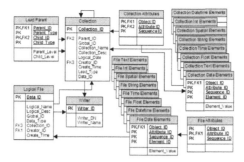

Fig. 3. Simplified relational schema of the myLEAD database. The organizational details (experiments, projects, etc.) and application attributes are coded in the data and not in the schema. This gives the catalog independence from the scientific domain.

database table of the same name. As depicted in Figure 3, an Attribute is implemented in the database schema as attribute and element tables. In the attribute table, the name and structure (i.e., data type) of a possibly complex Attribute are defined. The element table specifies a ⟨name, value⟩ pair belonging to one or more entries in the attribute table.

The attribute table defines attributes as containing one or more elements. Here, an attribute can be added on-the-fly by adding a new row to the attribute table. Although it is slightly more complicated because the attribute must be declared before an instance is created, this design decision reflects the balance we maintain between support for annotations after-the-fact and efficient querying. Additional details on the schema and database support can be found in [18].

4.2 Storing and Querying Metadata by a Hybrid Approach

In the myLEAD metadata catalog, the metadata of the data product is shredded into both Character Large Objects (CLOB) and relational tables. Due to the focus of the catalog on locating data objects that meet a specified criteria, the XML LMS document is stored using a hybrid technique employing both *inlining* and *shredding* [18]. Parts of the document received at the catalog are stored as CLOBs in the database for faster reconstruction. Key pieces of the schema are shredded (broken apart) for fast querying. This eliminates the need for achieving lossless shredding from XML since the shredded data is no longer needed to construct the XML documents returned in query responses.

4.3 Service Architecture

The myLEAD personal workspace is a distributed tool as depicted in Figure 4. At the lowest layer, there are set of distributed storage services such as the Distributed Replica Service (DRS) [7] for the personal data products and Unidata's

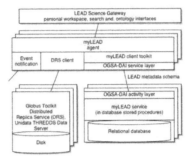

Fig. 4. Architecture of myLEAD personal workspace. The agent is a single service layer on top of the storage repository and the metadata catalog. It intercepts workflow activities by listening on event notification channels.

THREDDS Data Server (TDS) [8] for the public data products. Metadata on personal data products is managed by the myLEAD service and stored to a relational database. Much of the logic is implemented as database stored procedures. The data products themselves are either co-located with the metadata in the database (as in the case of workflow scripts), or passed to a replica manager, such as DRS. We envision providing support for TDS in the future, which provides features specific to the meteorology domain, such as sub-setting and aggregating files, and extracting fields from binary netCDF file. The server is a long-lived grid service built on top of a relational database. It is built on the OGSA-DAI service [2] interface layer.

The myLEAD agent provides client-side services for human users working interactively through the portal, and to other services in the LEAD system, particularly the workflow execution engine. The myLEAD agent responds to activities being carried out on the LEAD Cyberinfrastructure by listening on an event notification channel [17] on which status events about workflow progress are published. The agent uses the notification messages to determine the current state of a particular workflow, and actively manages the user space by, for instance, creating a new collection when a major mode transition has taken place [29]. Users interact with the tools primarily through the LEAD Cyberinfrastructure [11]. However, we are building user interactive features beyond the portal, such as to download and visualize archived experiments on their laptops.

5 Karma: Provenance Framework

Provenance [34, 5] is a form of metadata that describes the causality of an event, and the context within which to interpret it. Provenance about workflow executions is vital for scientific workflows and experiments to ensure that the exact sequence of tasks executed in the experiment is recorded [34]. This log, called the *workflow provenance*, describes the events that took place during the course of a workflow's execution and tries to address the questions of what services were invoked, where the workflow and services ran, what their inputs and outputs were (including data products used and produced), who invoked the workflow, and so on. This type of provenance is necessary to verify and validate the experiments at a later time, and brings in accountability. It is a useful debugging tool post-execution and a monitoring tool while the experiment is running. It can also be used to track resource usage and help with scheduling future runs of the workflow.

Provenance about data generated by and used in workflows is termed *data provenance*. It attempts to answer questions about the origin of the data (in the form of workflows or services that created it), the input data that were transformed to create this data, and the usage trail for the data product. This form of provenance is necessary to discover the creator of the data, to provide insight on its quality, and may also help determine its copyright. The data usage trail also comes in handy when users of the data need to be notified of potential errors in the creation of the data.

The *Karma provenance framework* [35] collects both these forms of provenance for the scientific workflows running in the LEAD Cyberinfrastructure. The provenance model is designed around an abstract workflow model and activities defined at different parts of the workflow help collect provenance. A key application of the collected provenance is in estimating the quality of workflow derived data products in the LEAD system.

5.1 Provenance Model

The *Karma provenance framework* [35] used in the LEAD project uses an abstract model of a workflow, which it considers as a directed graph, with nodes representing services and edges representing the dataflow between them. Services are used as a layer of abstraction on top of scientific tasks to enable their use in a SOA [19]. As a workflow executes, different services are invoked in sequence by a workflow engine interpreting the workflow logic. Data products and other parameters are passed as inputs to the service, which subsequently emits the generated data products. Invoking a service consists of staging the input files to the service location, launching the scientific task that the service wraps (usually as a command-line application), monitoring the execution of the scientific application, registering the output result from the application with the myLEAD catalog, and staging the data to a central data repository. These files may be used by subsequent services invoked by that workflow or other workflows.

As can be seen, the workflow execution takes place at 3 levels: at the workflow engine level, at the service level, and at the scientific application level. The Karma provenance framework tracks provenance as *activities* that take place at different stages of the workflow. These activities in a workflow are distributed across various dimensions, one of them being the level. The activities, such as `WorkflowStarts/Finishes`, `ServiceStarts/Finishes`, and

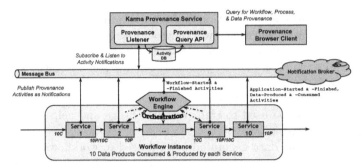

Fig. 5. The Karma Provenance Architecture. Workflows executing at the bottom publish provenance activities to a notification broker in the middle. These XML activities are subscribed to by the Karma provenance service at the top and recorded in a database. The provenance graph is reconstructed just-in-time and disseminated when queried for by clients.

`ApplicationStarts/Finishes`, take place at the boundaries between different levels. In addition, the activities contain a logical timestamp that helps order them and tracks the causality of the events. A third parameter present in the activity is the host where the event took place, which captures the distributed nature of the execution across organizational boundaries. Finally, two activities, `DataProduced/Consumed`, generated by the applications, help to track the dataflow between the applications.

Based on these activities generated by the various components of the workflow, a dynamic model of the workflow execution and the dataflow between the services can be constructed at workflow runtime. These activities are collected by the central provenance service, and used to build the workflow and data provenance graphs, and query upon them. Figure 5 shows the architecture of Karma. As the workflow executes at the bottom, its components produce activities, represented as XML notifications published to a pub-sub notification system [17]. The Karma provenance service subscribes to these activities and records them in a relational database. When a client queries the Karma service for workflow or data provenance through its web-service interface, the activities are reconstructed and composed together to form the workflow or dataflow graph, and returned to the client as an XML provenance document. Client libraries and the Application Service Toolkit [19] automate and ease the user's burden of generating these activities. Empirical performance measures have shown the overhead for collecting provenance activities to be under 1% of the application run time [36].

5.2 Provenance and Data Quality

One novel use that provenance is being applied to in LEAD is in predicting the quality of data products generated from the workflows. It is intuitive that the way a data is created has a bearing on its quality. Since provenance describes the

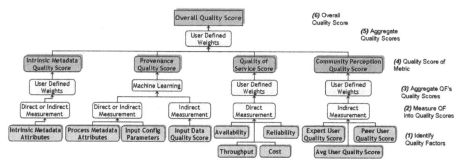

Fig. 6. Model to evaluate quality score of data product using various metrics applied to metadata attributes based on user-defined quality constraints. At the bottom are the attributes that affect the data's quality, and they are aggregated, using various metrics and user-defined constraints, to the overall quality score for the data at the top.

derivation history of data created by a workflow, it can be leveraged to estimate the data quality. Provenance forms a key attribute in the generic quality model [37] being used to quantify the quality of data products in LEAD. Such a quantification is necessary to allow comparison of data products when a user is trying to locate data for input to a workflow or for visualization and analysis. Typical search techniques for scientific data depend on the user to provide values for attributes that are then matched. These usually end up being too broad resulting in a large number of results with little to distinguish between them. Our quality model brings in not just the *intrinsic metadata* available for the data product, but also hidden (or indirect) metadata such as the *quality of service* of accessing the data product, the *community's perception* of the data, and *data provenance*.

Recognizing that quality is a very subjective matter, our quality model allows the users to define *quality constraints* on the intrinsic and hidden attributes of data products at a fine granularity [37]. The constraints are rules that define the relative importance of each attribute, which can then be evaluated for each matching data product and aggregated into a numerical *quality score* for the data product. This score then forms the basis for filtering query results and presenting only the most relevant data products in a sorted order to the user.

The quality model [37] used to evaluate the user's quality constraint is shown in Figure 6. Starting at the bottom, we have various intrinsic metadata attributes and indirect attributes available for a data product, including the provenance, represented as process metadata and input parameters. Based on the type of the attribute, different techniques are used to measured and converted them into a numerical estimate. For example, provenance is used to construct a quality model for the process deriving that data, and this model is used to generate a provenance quality score for the data. *Quality metrics* modeled as weighting functions are applied to the quality scores for attributes, guided by the user's constraints. These result in an aggregate quality score for

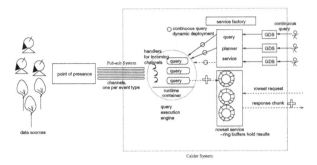

Fig. 7. Calder Architecture.

each metric, that are further combined into a single *overall quality score* for the data product. This score can then be used to rank the data product and help in the data search process.

6 Calder: Stream Mining of Environmental Data

In LEAD, the forecasting application is a special kind of data driven application that is triggered when an abnormal weather event is detected. Dynamic execution of forecast models is specified using a *rule-action* paradigm. A *rule*, defined by a user and run for a specific period of time, is a combination of filtering tasks and data mining actions triggered by the occurrence of certain events. The *action* portion of the rule-action paradigm is an invocation that kicks off a latent forecast model. Continuous data mining is performed in LEAD using the *Calder system*. A brief description of the dynamic adaptation scenario in LEAD is provided in [43].

Calder [41, 25] is a web-service that performs continuous query execution over real time streams of observational data (Figure 7). The query submission, modeled on OGSA-DAI [2], is through a data service that implements an extended realization of the GGF DAIS specification to stream systems [24]. Queries are expressed as *event-action* SQL queries deployed into the system dynamically at runtime with an associated lifetime. Calder is responsive to asynchronous stream rates and has sophisticated event scheduling mechanisms that improve the service time compared to conventional stream processing [27]. The Calder system contains a distributed query service and a stream provenance service. The distributed query planner optimizes the queries and distributes them among computational resources using a cost-efficient model [23]. The provenance service uses different models [42] to track the provenance of streams and queries in the system.

In LEAD, Calder is invoked from within a workflow as shown in Figure 8, which shows the execution of the data mining algorithm on the observational NexRad Level II data. The request to the Calder stream query service returns

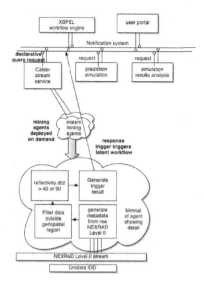

Fig. 8. Stream processing to detect vortices in Doppler radar data (below) as part of a larger workflow (above).

when the data mining results in a response trigger, such as "bad weather found". The Calder system communicates with external LEAD components using a common notification bus that transports WS-Eventing messages [17], and a separate, internal event channel for the transfer of data streams. Calder's query execution engine subscribes to channels that stream in observational data as events. These events are either described by XML metadata or arrive as *bzipped* binary data chunks.

When the query is instantiated at the computational node, it executes the filtering/data mining loop depicted at the bottom of Figure 8 for every incoming NexRad Level II Doppler radar volume scan. If the classification algorithm detects a vortex pattern whose intensity exceeds a pre-defined threshold (MDA algorithm [22]) or detects possible storm centers where the reflectivity exceeds a pre-defined threshold (SDA algorithm), a response trigger is issued to the WS-Eventing notification channel. The workflow engine subscribes to the notification channel, and acts on the message by waking up the dormant prediction simulation. We are currently expanding the continuous mining scenario in LEAD to include mining over multiple radars and aggregation of mining outputs that could be used to monitor the movement of storms over a spatial region, thereby providing more meaningful information to the forecast system.

7 Conclusions

The LEAD Cyberinfrastructure is providing essential data management tools that enable computational weather scientists to carry out investigations that are dynamically adaptive to weather. These tools, described in this article, allow scientists to manage experimental data in a grid-embedded workspace by automatically cataloging all pieces in the e-Science experiment; precisely track the execution of the workflow and creation of the data products as provenance to help scientists verify their results at a later time and to help the community in evaluating and reusing the data through quality metrics; and in mining observational weather data in real time to automatically respond to weather events by configuring and running computational models, the results of which could potentially save lives.

LEAD has a major commitment to providing facilities to educational users. The same tools being developed for weather researchers can also be configured for students and teachers to run simple weather forecasting models through the LEAD portal as part of class assignments. Glossaries and ontological dictionaries are being developed to assist beginners in learning key concepts about weather, and techniques such as community quality perception indices used by the quality model can possibly serve as means for knowledge transfer between researchers and students.

The data management tools developed for LEAD are also being applied to other data driven computational science domains with similar dynamic and adaptive properties. Our contributions, highlighted in this article, make it easier for the scientist to locate, understand, and use their data, allowing them to advance the frontiers of science more rapidly.

8 Acknowledgments

The authors would like to thank our collaborators in the LEAD project, notably Dennis Gannon, Kelvin Droegemeier, Dan Reed, Mohan Ramamurthy, Bob Wilhelmson, Sara Graves, and Rich Clark; students who contributed to this work, Scott Jensen, Ying Liu, and Yiming Sun; and the National Science Foundation (ATM-0331480, CDA-0116050, EIA-0202048) and the Department of Energy (DE-FG02-04ER25600) whose grants enabled this work.

References

1. Tony Andrews, Francisco Curbera, Hitesh Dholakia, Yaron Goland, Johannes Klein, Frank Leymann, Kevin Liu, Dieter Roller, Doug Smith, Satish Thatte, Ivana Trickovic, and Sanjiva Weerawarana. *Business Process Execution Language for Web Services Version 1.1*. BEA Systems and International Business Machines Corporation andMicrosoft Corporation and SAP AG and Siebel Systems, 2003.
2. Mario Antonioletti, Malcolm Atkinson, Rob Baxter, Andrew Borley, Neil P. Chue Hong, Brian Collins, Neil Hardman, Alastair C. Hume, Alan Knox, Mike Jackson, Amy Krause, Simon Laws, James Magowan, Norman W. Paton, Dave Pearson, Tom Sugden, Paul Watson, and Martin Westhead. The design and implementation of grid database services in ogsa-dai: Research articles. *Concurrency and Computation: Practice and Experience*, 17(2-4):357–376, 2005.

3. Rob Armstrong, Dennis Gannon, Al Geist, Katarzyna Keahey, Scott Kohn, Lois McInnes, Steve Parker, and Brent Smolinski. Toward a common component architecture for high-performance scientific computing. In *High Performance Distributed Computing Conference*, 1999.

4. Gordon Bell, Jim Gray, and Alex Szalay. Petascale computational systems. *Computer*, 39(1):110–112, 2006.

5. Rajendra Bose and James Frew. Lineage Retrieval for Scientific Data Processing: A Survey. *ACM Computing Surveys*, 37(1):1–28, 2005.

6. Charlie Catlett. *The TeraGrid: A Primer*. TeraGrid, 2002.

7. Ann Chervenak, Robert Schuler, Carl Kesselman, Scott Koranda, and Brian Moe. Wide area data replication for scientific collaborations. In *Workshop on Grid Computing*, 2005.

8. Ben Domenico, John Caron, Ethan Davis, Robb Kambic, and Stefano Nativi. Thematic real-time environmental distributed data services (thredds): Incorporating interactive analysis tools into nsdl. *Digital Information*, 2(4), 2002.

9. Kelvin K. Droegemeier, Dennis Gannon, Daniel Reed, Beth Plale, Jay Alameda, Tom Baltzer, Keith Brewster, Richard Clark, Ben Domenico, Sara Graves, Everette Joseph, Donald Murray, Rahul Ramachandran, Mohan Ramamurthy, Lavanya Ramakrishnan, John A. Rushing, Daniel Weber, Robert Wilhelmson, Anne Wilson, Ming Xue, and Sepideh Yalda. Service-oriented environments for dynamically interacting with mesoscale weather. *Computing in Science and Engineering*, 7(6):12–29, 2005.

10. Ian Foster, Hiro Kishimoto, Andreas Savva, Dave Berry, Andrew Grimshaw, Bill Horn, Fred Maciel, Frank Siebenlist, Ravi Subramaniam, Jem Treadwell, and Jeffrin Von Reich. *The Open Grid Services Architecture, Version 1.5*. Global Grid Forum, 2006.

11. Dennis Gannon, Jay Alameda, Octav Chipara, Marcus Christie, Vinayak Dukle, Liang Fang, Matthew Farellee, Geoffrey Fox, Shawn Hampton, Gopi Kandaswamy, Deepti Kodeboyina, Charlie Moad, Marlon Pierce, Beth Plale, Albert Rossi, Yogesh Simmhan, Anuraag Sarangi, Aleksander Slominski, Satoshi Shirasauna, and Thomas Thomas. Building grid portal applications from a web-service component architecture. *Proceedings of the IEEE*, 93(3):551–563, 2005.

12. Dennis Gannon, Beth Plale, Marcus Christie, Liang Fang, Yi Huang, Scott Jensen, Gopi Kandaswamy, Suresh Marru, Sangmi Lee Pallickara, Satoshi Shirasuna, Yogesh Simmhan, Aleksander Slominski, and Yiming Sun. Service oriented architectures for science gateways on grid systems. In *International Conference on Service Oriented Computing*, 2005.

13. Dennis Gannon, Beth Plale, Suresh Marru, Gopi Kandaswamy, Yogesh Simmhan, and Satoshi Shirasuna. *Workflows for eScience: Scientific Workflows for Grids*, chapter Dynamic, Adaptive Workflows for Mesoscale Meteorology. Springer-Verlag, 2006.

14. Carole Goble, Chris Wroe, Robert Stevens, and the myGrid consortium. The mygrid project: services, architecture and demonstrator. In *UK e-Science programme All Hands Meeting*, 2003.

15. N. Halbwachs, P. Caspi, P. Raymond, and D. Pilaud. The synchronous dataflow programming language LUSTRE. *Proceedings of the IEEE*, 79(9):1305–1320, 1991.

16. Elias N. Houstis, John R. Rice, Efstratios Gallopoulos, and Randall Bramley, editors. *Enabling Technologies for Computational Science: Frameworks, Middleware and Environments*, chapter 1, pages 7–17. Kluwer Academic, 2000.

17. Yi Huang, Alek Slominski, Chatura Herath, and Dennis Gannon. WS-Messenger: A Web Services based Messaging System for Service-Oriented Grid Computing. In *Cluster Computing and Grid Conference*, 2006.

18. Scott Jensen, Beth Plale, Sangmi Lee Pallickara, and Yiming Sun. A hybrid xml-relational grid metadata catalog. In *International Conference Workshops on Parallel Processing*, 2006.

19. Gopi Kandaswamy, Liang Fang, Yi Huang, Satoshi Shirasuna, Suresh Marru, and Dennis Gannon. Building Web Services for Scientific Grid Applications. *IBM Journal of Research and Development*, 50(2/3):249–260, 2006.

20. Richard A. Kerr. Storm-in-a-box forecasting. *Science*, 304(5673):946–468, 2004.

21. Sriram Krishnan, Randall Bramley, Dennis Gannon, Rachana Ananthakrishnan, Madhusudhan Govindaraju, Aleksander Slominski, Yogesh Simmhan, Jay Alameda, Richard Alkire, Timothy Drews, and Eric Webb. The xcat science portal. *Journal of Scientific Programming*, 10(4):303–317, 2002.

22. Xiang Li, Rahul Ramachandran, John Rushing, Sara Graves, Kevin Kelleher, S. Lakshmivarahan, Douglas Kennedy, and Jason Levit. Mining nexrad radar data: An investigative study. In *Interactive Information and Processing Systems*. American Meteorological Society, 2004.

23. Ying Liu and Beth Plale. Query optimization for distributed data streams. In *Software Engineering and Data Engineering Conference*, 2006.

24. Ying Liu, Beth Plale, and Nithya Vijayakumar. Realization of ggf dais data service interface for grid access to data streams. Technical Report 613, Indiana University, Computer Science Department, 2005.

25. Ying Liu, Nithya N. Vijayakumar, and Beth Plale. Stream processing in data-driven computational science. In *Grid Conference*, 2006.

26. Acopia Networks. File virtualization with the acopia arx. Technical report, Acopia Networks, 2005.

27. Beth Plale. Leveraging run time knowledge about event rates to improve memory utilization in wide area data stream filtering. In *High Performance Distributed Computing Conference*, 2002.

28. Beth Plale. Usage study for data storage repository in lead. Technical Report 001, LEAD, 2005.

29. Beth Plale, Dennis Gannon, Yi Huang, Gopi Kandaswamy, Sangmi Lee Pallickara, and Aleksander Slominski. Cooperating services for data-driven computational experimentation. *Computing in Science and Engineering*, 07(5):34–43, 2005.

30. Beth Plale, Rahul Ramachandran, and Steve Tanner. Data management support for adaptive analysis and prediction of the atmosphere in lead. In *Conference on Interactive Information Processing Systems for Meteorology, Oceanography, and Hydrology*, 2006.

31. Arcot Rajasekar, Michael Wan, and Reagan Moore. Mysrb & srb: Components of a data grid. In *High Performance Distributed Computing Conference*, 2002.

32. Kurt Riesselmann. 600 US scientists + 3500 scientists from other countries = The New High-Energy Frontier. *Symmetry*, 2(3):18–21, 2005.

33. Satoshi Shirasuna and Dennis Gannon. Xbaya: A graphical workflow composer for the web services architecture. Technical Report 004, LEAD, 2006.

34. Yogesh Simmhan, Beth Plale, and Dennis Gannon. A survey of data provenance in e-science. *SIGMOD Record*, 34(3):31–36, 2005.

35. Yogesh L. Simmhan, Beth Plale, and Dennis Gannon. A Framework for Collecting Provenance in Data-Centric Scientific Workflows. In *International Conference on Web Services*, 2006.

36. Yogesh L. Simmhan, Beth Plale, and Dennis Gannon. Performance evaluation of the karma provenance framework for scientific workflows. *LNCS*, 4145, 2006.
37. Yogesh L. Simmhan, Beth Plale, and Dennis Gannon. Towards a Quality Model for Effective Data Selection in Collaboratories. In *IEEE Workshop on Scientific Workflows and Dataflows*, 2006.
38. Gurmeet Singh, Shishir Bharathi, Ann Chervenak, Ewa Deelman, Carl Kesselman, Mary Manohar, Sonal Patil, and Laura Pearlman. A metadata catalog service for data intensive applications. In *ACM Supercomputing Conference*, 2003.
39. Alek Slominski. *Workflows for e-Science*, chapter Adapting BPEL to Scientific Workflows. Springer-Verlag, 2006. In Press.
40. Dennis E. Stevenson. Science, computational science, and computer science: at a crossroads. In *Conference on Computer Science*. ACM Press, 1993.
41. Nithya N. Vijayakumar, Ying Liu, and Beth Plale. Calder query grid service: Insights and experimental evaluation. In *Cluster Computing and Grid Conference*, 2006.
42. Nithya N. Vijayakumar and Beth Plale. Towards low overhead provenance tracking in near real-time stream filtering. *LNCS*, 4145, 2006.
43. Nithya N. Vijayakumar, Beth Plale, Rahul Ramachandran, and Xiang Li. Dynamic filtering and mining triggers in mesoscale meteorology forecasting. In *International Geoscience and Remote Sensing Symposium*, 2006.

PART 6

APPLICATIONS I

M. Thuné, Session Chair; I. Reid, Discussant

M. Garbey: *Efficient Algorithm to Compute PDEs on the Grid* (Abstract)

J. Alameda: *On the Use of Services to Support Numerical Weather Prediction*

J. Padget: *Mathematical Service Discovery*

Panel Discussion

Efficient Algorithm to Compute PDEs on the Grid

Marc Garbey

University of Houston

Abstract. This presentation will discuss the design of numerically efficient algorithm to solve PDEs on the Grid. Efficiency of numerical algorithms are strongly dependent on the features of computer architecture. In western countries the architecture of large scale parallel computer is essentially driven by industrial cost. Large "Uniform" Multi-Processors Architecture are replaced progressively by Multi-clusters Architecture or Beowulf systems that are cheaper. In such architecture Communication and/or memory access is generally very slow compare to the speed of the cpu units. Further cpu units may have several levels of cache and memory. It is then very difficult to achieve peak performance even on a single computer. The situation does not seems to improve: cpu flops still increases by a factor 2 every 18 months while bandwidth to access the memory is improving very slowly. An extreme situation is grid computing for which networks are at least one or two order of magnitude slower than internal network of parallel architecture. It is therefore a general problem to design numerical algorithm that can keep parallel efficiency in such environment. Meta-computing is a good test bed because it is probably the most challenging situation to achieve efficiency of a numerical scheme. Any numerical algorithm that will be efficient on Metacomputing Architecture such as a grid of parallel computers linked by a slow network should be of interest for large ASCI machine as well. There are some simple general idea that one may keep in mind to design numerical algorithm for PDE applications in grid environment: - ForWave propagation phenomenon: Speed of propagation of data in Memory should be the analogue of the speed of propagation of waves. - For Heat Transfer: Domain of influence of data in memory should be set according to decay of heat in space, i.e finite size depending on the level of accuracy. - For Steady flow: Data representation and space dependencies should match the memory Hierarchy. - For data transfer in Network, one may split the significant digits corresponding to required accuracy from the digits required for

Please use the following format when citing this chapter:

Garbey, M., 2007, in IFIP International Federation for Information Processing, Volume 239, Grid-Based Problem Solving Environments, eds. Gaffney, P. W., Pool, J.C.T., (Boston: Springer), pp. 337-338.

stability only. As a matter of fact in most of the applications, one look for a numerical result within one per cent accuracy and the need to carry all digits in communications should be review according to stability theory. In this paper we will concentrate on domain decomposition methods that are particularly efficient for large scale metacomputing.

On the Use of Services to Support Numerical Weather Prediction

Jay Alameda, Albert L. Rossi, Shawn Hampton
University of Illinois at Urbana-Champaign, National Center for
Supercomputing Applications, 1205 W. Clark St., Urbana, IL, 61801,
jalameda@ncsa.uiuc.edu

The challenges of building an effective grid-based problem solving
environment that truly extends and embraces a computational scientist's
traditional tools are multifold. It is far too easy to build simple stovepipes that
allow fixed use patterns, that don't extend a scientist's desktop, and fail to
encompass the full range of patterns that a scientist needs to find such a
problem-solving environment as a liberating and enabling tool. In the LEAD
project, we have focused on the most challenging users of numerical weather
prediction, namely, the atmospheric science researchers, who are prone to use
their own tools, their own modified versions of community codes such as the
Weather Research and Forecasting (WRF) model, and are typically
comfortable with elaborate shell scripts to perform the work they find to be
necessary to succeed, to drive our development efforts. Our response to these
challenges includes a multi-level workflow engine, to handle both the
challenges of ensemble description and execution, as well as the detailed
patterns of workflow on each computational resource; services to support the
peculiarities of each platform being used to do the modeling (such as on
TeraGrid), and the use of an RDF triple store and message bus together as the
backbone of our notification, logging, and metadata infrastructure. The design
of our problem-solving environment elements attempts to come to grips with
lack of control of elements surrounding and supporting the environment; we
achieve this through multiple mechanisms including using the OSGI plug-in
architecture, as well as the use of RDF triples as our finest-grain descriptive
element. This combination, we believe, is an important stepping stone to
building a cyber environment, which aims to provide flexibility and ease of
use far beyond the current range of typical problem solving environments.

Please use the following format when citing this chapter:

Alameda, J., Rossi, A. L., Hampton, S., 2007, in IFIP International Federation for Information Processing, Volume 239,
Grid-Based Problem Solving Environments; eds. P. W. Gaffney, Pool, J.C.T..; (Boston: Springer), pp. 339-348.

1   Numerical Weather Prediction as a science driver (Linked Environments for Atmospheric Discovery, LEAD)

Numerical Weather Prediction, in its current form, revolves around pre-scheduled computations, running models such as the Weather Research and Forecasting (WRF) [WRF] code on fixed grids, using observations statically obtained on a fixed schedule, to generate predictions of future weather, as depicted in Figure 1.

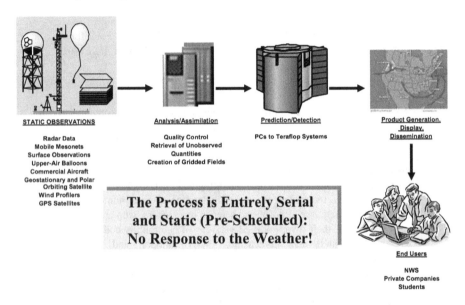

STATIC OBSERVATIONS   Analysis/Assimilation   Prediction/Detection   Product Generation, Display, Dissemination

Radar Data
Mobile Mesonets
Surface Observations
Upper-Air Balloons
Commercial Aircraft
Geostationary and Polar
Orbiting Satellite
Wind Profilers
GPS Satellites

Quality Control
Retrieval of Unobserved
Quantities
Creation of Gridded Fields

PCs to Teraflop Systems

The Process is Entirely Serial and Static (Pre-Scheduled): No Response to the Weather!

End Users

NWS
Private Companies
Students

Figure 1. Traditional Numerical Weather Prediction Methodology (credit: K. Droegemeier, U Oklahoma)

The National Science Foundation funded information technology research project, Linked Environments for Atmospheric Discovery (LEAD), was funded to address the shortcomings in the traditional forecasting methodology, and, for the first time, provide a means for people and technologies to interact with the weather [LEAD]. This project, a partnership of researchers from the University of Oklahoma, Indiana University, University of North Carolina at Chapel Hill, University of Alabama in Huntsville, the University of Illinois at Urbana-Champaign, Millersville University, Howard University, Colorado State University and University Corporation for Atmospheric Research (UCAR), is doing basic information technology research into the issues to enable models to respond to observations, as well as have models and algorithms drive sensors. This research is resulting in an integrated, scalable framework that allows analysis tools, forecast models and data repositories to be used as dynamically adaptive, on-demand systems that adapt in response to the weather, respond to users, initiate processes automatically, steer remote observatories, and operate independent of data format and location, as well as location of compute resources. The group at Illinois has been focusing on the use cases provided by our atmospheric science researchers. These researchers can be characterized by:

- having their own research computing allocations
- need to modify community codes or write their own codes
- work both remotely and locally on their own workstation
- always looking to innovate by asking tough questions: i.e., what will the weather look like with today's moderate risk of severe weather?
- Need to work with tens to hundreds of simulations

In this paper, we will describe the particular infrastructure we developed to meet these requirements, starting with our context within the LEAD Architecture.

2   LEAD Architecture

The LEAD project has broadly defined a service architecture, depicted abstractly in Figure 2. In this figure, user interfaces are clients of a set of crosscutting and configuration and execution services, which in turn access distributed resources through resource access services, such as those provided by the Globus Project [Globus]

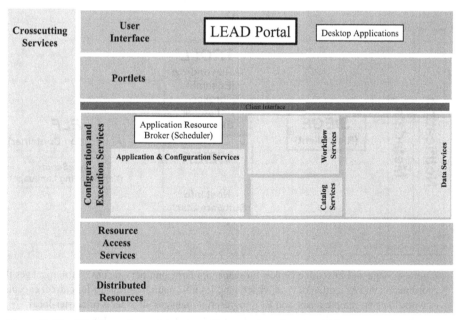

Figure 2. The LEAD service architecture. The majority of work within LEAD is in the area of crosscutting services, user interfaces, and configuration/execution services.

For our work with researchers, our focus has been on services and interface elements as depicted in Figure 3.

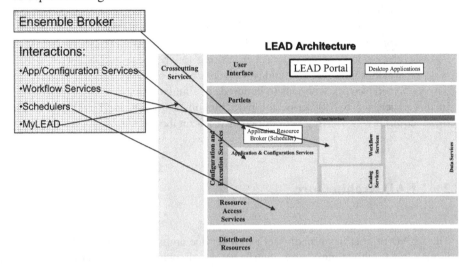

Figure 3. Context of UIUC contributions to LEAD within the LEAD service architecture. We are building a facility for managing atmospheric science ensembles, the Ensemble Broker, and a group of supporting services for this facility.

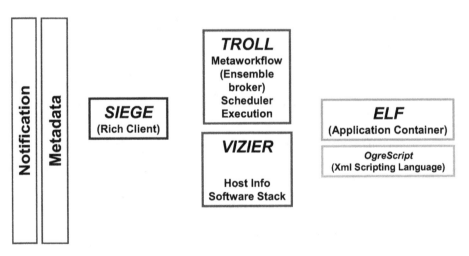

Figure 4. Siege and Ensemble Broker for managing large numbers of runs. Troll manages the coordination and execution of runs, vizier supplies information necessary for correct execution of workflows on remote hosts, and ELF+ogrescript manages all aspects of cluster-local execution. Tying this all together is notification and metadata (in progress).

Our application partners have the following requirements that have shaped our work. First, they need a facility to manage a large number of runs. Secondly, they need efficient interactions with their desktop platform. Thirdly, they need to be able to make modifications in a simple and powerful way – for instance, to add their own application, or to change their pattern of work. As a result, we developed a simple workflow description (ensemble builder to describe the overall interactions between jobs, and ogrescript for the compute resource-local orchestration), and a desktop tool (Siege) to manage their work. These pieces, which fit in the context of Figure 3, can be depicted schematically in Figure 4, which shows the desktop client, Siege [Siege], which interacts with the Troll ensemble broker stack and Vizier information services, to deploy applications controlled by the remote application container, ELF, which implements our own scripting language, OgreScript. Tying the system together are the notification systems, currently using the Java Messaging Service (JMS) [JMS] channel ActiveMQ [ActiveMQ], and a metadata system (we are planning to integrate myLEAD into the JMS channel, to be able to create LEAD metadata objects [LMS] from metadata events published to the channel).

The Siege desktop client is built using the Eclipse Rich Client Platform (RCP) [RCP], which has many advantages including ease of interface mockup, pluggable modules, and well-defined extension points. We are also using RCP to build our services, as it provides a nice modularity to better manage dependencies, especially on third-party libraries such as the jglobus [jglobus] client libraries that we use to access grid capabilities such as job submission and file management.

With Siege, the user authenticates to a myproxy server backed with a Kerberos realm [myproxy] to allow delegation of short term grid credentials to the Siege client by mere use of a user's Kerberos login at NCSA or on TeraGrid. This login, which is granted as normal part of a user's allocation at NCSA, allows users seamless access to computational resources through Siege, by use of their familiar Kerberos login (as depicted in Figure 5).

Figure 5 Siege MyProxy login, which uses Kerberos authentication for NCSA and TeraGrid.

Siege provides simple mechanisms for describing, executing and monitoring workflows. For instance, a user can directly edit the xml description of the workflow, as depicted in Figure 6. One such user prefers this, as the user can directly manipulate ranges of parameters to be explored in a parameter space study. The XML description of the ensemble is expanded into the full graph of execution at job submission time.

We are also prototyping user interfaces which guide the user to describe ranges and intervals of variables to be studied, in this case for a research weather code. The prototype, shown in Figure 7, depicts indication of default ranges and variable value possibilities as well.

Finally, we have prototyped a specific interface which is designed to allow the user to use Unidata's Integrated Data Viewer (IDV) [IDV] to select the center of a

Figure 6. Direct editing of ensemble-builder workflow description is provided as one possibility within Siege. The XML description of the ensemble is expanded into the full graph of execution at job submission time

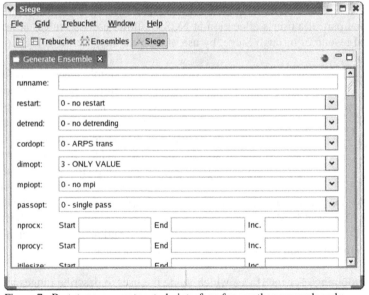

Figure 7. Prototype parameter study interface for weather research code

domain to model the atmosphere using WRF, and then simply launch and monitor the resulting model on TeraGrid resources. This interface was integrated to allow straightforward visualization of the model results in IDV as well, and is depicted in Figure 8.

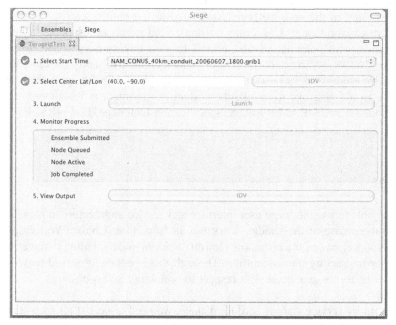

Figure 8 Simplified Unidata Workshop facility, which is integrated with the Unidata IDV, and allows simple selection of domain center latitude and longitude, as well as the NAM dataset for model initialization.

3 Real Grid Resources

The cyber infrastructure we have described so far, Siege plus its supporting services, are designed to work with grid resources [grid] as their target for supporting computations. In the context of NSF-funded computational resources, all computational resources are under the TeraGrid [TeraGrid] umbrella. The implications of this are multifold – first, one desirable result is that all TeraGrid platforms support common grid services. Secondly, there is supposed to be a common environment on all platforms (a goal which has proven harder to achieve than previously suspected), and lastly, there are no other grid resources available for a user to check against teragrid – unless you had your own test bed. One additional complexity: in TeraGrid in 2006, over 20 completely different computational architectures are represented. This means that the pain of porting and validation are very much there – not to mention performance optimization for each platform.

The mechanism used in TeraGrid to invoke the correct environment is softenv. Softenv essentially sources a script, establishing all relevant paths. The configuration of the environment is controlled through a user-configurable ".soft" file, which in the end establishes the source file. This is fine for users that are using the resources in a traditional fashion, i.e., doing local batch submissions of codes and problems that were built on the resource in question, but, it makes little sense for users of Siege who, in the end, we hope don't need to log onto a resource to take advantage of its capabilities. So, as a rule, we don't want to rely on users modifying their ".soft" files, with potential adverse effects to their environment – and, to be sure, we even want to use accounts where users may have inadvertently broken their environment, by establishing a correct environment for the scientific application in question. We would also like to invoke the correct environment at job-submission time, through the Globus GRAM Resource Specification Language (RSL) [RSL].

4   Results

We have been able to use the Siege user interface and service architecture to manage runs made in the course of the Unidata workshop in July 2006 [UnidataWorkshop], as well as to support one of the coauthors (Jewett) work in understanding parametric sensitivities for interacting thunderstorms. Through this, we have observed that we have a number of issues to address with respect to scalability and robustness – in no particular order:

- in-memory service state is hard to manage, we need to persist all such state to a relational database so that services can be brought back up seamlessly without loss of information
- gridFTP servers appear to have an issue handling many clients, with difficult-to-diagnose failures as a result
- the web services in the stack need to be few in number, as well as close to transactional as possible, with small items being used per interaction rather than complex objects

But, even with the issues identified for resolution, we were able to successfully support the modeling efforts of the workshop attendees as well as our coauthor, and have charted a path for improved performance and scalability of the underlying service stack. We also have shown that the Eclipse Rich Client Platform provides a powerful, flexible alternative user interface which integrates well with a user's desktop platform. The use of JMS for messaging has also proven to be a good choice, for its inherent flexibility and malleability to a variety of other messaging systems, as well as its performance, and finally, the ability to perform cluster-local orchestration readily facilitates local monitoring of batch processes

5   Acknowledgements

LEAD is a Large Information Technology Research (ITR) Grant funded by the National Science Foundation under the following Cooperative Agreements: ATM-0331594 (University of Oklahoma), ATM-0331591 (Colorado State University), ATM-0331574 (Millersville University), ATM-0331480 (Indiana University), ATM-

0331579 (University of Alabama in Huntsville), ATM03-31586 (Howard University), ATM-0331587 (University Corporation for Atmospheric Research), and ATM-0331578 (University of Illinois at Urbana-Champaign, with a sub-contract to the University of North Carolina). This work has also been supported by SCI03-30554, SCI04-38712, and SCI96-19019. Any opinions, findings, conclusions, or recommendations expressed in this material are those of the authors and do not necessarily reflect those of the National Science Foundation.

6   References

[WRF] The Weather Research & Forecasting Website, http://www.wrf-model.org/index.php.

[LEAD] Droegemeier, K. K. and Co-Authors, 2004: Linked environments for atmospheric discovery (LEAD): A cyberinfrastructure for mesoscale meteorology research and education. Preprints, 20th Conf. on Interactive Info. Processing Systems for Meteorology, Oceanography, and Hydrology, Seattle , WA , Amer. Meteor. Soc

[Globus], The Globus Toolkit, http://www.globus.org/toolkit/.

[grid], Grid Computing, Wikipedia, the free encyclopedia, http://en.wikipedia.org/wiki/Grid_computing.
[TeraGrid] TeraGrid, http://www.teragrid.org/.

[Siege] Siege – MRD-Public – Confluence, http://torcida.ncsa.uiuc.edu:8080/confluence/display/MRDPUB/Siege

[JMS] Java Message Service, http://java.sun.com/products/jms/

[ActiveMQ] ActiveMQ Home, http://www.activemq.org/site/home.html

[LMS] LEAD Metadata Schema Repository, http://www.extreme.indiana.edu/rescat/metadata/.

[RCP], Rich Client Platform, http://wiki.eclipse.org/index.php/Rich_Client_Platform.

[jglobus] CoG jglobus, http://dev.globus.org/wiki/CoG_jglobus.

[myproxy] Myproxy Credential Management Service, http://grid.ncsa.uiuc.edu/myproxy/

[TeraGrid] TeraGrid, http://www.teragrid.org/.

[IDV] Unidata Integrated Data Viewer (IDV),
http://www.unidata.ucar.edu/software/idv/.

[UnidataWorkshop] 2006 Unidata Users Workshop: Expanding the Use of Models as
Educational Tools in the Atmospheric & Related Sciences,
http://www.unidata.ucar.edu/community/2006workshop/

[RSL] GT 2.4http://www.globus.org/toolkit/docs/2.4/gram/rsl_spec1.html

Q&A – Jay Alameda

Questioner: Bill Gropp

What did you need to modify in the GSI Authorisation service? Was there some missing feature or functionality?

Jay Alameda

No problem building a simple stateless service ... we just wanted to add transport level security. We documented our experience on our wiki, at http://torcida.ncsa.uiuc.edu:8080/confluence/display/MRDPUB/Building+Web +Services

Questioner: Mary Thomas

Can your client run using dynamic IP addresses?

Jay Alameda

So far it has worked pretty well from hotel networks etc. Biggest problem has been gridFTP - need one way connections ... problems with firewalls. This is well documented at http://www.globus.org/toolkit/security/firewalls/.

Questioner: Gabrielle Allen

Can you explain more about your monitoring infrastructure, in particular how reliable is it?

Jay Alameda

We use JMS natively as our messaging/monitoring infrastructure, with activeMQ as the implementation of choice. Out of the box, this has worked well, though we have found some edge cases where "message storms" will bring down the channel. We are investigating message bus reliability techniques such as channel federation to address these issues.

Questioner: Brian Smith

You mentioned problems of porting your large application between the various TeraGrid sites. Can you briefly summarise the nature of the problems encountered?

Jay Alameda

Managing the software environment in a consistent fashion is one large problem on TeraGrid; coupled with uneven compiler and library quality across the wide range of resources of the machines, as well as specific uncontrolled configuration differences in service and machine configurations that cause surprising side effects, make managing functional builds of scientific codes a challenging endeavor.

Comment: Bill Gropp

When looking for a common environment, you need the same semantics not just syntax. It is important for the users to be engaged in this, not to just ask for the same syntax for routines/calls/services.

Questioner: Bill Gropp

You mentioned scaling issues which Pete Beckman has called the "system call storm"; you experienced that with JMS. Should components provide, as quality of service, information on their scalability (either tested or designed)?

Jay Alameda

Would be great - really like that idea.

Questioner: Michael Thuné

There are many technical details here, but the ultimate goal is to have a system that is useful and convenient to the users. Now, you had this interesting LEAD day with 50 users involved. Can you describe the methods you are using to collect the experiences of these users and to feedback into the technical design?

Jay Alameda

Have started process ... evaluations formal and informal, including social studies people. This has resulted in a report from the workshop, and is now continuing with a more formal test program and feedback channel.

Mathematical Service Discovery

Julian Padget[1] and Omer Rana[2]

[1] Department of Computer Science
University of Bath, Bath, UK jap@cs.bath.ac.uk
[2] Department of Computer Science
Cardiff University, Cardiff, UK o.f.rana@cs.cardiff.ac.uk

Abstract. Matchmaking has been a subject of research for many years, but the increasing uptake of service-oriented computing, of which the Grid can be seen as a particular instance, has made effective and flexible matchmaking a necessity. Early approaches to matchmaking and current schemes in the Grid community, like ClassAds, take a syntactic point of view, essentially matching up literals or satisfying some simple constraints for the purpose of identifying computational resources. The increasing availability of web services shifts attention to the function of the service, but WSDL can only publish (limited) information about the signature of the operation which tells the client little about what the service actually does. The focus in the MONET (www.monet.nag.co.uk) and GENSS (genss.cs.bath.ac.uk) projects has been on describing the semantics of mathematical services and developing the means to search for suitable services given a problem description. In this paper we discuss (i) the schema extending WSDL that we call Mathematical Service Description Language (MSDL), (ii) a number of ontologies for describing various properties of mathematical services, (iii) an approach to describing pre- and post-conditions in OpenMath (www.openmath.org) and (iv) an extensible, generic matchmaking framework along with a suite of match plug-ins that are themselves web services.

1 Relevance to Computational Science

A long term vision for computational science is the realization of a desktop environment for scientific research, where the scientist is as easily able to find data sets, the algorithms to manipulate them and the means to display them — in silico experiments — as they currently do with physical materials in the laboratory — in vivo experiments.

The ability to solve large computational science by the coordinated use of distributed resources has been advocated by a number of researchers. Work in this area has primarily focused on the development of "Problem Solving Environments" (PSEs). A PSE is a complete, integrated computing environment for composing, compiling, and running applications in a specific area [10]. In many ways, a PSE is seen as a mechanism to integrate different software construction and management tools, and application specific libraries, within a particular problem domain. One can therefore have a PSE for financial markets [4], for gas turbine engines [8], etc. Focus on implementing PSEs is based on the observation that previously scientists using computational

Please use the following format when citing this chapter:

Padget, J., Rana, O., 2007, in IFIP International Federation for Information Processing, Volume 239, Grid-Based Problem Solving Environments, eds. Gaffney, P. W., Pool, J.C.T., (Boston: Springer), pp. 351-368.

methods wrote and managed all of their own computer programs – however now computational scientists must use libraries and packages from a variety of sources, and those packages might be written in many different computer languages. Engineers and scientists now have a wide choice of computational modules and systems available, enough so that navigating this large design space has become its own challenge. A survey of 28 different PSEs by Fox, Gannon and Thomas (as part of the Grid Computing Environments WG) can be found in [9], and practical considerations in implementing PSEs can be found in Li et al. [14]. Both of these indicate that such environments generally provide "some back-end computational resources, and convenient access to their capabilities". Furthermore, work-flow features significantly in both of these descriptions. In many cases, access to data resources is also provided in a similar way to computational ones.

In [7] the authors identify how the original multiphysics problem – in this case a gas turbine engine simulation – may be considered as a set of smaller simulation problems on simple geometries that need to be solved simultaneously while satisfying a set of interface conditions. These simpler problems may be chosen to reflect the underlying structure/geometry/physics of the system to be simulated, or artificially created by scientific computing techniques such as domain decomposition. For physical systems and devices, these sub-problems are usually modelled by partial differential equations. The next step is to create a network of collaborating solver agents in which each such agent deals with one of the sub-problems defined earlier. This work therefore also can be considered as an aspect of PSEs, where a larger problem is decomposed and handed off to independent agents which can then aggregate their results.

Looking at these two aspects of PSEs together, we can see the need for a "matchmaking" process, which is able to: (i) decompose a larger problem into smaller components, based on very specific domain dependent information; (ii) map each of these smaller problem components to particular solvers that can be found in a registry. The granularity of the decomposition process and the capability inherent within each problem solver provides two constraints on the usefulness of this approach.

2 Technical Background

The work reported here stems from a series of projects, each focusing on different contributions to the goal of building a computational environment for scientific research:

- **OpenMath** provides an extensible framework for the authoring of mathematical ontologies
- **MONET** demonstrates feasibility of semantic processing from user query to service invocation [5]
- **GENSS** generalizes the matchmaking/brokerage component [16] and extends matching to conditions and effects [18]
- **KNOOGLE** implements an open architecture for matchmaking and brokerage [12]

We will now discuss each of these and their contribution in some more detail.

2.1 OpenMath

The objective of OpenMath is to provide both a framework for authoring mathematical ontologies and to provide some fundamental ontologies. We write of ontologies in the plural because OpenMath supports a structured collection of ontological information built from components called content dictionaries — referred to as CDs. OpenMath does not attempt to be a complete ontology of mathematics, but rather provides a comprehensive core, including the basic mathematical structures (group, ring, field etc.), key constants and common operations/functions (trigonometric, hyperbolic, integration, differentiation etc.). New specialized mathematical ontologies can be added as the need arises and thus contribute to the broader corpus of mathematical ontologies, including private CDs (subject to a validation process defined and implemented by the OpenMath Foundation).

Many browsers support the presentation of mathematical markup through a plug-in for the W3C recommendation MathML, which takes two aspects depending usage: (i) MathML-P is for *presentation* and (ii) MathML-C is for *content*. The purpose of the latter is similar to OpenMath, namely to provide a neutral format for the communication of mathematical information between software components. However, MathML-C is a fixed ontology that only handles a subset of mathematics. OpenMath complements MathML-C by being extensible and by being the defined extension language for MathML-C.

OpenMath markup to some extent still reflects the period of its inception, when XML was a developing language. Consequently, there is little use of the more recent more sophisticated features of XML. OpenMath is intended to be as lightweight as possible so there are relatively few markup tags (see The OpenMath Standard v2.0 [26] for more detail: what follows is an abstracted summary from the standard for the sake of making this article self-contained):

- OMS: denotes a symbol, where the string name of the symbol and the CD in which it is defined are attributes of the tag: `<OMS cd="arith" name="minus">`
- OMV: denotes variable, where the string name of the variable is given in the `name` attribute of the tag
- OMI: denotes integer, for example `<OMI>2</OMI>`
- OMB: denotes a byte array and wraps a base64-encoded XML string
- OMSTR: denotes a string value
- OMF: denotes IEEE floating point number and the attributes may indicate size and even a value represented as a hexadecimal string
- OMA: denotes application, where its first child is the operator and the remaining children are the operands.
- OMBIND: denotes the binding constructor which has three children, a *binder*, a variable (specified by OMBVAR) and a body
- OMBVAR: variables used in binding constructor as above
- OME: error constructor, which has an arbitrary number of children, the first denoting the error and the remainder being OpenMath object relating to the error.

```
<om:OMOBJ><om:OMA>
  <om:OMS cd="arith1" name="minus"/>
  <om:OMA>
    <om:OMS cd="arith1" name="power"/>
    <om:OMV name="x"/>
    <om:OMI>2</om:OMI>
  </om:OMA>
  <om:OMA>
    <om:OMS cd="arith1" name="power"/>
    <om:OMV name="y"/>
    <om:OMI>2</om:OMI>
  </om:OMA></om:OMA>
</om:OMOBJ>
```

Fig. 1. OpenMath representation of $x^2 - y^2$

- OMATTR: the attribution constructor is used to wrap a sequence of attribute pairs which is how additional textual and semantic annotations of objects are constructed.
- OMATP: the attribute pair constructor is used in conjunction with OMATTR above.
- OMFOREIGN: the foreign constructor, which allows the inclusion of arbitrarily encoded data, such as:

```
<OMFOREIGN encoding="text/x-latex">\sin(x)</OMFOREIGN>
```

By way of illustration the OpenMath representation of $x^2 - y^2$ is shown in Figure 1. Detailed information about OpenMath, including the OpenMath 2.0 standard (June 2004) are available from the OpenMath website at www.openmath.org.

By providing the means to structure, author and publish markup for any aspect of mathematics, OpenMath establishes a way to describe both the functionality of any piece of mathematical software and the data that it inputs and outputs in an application and network neutral format. Thus it contributes to the goal of enabling the inter-operation of mathematical software components wherever they may be deployed.

2.2 MONET

MONET — Mathematics On the NET — had the objective of demonstrating the potential of semantic web techniques in service discovery, and given the partners' previous work with OpenMath, specifically mathematical service discovery, composition and invocation. Project details are available via http://monet.nag.co.uk, but we now summarize the main contributions of the project.

An important problem to solve at the outset was how to publish information about mathematical web services in a way that could be used to help achieve the project goals. Consequently, an embedding of WSDL [28], called Mathematical Service Description Language (MSDL)[1] was defined to incorporate the necessary semantic information to support the discovery process. As with some OpenMath design decisions, MSDL is a product of its time: OWL-S was not completed and the tools for DAML-S were relatively experimental, so while the structure of MSDL documents mimicked these more general approaches to service description, they were under project control and allowed demonstration of principle. A complementary Mathematical Query Description Language (MQDL) was defined for posing queries. The structure of the two schemas is necessarily very similar, comprising the following elements:

Classification: The specification of what the service does (a more detailed description appears in [5] and [16]):
- Reference to a problem description library — terms supplied by the Mathematical Problem Description Language (MPDL).
- Reference to taxonomies, e.g. to GAMS (Guide to Available Mathematical Software) [3].
- Supported Semantics, such as which OpenMath CDs the application can process.
- Supported Directives, such as *solve*, *prove* and *decide*.

Implementation Details: information about the specific service
- A reference to an Algorithm Description, using entities from the OpenMath CD containing symbols for describing algorithmic complexity.
- Software Details – information about the hosting software package.
- Hardware Details – self explanatory.
- Algorithmic Properties, including attributes such as accuracy and resource usage.
- Descriptions of actions needed to solve a problem.

It should be noted that not all of the Classification or Implementation details are mandatory.

Service Interface Description: Typically a WSDL document.

Service Binding Description: Map from abstract problem components and actions to elements of the service interface.

Broker Interface: The API exposed to the broker. Typically, this is a service URI and an interface description.

The demonstrator architecture is shown in Figure 2 and allows us to trace out two scenarios:

- Service registration: the provider registering a service submits a MSDL document, elements of which refer to the MONET and the OpenMath ontologies. The registry manager then processes elements of the mathematical service description into OWL because that is the representation over which the Instance Store operates. That description is then entered into the repository and the process is complete.
- Service discovery and invocation: the client seeking a service submits a Mathematical Query Description Language (MQDL) document to the Plan Manager.

---

[1] The XSD schema for MSDL is available from `http://monet.nag.co.uk/cocoon/monet/publicdocs/index.html`

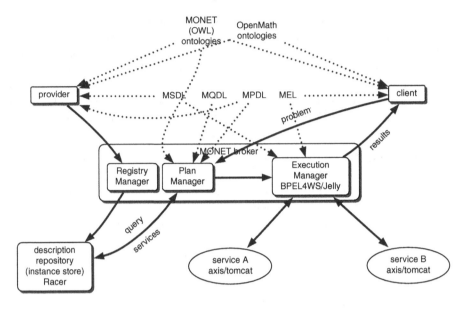

Fig. 2. The MONET Architecture

The mathematical elements of the problem description are then translated into OWL and passed to the Instance Store to find any candidate services according to a description logic querying process. The plan manager selects one of the candidate services and then invokes the execution manager to handle the actual calling of the web service. The results are then returned as a Mathematical Explanation Language (MEL) document to the client.

From a practical point of view the MONET architecture demonstrated the feasibility of semantic match making, but the demonstrator was very limited in that there is only one repository, one matching technique and one selection policy. Furthermore the matching technique was essentially using signature information and computing the equivalent of a multi-method look-up. Nevertheless, by demonstrating end-to-end support for computational problems using ontological information and web services it had established the viability of the approach and raised awareness of the direction future semantic grids research might take.

2.3 GENSS

The purpose of the GENSS (Grid-enabled Numerical and Symbolic Services) was to build on the outputs of MONET and, in particular to tackle the more complex problems inherent in reasoning about the conditions and effects of services, while building links with the UK's e-Science research program, arguing that semantic discovery of (mathematical) services was an important enabling activity for e-Science. The main outputs of the project are more sophisticated approaches to mathematical service matching, including mathematical analysis of the conditions and effects, the use of multiple matching techniques and access to multiple registries. A detailed report on the matching techniques appears in [16] while the revised architecture is discussed in [12]. We now summarize the main contributions of the project.

GENSS Matchmaking Strategy The information source for the matchmaking process remains as for MONET: the MQDL describing the query and the MSDL document describing the service, but now attention was focused on working with the information about the conditions and effects in each case. One of several difficulties is that the expressions marked up with OpenMath in the condition and effect fields of the problem and service description may be equivalent semantically, but be written very differently. To begin to tackle this problem the expressions are normalized — not in the sense that there is any absolute normal form for mathematics, just the right one for the current purpose. Thus a fairly standard set of transformation is carried out dealing with:

- Logical equivalences — using standard rewrites
- Associative operators — are flattened, so for example the OpenMath equivalent of (+ a (+ b c)) becomes (+ a b c).
- Context dependent equivalences — for example $i + 1 > 0 \Rightarrow i >= 1$ if $i \in \mathbb{Z}$, but not if $i \in \mathbb{Q}$.
- Alpha conversions — consistent naming of variables in problem and service, so that name comparison is meaningful
- Commutative operators — reorder arguments to bring constants towards the operator (and subsequently evaluate constant combinations) and so that the left hand side is less than the right hand side.
- Conversion to disjunctive normal form to capture, if present, the alternatives between pre- and post-conditions.

As a result, the conditions and effects take on the form $Q(L(R))$ where:

- Q is a quantifier block e.g. $\forall x \exists y$ s.t. $\cdots$
- L is a block of logical connectives e.g. $\wedge, \vee, \Rightarrow, \cdots$
- R is a block of relations. e.g. $=, \leq, \geq, \neq, \cdots$

With a summary of the normalization process in place, the two scenarios of registration and discovery become relatively straightforward: in the first case, the service description is normalized and stored in the registry; in the second the query is normalized and the registry is traversed calculating a similarity value between the query and each service. This latter results in a list of URIs ordered by similarity value.

Matching techniques A major development in GENSS was the idea of a matchmaker shell within which several match modes could be applied to the service and aggregate match scores computed. Thus, several matchers were deployed for use in the GENSS matchmaker:

- Structural: used to determine whether task and capability match exactly; cheap if not often very successful
- Syntax+Ontology: used to compare elements and attributes in task and capability using the taxonomic structure of types to test for inclusion relations
- Ontological reasoning: as had previously been demonstrated in MONET (described in section 2.2)
- Function: use conditions and effects expression to establish whether: $T_{cond} \Rightarrow C_{cond} \wedge C_{eff} \Rightarrow T_{eff}$; in other words do the conditions of the capability subsume those of the task and do the effects of the task subsume those of the condition. In fact, the tests applied aim to establish the *equivalence* of the given expressions:
  - *Algebraic equivalence*: where we wish to show that $Q - S = 0$ algebraically by translating the expression into the input syntax of a computer algebra system and calculating the difference. In general undecidable, but the approach outlined may be useful in practice. For example: $x^2 - y^2$ and $(x+y)(x-y)$. The idea stems from the work of Richardson [21] on the identification of zero.
  - *Value substitution*: where we wish to show that $Q - S = 0$ by substituting random values for the variables in the relation sub-expressions in the $Q(L(R))$ structure outlined above. This must be done with care: variables must be renamed consistently and the same random value substituted for a given variable in each expression. If the result is zero, it is only *evidence* not *proof* of equivalence. This relies on later work also by Richardson [22] on the so-called Uniformity Conjecture

The computation of the similarity score is quite detailed and not easily summarized, so the interested reader is referred to [16].

GENSS Architecture and Critique The GENSS architecture is shown in Figure 2.3 in which we can identify the various differences with MONET. The most obvious is that not only are there multiple matcher mechanisms, but those matchers are deployed as web services that are accessed from the matchmaker. The second key difference is the adoption of a standard registry component, namely a UDDI registry. However, there are still several aspects of this design that can be criticized: (i) the matcher work-flow is fixed (ii) UDDI registry searching is based on textual information (iii) the selection policy is fixed as the service with the highest similarity score

Work-flow enactment In a further development from MONET where we had posited a stand-alone broker, in GENSS we also demonstrated how the matchmaker shell could be turned into a web service and then built into a work-flow. The enactment system used was Triana[2]. Like other such systems, it works by scouring specified resources, such as UDDI registries for services and then displays them in a selection palette on the side. In Figure 4, the broker has simply been interposed between a widget to read input from the user and another for the display of results, while in Figure 5 the output from running the query are displayed. Although this only demonstrates the functionality, it also suggests the capability, given sufficient suitable services in available registries, of

---

[2] Details of Triana can be found via www.trianacode.org

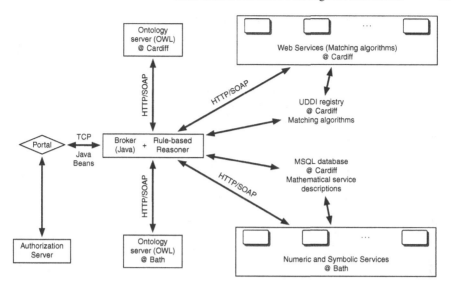

Fig. 3. The GENSS Architecture

constructing work-flows including proxy services. By "proxy" service, we mean that some work-flow elements are instances of the broker that when invoked can discover and call the appropriate service to meet the requirements, which may themselves have only been established dynamically earlier in the work-flow.

Generation of Semantic Descriptions The final contribution from GENSS has been an initial investigation of how mathematical information may be used to help generate service descriptions automatically. It is widely appreciated that authoring WSDL is a tedious and error-prone process, so that several Java IDEs will now generate it automatically for the user. However, we need to generate MSDL, including pre- and post-condition information.

We had been working with the Aldor language[3] and its algebra package as a means to remove the GENSS broker's dependency on Maple and thus on licensed software. The Aldor type system derives from that of Axiom/Scratchpad and provides a two-level categorical-style polymorphic dependent-type structure that has been established is adequate, while still remaining decidable for checking, to capture correctly the many mathematical relations required in building a strongly-typed computer algebra system. The consequence of this expressive power is that because the type system actually captures the necessary mathematical knowledge about the function it implements, it can be used for:

– Automatic wrapper generation

---

[3] The detailed history of Aldor is quite complicated, but it is probably sufficient to say that it inherits from the computer algebra system Axiom (market by Numerical Algorithms Group for some years) and Scratchpad (developed by IBM over many years) and is BSD-license software

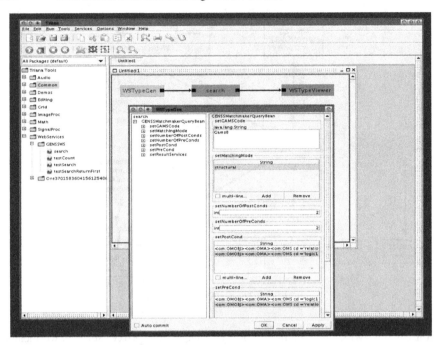

Fig. 4. A Triana work-flow with matchmaker (Screenshot provided by Tom Goodale)

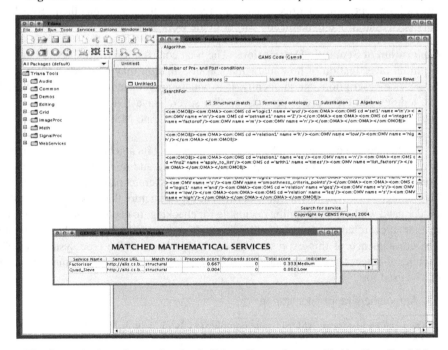

Fig. 5. Results from the matchmaker in Triana (Screenshot provided by Tom Goodale)

- Automatic generation of OpenMath for service description signatures and for (part of the) conditions and effects

However, it should be emphasized that the OpenMath generation depends on the availability of the appropriate CDs in OpenMath to reflect the corresponding types in Aldor. There are several other delicate technical issues that are covered in detail in [18].

GENSS Outcomes The contributions of the project are outlined above, but to put them in the context of this article, the project demonstrated that it was possible to go further on the problem of service discovery to examine conditions and effects and that it was practical to deploy and invoke multiple matchers using the basic technology of the semantic web — web services — and even to integrate the broker with work-flow enactment, thus making the broker work with the primary components for computational science.

3 A generic matchmaker/broker

Reflection on the design and limitation of the GENSS architecture have fed into a further project called KNOOGLE (pronounced noo-gl), in which the previous system is being re-factored to produce robust generic tools, and demonstrated in the context of other current UK e-Science projects.

From a client point of view, the brokerage function can be parameterized by three requirements:

- Where to find descriptions of entities to match against
- How to match the query against a description
- How to choose between the matched descriptions

Some clients may like to have each of these fixed, whereas others might like the opportunity to control some or even all of these at the point of calling the broker. Thus there is a complete spectrum ranging from no fixed actions to all three being fixed. For each case, we specify what information the client must provide:

- A set of registries identifies the places to look for candidate services
- A set of matchers, deployed as web services, identifies how to calculate a similarity score between the query and a service (note: each matcher web service must take a query description and a service description as arguments and deliver a score in the range $[0, 1]$)
- A selection policy, defined as a query over the match results, identifies one or no service to invoke. More details about specifying selection policy appear later.

These three issues lead to a refinement of the GENSS architecture of Figure 2.3 resulting in the KNOOGLE architecture of Figure 6, where:

- The registries have been replaced by the UDDI-compliant Grimoires registry, which supports semantic querying for services and the annotation of services with various forms of metadata (string, URL and RDF). The broker now accepts a list of such registries to search for candidate services

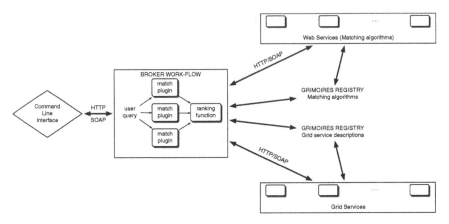

Fig. 6. The KNOOGLE Architecture

- The matchers are specified as a list of URLs identifying WSDL service descriptions. These matchers are treated as alternatives in that each matcher is invoked with the query and the service description, resulting in a match-score. This score is then asserted into a RDF store associating matcher, service and score for subsequent assessment by the selection policy.
- The selection policy is specified as a query in the RDQL language over the set of RDF triples that resulted from the matching process. This query should result in the identification of either no service, in the case that none satisfies the selection policy, or one service that does.

Current Developments The KNOOGLE project [20] is currently running and has the target of delivering tools for end-user construction and deployment of brokers by the middle of 2007. The broker functionality is planned for demonstration in the context of two related current projects (also in the UK): (i) GridSAM [6] which provides a client interface for the submission and monitoring of jobs using the JSDL [1] framework and (ii) Taverna, which is a work-flow enactment system that has seen much use in the bio-informatics domain. We now describe these two demonstrators in more detail.

　　GridSAM: The aim of the GridSAM project is to provide an executable submission and monitoring service. Each GridSAM instance has a set of processors on which it may execute programs. The clients of the GridSAM instances must provide their input data and the executable they wish to run, they must also provide a JSDL document which gives constraints on where and how their program is to be run. The GridSAM instance creates a DRMConnector, which translates the JSDL to processor-specific JCL and executes the job on the distributed resources. The GridSAM instance also provides tools to monitor the job's progress.

　　One problem with this architecture is the requirement that the client is in possession of the executable of the code they wish to execute. The client could be relieved of this task by keeping the code in a repository, accessible to a broker. Our first use case addresses this issue by placing the broker between the client and the GridSAM instance, so the client sends a description of the problem to the broker, which retrieves the executable from a repository, sends this to the GridSAM instance, then receives the results back from the GridSAM instance and forwards these back to the client.

A second problem is that the client may not be aware of the resources available, but would like to search for suitable resources based on some description of needs. This too can be addressed by brokerage. Thus in the second use case, the client provides the executable, which the GridSAM instance sends to a DRMConnector augmented by a brokerage function. The DRM-broker determines what resources are available to be used, communicates this to the DRMConnector which then deploys the job, receives the results and passes these back to the client.

Taverna: The Taverna workbench [19] is a graphical environment with which users can construct, edit, browse and share work-flows. The application provides three views: one on available services found either locally or in specified registries, another depicting the work-flow diagram and a third called the model explorer. This last allows the user to specify input sources and output locations for the work-flow along with the actual services that will do the work.

There are numerous components associated with the Taverna system including the FreeFluo work-flow enactor, the KAVE metadata store and the FETA service discovery component. FETA uses the myGrid service ontology [29], which provides descriptions of bioinformatics tasks and data types, to express descriptions of the kind of bioinformatics services sought. However, functional descriptions of bioinformatics services are hard to formulate because the datatypes involved are usually not defined in any formal type language[15]. Consequently that service information is typically limited to the name of the service — which might in itself be descriptive, but such information is hard to recover — the names of the operations supported and the names of the input and output parameters. Thus, the lack of type information means there is even less than a type signature available, so queries are most likely to be stated in terms of the name of the service sought. Although the query technology is based on JENA and RDQL, myGrid users apparently do not normally construct their own RDQL queries: instead they are provided with some prepared queries from which to choose. Taverna then presents the results in a similar way to that in which other services which are listed and they can then be dragged into the work flow like any other service.

The objectives of integrating the KNOOGLE broker with Taverna are

- To demonstrate the integration of the broker with a work-flow enactment system. This has already been achieved with Triana, but Taverna is the approved work-flow environment for OMII projects.
- To enhance Taverna through the provision of a flexible external matchmaking facility to complement the built-in FETA system described above, as well as providing access to external registries and the adding options for (i) the creation of bespoke matcher/broker components (ii) access to a range of different matching technologies (iii) the means to embed proxy services in work-flows that can be resolved into actual services through the function of the broker, as described earlier in section 2.3.

It is perhaps paradoxical that the result of the evolution of the brokerage architecture described here is now little more than a shell, with almost no function in itself: an instance of the KNOOGLE broker has no registries, no matching function and no selection function; it can do nothing except wait to be supplied with these three pieces of information. The result of re-factoring has been to hollow out the original architecture and delegate the functions either to client-specified parameters or externally supplied web services. Yet the result is potentially more useful, more flexible and more customizable than the original. Perhaps evidence of the validity of the statement "less is more".

4 Related Work

A variety of matchmaking systems have been reported in the literature over the last couple of decades, although it seems that almost all are relatively special-purpose or domain-specific in some way or another and there is little to indicate success in re-application outside the domain of their original development. Nevertheless, there are some valuable ideas to be found as we attempt to show in our review below. From a computational science perspective, we observe that much of the prior art in matchmaking has focused on AI or free text and it is only in the last five years or so, with the advent of widely accepted ontological frameworks, that there has been rising interest in services and service matching. Parts of this survey have appeared in earlier publications [16, 12].

The SHADE (SHAred Dependency Engineering) matchmaker [13] operates over logic-based and structured text languages. The aim is to connect information sources dynamically. The matchmaking process is based on KQML (Knowledge Query and Manipulation Language) communication [25]. The content languages of SHADE are a subset of KIF (Knowledge Interchange Format) [11] as well as a structured logic representation called MAX (Meta-reasoning Architecture for "X"). Matchmaking is carried out solely by matching the content of advertisements and requests. There is no knowledge base and no inference performed, however rules may be added dynamically making MAX flexible and adaptable.

COINS (COmmon INterest Seeker) [13] is a matchmaker over free text descriptions.. The motivation behind COINS is given as a need for matchmaking over large volumes of unstructured text on the Web and the unsuitability of existing matchmaking technology for such an application domain. Initially the free text matchmaker was implemented as the central part of the COINS system but it turned out that it was also useful as a general purpose facility. As in SHADE the access language is KQML. The System for the Mechanical Analysis and Retrieval of Text (SMART) [23] information retrieval system is used to process the free text, producing a document vector using SMART's stemming and "noise" word removal, after which document vectors are compared using inverse document frequency. Such technology could usefully be redeployed now as a web service and straightforwardly incorporated into a broker using the architecture outlined above.

LARKS (Language for Advertisement and Request for Knowledge Sharing) [24] was developed to enable interoperability between heterogeneous software agents and had a strong influence on the DAML-S specification. The system uses ontologies defined by a concept language ITL (Information Terminology Language). The technique used to calculate the similarity of ontological concepts involves the construction of a weighted associative network, where the weights indicate the belief in relationships. While it is argued that the weights can be set automatically by default, it is apparent that the construction of realistically weighted relationships requires human input and thus impacts the general deployment of such technology.

InfoSleuth [17] is described as a system for discovery and retrieval of information in open and dynamically changing environments. The brokering function provides reasoning over the advertised syntax and the semantics. InfoSleuth aims to support cooperation among several software agents for information discovery, where agents have roles as core, resource or ontology agents. There is a distinguished broker agent encapsulating a matching function, which serves to bring agents requiring services together with those offering. The matching operations are a mixture of syntactic, structural and ontological proximity, inspiring the similar mechanisms developed in GENSS.

The GRAPPA [27] (Generic Request Architecture for Passive Provider Agents) system allows multiple types of matchmaking mechanisms to be employed within a system. It is based on receiving arbitrary matchmaking offers and requests, where each offer and request consist of multiple criteria. Matching is achieved by applying distance functions which compute the similarities between the individual dimensions of an offer and a request. Using specialized aggregation functions, the similarities are projected to a single value to constitute a match score. There is a clear link between the ideas in GRAPPA and our final KNOOGLE architecture.

MathBroker [2] is a project at RISC-Linz with some elements in common with those described here, including providing semantic descriptions of mathematical services. It too uses MSDL, however it seems that most of the matchmaking is achieved through traversing taxonomies, while actual understanding of the pre- and post-conditions is still regarded as an open problem.

In the main, matchmaking research projects have tried to deliver generic results, capable of being adapted subsequently for particular domains. However, the motivation for many such projects has primarily been e-commerce (as a means to match buyers with sellers, for instance), where it is hard to describe accurately the actual function of a service, compared to the case of mathematical functions. In other cases, the work has been driven by a specific language, notably KQML in some cases above, which although powerful, does not enjoy widespread appeal.

In contrast, we believe that the approach we have outlined here, has attempted to learn from this history, by putting as little as possible in the matchmaker/broker itself and building on the power of web services and work-flow enactment, technologies that at present appear to have good prospects for the medium-term, to provide a "late-binding" of whatever functionality is desired, while also offering a degree of future-proofing through the means to publish new matching techniques and rapidly deploy new brokers using them.

5 Conclusions

We have presented a short history of a selection of closely related projects that have fortuitously led one into another to deliver a series of outputs that could be very beneficial for the provision and up-take of computational science services. From Open-Math, we obtain a general framework for mathematical semantic annotation of services, (as well as a *lingua franca* for communication between mathematical services). From MONET we get the confirmation that ontological reasoning can help in service discovery. From GENSS, we see how mathematical reasoning over the ontological description of conditions and effects can make that discovery process more precise. And finally in KNOOGLE, with the benefit of hindsight, we see better how to engineer an architecture to deliver past and future matching technology using both mathematical and a wide range of other techniques.

Acknowledgements

The work reported here has been partially supported by the European Commission and the Engineering and Physical Sciences Research Council of the UK. Specifically: (i) OpenMath I and II were funded by the CEC (ESPRIT Project 42969 and project IST-2000-29719); partners: Numerical Algorithms Group Ltd (United Kingdom), University of Bath (United Kingdom), Stilo Technology Ltd (United Kingdom), INRIA Sophia-Antipolis (France), University of St Andrews (United Kingdom), Technical University of Eindhoven (Netherlands), Springer Verlag (Germany), The University of Nice (France), Konrad-Zuse Zentrum für Informationstechnik (Germany), Nibbles.it (Italy), Research Institute for Symbolic Computation (Austria), German Research Centre for Artificial Intelligence (Germany), University of Helsinki (Finland), International University of Bremen (Germany), University of Köln (Germany) (ii) MONET was funded by the CEC (project IST-2001-34145); partners: NAG Ltd., Stilo Ltd., University of Eindhoven, Université de Nice/INRIA Sophia Antipolis, University of Bath, University of Manchester, University of Western Ontario (iii) GENSS was funded by the EPSRC (UK) under the Semantic Grids call of the e-Science program (project GR/S44723/01); partners: University of Bath and Cardiff University (iv) KNOOGLE is funded by the Open Middleware Infrastructure Institute managed program, which in turn is funded by the EPSRC (UK); partners University of Bath and Cardiff University. Finally, particular thanks are due to Omer Rana for input on the computational science context and to Bill Naylor for commenting on drafts of this article.

References

1. Stephen McGough Ali Anjomshoaa, Darren Pulsipher. Job Submission Description Language WG (JSDL-WG), 2003. Available from `https://forge.gridforum.org/projects/jsdl-wg/`.
2. Rebhi Baraka, Olga Caprotti, and Wolfgang Schreiner. A Web Registry for Publishing and Discovering Mathematical Services. In *EEE*, pages 190–193. IEEE Computer Society, 2005.

3. R.F. Boisvert, S.E. Howe, and D.K. Kahaner. GAMS: A Framework for the Management of Scientific Software. *ACM Transactions on Mathematical Software*, 11(4):313–355, December 1985.

4. O. Bunin, Y. Guo, and J. Darlington. Design of problem-solving environment for contingent claim valuation. In *Proceedings of EuroPar 2001*, volume 2150 of *LNCS*. Springer Verlag, 2001.

5. Olga Caprotti, Michael Dewar, James Davenport, and Julian Padget. Mathematics on the (Semantic) Net. In Christoph Bussler, John Davies, Dieter Fensel, and Rudi Studer, editors, *Proceedings of the European Symposium on the Semantic Web*, volume 3053 of *LNCS*, pages 213–224. Springer Verlag, 2004. ISBN 3-540-21999-4.

6. John Darlington. Gridsam grid job submission and monitoring web service. `http://www.omii.ac.uk/projects/`, 2004. Last visited September 2006. See also `http://www.lesc.ic.ac.uk/gridsam/`.

7. Tzvetan Drashansky, Elias N. Houstis, Naren Ramakrishnan, and John R. Rice. Networked agents for scientific computing. *Communications of the ACM*, 42(3):48–54, 1999.

8. S. Fleeter, E. Houstis, J. Rice, C. Zhou, and A. Catlin. A problem solving environment for simulating gas turbines. In *Proceedings of 16th IMACS World Congress*, pages 104–105, 2000.

9. G. Fox, D. Gannon, and M. Thomas. A summary of grid computing environments. *Concurrency and Computation: Practice and Experience (Special Issue)*, 2003.

10. E. Gallopoulos, E. N. Houstis, and J. R. Rice. Computer as thinker/doer: Problem-solving environments for computational science. *IEEE Computational Science and Engineering*, 1(2), 1994.

11. M. Genesereth and R. Fikes. Knowledge Interchange Format, Version 3.0 Reference Manual. Technical report, Computer Science Department, Stanford University, 1992. Available from `http://www-ksl.stanford.edu/knowledge-sharing/papers/kif.ps`.

12. Tom Goodale, Simone A. Ludwig, William Naylor, Julian Padget, and Omer F. Rana. Service-oriented matchmaking and brokerage. In Paul Watson, editor, *Proceedings of UK e-Science All Hands conference*. EPSRC, 2006.

13. D. Kuokka and L. Harada. Integrating information *via* matchmaking. *Intelligent Information Systems 6(2-3), pp. 261-279*, 1996.

14. M. Li, O. F. Rana, D. W. Walker, M. Shields, and Y. Huang. *Component-based Software Development*, chapter Component-based Problem Solving Environments for Computational Science. World Scientific Publishing, 2003.

15. Phillip Lord, Pinar Alper, Chris Wroe, and Carole Goble. Feta: A light-weight architecture for user oriented semantic service discovery. In A. Gómez-Pérez and J. Euzenat, editors, *European Semantic Web Conference*, pages 17–31. Springer-Verlag, 2005.

16. Simone Ludwig, Omer Rana, William Naylor, and Julian Padget. Matchmaking Framework for Mathematical Web Services. *Journal of Grid Computing*, 4(1):33–48, March 2006. Available via `http://dx.doi.org/10.1007/s10723-005-9019-z`. ISSN: 1570-7873 (Paper) 1572-9814 (Online).

17. W. Bohrer M. Nodine and A.H. Ngu. Semantic brokering over dynamic heterogenous data sources in InfoSleuth. In *Proceedings of the 15th International Conference on Data Engineering, pp. 358-365*, 1999.

18. William Naylor and Julian Padget. From untyped to polymorphically typed objects in mathematical web services. In William Farmer, editor, *Proceedings of MKM2006*. To appear in Springer LNCS, 2006.

19. Tom Oinn, Mark Greenwood, Matthew Addis, M. Nedim Alpdemir, Justin Ferris, Kevin Glover, Carole Goble, Antoon Goderis, Duncan Hull, Darren Marvin, Peter Li, Phillip Lord,

Matthew R. Pocock, Martin Senger, Robert Stevens, Anil Wipat, and Chris Wroe. Taverna: lessons in creating a workflow environment for the life sciences: Research articles. *Concurr. Comput. : Pract. Exper.*, 18(10):1067–1100, 2006.

20. Julian Padget. Knoogle matchmaking and brokerage framework. `http://www.omii.ac.uk/projects/`, 2006. Last visited September 2006.

21. D. Richardson. Some Unsolvable Problems Involving Elementary Functions of a Real Variable. *Journal of Computational Logic*, 33:514–520, 1968.

22. Daniel Richardson. The uniformity conjecture. In Jens Blanck, Vasco Brattka, and Peter Hertling, editors, *CCA*, volume 2064 of *Lecture Notes in Computer Science*, pages 253–272. Springer, 2000.

23. G. Salton. *Automatic Text Processing*. Addison-Wesley, 1989.

24. K. Sycara, S. Widoff, M. Klusch, and J. Lu. Larks: Dynamic matchmaking among heterogeneous software agents in cyberspace. *Journal of Autonomous Agents and Multi Agent Systems*, 5(2):173–203, June 2002.

25. D. McKay T. Finin, R. Fritzson and R. McEntire. KQML as an agent communication language. In *Proceedings of 3rd International Conference on Information and Knowledge Management, pp. 456-463*, 1994.

26. The OpenMath Society. The OpenMath Standard, June 2004. Available from `http://www.openmath.org/standard/om20-2004-06-30/omstd20.pdf`.

27. D. Veit. *Matchmaking in Electronic Markets*, volume 2882 of *LNCS*. Springer, 2003. Hot Topics.

28. W3C. *Web Services Description Language (WSDL) Version 1.2 W3C Working Draft*. W3C, 2002-2003. Available from `http://www.w3.org/TR/wsdl12`.

29. Chris Wroe, Robert Stevens, Carole Goble, Angus Roberts, and Mark Greenwood. A suite of DAML+OIL Ontologies to Describe Bioinformatics Web Services and Data. *The International Journal of Cooperative Information Systems*, 12(2):597–624, 2003.

Q&A – Julian Padget

Questioner: Ron Boisvert

Could you provide some example scenarios in which your system might be used? For example, what types of services would this sit on top of? Who would be the users - people? Software agents?

Julian Padget

Both, although I think it will take some experience of use for scientists to be prepared to delegate some part of the decision-making to software agents. So initially, the clients will be human, but this is essentially a trust-building exercise in which people describe a problem and the system finds a service – or service work flow – that can solve the problem for them. As people find those answers satisfactory – and various techniques can be used to have the system better meet users expectations – they may be increasingly willing to let software make choices for them.

Questioner: Brian Ford

What ideal are you working towards in terms of the systems you wish to develop?

Julian Padget

That they should be invisible! Or perhaps to be more realistic they should not get in the way – be part of the solution, not as so often with computers, part of the problem. So the ideal scenario is that a problem description be posed and all the appropriate software and the resources on which to run it are arranged to deliver the results where and when they are needed with only as much intervention from a human as they wish.

Questioner: Brian Ford

Tony Hoare always wished to replace computer software written in languages such as Algol68 and Fortran with logically, provable programs. In a similar manner do you wish to replace computation in "numerical analysis" with more rigorously based mathematical solutions?

Julian Padget

I don't see that as the main thrust. I'm certainly not trying to supplant numerical analysis, rather trying to enhance its accessibility to the person with a problem – who doesn't necessarily know which is the right NAG (for instance) routine to use.

Questioner: Mary Thomas

Is this a possible usage scenario: running Mathematica, my matrix multiply is running locally and is too slow. I'd like to access a web service to help me find a faster service to run my job.

Julian Padget

Yes, in principle. This goes back to the invisibility point I made earlier. It would be great if the integration of software was at the level to enable something like that to happen. There is still the question of whether you want that to happen automatically or under your control, but there are a lot more engineering problems to resolve before we get to that issue.

Questioner: Ron Boisvert

The EU funding for the OpenMath project has recently ended. They have produced some very good work, Is more needed to be done to support its use in systems like yours? Is the OpenMath technology sustainable?

Julian Padget

Yes, more does need to be done: there are not that many content dictionaries in place – we had to write more as the GENSS project progressed because there was nothing that allowed us to describe some services' functionality at the right level. A case in point involved matrix operations and yes, we could have described the service semantics in terms of operations on individual matrix elements, but that was just too detailed: we needed to describe pre- and post-conditions in terms of whole matrix properties. Fortunately we had someone who was experienced in writing OpenMath CDs working for us. I'm not sure it would have been so easy otherwise. So, I do have some concern about the sustainability of OpenMath as long as the experience of use in the wider community remains limited.

Thursday AM Panel Discussion

Panel

- Jay Alameda
- Julian Padget

Questioner: Richard Hanson

Addressed to: Jay Alameda

What are some examples of using Teragrid besides weather prediction?

Jay Alameda

The TeraGrid website, www.teragrid.org, has a continually updated set of success stores from scientists and engineers using the resources. They span many directorates at NSF, from physics, to materials science, to biology and beyond.

Addressed to: Jay Alameda

How does a potential user get onto Teragrid?

Jay Alameda

This is well documented at www.teragrid.org; normally, one would use a development allocation (DAC) to get started (this is an easy submission); which is meant as a mechanism for preparation for a formal peer reviewed proposal.

Comments: Jim Pool

The Teragrid Web pages provide both descriptions of a broad array of applications and information about obtaining access to Teragrid resources.

Comment: Craig Douglas

Getting a starter account on the Teragrid is relatively simple:

1. *Pick a login / password*
2. *Go to starter allocation request*
3. *Title of project*
4. *Abstract*
5. *PI info (including grants)*
6. *CV's*
7. *Submit*

Regular allocations require more information:

1. *Computational proposal*

2. Resource justification
3. Code scaling
4. $100,000 bank transfer (just kidding).

Questioner: Mary Thomas

Each of you represents a layer in a grid user interface: Jay = GUI, Julian = service protocol, Marc = grid computation. How do you see these layers changing the way I can use a tool such as Mathematica?

Julian Padget

It should change what you can do, but not necessarily how you do it: this is a good encapsulation of the vision where access to grid deployed mathematical services essentially becomes transparent, as if it were built into the source language, whether that is Mathematica, Maple or Matlab (+ others). There is an incredible amount of work yet to be done to make functional service brokerage good enough that users might begin to trust it and likewise a lot of work to do to bring together familiar desktop packages and grid problem solving environments.

Comment: Brian Ford

The interface between the rigorous mathematical solution and practical solution through algorithms in a numerical library is a challenging one. An attempt at this is being made through the inclusion of a numerical algorithms library contents in a commercial symbolic solving package, and this has thrown-up the discontinuity between mathematical foundations of the symbolic approach and the more practical base in the algorithmic approach.

There is some genuine mapping between the two, but the mathematical imprecision of definition in the algorithmic approach makes a continuity of solution challenging. But numerical algorithms do provide effective solutions in many application areas and the mathematical base is becoming stronger.

Comment: Mary Thomas

*I can see someday running Matlab, and for a problem such as A+B*C, picking the right remote math service. This development environment could help move computational scientists off the mainframe so their codes are not tied to one host. Also, some code development time could be saved in compilation because the service is already compiled and optimized.*

PART 7

APPLICATIONS II

M. Vouk, Session Chair; P. Hemker, Discussant

H. Usami: *A Problem Solving Environment based on Grid Services: NAREGI-PSE*

M. Aoyagi: *Grid Enabling of Nano-Science Applications in NAREGI* (Abstract)

S. Goasguen: *Grid Architecture for Scientific Communities* (Abstract)

B. Applebe: *Scientific Software Frameworks and Grid Computing – Improving Programming Productivity*

Panel Discussion

A Problem Solving Environment based on Grid Services: NAREGI-PSE

Hitohide Usami[1], Hiroyuki Kanazawa[2], and Shigeo Kawata[3]

1 National Institute of Informatics, 2-1-2 Hitotsubashi, Chiyoda-ku,
Tokyo 101-8430, Japan, usami@grid.nii.ac.jp,
WWW home page: http: //www.naregi.org/
2 Fujitsu Limited, Shiodome 1-5-2, Higashi-Shinbashi, Minato-ku,
Tokyo 105-7123, Japan, kanazawa.h@jp.fujitsu.com
3 Utsunomiya University, 7-1-2 Yohtoh, Utsunomiya 321-8585,
Japan, kwt@cc.utsunomiya-u.ac.jp

Abstract. The National Research Grid Initiative (NAREGI) program is trying to develop NAREGI-PSE, which is a part of the NAREGI middleware. It provides services for deploying and executing large scale scientific computer simulation software on a grid's distributed and heterogeneous computer system. NAREGI-PSE has a PSE server that handles the applications residing on the distributed computers, and co-shares the application know-how, such as the source codes shared by the research community. This PSE server consists of an application pool and four PSE services. Users access the distributed computers through the NAREGI portal and the NAREGI application environment, which includes the NAREGI-PSE. The PSE server's main purposes are: (1) simple and easy execution of a user's application program in the grid environment, (2) simple and easy deployment of a user's program onto the distributed computer environment, (3) simple and easy software plug-in system into the application pool in the PSE server for software-reuse, and (4) application archive for a co-sharing application and it's know-how among the research communities, which is achieved by grid virtual organization (VO). NAREGI middleware is designed and developed based on grid services according to OGSA/WSRF frameworks.

1 Introduction

Using network connections spread out over a wide area, the large-scale grid project to integrate high performance computer resources that will be geographically dispersed is promoted in many countries. For example, TeraGrid in the United States integrates resources including more than 102 teraflops of computing capability and

Please use the following format when citing this chapter:

Usami, H., Kanazawa H., Kawata, S., 2007, in IFIP International Federation for Information Processing, Volume 239,
Grid-Based Problem Solving Environments, eds. Gaffney, P. W., Pool, J.C.T., (Boston: Springer), pp. 375-390.

more than 15 petabytes of online and archived data storage [1]. In Japan, the NAREGI program was instituted to research and develop high-performance, scalable grid middleware for a nationwide grid environment for scientific research.

In a large-scale grid environment, it is quite difficult for users to know the detailed specifications of a distributed computer system they can use. Most grid users will not write programs. Instead, they will use grid-enabled applications that make use of grid resources. These applications may be widely distributed general purpose software or applications that are used only in specific fields. In advanced scientific research, the latter is very important. Such applications are probably developed by small groups of researchers, and most researchers only use it on the grid resources.

We had to address the need for application developers and users in the field of advanced science research. Application users want to use applications with minimum knowledge of the applications and grid environment. Therefore, application developers should prepare information for the applications prior to release. NAREGI-PSE focuses on the functions to share applications, to deploy applications onto the grid, and to compose workflows using shared applications.

NAREGI-PSE consists of the following subcomponents: 1) a retriever and the application information setup, 2) the application and application information registration, 3) the compilation, test run, and comparison of the outputs with the desired results in the register phase in order to check if the program can be correctly run on the target computer systems, 4) an application search component to find the required programs from the application pool, 5) the application deployment, 6) the application and workflow search and registration in the application pool, and 7) a search for the appropriate computers based on the application information that is retrieved. This article at first briefly focuses on the NAREGI program itself, but later mostly on the NAREGI-PSE activities, including the design concepts, configuration, functions, and user scenario.

2   NAREGI Program

The NAREGI project is a five-year project that was instituted in fiscal 2003 in Japan. In 2006, the NAREGI project restarted as a new five-year project called the "NAREGI program" under the Development and Application of Advanced High-performance Supercomputer Project initiated by the Ministry of Education, Culture, Sports, Science and Technology (MEXT). NAREGI aims to research and develop high–performance, scalable grid middleware for the national scientific computational infrastructure. Such middleware will help facilitate computing centers within Japan as well as worldwide in constructing a large-scale scientific "research grid" for all areas of science and engineering, to construct a "National Research Grid" [2][3].

As a representative application area, NAREGI has adopted nanoscience, and large-scale nanoscience simulations have been performed. We assume that the future computational environment for scientific research will have a computational scale well beyond 100 teraflops and tens of thousands of users online. As such, the grid-enabled nanoscience applications associated with NAREGI will serve as the hallmarks of the project to evaluate the effectiveness of the grid middleware that we will develop. The experimental deployment of these applications will be significant in terms of the scale of the computational requirements. It will also provide a virtual distributed computing environment with a large number of users in nanoscience and nanotechnology, and from the areas of academia as well as industry.

The middleware R&D work is being conducted at the newly established Center for Grid Research and Development, hosted by the National Institute of Informatics (NII) in Tokyo, Japan. The grid-enabled nanoscience application work is under the auspices of the Center for Applications Research and Development, hosted by the Institute for Molecular Science (IMS) in Okazaki, Japan. These two centers are collaborating to establish and operate a dedicated NAREGI test bed with Japan's SuperSINET as the underlying network infrastructure. The test bed will facilitate nearly 18 teraflops of computing power distributed over nearly 3000 processors. Both the developed grid middleware and the grid-enabled nanoscience applications will be under scrutiny and expected to achieve a performance over a predetermined scale, as well as serving to test the stability and manageability of future grids hosted by the two centers and utilized by various application domains.

3   NAREGI middleware framework

The grid middleware R&D work consists of six research and development groups, as shown in Figure 1, which are referred to as "Work Packages" (WPs). WP-1 focuses on the lower- and middle-tier middleware for resource management, such as a Super Scheduler, GridVM (providing local resource controllers), and information services on the grid. WP-2 covers the basic parallel programming tools for the grid, mainly consisting of two key middleware pieces, GridRPC (for task-parallel applications) and GridMPI (for data-parallel applications). WP-3 works on the grid tools for end users, including the grid workflow, the problem solving environment (GridPSE), and the grid visualization tools. WP-4 deals with the data grid for the federation of databases spread worldwide on the grid environment, while WP-5 investigates networking, security, and user management issues for high-performance grid infrastructures, such as real-time traffic measurements, QoS provisioning, and optimal routing for VOs and robust file and data transfer protocols. Finally, WP-6 acts as a liaison with the Center for Applications Research and Development, developing application-specific middleware components in order to grid-enable large-scale nanoscience applications, including those that require the coupling of multiple applications on the grid.

3.1 Lower- and middle-tier middleware (WP-1)

The requirements for a scheduler that can handle the widely distributed computing resources of a grid environment include a high level of scalability, fault tolerance, and collaborative scheduling functions coordinating between multiple sites. This area of research and development covers such components as a "Super Scheduler", which can manage all scheduling over a wide area, a broker that can secure the computational resources meeting the user requirements, such as the number of CPUs, urgency, and cost, a scheduler for the cluster environment, middleware for computational resources, networks, and grids, and tools for monitoring information and managing system configurations for the various applications [4].

1) Super Scheduler: This is a meta-scheduling system for the large-scale control and management of a wide variety of resources shared by different organizations in the grid environment. The system will be aimed primarily at identifying resources that can meet requests from batch job users and allocate these resources to specific jobs.

2) GridVM (local resource controllers): This is a new grid middleware that deploys a virtual layer of computing resources in the grid environment and facilitates resource utilization, resource protection, and fault tolerance.

3) Information services: A secure, scalable resource information management service will be established for the purpose of running a large-scale, multi-discipline grid computing environment.

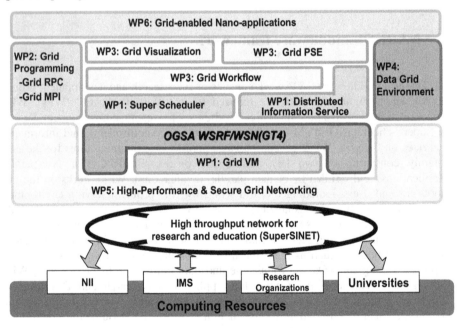

Fig. 1. NAREGI grid middleware stack

3.3 Grid programming environment (WP-3)

For this grid environment to be widely accepted by researchers, who are the end users, the grid software environment must be easy for them to use. To this end, research and development will be conducted in areas, such as the design of a workflow description language for controlling jobs on the grid, grid workflow tools for executing jobs in cooperation with the resource management mechanism, software tools for visualizing massive computational results distributed over the grid remotely with a light network load, and GridPSE to act as a software environment that can easily enable the execution, linkage, and coordination of the applications, computational modules, data, and other resources used by researchers over a wide area.

1) Grid workflow: A visual tool for seamlessly preparing, submitting, and querying distributed jobs running on remote computing resources. It explicitly handles programs and data, and is independent of the specific Grid middleware. Complex workflow descriptions, such as loops and conditional branches, are supported for nanoscience applications. Graphically described workflow jobs are converted to an enhanced workflow language based on Grid Services Flow Language (GSFL), which may be a common interface with other systems such as the PSE.

2) GridPSE: A Problem Solving Environment (PSE) for a scientific grid that facilitates the development and execution of application programs in nanoscience technology applications and other areas, without detailed computer-related knowledge or skills on the grid from the user's side. NAREGI-PSE is the software product name of this sub-project and the details for it are described in Section 4.

3) Grid visualization: A real-time, post-processing visualization system for nanosimulation, capable of reducing network loads that may interfere with smooth visualization, through flexible distribution of visualization tasks in the grid environment. This system is also characterized by having functions for large-scale parallel visualization, visualization for coupled simulation, and collaboration.

3.4 Data Grid environment (WP-4)

The research subjects are data grid fundamental technology, search control technology for a database federation, and metadata-based information integration for heterogeneous data resources. These technologies are under research and development for the federation of numerous databases spread throughout the Internet on the grid environment. The technologies include the Data Grid fundamental technology for managing and querying data resources using the WSRF-based OGSA infrastructure, search control technology (preventing combinatorial explosions caused by searching across many databases), and information integration technology with metadata that mediates heterogeneous data resources. Their developments are carried out in cooperation with the other grid environment.

3.5 High-performance and secure grid networking (WP-5)

This section discusses the research and development of high-performance and secure grid networking in the NAREGI project. In the last decade, network infrastructures have become a very complicated combination of different sub-infrastructures, with wide ranges of throughput, delay, error rate, and jitter supported by different technologies, such as Multi-Protocol Label Switching (MPLS), differentiated services (diffserv), and optical networking. Because of the nature of distributed computing, the performance of grid computing may be considerably degraded by certain conditions of underlying networks, such as poor bandwidth, long delay, or temporal failures. Thus, we should be aware of the network resources as well as the computing resources [5]. The goal of the project's high-performance and secure grid networking subgroup is to develop a reliable, easy-to-use, high–performance, secure networking infrastructure for grid computing by taking into consideration the requirements of various applications; that is, the goal is to develop a high-performance "managed network". For this purpose, we have set up the following three subgroups:

1) Network function infrastructure: In developing high-performance networks, over-provisioning and strict static reservation of the network resources are potential solutions, but neither are scalable nor cost-effective. Therefore, our goal for the network function infrastructure is to develop a system of measurement, management, and control for adaptively using and assigning network resources in order to avoid resource conflicts and cost-effectively maintain the network quality for grid computing.

2). Communication protocol infrastructure: The currently deployed version of TCP cannot detect network congestion until a packet loss occurs, so that many packets will be discarded. As either the network bandwidth or the router buffer size increases, the number of lost packets grows, significantly degrading the TCP throughput. Therefore, our goal for the communication protocol infrastructure is to develop a communication protocol optimized for grid computing and a method of evaluating the network performance.

3). Grid security infrastructure: Security problems in grid computing may occur in accessing the distributed resources over the network. Our goals for the grid security infrastructure are to develop a security model for grid computing based on PKI and to implement authentication and VO management across multiple organizations [6].

3.6 Grid-Enabled Nano Applications (WP-6)

WP6 is developing application-specific middleware components to grid-enable large-scale nanoscience applications, including those that require coupling of multiple applications on the grid. One example of such applications is multi-scale simulation, where each application component utilizes different mathematical and physical modeling approaches and cooperates on spatially or temporally different calculations. To advance such multi-scale applications, and more generally, multiple applications, users have wasted a lot of effort in developing custom codes and decomposing original codes for semantic-level communication between heterogeneous scientific application components.

3.7 Services Architecture of NAREGI Middleware

NAREGI middleware is designed and developed based on OGSA/WSRF. WSRF is a messaging model and provides the ability to model state-full resources in a framework of web services. WSRF defines the conventions for managing "state", so that applications can reliably share dynamically changing information. Major NAREGI middleware components are developed as grid services using GT4 [7] based on WSRF. The NAREGI middleware services architecture is shown in Figure 2. Each component works as an independent service and communicates with the others according to the grid service access protocol.

The top layer is the services for the end user, and this layer is usually provided as a portal for corresponding to the research community realized by VO. The second layer is the gateway services, and this layer provides several services building science gateway in TeraGrid. The third layer is the core grid services, and this layer provides core grid services, such as resource management, security services, and data services. The fourth and fifth layers are the physical resource infrastructure, which includes the network resources. NAREGI-PSE tightly co-works with workflow services and other layer services, such as information service and Super Scheduler, and is located in the gateway services layer.

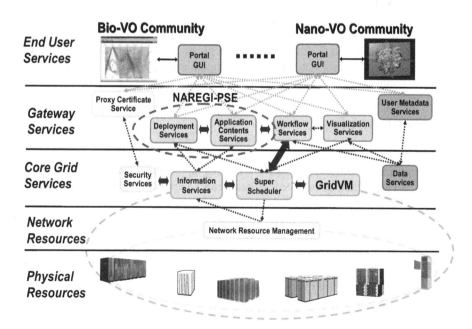

Fig. 2. NAREGI middleware service architecture

The workflow services are a visual tool for seamlessly preparing and submitting distributed jobs running on remote computing resources. It handles programs and data explicitly, and is independent of the specific Grid middleware. Complex workflow descriptions, such as loops and conditional branches, are supported for nanoscience applications. Graphically described workflow jobs are converted to an enhanced workflow language based on a workflow modeling language (WFML), which is a common interface with other systems, such as the PSE. The user imports the application information from an application contents service (ACS) in NAREGI-PSE and builds the application scenario using that application information on the workflow graphical user interface (GUI).

The information service contains various kinds of information; CPU, memory, OS, job queue, account, usage record, etc. These contents are aggregated and hierarchically accumulated in relational databases. A common information model (CIM) based schema is used to describe the resources in the computing grid [8]. The access control information for the applications in VO is supplied by the information service.

The Super Scheduler is a scheduling system for large-scale control and management of a wide variety of resources shared by different organizations in the grid environment. The system will be aimed primarily at identifying resources that can meet requests from batch job users and allocating these resources to specific jobs.

4   NAREGI-PSE

NAREGI-PSE is a part of the results of a grid application environment (WP3) group activity. NAREGI-PSE facilitates the deployment and execution of application programs in nanoscience technology applications and other areas, without detailed computer-related knowledge or skills for the grid on the user's side. [9-18]

4.1 NAREGI-PSE Design Concept

The design and development concepts of NAREGI-PSE are as follows:
(1) Provide a framework to distributed users' applications on a grid
- Users can register, deploy, and retrieve applications by using NAREGI-PSE for real-time collaborations.
- Application developers distribute and share their applications with research community members.
- Application users find it easy to use the latest research applications without a compilation or test run.
(2) Focus on a legacy application

- Deploy application binaries for specific target machines.
- Compile source programs, if needed.

(3) Design and development policy

- Simple and easy execution of users' application programs on distributed computers.
- Simple and easy deployment of users' programs onto the distributed computer environment.
- Simple and easy software plug-in into the application pool in the PSE server to provide a software-reuse environment. In this mechanism the PSE server supports users to reuse previous software for their own purposes.
- A problem solving scenario written by the workflow stored in the application pool in the same way as for a single application. End users easily reuse the stored workflows developed by themselves or by others for a new problem solving scenario.

4.2 NAREGI-PSE Configuration

The configuration of NAREGI-PSE is shown in Figure 3. NAREGI-PSE serves four WSRF-based grid services and a client GUI.

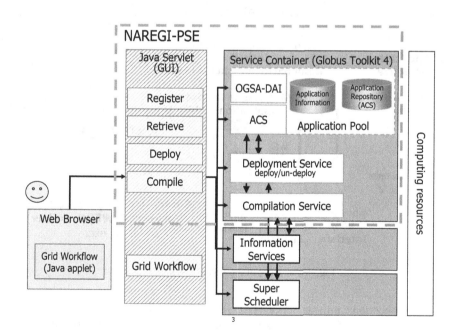

Fig. 3. NAREGI-PSE System Configuration

The NAREGI-PSE client GUI delivers a user interface to users, who work on distributed computer systems. The deployment service provides the function where they can transfer files of an application to remote computing resources, and execute a "post-procedure" to configure and/or examine a deployment. The compilation service provides the service that transfers the source files of an application to remote computing resources, and executes a script compilation, then collects and stores the binary files to ACS if the script compilation succeeds.

The application pool is implemented by using the application repository (AR) interface and application archive (AA) format from the ACS specifications. In addition, the application information utilizes OGSA-DAI and PostgreSQL.

4.3 Application pool

The application pool consists of two databases, the application information database and the ACS database as shown Figure 4. The application information database contains the meta-information related to the application, including the resource requirements (JSDL), and the ACS database contains the application entities, including the source codes.

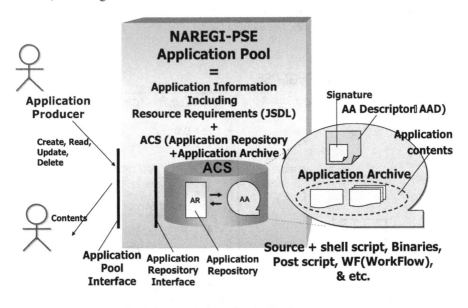

Fig. 4. Structure of Application Pool

(1) Application Contents Service (ACS)

ACS is a set of requirements and specifications that is being worked on by the Application Contents Service Working Group (ACS-WG) [19] within the Global Grid Forum (GGF) [20], which is an international standards and community body focusing on Grid technologies. The ACS specification documents define a standardized way to manage and handle a grid application as a deployable logical unit, so as to maintain consistency, reduce management overhead, and enable automation throughout the lifetime of an application.

The ACS architecture is described as follows. The ACS provides a repository for grid applications. The application producer creates application archive (AA) instances accompanied with the meta-information describing the contents. The AA is a logical bundle of files that is used for provisioning and executing a task in a Grid system. Such information may include, but is not limited to, the application executable code, configuration data necessary for initial deployment of the application, and the deployment descriptor documents.

An AA consists of an Application Archive Descriptor (AAD) and zero or more application contents. The ACS repository will parse and make use of the AAD. The AAD may contain information, such as the identification, access constraint policy, and information associated with the structure, of the AA contents. In order to achieve application contents retrieval, the ACS repository needs to know the meta-information of the application content files, such as the names and types of the files. They should be provided by the Application Provider and be included in the AAD.

(2) Application Archive

The Application Archive of a single application contains the following materials:

- Source files (optional)
- An executable file (required, but it may be generated by a compilation procedure.)
- A compilation procedure (optional)
- A deployment procedure (required)
- Files required for executing the application (optional)

An application stored in the Application Repository will be a part of a complex application, using the grid workflow. A workflow consists of some applications that can be registered in NAREGI-PSE, too. The Application Archive of a workflow contains a workflow file described in WSML. The resource requirements of applications in NAREGI-PSE are described based on the Job Submission Description Language (JSDL). The application with a different resource requirement is stored as another application archive, as shown in Figure 5.

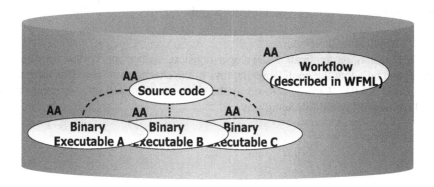

Fig. 5. Structure of Application Archives

4.4 Compilation and Deployment Services

The following two services are the key services in NAREGI-PSE.
(1) The compilation service
The compilation service provides the remote compilation function, according to the following procedures.

- Retrieve and select an application to compile.
- Display the candidate set of the computing resources from the resource requirements of the application.
- Select (a) computing resource(s) for the compilation.
- Transfer files to the selected computing resources and execute the compilation.
- If the compilation succeeds, the resulting files are stored in the application repository.

(2) The deployment service
The deployment service provides the deployment function, according to the following procedures.

- Retrieve and select a application to deploy.
- Display the candidate set of computing resources from the resource requirement of the application.
- Select (a) computing resource(s) for the deployment.
- Transfer files to the selected computing resources and execute the "post-procedure"
- If the post-procedure succeeds, the deployment information is stored in NAREGI-information service (NAREGI-IS).

4.5 NAREGI-PSE Using Scenario

NAREGI-PSE assumes two types of users, one is the application developer and the other is the application user. The application user just uses applications that were developed by other researchers or by his/herself.

(1) Application developer
In Figure 6, an application developer registers his/her application with the PSE server and tells that the application deploys to the execution server. This information is put into NAREGI-IS. Developed applications are deployed and registered to the application pool in the following way.

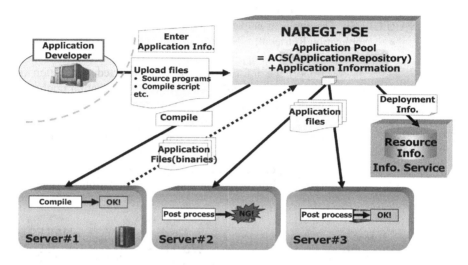

Fig. 6. NAREGI-PSE Usage Scenario (I)

- Upload to PSE server:
  - Upload files (e.g., source code/executables, compile script, post-process script, initial input files, etc.) to the PSE application pool.
  - Upload information (e.g., description, system requirements, etc.) associated with the uploading application to the application pool.
- Compilation (if needed):
  - Select an application and then select a server for the compilation matching to a resource requirement.
  - The PSE transfers the necessary files (e.g., source code) from the application pool to the compile server.
  - The PSE compiles and verifies them on the server.
  - The PSE transfers files (e.g., executable) from the compile server to the application pool.
- Deployment
  - Select an application and servers that meet the system requirements for the application deployment.
  - The PSE transfers the executables in the application pool to the selected servers.
  - Executes a post-process defined by user to configure and/or verify deployment on each server. (Optional)
- PSE registers information on the deployed servers to the information service

(2) Application User

Figure 7 shows the application user executing the registered application in NAREGI-PSE. The application executing processes are as follows.

- Application Retrieval:
    - o Retrieve the application using GUI
    - o Import the information from the selected application (system requirements - JSDL, etc.) from the application pool to make a workflow icon of the Grid Workflow
- Execution:
    - o Compose a workflow job from the registered workflow icon.
    - o The PSE submits a job to the Super Scheduler.
    - o The Super Scheduler dispatches the resources referring the resource information provided by Information Service.

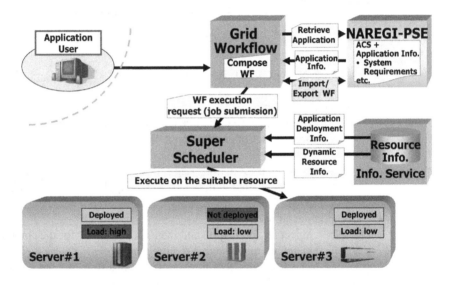

Fig. 7. NAREGI-PSE Usage Scenario (II)

5   Conclusions

The NAREGI program is now in the middle of its fourth year. The beta version of NAREGI middleware was released in May 2006. The program is now fully engaged in software development for delivering the final version of a NAREGI-integrated (NAREGI V1.0) Grid middleware at the end of the next fiscal year. The research projects under the NAREGI program have made considerable progress in the development the a prototype software, and some of them have already produced preliminary results, including GridRPC, GridMPI, and NAREGI-Certification Authority (NAREGI-CA). NAREGI-PSE also has developed a beta version and delivered it to IMS and several other user sites. The role and viability of PSE in the distributed computer system have been demonstrated. The PSE server provides a smooth and flexible environment in the HPC on distributed computers, and encapsulates the complex information of distributed systems, so that on the PSE server users can perform HPC as if distributed computers are under the users' hands. The PSE server may open a new environment for the HPC world.

Finally, we regard Grid as one of the fundamental technologies of the IT infrastructure in the 21st century, and expect that the results of the NAREGI program will greatly advance research and development in the scientific fields, improve Japan's international competitiveness, and have a major economic impact.

Acknowledgments

This work was partly supported by a grant from the Ministry of Education, Sports, Culture, Science and Technology (MEXT) of Japan through the NAREGI (National Research Grid Initiative) Program. We would like to express special thanks to Prof. Kenichi Miura (NII), Prof. Mutsumi Aoyagi (Kyushu University), Prof. Yoshio Tago (Kanazawa University), and other members of the NAREGI project for their valuable discussions and useful comments.

References

[1] TeraGrid: http://www.teragrid.org/
[2] S. Matsuoka, S. Shimojo, M. Aoyagi, S. Sekiguchi, H. Usami, and K. Miura, "Japanese computational grid research project: NAREGI", Proceedings of the IEEE, Vol. 93, NO. 3, pp. 522-533, March 2005.
[3] NAREGI: National Research Grid Initiative
http://www.naregi.org/⊔ National Institute of Informatics⊔
http://nanogrid.ims.ac.jp/nanogrid/⊔ Institute for Molecular Science⊔
[4] I. Foster and C. Kesselman, "The GRID Blueprint for a New Computing Infrastructure," Morgan Kaufman Publishers, 1998
[5] Y. Kitatsuji and K. Yamazaki, "A Distributed Real-time Tool for IP-Flow Measurement," In Proc. of the 2004 Int'l Symposium on Applications and the Internet, pp. 91-98, Tokyo, January 2004
[6] Common Component Architecture Forum, http://www.cca-forum.org/
[7] Globus Toolkit: http://www-unix.globus.org/toolkit/
[8] G. Wasson and M. Humphrey, "Toward Explicit Policy Management for Virtual Organization," IEEE 4th International Workshop on Policies for Distributed Systems and Networks, pp. 173-182, 2003

[9]   E. Gallopoulos, E. N. Houstis, and J. R. Rice, "Computer as thinker/doer: Problem solving environments for computational science," IEEE Comp. Sci. and Eng., Vol. 1, 1994, pp. 11-23.

[10] E. N. Houstis, E. Gallopoulos, J. R. Rice, and R. Bramley, eds., "Enabling Technologies for Computational Science," (Kluwer Academic Publishers, Amsterdam, 2000).

[11] K. Schuchardt, B. Didier, and G. Black, "Ecce: A Problem Solving Environments Evolution Toward Grid Services and a Web Architecture," Available at http://citeseer.nj.nec.com/459199.html

[12] Y. Umetani, M. Tsuji, K. Iwasawa, and H. Hirayama, "DEQSOL: A Numerical Simulation Language for Vector/Parallel Processors," Proc. of IFIP WG2.5 Working Conference on Problem Solving Environments for Scientific Computing, Sophia Antipolis, France1, 1987, pp. 147-162.

[13] C. Konno, M. Yamabe, M. Saji, N. Sagawa et al., "Automatic Code Generation Method of DEQSOL," Journal of Information Processing, Information Processing Society of Japan, Vol. 11, No. 1, pp. 15-21.

[14] Y. Umetani, C. Konno, and T. Ohta, "Visual PDEQSOL: A Visual and Interactive Environments for Numerical Simulation," Proc. of IFIP TC2/WG2.5 Working Conference on Programming Environments for High-Level Scientific Problem Solving, Karlsruhe, Germany, 1991, pp. 259-267

[15] S. Kawata, K. Iijima, C. Boonmee, and Y. Manabe, "Computer-assisted scientific-computation/simulation-software-development system - including a visualization system -," IFIP Transaction, Vol. A-48, 1994, pp. 145-153.

[16] C. Boonmee and S. Kawata, "Computer-Assisted Simulation Environment for Partial-Differential-Equation Problem: 1. Data Structure and Steering of Problem Solving Process," Trans. of Jpn. Soc. Comp. Eng. and Sci., Paper No. 19980001, 1998

[17] C. Boonmee and S. Kawata, "Computer-Assisted Simulation Environment for Partial-Differential-Equation Problem: 2. Visualization and Steering of Problem Solving Process," Trans. of Jpn. Soc. Comp. Eng. and Sci., Paper No. 19980002, 1998.

[18] CACTUS: http://www.cactuscode.org/

[19] ACS-WG: https://forge.gridforum.org/projects/acs-wg/

[20] GGF: Global Grid Forum http://www.ogf.org/

Q&A – Hitohide Usami

Questioner: Mladen Vouk

Can you estimate how many users of the prototype system there may be?

Hitohide Usami

Now over 50 users had downloaded the NAREGI Grid Middleware Version Beta1.0, but I guess only few users finished install and setup.

Questioner: Mladen Vouk

Can you please comment on the interoperability properties of the NAREGI?

Hitohide Usami

We are now discussing with EGEE group about the way of the interoperability. We are planning demonstrations of interoperability between NAREGI and EGEE at the next SC2006. We belong to GGF GIN(Grid Interoperation / Interoperability Now)-WG, and discuss interoperability from the viewpoints of standardization.

Questioner: Bill Gropp

Did you find that the original design of NAREGI into six areas and the interfaces between them needed to be changed as you developed the Grid application environment?

Hitohide Usami

The original design of NAREGI (prototype system) was developed based on UNICORE, but the current version is based on OGSA/WSRF. So, the interfaces between each component are drastically changed.

Questioner: Bill Gropp

Do you have measures for the success of the components of the projects, such as performance or scalability?

Hitohide Usami

We are measuring performance, scalability, reliability, stability, robustness, etc as the success of the middleware.

Questioner: Bill Appelbe

What "off the shelf" or existing software are you using, e.g., scheduling?

Hitohide Usami

NAREGI Grid Middleware Version Beta1.0 using PBSpro (for Linux machine) or LoadLeveler (for AIX machine) as "off the shelf" software.

Questioner: Brian Ford

Japan suffers earthquakes from time to time. Are there special disaster recovery demands in the design of NAREGI to overcome likely problems?

Hitohide Usami

NAREGI Grid Middleware Version Beta1.0 does not yet support special disaster recovery functions. These functions are closely depended on the local scheduling "out of NAREGI" software, we are now discussing about these functions including application level checkpoint restart function.

Grid Enabling of Nano-Science Applications in NAREGI

Mutsumi Aoyagi

Kyushu University

Abstract. Grid-Enabling Team(WP6) in National Research Grid Initiative(NAREGI)1 is developing application-specific middleware components to grid-enable large-scale nano-science applications, Chemistry applications, including those that require coupling of multiple applications on the grid. One example of such applications is multi-scale and/or multi-physics simulation, where each application component utilizes mathematically and physically different modeling and cooperates on spatially or temporally different calculations. To advance such multi-scale and/or multi-physics applications, users have made an every kind of efforts in developing custom codes and decomposing original codes for semantic-level communication between heterogeneous scientific application components. To facilitate easier usage and minimize customization processes of original user programs which may be legacy codes, we have been developing a middleware system, called a _Mediator_ on top of the GridMPI2, that provides high-level transparency in automatically transferring and transforming data between heterogeneous application components. The Mediator focuses on a data-handling specification that correlates different discrete points in finite difference method (FDM), finite element method (FEM), or particle simulations such as Molecular Dynamics(MD) in the unified way. It supports a variety of techniques for semantically transforming the values associated with the correlated points, e.g., in-sphere, first nearest neighbors, and nearest points. The Mediator provides three types of Application Programming Interface (API), which (1) manage a task identification and construct an association between Mediator and application processes in parallel programming style such as Single Program Multiple Data and Master-Worker, (2) register different levels of discrete points, search the correlated discrete points, and determine processes and (3) transfer messages incorporating the extraction and the transformation of the values associated with the correlated points. The prototype system has been applied to multi-scale simulations in nano-science, in which

Please use the following format when citing this chapter:

Aoyagi, M., 2007, in IFIP International Federation for Information Processing, Volume 239, Grid-Based Problem Solving Environments, eds. Gaffney, P. W., Pool, J.C.T., (Boston: Springer), pp. 393-394.

RISM (Reference Site Model) and FMO (Fragment Molecular Orbital) are coupled to analyze an entire electric structure of large-scale molecules immersed in infinite solvent. RISM is employed to analyze the pair correlation functions of molecular sites between a solvent and a solute, while FMO is used to calculate the total electronic energy and the molecular structure of the solute. The interoperability between nano-science applications on the grid might require the functionality to reuse application codes and data from one application domain to another as well as to retrieve and transport data. In the execution step of nano-applications, we have to focus on providing the grid-ready environment which could easily enable the execution, linkage, and coordination of the application modules and the data. To achieve this end, Grid Application Environment Team(WP3) in NAREGI has been developing Workflow Tool, GridPSE and Grid Visualization Tools in cooperation with the resource management mechanism. We expect that these middlewares and tools could be a key component for enabling gateway developers to manage and provide applications on the computational resources for execution and for analyzing linked data sets from related domains, such as Monte Carlo calculations, molecular dynamics, electronic structure studies, and further cross-disciplinary data mining.

Q&A – Mutsumi Aoyagi

Questioner: Brian Ford

Congratulations on your computation of a very large molecule in this way! Have you found that the computing method you have chosen confirms and supports your chemical intuitions? As the molecular groups within the ensemble rotate, do you anticipate changing the strategy of your computation?

Mutsumi Aoyagi

Thank you very much. I found that the fragment Molecular Orbital (FMO) method works very well for the decomposition on simple chemical bonds like a single bond, but for molecules having multiple-bonds or delocalized electrons, we must carefully apply the FMO method to such systems.   Yes, we realize that different decomposition schemes have to be applied according to large changes of molecular structure, such as a rotation of molecular groups.

Questioner: Mladen Vouk

In your multi-scale and/or multi-physics simulation example, the large molecule is immersed in water. What happens to the possible hydrogen bonding between the molecule and "thin" water layer around it? Is it computed by the FMO code or by the water "integral" code?

Mutsumi Aoyagi

Yes, hydrogen bonding of surrounding water molecules with solute, such as large protein molecule, plays an important role in solvation dynamics of protein. So the surrounding water molecules located at the 1st layer are treated as the part of solute. In other word, hydrated protein with thin water is calculated by FMO, and surrounding water molecules located at 2nd layer are treated through statistical method in our multi-scale and/or multi-physics simulation.

Questioner: Mladen Vouk

In your slides which show decomposition of the FMO code into modules, does your grid system automatically adapt the code (through automatic recompilation) if mapping onto computing resources offers a platform for which you may not have precompiled/optimized executables?

Mutsumi Aoyagi

Our grid system, NAREGI-PSE, does not have automatic recompilation functionalities. Instead, since the compilation conditions required for each module are registered on the application information service, NAREGI-PSE can deploy our modules onto the appropriate computing resources automatically.

Questioner: Bill Applebe

Is the water molecule display purely for one time-step?

Mutsumi Aoyagi

Yes, the calculated results correspond only to one time-step, and in order to investigate the dynamical aspect of solvated molecule, including the analysis of free energy surface, we need to iteratively solve the RISM equation for solvent according to the structural changes of solute.

Grid Architecture for Scientitic Communities

Sebastien Goasguen

Purdue University

Abstract. Sharing of resources among virtual organizations (VO) has been termed the grid problem. At the heart of this problem is development and acceptance of a protocol to share, discover and compose services. However significant challenges arise in monitoring, accounting and securing any grid infrastucture. VOs of any size should be able to build their own cyberinfrastructure (CI) by discovering and then composing services to build higher level capabilities that they need. These community's CI could be dynamically expandable, persistent and migratable while using resources across adminstrative domains. In this paper we will present several VO based grid architecture and focuse on the nanotechnology community CI called the nanoHUB. The nanoHUB uses virtualization technologies to isolate the infrastructure from the local administrative domain. Virtual machine migration and virtual networking techniques allow the infrastructure to be dynamic and adapt to the underlying physical system. Moreover by using virtual machine the users are provided with a sand box that serve as a development platform for their software an as a entry point to physical grids. Finally, we will cover the security issues in VO access to multiple grid infrastructure and present our work towards using shibboleth witin the nanoHUB.

Please use the following format when citing this chapter:

Goasguen, S., 2007, in IFIP International Federation for Information Processing, Volume 239, Grid-Based Problem Solving Environments, eds. Gaffney, P. W., Pool, J.C.T., (Boston: Springer), pp. 397.

Q&A – Sebastien Goasguen

Questioner: Bill Applebe

Is the nanoHUB installed elsewhere, or is there a plan to distribute it more widely or make it compatible with other grid hubs?

Sebastien Goasguen

Currently the nanoHUB infrastructure is centralized and operated from Purdue. Remote resources on TeraGrid and Open Science Grid are used but the virtual infrastructure is based at Purdue. We have started work towards a much more distributed infrastructure using some virtual networking technologies. Resources at the University of Florida are being used to test migration of virtual machines between Purdue and UF. We also plan to package the middleware to make it available to other communities.

Questioner: Mladen Vouk

What are the failover (fault-tolerance) provisions in your system?

VMWare seems to have nicer failover properties (automatic migration to backup servers). Is there are reason you chose to use XEN?

NC State has a system that is in many ways similar to what you have. Ours is called Virtual Computing Laboratory and uses RDP as the remote desktop access protocol (and within web window display). Is there a reason you chose VNC? In my experience VNC sometimes has difficulties with graphics.

Sebastien Goasguen

The In-VIGO middleware has been deployed at Purdue and a reference implementation is used in Production. This implementation has been enhanced with monitoring tools such that user sessions, file system, connection to back-ends, VNC servers are being checked regularly and restarted if they fail. This system also allows us to stress test the middleware and simulate high user load.

We currently do not have automatic migration in our infrastructure. Migration is being used in our virtual cluster to adapt to the load and run time characteristics of the applications. When the project started we purchased two licenses of the Vmware GSX server. We ended up transitioning to the open source Xen system which is a patch to the Linux kernel. It offers less overhead and through experience has shown to be more reliable. Now that Vmware has released a free version of their player and their server we are starting to re-introduce some Vmware technologies, especially the player which allows us to give a "nanohub appliance" to our users.

So far VNC has seemed able to meet our needs. We are aware that there maybe some networking issues when applications have heavy graphics.

Questioner: Ron Boisvert

There are many simulation applications available to users of the nanoHUB. Presumably, these are contributed by the research community. On average, how much work is required to take one of these apps and make it presentable/reliable for use in the nanoHUB, and who does this work?

Sebastien Goasguen

Anyone can contribute an application to the nanoHUB. A project is created in our subversion repository and the contributor can upload his or her applications. The Network for Computational Nanotechnology has developed its own graphical user interface builder called Rappture, which can be used easily to create a nice GUI. An undergraduate can create the interface in a couple of hours. More complex applications can take weeks, but mostly due to a review process that has several iterations before an application is made publicly available. However the strength of the middleware is that any application can be made available, so technically it takes as much time as to get the source and compile the code.

Questioner: Xiaoge Wang

Will and how does this middleware affect the way that scientists work?

Sebastien Goasguen

Users of the applications can access them through their browser without installing or compiling any software components. More advanced users who develop applications can benefit from a standard development environment available through the workspaces. If developers wish to adopt Rappture to create their applications interface they will need to learn the Rappture API that they will use in their code. If we consider the access to remote resources outside the nanoHUB, the scientists need only know how to use condor and pbs. They actually don't have to learn too many new things from their standard mode of operation.

Scientific Software Frameworks and Grid Computing

Improving Programming Productivity

Bill Appelbe[1], Louis Moresi[2], Steve Quenette[1], and Patrick Sunter[1]

1 Victorian Partnership for Advanced Computing (VPAC)
PO Box 201, Carlton South, Victoria 3188 Australia
{bill, steve, pat}@vpac.org
2 School of Mathematical Sciences
Monash University, Clayton, Victoria 3800, Australia
louis.moresi@sci.monash.edu.au

Abstract Scientific research applications, or codes, are notoriously difficult to develop, use, and maintain. This is often because scientific software is written from scratch in traditional programming languages such as C and Fortran, by scientists rather than expert programmers. By contrast, modern commercial applications software is generally written using toolkits and software frameworks that allow new applications to be rapidly assembled from existing component libraries. In recent years, scientific software frameworks have started to appear, both for grid-enabling existing applications and for developing applications from scratch. This paper compares and contrasts existing scientific frameworks and extrapolates existing trends.

Introduction

A *software framework* is *an organized collection of reusable software components that is used to implement software applications.* Software frameworks are now in widespread use in commercial software development, and software development using such frameworks is referred to as Component Based Software Development or Engineering [1]. The two most widely used commercial software frameworks are SUN's Java J2EE, and Microsoft's .NET. The J2EE and .NET frameworks consist of many thousands of classes that provide the basic infrastructure necessary to implement GUIs, web sites and web services, and relational database interfaces. Frameworks provide significant software productivity improvement through reuse of their components [2].

Please use the following format when citing this chapter:

Applebe, B., Moresi, L., Quenette, S., Sunter, P., 2007, in IFIP International Federation for Information Processing, Volume 239, Grid-Based Problem Solving Environments, eds. Gaffney, P. W., Pool, J.C.T., (Boston: Springer), pp. 401-413.

The notion of *grid computing* [3] has several interpretations, ranging from a rather restricted interpretation (an application run remotely), to a much more expansive view of an application that is in use by a distributed community that uses the grid to share and exchange models (developed using the application), data, and research outcomes. In this paper, we adopt the more expansive view of a grid-based application, in line with the evolution and growth of the grid and communities that use it.

So the key aim of software frameworks, as applied to scientific grid-based applications, is to reduce the development, maintenance, and support time for scientific applications and models, comparable to that achievable for commercial software development by reuse.   Realistically, widespread large productivity increases for scientific software are unlikely for a variety of reasons, not the least of which is the limited "market" for specialized scientific applications and the corresponding lack of resources.   However, it is arguable that the progress in scientific software frameworks has been significant over the past few years, with both successes and failures, which point to emerging opportunities and likely evolution.

The definition of software frameworks adopted above (or equivalent definitions such as in www.wikipedia.org) is inherently subjective and qualitative – it provides no clear measure of what is, and is not, a framework. However, the definition of frameworks adopted above does leads to several key characteristics of software frameworks that can be used to assess, or quantify, the extent to which a software product, library, or *toolkit,* is a framework:

1. *Extensibility* – to what extent can the framework be extended or adapted, by mechanisms that include specialization, introduction of new components, and modification of existing components? Inevitably, extensibility implies object-orientation – in the architecture and implementation of the framework.
2. *Integration* – to what extent can the components of the framework be combined or interoperate? Is there an underlying architecture that facilitates assembly of components?
3. *Scope* – what fraction of an application can be implemented by applying framework components?   This fraction is obviously dependent upon the application and the extent to which customization or adaptation is needed. A broad framework scope provides for significantly reduced development time, but comes at a corresponding cost and complexity of the framework.

Frameworks for Grid Computing

One view of grid computing is that it will eliminate or reduce the need for traditional "command line" scientific computing – where a user logs in to a remote or local computer, typically running Linux, then runs the scientific application as a batch job, supplying it with whatever files and command arguments are required. Such command-line computing has been the standard model for using scientific software since the 1960's. Command-line computing often requires considerable application expertise to configure and run, as every application has its own input and output formats, files, and constraints. In addition, there are typically suites of applications or programs that need to be run to create model and post-process the output (e.g., to create a visualization or plots). When used repetitively, such a suite of applications and programs is referred to as a *workflow*[4]

Grid computing can simplify scientific computing by replacing the command line model by a *web portal*, that uses web pages to provide a standardize www interface for scientific data and computations – setting up, running, archiving, and post-processing output of scientific applications running on remote computing systems (e.g., blast searches on NCBI's website [5]). The goal of web portals is to provide a scientific computing www environment that is as convenient and simple as that for www applications such as online news, encyclopedias, or travel.

For well-developed and standardized scientific applications, such as blast, web portals can be highly successful. However, it is often very labor intensive to create and maintain effective customized web portals for less widely used scientific applications (in spite of the availability of robust toolkits such as gridsphere for creating web portals). Thus there are two key limitations of the strategy of replacing command line scientific computing with web portals:

1. Individual scientists and applications often have their own nuances and techniques for using scientific applications, based on their research objectives and peculiarities of the application – a "one size fits all" approach for scientific computing is not feasible. The strength of command-line computing is its flexibility, albeit at a cost in complexity. Conversely, the weakness of portal-based computing is that it is limited by whatever workflows and input are built into the portal to support the user community.

2. The other limitation of portals is that they do not provide for customization of the scientific application – beyond what customization was provided for by the implementer of the scientific application. Almost invariably, the implementer of the portal is not the same as the implementer of the application (as portals and scientific applications use different skills and programming technology). In effect, a portal "shrink wraps" an application, but does not readily provide for customization of the scientific application inside of the shrink-wrapping (such as changing a solver or a constitutive law).

A partial solution to the lack of flexibility in portals, and the lack of standardization of inputs to scientific applications is *superstructure frameworks*. A superstructure framework is simply a framework that provides components to replace the "top-level" of an application, and/or tie together applications or application components into a workflow. Notable examples of such superstructure frameworks include:

- Kepler [4] – for workflows
- Pyre [6] – a Python toolkit for staging, monitoring, and visualization scientific applications.

While superstructure frameworks do provide more capability for customization of applications and their interfaces than web portals, they still do not facilitate the internal customization of an application. Superstructure frameworks generally use interpreted languages and tools that are unsuited to customization of low-level high-performance numerical algorithms used by scientific applications. A further limitation of superstructure frameworks is that they require the end-user to become familiar another programming paradigms – that of the superstructure framework. By contrast, web portals generally do not require any end-user knowledge of the portal technology/framework. Of course, specialist applications support developers can provide the expertise needed for end-users of superstructure frameworks, but that just shifts, rather than removes, the complexity introduced by superstructure frameworks.

Superstructure frameworks do have an important niche in interfacing scientific applications and standardizing interfaces to scientific applications. However, they do not significantly simplify the development and support of the algorithms and data structures of parallel scientific applications. For such a task, it is necessary to develop frameworks that reduce the development and maintenance cost for applications themselves. Such frameworks are referred to either as *infrastructure* or *scientific frameworks*.

The Evolution of Scientific Applications

Scientific applications software is always faced by the challenge of the moving target of scientific research and models. Once a problem is "solved" it is no longer research, and the frontier of research is always moving towards ever more complex problems and models. This is the "catch-22" of scientific software for research – software application and models often need to evolve to be relevant to the research community. In disciplines with large research communities and well-understood physics, such as quantum chemistry and atmospheric physics, the community may be supported by commercial or *community codes* – well-established scientific applications that are in widespread use and supported by a funded development and support team (e.g., Gaussian or NAMD [7] for Chemistry). In such disciplines, the community need is for maintenance and extension of existing codes, rather than development of new codes. However in other research disciplines, such as geosciences, there are relatively few well-supported community or commercial codes in widespread use. In such disciplines, software development and modeling is dominated by a patchy landscape of specialized codes each with a small band of loyal followers. Reflecting on the difficult environment in which these codes originated and thrive, they are colloquially referred to as *"hero codes"* [8].

A hero code is simply a scientific application that was written to model a specific scientific research problem. Common characteristics of hero codes include:

- Design and coding is done by one person, often a scientist with relatively little formal training in programming or software design
- High priority is given to modeling a very specific problem, or family of problems, for a publication or graduation deadline
- Low priority is given to documentation, adaptability, or reuse of the software
- The user-community for a given code often coincides quite closely with a particular school of thought within a discipline

Hero codes correspond to what is known in commercial software as a *rapid prototype* – where speed of development is initially a primary goal. Rapid prototypes are intended to be "throw away" code [9] – used once, but then thrown away as the code was never built with maintainability and robustness. However, experience in commercial software and scientific computing is that such prototypes, or hero codes, are rarely thrown away. Instead what happens is that successful hero codes are copied and adapted, sometimes very painfully, to meet new requirements, such as:

- Changed scope of boundary and initial conditions beyond those originally foreseen in the initial code development.
- Different discretizations of the primary variables such as new meshes, elements, or interpolation functions of higher order or adaptive refinement.
- Changing the solution scheme, for performance or accuracy reasons
- Applying the code to include additional physics or to work on multi-scale, multi-physics (coupled) problems
- Scaling the code up to much larger problems – inevitably by parallelizing the code in one or more dimensions to be run in parallel on dozens or hundreds of processors

Inevitably, once the original successful hero code is made available to a community it is copied and adapted by individual researchers, with little coordination or consistency in adaptation. Multiple version of the hero code exist, and each new version just adds more complexity – there is often no incentive or funding mechanism for an individual researcher or research organization to perform a "cleanup" of the hero code and its versions. By contrast, in commercial software, the maintenance costs of software a budget line-item, so there is strong incentive to drop or replace legacy applications that are expensive to maintain, or incrementally improve legacy applications through *refactoring* [10] – preserving the same functionality, but making incremental improvements in the design to enable reuse and extension.

Scientific Software Frameworks

Math libraries have been widely used for numerical software development since the 1950's. The evolution of such libraries gradually extended from simple scalar functions (e.g., sine or exp), to higher-level libraries:
- BLAS (Basic Linear Algebra Subprograms, 1979) – matrix and vector operations
- LINPACK and LAPACK (1990) [11] – solvers, built on BLAS

These libraries gradually evolved to the point that optimized versions were available for most shared memory and vector processors by the 1990's. However, the rise of distributed memory systems complicated the implementation and use of such libraries. Such libraries generally did not meet the criteria of a framework (extensibility, integration, and scope), and were functional rather than being object-oriented. Several key evolutionary steps were needed before libraries could evolve into frameworks that effectively support portable scientific applications for distributed memory systems:

a) A portable standard for message passing (MPI, 1992)

b) Decoupling the library implementations of matrices and vector (e.g., sparse, dense, and how these are distributed across processors) from the interface to these abstractions. This decoupling of interfaces from implementations is a powerful object-oriented mechanism for adaptability – the client sees only the interface, which can be dynamically replaced by any implementation of the interface.

c) Provision of partial differential equation (PDE) solver libraries – where much of the complexity of many applications lies, with the greatest opportunities for reuse and productivity gains.

d) Implicit parallelism – hiding the details of parallel decomposition and communication from users of the library (while allowing a choice of parallel decompositions through interfaces). The design and implementation of portable, scaleable, and efficient parallel numerical methods requires considerable specialist labor and expertise.

PETSc (1994) [12], the Portable Extensible Toolkit for Scientific computation was the first scientific library in wide use to incorporate these features. The main application domain for PETSc is scientific applications based around linear solvers, although it includes support for other domains such as non-linear solvers.

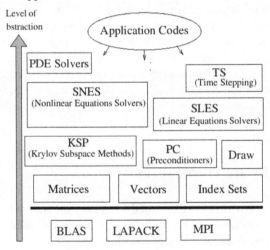

Fig. 1. The Architecture of PETSc

What distinguishes PETSc from earlier numerical libraries is its use of object-oriented abstractions, and an overall architecture. Even a solver is an object, or *context*, that is filled in at runtime with information about the solver. Within the domain of PDE solvers, PETSc is arguably the first scientific framework, as it satisfies the three key criteria of extensibility, interoperability, and scope (a large fraction of a many PDE based scientific applications can be implemented in PETSc).

PETSc has been widely used, deployed, and extended. Since PETSc, there have been several other frameworks for scientific computing developed, with somewhat different goals notably: Trilinos [13], CCA [8], and StGermain [14, 15].

Trilinos has a somewhat different philosophy and implementation style to PETSc. Firstly, it is implemented in C++, rather than C. Secondly, it is composed of contributed packages, as opposed to PETSc's structure of a single integrated subroutine library. The use of C++, which is an object-oriented "extension" of C scientific computing is increasing, and it is arguable that since almost any framework will be object-oriented, it is better to implement frameworks in an object-oriented programming language. The downside of using C++ is that C++ is a considerably more complex programming language than C, especially when using advanced features of C++ such as templates and the BOOST libraries. Such complexity may make it difficult for end-users, who are scientists rather than computer scientists, to use the framework. In addition, the package structure and "contributed component" structure of Trilinos may lead to inconsistencies and incompatibilities between components as Trilinos evolves. Arguably, a consistent modular architecture is central to the success and evolution of frameworks.

Both PETSc and Trilinos use object-oriented abstractions, and interfaces, between components, and abstractions for the foundation classes of numerical software (Matrices and Vectors – the Petra libraries in Trilinos and the implicit Mat and Vec abstractions in PETSc). This means that PETSc and Trilinos should be interoperable, if appropriate wrappers and adapters are built.

CCA, the Common Component Architecture, is an alternative approach to frameworks based on standardization of component interfaces, including a formal specification of the architecture. So CCA is not really a software framework itself, but rather a meta-framework. The success of CCA will depend upon the extent to which is adopted by the community and the perceived value of such a framework. In practice, such "top-down" standardization efforts have not been very successful in the past (e.g., HPF). Standardization works best in a "bottom-up", tightly integrated fashion where the standard covers a quite limited application domain (e.g., MPI).

StGermain

StGermain is a framework, like PETSc or Trilinos, but has key architectural differences:

- It is component-oriented (using classes, implemented in C, and a component-architecture)
- It is hierarchical

The traditional definition of object orientation is that all data is encapsulated in classes, and common behavior is factored out using inheritance and polymorphism (dynamic binding of methods or functions). But merely being object-oriented does not ensure that an application or framework can be readily extended or adapted. Thus modern software frameworks have extended object-orientation into component-orientation, to facilitate reuse of components using a variety of programming techniques, design patterns [16], and architectural principles. These include:

1. Run or load-time class definition – new classes can be created "on the fly", and the data and methods of those classes specified at runtime
2. Reflection [17] – at runtime, an application can query the properties of any class or object
3. Factories [16] – once a class is defined, it is registered in a factory. An application can create objects dynamically of any registered class

Such component orientation is needed to support declarative programming [18] – a scientist specifies *what* the model should be, in a declarative language such as XML, rather than *how* the model should be implemented, in an imperative programming language such as C or Fortran. The objects and classes are then generated from the declarative language. StGermain supports this approach. The advantage is that at the top-level, a scientist who is not a programmer can specify a model using XML

A scientific application can be viewed at several different levels or layers, depending on the expertise and objective of the user at that layer

Model Layer - Scientist
- Models or solves real world problems, using applications frameworks developed by computational scientist

– –

Application Layer - Computational Scientist
- Develops application framework from constitutive laws (equations) using solver frameworks

– –

Solver Layer - Numerical Methods Developer
- Implements numerical methods and solver frameworks using generic software components

– –

Component Layer - Software Engineer
- Implements generic software components (e.g., Object, Class, Entry Points, Mesh, Particle Swarms) and interfaces

Hierarchical software design and minimizing coupling between software components, have long been recognized as foundations of good software design (Myers, 1978 [19]). However, most scientific applications and other frameworks such as PETSc and Trilinos, do not tend be hierarchical: application I/O and model setup, physics, solvers, and component library calls are intermixed. This makes scientific programs very difficult to understand and maintain (as a user or maintainer needs to understand all the layers). By contrast, in StGermain the layers are all separate and hierarchical. Such separation also facilitates reuse. On top of the one component layer, many solver layers can be built, and on each solver layer many application frameworks can be built (by solver, we mean any numerical or analytical method for solving a collection of PDEs, not just an implicit "Ax=B" solver). We use the term application framework, as a StGermain application is highly parameterized – the input to the application can control the solvers and constitutive laws used, as well as the initial and boundary conditions. The application layer input is an XML file (a Model).

The Component Layer of StGermain is *StgDomain* and it includes approximately 200 classes (implemented using C structs). The key components of the StgDomain are:

- Object and class support
- Local generic data structures: e.g., Vector, Set, Dictionary, and BTree
- Local numerical classes: e.g., Topology, Tensor, and ConvexHull
- Distributed numerical classes: e.g., Decomposition, Field, Mesh, and Swarm (particle collection)

The StgDomain layer contains no "solver" components, such as Matrices (and hence makes no use of solver libraries such as PETSc). Abstractions such as Vector and Set are there to hide or encapsulate the implementation of data structures such as a bitset or C vector. Both Mesh and Swarm use the Decomposition class and are abstract classes (almost interfaces, but they have properties associated with them). Implementations of these classes can be created at load time. The distributed numerical classes use MPI for communication.

Many different solvers can be built on the StgDomain layer, such as Finite Element, Finite Difference, and Explicit solvers such as SPH. In most cases, it is not necessary or worthwhile to develop new Matrix solvers from scratch, as there is a wealth of existing solvers available, from toolkits such as PETSc and Trilinos. So StGermain often follows the strategy of "wrapping" existing solvers, in particular StGermain solvers make frequent use of PETSc for implicit solvers and the preconditioner and multigrid abstractions of PETSc. Despite the frequent use of PETSc solvers (and solvers that PETSc itself wraps, such as HYPRE), it is not really correct to say that StGermain is "built on" PETSc, but rather that StGermain "uses" PETSc, where appropriate, though a fairly narrow interface that allows other solvers to be incorporated.

The following solvers have been developed on top of StgDomain and are in production use:
1. StgFEM – an implicit finite element solver framework, that uses PETSc
2. PICellerator – a Particle In Cell (PIC) Lagrangian integration scheme and constitutive rule framework, that uses StGFEM. PICellerator is a successor to the PIC algorithms and technology first developed in Ellipsis [20]
3. Snac – a explicit finite-element continuum solver, similar in formulation to FLAC (Finite Lagrangian Analysis of Continua)
4. SPModel – a surface-process (erosion and transport) solver framework, that extends the technology used in Cascade

The Solver layer includes software tools, built using StgDomain, such as gLucifer – a visualization framework that provides both interactive and background rendering but concentrates on the latter for rendering frames of computationally intense, remotely running applications (i.e. generates 4-D streaming movies while the calculation is running). It uses open source, freely available libraries such as OpenGL, X11, VTK, and libfame (a movie encoder).

All the StGermain solver frameworks are 3D and 2D parallel, and distributed (using MPI and parallel libraries such as PETSc).

Computational scientists can develop new applications from scratch by using solvers programmatically, but many scientists prefer to specify models just from a configuration file or script to an application framework. A StGermain Application Framework specializes a StGermain Solver to an application domain, adding precompiled components and plug-ins appropriate to that domain, and makes all this available to a scientist using a declarative XML model configuration. The StGermain application frameworks include:

1. Underworld – for geodynamics applications (stokes flow) built on PICellerator
2. Xanthus – for metal alloy deformation modeling, built on PICellerator
3. Gale – for geodynmics applications (long-term lithospheric deformation), a Generalized Arbitrary Lagrangian Eulerian model, built on PICellerator

Each application framework takes an XML model configuration file as input, which controls:

- Geometry and mesh setup – dimensionality, mesh size and shape
- Simulation parameters – e.g., timesteps and convergence/error tolerances
- Boundary and initial conditions
- Output – variables output to a journal file, visualization parameters (viewports)
- Contexts and plug-ins (e.g., for PDEs or material laws)

StGermain applications make heavy use of both contexts and plug-ins, which are object-oriented design patterns that facilitate code adaptation. A context is a set of functions that can be used to customize the behavior of a solver or model. For example, viscosity can be calculated using several different laws in Underworld, including:

- Arrehenius (viscosity is a function of depth and temperature)
- Frank Kamenetskii (viscosity is a function of temperature)
- Non-newtonian (viscosity is stress dependent)

Each of these laws is implemented by a different function, or *strategy*, called from the same places in the solver, with the same interface (function specification). In traditional scientific applications, alternative strategies would be supported either by editing and recompiling the code or by "case" statements that control which strategy is called. Experience is that maintaining applications with many case statements soon becomes unmanageable due to the interdependencies between various case statements and the tight coupling between the strategy functions and the code that they are embedded in. In StGermain, strategies are bundled together into contexts, and at link-time the strategies used by a model are specified by the XML Configuration file written by the scientist. A computational scientist or numerical analyst can *extend* an application or solver framework respectively by defining a new strategy (e.g., a new viscosity law), or *generalize* an application or solver framework by replacing a fixed piece of code by a set of strategies (e.g., for calculating higher-order elements in a Finite Element Solver).

Conclusion

Scientific Software Frameworks for *superstructure*, such as web interfaces to scientific applications, are fairly well supported – there is no lack of toolkits for building websites or for producing bindings to legacy applications.

By contrast, scientific software frameworks for *infrastructure*, such as PETSc, Trilinos, or StGermain, face many challenges, including:

- *Portability* – to different programming languages and parallel computing platforms.
  While C/C++ and Fortran are the dominant languages for scientific computing, there are others. While there is not as much diversity of parallel computing platforms as there was a decade ago, there is still considerable diversity across Linux boxes, and many boutique parallel systems and emerging systems (such as Cell processors). Some scientific developers have gone down the track of using a specification or Interface Definition Language (IDL) that can be compiled or linked to any other language (e.g., Babel/SIDL [8]), but such efforts are more in a research stage than production, and IDLs have not historically had much impact (e.g., UNCOL).
- *Performance* – scalability to peta-scale computing platforms.
  There is a major push to scale scientific applications up to peta-scale computing (tens of thousands of processors). At such scales, any minor overheads in communication or load imbalance will have catastrophic performance impacts. Inevitably, peta-scale computing requires careful platform-specific tuning of an entire application, including and libraries used by the application. For scientific software frameworks, this presents a real challenge, as tuning the framework adds complexity, and tuning for one application/platform may detune the framework for another.
- *Install-ability* – of the framework on a new platform.
  Portability measures the effort or complexity of extending the framework by the *framework developers*. By contrast, install-ability measures the effort or complexity of installing and using the framework by *scientists*. Most frameworks have a high degree of dependence on other libraries and platform tools, and so installing and upgrading a framework can be daunting for scientists, who generally have limited programming expertise.
- *Complexity* – of the framework and its applications.
  A single scientific application, no matter how difficult to maintain, will always be "simpler" than a framework. As a framework grows in capability and sophistication it becomes more and more complex – and harder to learn and apply.

All the above challenges are solvable, but at a cost in development, support, documentation, and training that is high relative to the size of the community.

Inevitably, tradeoffs need to be made between such challenges. Also framework support costs cannot be justified by an economic return by commercialization of scientific software frameworks – the academic research community is just too small and under funded to justify extensive commercialization of scientific frameworks. The NAG framework is a commercial scientific framework; albeit somewhat less sophisticated than, say PETSc or StGermain. However, NAG has had fairly limited impact due to the scientific communities focus on open-source or free software. Another approach that has been mooted is the use of "plug-ins" to commercial packages such as Matlab or Mathematica. Matlab and Mathematica are interactive environments in widespread research and teaching use, with a mathematics-oriented input language, that enable scientists to create scientific models faster than with traditional programming languages such as C, C++, and Fortran. They both support parallel plug-ins, but little infrastructure support for developing parallel solvers or models. In effect, both Matlab and Mathematica are convenient superstructure frameworks that any infrastructure framework, such as PETSc or StGermain could be coupled to.

While the use of scientific software frameworks is increasing, the funding is low relative to the demand, and there have been many "false starts" on developing frameworks by well-intentioned computer scientists. Inevitably, the use of frameworks and their sophistication will increase, but it will be a long, slow process.

References

1. W. Kozaczynski, and G. Booch, Component-Based Software Engineering, *IEEE Software* 15(5), 34-36 (1998).

2. B. Boehm, Managing Software Productivity and Reuse, *IEEE Computer*, 32(9), 111-113 (1999)

3. http://en.wikipedia.org/wiki/Grid_Computing.

4. B. Ludäscher, I. Altintas, C. Berkley, D. Higgins, E. Jaeger, M. Jones, E. Lee, J. Tao, and Y. Zhao, Scientific Workflow Management and the Kepler System, *Concurrency and Computation: Practice and Experience* 18(10), 1039-1065 (2005)

5. http://www.ncbi.nlm.nih.gov/blast/

6. http://www.cacr.caltech.edu/projects/pyre/

7. http://www.ks.uiuc.edu/Research/namd/

8. B. Allan, R. Armstrong, A. Wolfe, J. Ray, D. Bernholdt, and J. Kohl, The CCA core specification in a distributed memory SPMD framework, *Concurrency and Computation: Practice and Experience* 14(5), 323-345 (2002)

9. http://en.wikipedia.org/wiki/Software_prototyping

10. M. Fowler, *Refactoring: Improving the Design of Existing Code* (Addisson-Wesley, New Jersey, 2000)

11. http://www.netlib.org/lapack/

12. S. Balay et. al., PETSc Users Manual, Argonne National Laboratory, Technical Report No. ANL-95/11 - Revision 2.3.2 (2006)

13. M. Heroux et. al., An Overview of Trilinos, Sandia National Laboratory, Technical Report No. SAND2003-2927 (2003).

14. https://csd.vpac.org/twiki/bin/view/Stgermain/

15. S. Quenette, B. Appelbe, M. Gurnis, L. Hodkinson, L. Moresi, and P. Sunter, An Investigation into Design for Performance and Code Maintainability in High Performance Computing, ANZIAM J. 46(e) pp. C1001—C1016, 2005

16. E. Gamma, R. Helm, R. Johnson, and J. Vlissides, *Design Patterns: Elements of Reusable Software* (Addison-Wesley, Massachusetts, 1995)

17. http://en.wikipedia.org/wiki/Reflection_%28computer_science%29

18. http://en.wikipedia.org/wiki/Declarative_programming

19. G. Myers, *Composite/Structured Design* (Van Nostrand Reinhold, New York, 1978)

20. L. Moresi, F. Dufour, and H. Mulhaus, A Lagrangian Integration Point Finite Element Method for Large Deformation Modeling of Viscoelastic Geomaterials, *Journal of Computational Physics*, 184, 476-497 (2003)

Q&A – Bill Applebe

Questioner: Brian Ford

How are you addressing issues of code maintenance and support?

Bill Applebe

At the moment, we are not widely distributing our software, so the issues of code maintenance and support are not large. Instead of wide distribution, we are working with individual users and research groups to support their development of new applications using our software framework. From a technical viewpoint, for code maintenance and support we currently use a range of tools including nightly regression testing, unit tests for many components, online documentation, and collective code ownership. As and when our software becomes more widely used, we could look to several different models to cover the cost of code maintenance and support, ranging from forming a strategic partnership with a software vendor to offer commercial maintenance and support, to partnerships and funding from research support agencies to provide such funding.

Questioner: Brian Ford

C code is notoriously difficult to monitor. Is the use of C consistent with your intention of providing reliable user service?

Bill Applebe

Robust C libraries and frameworks require a great deal of internal checks on the parameters passed to the framework, and within the framework code to detect internal errors. We have such checks in place in many instances, and will continue to harden our code. Unfortunately, C and Fortran (which is equally unreliable), are the languages of choice for high-performance parallel code. More reliable languages, such as Java or C#, do not have the performance or availability for scientific computing.

Questioner: Pat Gaffney

One thing NAG has given the community is quality of the mathematics, numerical algorithms, and implementations. What are you doing to assure a level of quality for all of these aspects?

Bill Applebe

For implicit solvers, we use PETSc, which has its own group working on numerical accuracy. For explicit solvers, we are working with the numerical community and using a variety of benchmarks to ensure accuracy.

Questioner: Julian Padget

Please comment on the fragility of base code. Also, please discuss storage management and impact on performance. Also, please comment on practices such as pair programming and time boxing software engineering practices in your environment.

Bill *Applebe*

Our base code is fairly stable, but we are presently continuing to re-factor it as we gain experience and insight from applying the framework to new applications. For storage management, we use wrappers around C allocation and do not allocate small individual objects (such as Grid points or Particles). Instead we allocate large collections and use offsets into these collections for individual objects. We do not use Pair programming, but do use collective ownership. We have project deadlines and deliverables that are fixed (such as demos for site visits), but most of our deadlines are a little loose (not strict time boxing) as the software is supporting research projects, not commercial development.

Thursday PM Panel Discussion

Panel

- Bill Applebe
- Hitohide Usami
- Mutsumi Aoyagi
- Sebastien Goasguen

Questioner: Jim Pool

While developing the systems have you discovered things the numerical software developers should have done or could have done to improve your systems?

Bill Applebe

Not really, from a "numerical software developer" viewpoint. We have discovered, and continue to discover, limitations of our software architecture, that we improve via re-factoring.

Mutsumi Aoyagi

I've been using several kind of numerical software, e.g. NAG, IMSL. There are no remarkable problems to improve our systems. With the help of this software, our nano-science applications have high level of portability, where machine dependent/independent parts are almost decoupled.

Hitohide Usami

I don't know well the numerical software developers, but general domain researchers are conservative for new programming methodology and new information technology. I think if they can change the mind more aggressive for using new information science, then their research and our system more improve simultaneously.

Questioner: Brian Ford

What percentage of time in the project was spent in preparing a specification (or iteratively in intermediate specifications) as compare with building your Grid/Grid-enabled systems? Did you get the balance correct?

Bill Applebe

We find that with scientific applications, it is very hard to get an exact specification out of users. About the best you can do is to get the PDE's, and some idea of a method of solution and boundary conditions. But these ideas and the users' needs often change during implementation. So we do not try to get or prepare detailed specifications. This contrasts with efforts such as CCA, the Common Component Architecture, which has devoted considerable time to specifications (only to find that when implementation commences, that the detailed specifications may contain errors, omissions, or ambiguities).

Mutsumi Aoyagi

Sum total 30 percents of time in our application development have been spent in preparing a specification, where the time spent for the first draft, the intermediate, and final version of specification are compared with the time for building systems. I think that these are well balanced.

Hitohide Usami

In NAREGI case, first year developed proto type system, second year developed alpha version and last year developed beta version. First year, a lot of time spent for specification through prototyping. Second year, specification time considerably decreased than first year. Last year, not so decrease than second year, because the core software changed from UNICORE to GT4 based on OGSA/WSRF.

Comment: Bill Gropp

Yes, PETSc does have a steep learning curve; however, learning it in a class is much faster than learning it on ones own.

Bill Applebe

The same is true of our framework, StGermain. If anything, it has a steeper learning curve than PETSc, as it is more sophisticated and built on top of PETSc for implicit solvers. The best way to learn StGermain is through apprenticeship with an expert. This will change over time at StGermain becomes more mature and we develop better and more comprehensive documentation, such as user manuals and case studies.

Mutsumi Aoyagi

I agree.

PART 8

GRID-BASED IMAGING

B. Ford, Session Chair; M. Vouk, Discussant

V. Boccia: *Monitoring and Migration of a PETSc-based Parallel Application for Medical Imaging in a Grid computing PSE*

D. Keyes: *Grid-based Image Registration*

Monitoring and Migration of a PETSc-based Parallel Application for Medical Imaging in a Grid computing PSE*

A. Murli[1], V. Boccia[1], L. Carracciuolo[2], L. D'Amore[1], G. Laccetti[1], and M. Lapegna[1]

[1] University of Naples Federico II, Naples, Complesso Universitario M. S. Angelo, Via Cintia, Naples (`almerico.murli, vania.boccia, luisa.damore, giuliano.laccetti, marco.lapegna`)`@dma.unina.it`
[2] Institute of High Performance Computing and Networking of CNR, Naples, ITALY, `luisa.carracciuolo@na.icar.cnr.it`

1 Introduction

In last decades, imaging techniques became central to the diagnostic process providing the medical community with a fast growing amounts of information held in images. This implies developing computational tools which allow a reliable, robust and efficient processing of data and enhanced analysis. Moreover, clinicians may have the need to explore collaborative approaches and to exchange diagnostic information from available data. A medical experiment often involves not a single approach but a set of processings that should be sometimes executed concurrently.

Grid computing is becoming a cost effective emerging technology for high performance computing aggregating resources that cannot be available locally [16]. In particular, grid technologies are a promising tool to deal with current challenges in medical domains. On the other hand, employing a distributed infrastructure, where nodes may be geographically scattered all around the world and not dedicated to a specific application, is not without a price. The challenge of the grid computing paradigm derives mainly from the dynamic nature of resource requirements. In this context, in particular, reliability is a key issue and critical to the correct diagnosis.

Here we are concerned with improvements and enhancements of a medical imaging grid enabled infrastructure, named MedIGrid, oriented to the transparent use of resource-intensive applications for the management, processing and visualization of biomedical images [5, 8, 6]. MedIGrid has been designed so that users can schedule reconstruction jobs needed in tomographic nuclear imaging or the denoising of ultrasound images arising in 3D echocardiography.

In this paper we focus on the optimization of the software routines of MedI-Grid for dynamically adapting to changes in the computational nodes. More

* This work has been partially supported by the 2004-2006 PRIN 200415818 Italian National Project and the 2000-2006 PON SCoPE Italian National Project.

Please use the following format when citing this chapter:

Murli, A., Boccia, V., Carracciuolo, L., D'Amore, L., Laccetti, G., Lapegna, M., 2007, in IFIP International Federation for Information Processing, Volume 239, Grid-Based Problem Solving Environments, eds. Gaffney, P. W., Pool, J.C.T., (Boston: Springer), pp. 421-432.

precisely, we deal with the monitoring and the migration of a parallel algorithm based on the PETSc library [3] for denoising of 3D ultrasound images.

The paper is organized as follows: in Sec. 2 a brief description of MedIGrid infrastructure is presented, in Sec. 3 the images reconstruction application is introduced, in Sec. 4 the Performance Contract System and its implementation inside the PETSc parallel algorithm is discussed, finally in Sec. 5 conclusions and future work are presented.

2 MedIGrid infrastructure

The testbed we are presently using, is made of acquisition systems and storage resources located in Florence (Careggi Hospital) and Genoa (S. Martino Hospital), computational resources in Naples and Lecce, grid access points in Naples and Genoa. The client side allows to set up the input and to monitor the reconstruction process by means of a user-friendly graphical interface. More precisely, the computational servers are:

IA-64-1 : cluster of 60 nodes operated by the INFN (Istituto Nazionale Fisica Nucleare). Each node of the cluster is composed by two Itanium 2 processors running at 1.4 GHz and with 4 GB of main memory. The nodes are connected by a switch Quadrics QSNet II. The operating system is Red Hat Enterprise 3 Linux, equipped with the hp-mpi, PETSc 2.2.1 and Autopilot;

IA-64-2 : cluster located at the University of Lecce with the same features of IA-64-1;

UniPart1 : cluster of 8 nodes located at the University of Naples, Parthenope. Each node is an Intel Pentium 4 HT running at 3 GHz with a main memory of 512 MB. The operating system is Fedora Core 3 Linux, equipped with mpich 1.2.7, PETSc 2.2.1 and Autopilot;

UniPart2 : cluster of 25 nodes operated by the University of Naples, Parthenope. Each node is an Intel Pentium 4 HT running at 2.8 GHz with a main memory of 512 MB. The operating system is Fedora Core 3 Linux, equipped with mpich 1.2.6, PETSc 2.2.1 and Autopilot.

The clusters in Naples are connected by a 1 Gbits metropolitan area network, while Naples and Lecce are linked by a 155 Mbits wide area network; the Globus 4 middleware has been used to build the computational grid.

More recently, the system has been upgraded with several new, advanced features, including grid services, available through the User Portal; an application oriented brokering service, as part of the application manager, to enable dynamic discovery and allocation of computing resources, an xml based configuration model to set parameters related to the execution of the software [7].

The following section describes the parallel algorithm that we have developed, using PETSc, for denoising a sequence of 3D ultrasound images of the heart [9].

3 The PETSc-based parallel algorithm

A 3-D image is the function

$$u_0(x_1, x_2, x_3) : \ \Omega \longrightarrow \Re_0^+, \quad \Omega \subset \Re^3; \tag{1}$$

a 3-D sequence of images is the function:

$$u_0(x_1, x_2, x_3, \theta) : \ \Omega \times I \longrightarrow \Re_0^+, \quad \Omega \subset \Re^3, \tag{2}$$

where $I := [0, T]$ is the time interval during which the acquisition of the sequence has been performed. We consider the following equation describing the denoising of the 3-D sequence:

$$\frac{\partial u}{\partial t} = clt(u)\nabla \cdot (g(|\nabla u_\sigma|)\nabla u); \tag{3}$$

[11, 22]. Equations are accompanied with zero-Neumann boundary conditions in space, initial condition is given by (2); finally, we suppose periodic boundary conditions in time.

The function $clt(u)$ is a scalar function representing a measure of coherence in time for the moving structures [21]; $g = g(s)$ is a continuous function satisfying:

$$g(0) = 1, \ lim_{s\to\infty}g(s) = 0, \tag{4}$$

and $u_\sigma := G_\sigma * u$ is obtained convolving u with a 3-dimensional Gauss function of zero mean and variance equal to σ,

$$G_\sigma = \frac{1}{(2\sqrt{\pi\sigma})^3} e^{-|x|^2/4\sigma}. \tag{5}$$

In order to compute u_σ we have to solve the Heat equation:

$$\frac{\partial u}{\partial t} = \nabla \cdot (\nabla u) \tag{6}$$

in $[0, \sigma]$ with initial condition u_0. We now briefly describe a common numerical scheme for the discretization of (3). Details can be found in [9].

Let $N = n1 \times n2 \times n3$ be the dimension of the 3-D frame, $nscales$ the number of scale steps that are performed and, finally, τ be the discrete scale step; let us consider a space-time sequence consisting of n_4 3-D frames of dimension N, and let $\theta := T/(n_4 - 1)$ be the discrete time step; we denote by u_j^i the jth frame in the ith scale step,

$$u_j^i(x_1, x_2, x_3) := u(i\tau, x_1, x_2, x_3, j\theta), \tag{7}$$

where

$$i = 0, 1, \cdots, nscales - 1,$$
$$x_1 = 0, 1, \cdots, n_1 - 1,$$
$$x_2 = 0, 1, \cdots, n_2 - 1,$$
$$x_3 = 0, 1, \cdots, n_3 - 1,$$
$$j = 0, 1, \cdots, n_4 - 1.$$

Numerical discretization has been performed by using a semi-implicit scheme in scale, that is the nonlinearities are treated using the previous scale step, then linearized, while the linear terms are handled implicitly. Semi-implicit discretizations of $u_j^i(x_1, x_2, x_3)$ is shown in Fig. 1.

$u(x, 0) = u_0$
% loop over the scales
for $i = 1, nscales$ **do**
　% loop over the frames
　for $j = 0, m$ **do**
　　solve $\frac{u_j^i - u_j^{i-1}}{\tau} =$
　　$clt(u_j^{i-1})\nabla \cdot (g(|\nabla(u_j^{i-1})_\sigma|)\nabla u_j^i)$
　endfor
endfor

Fig. 1. semi-implicit scheme for the numerical solution of (3).

The semi-linear discrete equations that arise, i.e. :

$$\frac{u_j^i - u_j^{i-1}}{\tau} = clt(u_j^{i-1})\nabla \cdot (g(|\nabla(u_j^\sigma)|)\nabla u_j^i), \tag{8}$$

are discretized in space via finite volume method [18]; we solve (6) with a semi-implicit scheme in scale as well, that is:

$$\frac{u_j^\sigma - u_j^{i-1}}{\sigma} = \nabla \cdot (\nabla u_j^\sigma), \tag{9}$$

where finite volume discretization in space has been used as for the equation (8).

Two main computational kernels arise, that is, the solution at each scale step i and for each frame j, of the linear systems:

$$\mathbf{A}_{HE}\, \mathbf{u}_j^\sigma = \mathbf{b}_j^i, \tag{10}$$

$$\mathbf{A}_{ME}\, \mathbf{u}_j^i = \mathbf{b}_j^i, \tag{11}$$

with

$$\mathbf{A}_{HE}, \mathbf{A}_{ME} \in \Re^{N \times N}, \mathbf{b}_j^i \in \Re^N,$$

where (10) refers to the space discretization of (9) and (11) to that of (8).
In Fig. 2. a schematic description of the algorithms that we have implemented
is shown. The matrix $\mathbf{A}_{HE}$ depends upon σ and the size of the space discretization grid, so it is built only once, while $\mathbf{A}_{ME}$ depends upon quantities that change their value both with the scale step and the frame. As a consequence, its entries have to be recomputed $m \times nscales$ times. Right-hand side $\mathbf{b}_j^i$ contains the values of $\mathbf{u}_j^{i-1}$, i.e. the frame at the previous scale.

---

build $\mathbf{A}_{HE}$
% loop over the scales
for $i = 1, nscales$ **do**
    % loop over the frames
    for $j = 0, m$ **do**
        1. Init $\mathbf{A}_{HE}\mathbf{u}_j^\sigma = \mathbf{b}_j^i$
        2. solve $\mathbf{A}_{HE}\mathbf{u}_j^\sigma = \mathbf{b}_j^i$
        3. build $\mathbf{A}_{ME}$
        4. solve $\mathbf{A}_{ME}\mathbf{u}_j^i = \mathbf{b}_j^i$
    endfor
endfor

Fig. 2. multiscale analysis of a sequence of 3-D frames: outline of the algorithm.

Both $\mathbf{A}_{HE}$ and $\mathbf{A}_{ME}$ are large, sparse and structured; more precisely, their non-zero elements are located along seven diagonals: the principal diagonal and the three upper and lower diagonals respectively. Since we use the same discretization scheme both for (9) and (8), $\mathbf{A}_{HE}$ and $\mathbf{A}_{ME}$ have the same symmetric sparsity pattern; finally, $\mathbf{A}_{HE}$ is symmetric with respect to its entries as well, while $\mathbf{A}_{ME}$ is not for the presence of function $clt(u)$ in equation (3).
$\mathbf{A}_{HE}$ and $\mathbf{A}_{ME}$ are positive definite M-matrices symmetric in their structure. $\mathbf{A}_{HE}$ is besides symmetric with respect to its entries too. The properties we mentioned motivate the effectiveness of two popular Krylov projection methods, the Conjugate Gradient (CG) and the General Minimal Residual (GMRES) [13]. Both CG and GMRES are provided by the PETSc library [3]. Parallel approach is domain decomposition-based, i.e., we distribute the image domain among processes. In particular, we choose the **Slice Partitioning**, that is, the image is partitioned along one single dimension. Let $\Omega \subset \Re^3$ be the image domain, as defined in (1) and (2); Ω is a rectangular domain, with n_1, n_2, n_3 be its three dimensions. We distribute the domain along the third dimension only: if p is the number of processes, each process id, $0 \leq id \leq p - 1$, will have

n_{id} slices of the 3-D image (that is, $n_1 \times n_2 \times n_{id}$ voxels), where:

$$n_{id} = \begin{cases} n_3/p + 1 \ id < (n_3/p) \\ n_3/p \quad otherwise. \end{cases} \tag{12}$$

Let (i, j, k) be the coordinates of a voxel V_l in the $n_1 \times n_2 \times n_3$ image; voxels are numbered in a row-major fashion on successive planes, so, since each voxel generates one equation of the linear system and l corresponds exactly to the number of the equation generated by V_l, it follows that the slice partitioning gives rise to a *row-block fashion* distribution of the system matrix, that is, blocks of contiguous rows are distributed among contiguous processes. Slice partitioning has been chosen because the row-block fashion distribution is the standard PETSc matrices decomposition, and redistribution before the solution of the linear systems, is avoided.

4 Monitoring and Migration of the algorithm

The software architecture of MedIGrid is composed of three main layers: *core services*, based on the Globus toolkit, *collective services*, including the Resource Broker (RB) and the Performance Contract System (PCS), and the *Application Manager* (AM) that collects the software units that deeply interact with the algorithms during their execution. Some previous works refer to the Performance Contract System and to the Resource Broker [10, 17]. Here we focus on the deployment of the PCS for steering the performance of the parallel algorithm as described in section 3 in Figure 2. To this aim, following [2, 4] the reference workflow of the AM can be sketched as follows: the AM invokes the Performance Modeler with input parameters and information related to the computational resource. The Performance Modeler provides an execution model of the algorithm. The execution model, the input parameters and the machine parameters are given as "contract" to a Contract Developer. If the contract is approved the AM provides to spawn the job on the given resource. The Contract Monitor, monitors the times taken by the application while the AM waits for the job to complete. The job can either complete or, in case of contract violation, suspend its execution. If the job has completed the AM exits. If the job is suspended, the AM collects new information given by the brokering service and by the Contract Developer and it starts the phase again. In this latter phase a migration of the application onto another available resource can occur in such a way that the performance contract is satisfied. Hence, the entire process consists of a Periodical rescue of the execution state (**recovery**); a Run-time check of the execution flow (**monitoring**); a Process resumption on alternative resource (**migration**).

The contract verification consists of comparing the execution time of the algorithm with the one stated in the Performance Contract itself. We consider, as expected performance, the execution time of a computational kernel of the algorithm. In particular, we consider the execution time needed for denoising frame 1 at scale 1.

To monitor the algorithm, the *Autopilot* library [20] is used. The algorithm is instrumented by means of *sensors* and *actuators* to enable it to adapt its flow according to the performance level.

The migration step is aimed to suspend and migrate the execution of the algorithm on another resource in such a way that the performance contract is satisfied. We enable the parallel algorithm for saving current state and for restarting on another resource. More precisely, as shown in Figure 2, the algorithm consists essentially of two nested loops: the outermost over scale i and the innermost over the frame j. Denoising a single frame at each scale is performed by four steps: the first (*init*) and the third (*build*) steps have a computational complexity that does not depend on i and j, whereas the computational cost of the second (the parallel CG) and the fourth (the parallel GMRES) depend on the number of iterations needed to reach the requested tolerance, hence it depends on i and j. Note that both CG's steps and GMRES's steps have a computational cost that depends only on the size of the frame.

In order to select a resource on the basis of its computational power it is a common way to run a benchmark by the Performance Modeler [1, 14]. As benchmark of the k-th computational nodes of the grid, we consider the execution time, $T^{(0)}(1,1)$, needed for denoising frame 1 at scale 1:

$$T^{(k)}(1,1) = T_{init}^{(k)} + T_{CG}^{(k)}(1,1) + T_{build}^{(k)} + T_{GMRES}^{(k)}(1,1) \qquad (13)$$

where:

- $T_{init}^{(k)}$ is the execution time of step 1
- $T_{CG}^{(k)}(1,1)$ is the execution time of step 2 on frame 1 at scale 1
- $T_{build}^{(k)}$ is the execution time of step 3
- $T_{GMRES}^{(k)}(1,1)$ is the execution time of step 4 on frame 1 at scale 1

Starting from the benchmark on the first frame we can provide an estimate of the execution time of the algorithm on a generic frame. Let:

- $\Delta_{CG}(i,j)$ be the number of iterations of step 2 on the frame j at scale i
- $\Delta_{GMRES}(i,j)$ be the number of iterations of step 4 on the frame i at scale j

then

$$\frac{\Delta_{CG}(i,j)}{\Delta_{CG}(1,1)} T_{CG}^{(k)}(1,1) \quad \text{and} \quad \frac{\Delta_{GMRES}(i,j)}{\Delta_{GMRES}(1,1)} T_{GMRES}^{(k)}(1,1)$$

provide respectively an estimate of the execution time of *CG* and of *GMRES* on frame i at scale j.

Using the benchmark given by (13), taking into account that both $T_{init}^{(k)}$ and $T_{build}^{(k)}$ do not depend on i and j, the expected execution time needed for denoising frame j at scale i on the k-th node, and used by the Performance Contract, is the following:

$$PC^{(k)}(i,j) = T_{init}^{(k)} + \frac{\Delta_{CG}(i,j)}{\Delta_{CG}(1,1)} T_{CG}^{(k)}(1,1) + T_{build}^{(k)} + \frac{\Delta_{GMRES}(i,j)}{\Delta_{GMRES}(1,1)} T_{GMRES}^{(k)}(1,1)$$

(14)

A first set of experiments has been executed with the aim of validating (14). These experiments are executed on clusters IA-64-1 and UniPart1. Tables 1 and 2 report results concerning the denoising of a sequence of 14 frames of size $151 \times 151 \times 101$. We show the Performance Contract $PC^{(0)}(1,j)$ related to node 0 for all values of j (the frames) and for $i = 1$ (one scale), and the execution time $T^{(0)}(1,j)$ (in seconds) for denoising the frame j. Further we show, in the last column, the relative error obtained estimating the actual execution time and that estimated by the Performance Contract. Note that the error is of 10% at most. Results refer only to node 0 because we did not observe significant differences with the other nodes of the clusters IA-64-1 and UniPart1.

Table 1. Monitoring on the cluster IA-64-1

Frame index	$PC^{(0)}(1,j)$ (in secs.)	$T^{(0)}(1,j)$ (in secs.)	Relative error
1	20.9512	20.9512	0.00
2	14.4678	13.3022	0.08
3	14.7625	13.5491	0.08
4	15.6466	14.4584	0.08
5	16.5307	15.3111	0.07
6	16.2360	15.0253	0.07
7	15.6466	14.3392	0.08
8	14.7625	13.5789	0.08
9	14.4678	13.2639	0.08
10	15.6466	14.3577	0.08
11	15.3519	14.0668	0.08
12	15.6466	14.3602	0.08
13	15.6466	14.2467	0.09
14	19.7724	18.8719	0.05

Migration is a crucial task, because it depends on the relative overhead. Of course, such overhead may drastically change if migration occurs on nodes of the same resource or it is needed to migrate on another resource. In the Table 3 we report, in the first column the time (in seconds) needed to migrate on other nodes of the same cluster (we refer to the *local* migration), in the second column we report the time (in seconds) needed to migrate on different resources of the same geographic area, and we consider the two clusters located in Naples. Finally, in the third column, we report the time (in seconds) needed to migrate on the cluster located in Lecce (we refer to these last two cases as to a *remote* migration).

Table 2. Monitoring on the cluster UniPart1

Frame index	$PC^{(0)}(1,j)$ (in secs.)	$T^{(0)}(1,j)$ (in secs.)	Relative error
1	28.0687	28.0687	0.00
2	21.9950	20.3260	0.08
3	22.2711	20.6368	0.07
4	23.0993	20.9746	0.09
5	23.9275	21.5562	0.10
6	23.6515	21.2710	0.10
7	23.0993	20.8936	0.10
8	22.2711	20.1092	0.10
9	21.9950	19.9545	0.09
10	23.0993	20.8051	0.10
11	22.8232	20.7351	0.09
12	23.0993	20.7394	0.10
13	23.0993	20.8089	0.10
14	26.9644	25.4509	0.06

Table 3. Local vs. Remote Migration time (secs.)

Task	Local	Naples area	wide area
New resources selection	0	240	240
Data moving (1 frame=3MB)	0	6	0.2
Application starting	1	1	1

As expected, the overhead introduced by the resource brokering in case of remote migration, is much larger than that for the local migration. Therefore, let:

- T_{mo} be the migration overhead, as reported in Table 3;
- R_{old} be the execution time needed to terminate the algorithm on the initial resource;
- R_{new} be the execution time needed to terminate the algorithm on the resource where it migrates;

then, a migration on another resource occurs if

$$R_{new} + T_{mo} < R_{old}$$

where R_{old} is estimated by the Migration Manager as follows:

$$R_{old} = \widehat{T} \cdot nscales \cdot RF$$

where $\widehat{T}$ is the average time needed on for denoising the frames before the migration, and RF is the number of frames not yet denoised. To estimate R_{new} the Migration Manager evaluates the ratio between the benchmarks on the two systems, as defined in (13). More precisely, let B_{old} and B_{new} respectively denote the average benchmarks computed on all nodes of the initial resource and of the alternative resource, then, the Migration Manager computes:

$$B_{new/old} = \frac{B_{new}}{B_{old}}$$

and we assume that:

$$R_{new} \simeq B_{new/old} R_{old}$$

From Tables 1, 2 and 3, we observe that a remote migration should occur only if a strong violation of the Performance Contract occurs while the algorithm is processing the first two or three frames. Otherwise, once first frames have been processed, the overhead makes the remote migration not convenient. However, in our experiments, the overhead relative to the remote migration is mainly due to the execution of the benchmark needed for the selection of an alternative resource. This step is executed at runtime when the Monitor detects a contract violation. Of course, to reduce this overhead, the benchmark values should have been already available.

5 Future Works

We are currently working on the introduction of a fault-tolerance mechanism into the PETSc based application combined with some kind of checkpointing [12, 19]. We are using an *algorithm-based* approach relying on FT-MPI [15] which provides the software tools needed to identify and manage faults. We are using a disk based checkpointing method, indeed the algorithm already writes onto the disk the vectors u_j^i for each i and j. Moreover, to compute the vector u_j^i we only need u_{j-1}^{i-1}, u_j^{i-1} and u_{j+1}^{i-1}. Then, in order to recover from a fault we restart from those i and j corresponding to the last computed u_j^i, and the check of faults is performed at the end of each step of the innermost loop of the algorithm.

FT-MPI allows to re-spawn failed processes and to decide if to drop, or not, all ongoing messages. Moreover, when FT-MPI is used, the MPI context is redefined after each process is re-spawned. The main drawback seems to be the heavy dependence of all the PETSc global objects on the MPI context: i.e. the PETSC_COMM_WORLD macro, used by all PETSc objects, is a "copy" of the underlying MPI_COMM_WORLD MPI context. This suggests to address the fault-tolerance by the following steps:

- check the status of the processes: if a process has been re-spawned, then:
  - destroy the PETSc environment with all its objects,
  - re-inizialize the PETSc environment and create all the PETSc objects that are needed,
- restart the iterations from the last computed and saved u_j^i.

References

1. ARNOLD, D., S. AGRAWAL, S. BLACKFORD, S., J. DONGARRA, M. MILLER, K. SEYMOUR, K. AND SAGI, K. AND SHI, Z. AND VADHIYAR, S. , *Users Guide to Netsolve* - Univ. of Tennessee Tech. Rep. ICL-UT-02-05, 2002.

2. AYDT R., C. MENDES, D. REED, F. VRAALSEN, *Specifying and Monitoring GRADS contracts*, http://hipersoft.cs.rice.edu/grads/publications/grid2001.pdf, 2001.

3. BALAY S., K. BUSHELMAN, W. GROPP, D. KAUSHIK, M. KNEPLEY, L. CURF-MAN MCINNES, B. SMITH, H. ZHANG, *Petsc Users Manual*, ANL-95/11- Revision 2.1.3, Argonne National Laboratory, 2003.

4. BERMAN F., TO CHIEN, K. COOPER, J. DONGARRA, I. FOSTER, D. GANNON, L. JOHNSON, K. KENNEDY, C. KESSELMAN, J. MELLOR-CRUMMEY, D. REED, L. TORCZON, R. WOLSKY , *The Grads Project: Software support for High Performance Grid Applications* - Int. Journal on High Performance Applications. Vol 15 (2001), pp. 327-344.

5. BERTERO M., P. BONETTO, L. CARRACCIUOLO, L. D'AMORE, A. FORMICONI, M. R. GUARRACINO, G. LACCETTI, A. MURLI AND G. OLIVA , *A Grid-Based RPC System for Medical Imaging*, chapter of Parallel and Distributed Scientific and Engineering Computing: Practice and Experience, (Y. Pan and L T. Yang editors), Nova Science Publishers, 2003, pp. 177-190.

6. BOCCIA V., L. CARRACCIUOLO, P. CARUSO, L. D'AMORE, G. LACCETTI, A. MURLI, *Sull'integrazione di un'applicazione basata su PETSc in ambiente di grid computing*, ICAR-NA-CNR Tech. Rep. TR-04-25, 2004.

7. BOCCIA V., L. D'AMORE, M. GUARRACINO, G. LACCETTI, *A Grid enabled PSE for Medical Imaging: Experiences on MedIGrid*, chapter of Computer Based Medical Systems CBMS 2005 , (A. Tsymbal and P. Cunningham editors), IEEE Press, 2005, pp. 529-536.

8. BONETTO P., G. COMIS, A.R. FORMICONI, M. GUARRACINO, *A new approach to brain imaging, based on an open and distributed environment*, Proceedings of 1st Int. IEEE EMBS Conference on Neural Engineering, 2003.

9. CARRACCIUOLO L. , L. D'AMORE, A. MURLI, *Towards a parallel component for imaging in PETSc programming environment: A case study in 3-D echocardiography*, Parallel Computing 32, 2006, pp.67-83.

10. CARUSO P., G. LACCETTI, M. LAPEGNA, *A Performance Contract System in a Grid Enabling Component Based Programming Environment*, chapter of Advances in Grid Computing - EGC 2005 (P.M.A. Sloot et al., editors), Lecture Notes in Computer Science n. 3470, Springer, 2005, pp. 982-992.

11. CHAN T.F., J. SHEN AND L. VESE , *Variational PDE Models in Image Processing*, Notices of American Mathematical Society, Vol. 50 n. 1, (2003) 14-26.

12. D'AMORE L., F. GREGORETTI, A. MURLI, *Diskless algorithm-based checkpointing in a fault tolerant medical imaging application*, Conferenza SIMAI, 2004, and FIRB Grid.it Italian National Project, WP9 working note WP9-39, 2004.

13. DUFF I.S., H.A. VAN DER VORST, *Preconditioning and Parallel Preconditioning*, in: J. Dongarra et al., Numerical Linear Algebra for High-Performance Computers (SIAM, Philadelphia, PA, 1998).

14. ELMROTH, E., J. TORDSSON, *A Grid Resource Broker Supporting Advance Reservation and Benchmark-Based Resource Selection*, chapter of Applied Parallel Computing. State of the Art in Scientific Computing (J. Dongarra, K. Madsen,

J. Wasniewski editors), Lecture Notes in Computer Science n. 3732, Springer, 2006, pp. 1061-1070.

15. FAGG G.E., A. BUKOVSKY , S. VADHIYAR, J. DONGARRA, *Fault-tolerant MPI for the Harness metacomputing system*, Lecture Notes in Computer Science 2073:355–366.

16. FOSTER I. , C. KESSELMAN , *The Grid: Blueprint for a New Computing Infrastructure* - Morgan and Kaufman 1998

17. GUARRACINO M.R., G. LACCETTI AND A. MURLI, *Application Oriented Brokering in a Medical Imaging: Algorithms and Software Architecture*, chapter of Advances in Grid Computing - EGC 2005 (P.M.A. Sloot et al., editors), Lecture Notes in Computer Science n. 3470, Springer, 2005, pp. 972-982.

18. LEVESQUE R.J., *Finite Volume Methods for Hyperbolic Problems*, Cambridge University Press, New York, 2002.

19. MURLI A. , L. D'AMORE AND F. GREGORETTI , I/O Tolerance e Fault-Tolerance nell'algoritmo del gradiente coniugato, FIRB Grid.it Italian National Project, WP9 working note WP9-28, 2004.

20. REED D.A. , R. RIBLER, H. SIMITCI, J. S. VETTER, *Autopilot: Adaptive Control of Distributed Applications*, Proceedings of the Seventh IEEE International Symposium on High Performance Distributed Computing (HPDC), 1998.

21. SAPIRO G., *Geometric Partial Differential Equations and Image Processing*, Cambridge University Press, New York, 2001.

22. SARTI A. , K. MIKULA, F. SGALLARI, *Nonlinear Multiscale Analysis of Three-Dimensional Echocardiographic Sequences*, IEEE Transactions on Medical Imaging, Vol. 18, N. 6 (1999), pp. 453-466.

Q&A – Vania Boccia

Questioner: David Keyes

PETSc, Aztec, Scalapack and other scientific libraries that you propose to be modified for fault-tolerance are in use worldwide and there is a potentially enormous interest in such a development. I recommend that any such modifications, to be accepted, be undertaken in conjunction with the developers. Please comment.

Comment: Bill Gropp

The PETSc group is interested in understanding the best ways to integrate the changes or extensions you need to PETSc.

Vania Boccia

The introduction of fault tolerance mechanisms as those described in the talk, on our PSE's numerical kernels requires the modification of the algorithms source code. In the case of MEDITOMO library in fact, we worked on its two algorithms (Conjugate Gradient and Expectation Maximization) to enable them to do fault management, by modifying their source codes. This is the reason because we didn't introduce these mechanisms on the second PSE library (ECOCG). It is based on the PETSc library and we thought that every eventual modification in a such used library, should be done together with library developers.

Questioner: Brian Ford

Who pays for each analysis? Do Doctors keep their own copy of each image (as well as the copy in the system database), and are the patients given a copy? How is this provided?

Vania Boccia

At present the project has an experimental status - it is sponsored from the two basic research projects I cited in the talk and nobody pays for any analysis. In this phase the doctors have some authorized test images stored in their database at the hospitals. Regarding to the personal copy of the images I don't know if patients have it; this matter is managed directly by the doctors.

Comment: Pat Gaffney

Transporting images to patients in order satisfy the UK Data Protection act, comes under the category of MOVING data, which the speaker mentioned. Most Western countries have restrictions on MOVING medical patient data. What the patient does with his or her data is not the concern. It is the movement that must be secure.

Vania Boccia

The data movement in the environment is granted by the secure channel provided by the Globus GridFTP protocol. Furthermore data about the patient identity is not present in the data moved. This information remains at the hospital database. Anyway, at present this problem has not been faced, but we are investigating local laws and how other research groups think to solve security issues.

Questioner: Brian Ford

Why is the limit of 10 set on the iteration count for CG?

Vania Boccia

To "cure" the problem's ill conditioning, iterative methods that have the so called *semi convergence* property are used. For these methods, there exists an optimal number of iterations that gives the least value of the residual at the solution. Numerical experiments gave the proof that the optimal iteration number for the CG algorithm is ten while for EM it is six.

Questioner: Brian Ford

Presumably the physician can always seek a reprocess if he feels that fault correcting processes have not been sufficiently successful for his needs. Note the difficulty of comparing the two images in such systems.

Vania Boccia

The doctor can require every time he wants to process again the data that have been already processed. He can for example ask for reprocess these data with different algorithms and make a comparison. This is possible and not difficult in actual version of the PSE. Output images are stored and there is a little search engine to find set of images to be compared.

Grid-based Image Registration

William Gropp[1], Eldad Haber[2], Stefen Heldmann[2], David Keyes[3], Neill Miller[1], Jennifer Schopf[1], and Tianzhi Yang[3]

[1] Computation Institute, University of Chicago, Chicago, IL 60637
{gropp,neillm,schopf}@mcs.anl.gov
[2] Mathematics & Computer Science, Emory University, Atlanta, GA USA 30322
{haber,heldmann}@mathcs.emory.edu
[3] Applied Physics & Applied Mathematics, Columbia University
New York, NY USA 10027 {david.keyes,ty2109}@columbia.edu

We introduce and discuss preliminary experience with an application that has vast potential to exploit the Grid for social benefit and offers interesting resource assessment and allocation challenges, having real-time aspects: image registration. Image registration is generally formulated as an optimization problem that satisfies constraints, such as coordinate displacements that are affine or volume-preserving or that obey the laws of elasticity. Three-dimensional registration of high-resolution images is computationally complex and justifies parallel implementation. In turn, ensembles of registration tasks exploit concurrency in the simpler sense of job farming.

Registration is an elementary example of a much larger class of large-scale mesh-based computations that are in principle amenable to execution on the Grid, but are sensitive to workload-to-capability balance at synchronization points. While better resource assessment and allocation tools lift all such applications, reducing sensitivity to synchronization within an individual application is a complementary and equally important objective. We therefore examine the potential for weakening the synchronization sensitivity of general mesh-based bulk synchronous computations through less restrictive programming paradigms.

Keywords: Medical image registration, asynchronous numerical algorithms, Grid-based processing, MPI-based parallelization

Introduction

Imaging is exploding and, with it, so are the needs and opportunities for image registration. A recent catalog of books and journals on imaging from a single publisher [26] lists 5 pages of imaging journals, 13 pages of books on imaging techniques (CT, fMRI, ultrasound, etc.), 29 pages of books on diagnostic imaging of specialized anatomical domains, and 6 pages of books on radiotherapy and image-based intervention. Telling as well, with respect to clinical applications, is the formation of a new *Journal of Real-time Image Processing*.

Please use the following format when citing this chapter:

Gropp, W., Haber, E., Heldmann, S., Keyes, D., Miller, N., Schopf, J., Yang, T., 2007, in IFIP International Federation for Information Processing, Volume 239, Grid-Based Problem Solving Environments, eds. Gaffney, P. W., Pool, J.C.T., (Boston: Springer), pp. 435-448.

Imaging applications are ripe for the Grid. The Globus-based MEDICUS system has already "broken the medical image communication barrier" [17], in the sense that raw images can be shared with unprecedented speed and transparency. The communication breakthroughs of the Grid create opportunities in Grid-enabled processing, as well, by opening up vast possibilities for registration of images that were previously not simultaneously available.

Numerical computing on the Grid, of which image registration is an example, is, in turn, only one of several categories of Grid-based applications, and has not so far been a significant driver of the Grid overall. The Grid is yet to be exploited by most computational scientists, though it is potentially very useful for applications requiring real-time solution or exceptional amounts of memory. This potential will be realized after two independent trends, each with its own inertia, converge: better tools for understanding and harnessing the dynamic performance capabilities of the Grid, and better asynchronous algorithms implemented in consistency-relaxed parallel programming models.

A basic problem that motivates this work can be posed as follows: given a number of images that require registration, an MPI-based program to perform the registration, and a collection of Grid-enabled compute resources, compute the registrations by a specified time or estimate for the user what portion of the registrations can be completed before a given time. A currently available affine linear registration code has complexity roughly linear in the voxel volume. The target images are 1024^3. Our test images of 128^3 voxels require approximately 5 minutes of processing on a commodity cluster of 8 dual nodes. The targets should therefore take approximately two days to run on such a cluster. The kernel that dominates CPU cycles is multivariate interpolation. The task is easily partitioned into arbitrary working-set distributions by apportioning subdomains (subvolumes) of the image space to processors. The processing that needs to be done to back out the parameters that specify the three-dimensional affine map is negligible in comparison to the easily partitioned interpolation work. However, there is synchronization at regular intervals between interpolation steps. Although our demonstration is confined to affine registration, the techniques are extensible with the same computational issues to more general registrations of clinical importance.

In Section 1, we consider the motivation for real-time registration, some registration algorithms, an example of registration, and an initial feasibility demonstration of registration recently conducted on the Grid. Section 2 backs up from registration as a particular application and examines advances in asynchronous algorithms more generally, in terms both of algorithms and software infrastructure. We conclude in Section 3 with some speculations.

The philosophy of this presentation is that algorithms must be adapted or created to bridge to "hostile" architectures to support applications, taking both the applications and the architectures as givens. The interplay of applications and architectures with algorithms is a two-way street, generally. Knowledge of algorithms can influence the way applications are formmulated and the way architectures are constructed. More often than otherwise, however, it is the algorithms that must adapt to inflexible architecture and nonnegotiable formulations of the application.

1 Image registration

Real-time registration has numerous applications. In medicine, alone, registration arises in many contexts. Diagnosis and surgery planning make use of patient-to-reference anatomy registration. The evaluation of fitness for transplants makes use of patient-to-patient registration. In addition, patient-to-self registration of images taken at different times may be useful in monitoring progress. Besides clinical applications, real-time registration arises in automated surveillance, in which the goal is to recognize people whose images are stored in a database. In the area of robotics, manipulation of and navigation in the environment depends upon recognition of objects, which can include real-time registration aspects. Finally, we mention as a motivation for the importance of performing image registration tasks quickly the novel technique of super-resolution [9], which relies upon repeated registrations of an object that is moving with respect to the viewer. As its name implies, super-resolution is able to produce high-resolution images by comparing a series of low-resolution images of the same object. Intuitively, information at sub-pixel resolution that is "lost" in any one image can be recovered from staggered images in which the underlying information is captured in pixels that are displaced by a fraction of a pixel cell. This powerful technique allows a tradeoff between the quality of the instrument capturing the image in digital form and the capability of the computer system processing the resulting data.

1.1 Mathematical setting of registration

The typical mathematical setting of registration is optimization. One posits an objective function whose minimization is designed to minimize mismatch between a pair of images and seeks a transformation of one image into the other. This sounds simple in principle, but the simplicity can be deceptive. One must be careful, for instance, not to allow uncorrelated pixel-to-pixel matches from a list of pixels in one image to those of another, or else continguity of the transformation could be lost. Constraints may be imposed to preserve contiguity, to preserve volume, to map certain key points, etc. Since the number of constraints is generally vastly smaller than the number of parameters to be determined in a deformation map of one image into another, regularization is almost always required to remove ill-posedness.

Many optimization problems that arise in registration, as in other fields, require the solution of discretizations of elliptic partial differential equations; hence numerical ill-conditioning is often present. The data sets may be large-scale, with multiple billion-voxel images (thousand-fold resolution in each of

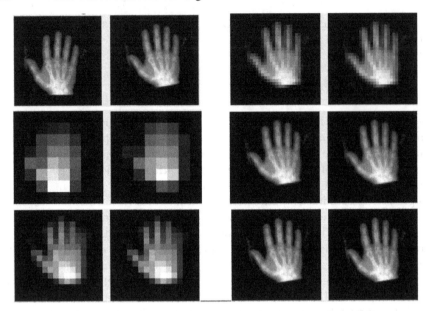

Fig. 1. Registration of hand images by a multilevel technique. The original pair of images is in the upper left. The next four pairs of images show successive stages of the registration process at successively finer resolutions, ending with the registered pair in the lower right.

three dimensions) coming on line, requiring parallel computing for each registration, in addition to distribution of registration of multiple image pairs over the Grid.

The field of image registration is mathematically rich, with both new theory and new heuristics playing roles in moving it forward.

Finally, in production mode, registration presents challenges in terms of managing the computational workflow, with issues of transparent archiving, remote access, and security requirements arising in conjunction with large data sets.

Mathematical descriptions of registration The problem of image registration can be posed intuitively as follows [22]: "given a template image and a reference image, find a transformation of the template image such that it becomes similar to the reference image." Images may be considered as fields over domains, in which a template image $T(\mathbf{x}) = T(x_1, x_2, x_3)$ and a reference image $R(\mathbf{x}) = R(x_1, x_2, x_3)$ are given and a transformation $\mathbf{u}(\mathbf{x}) = [u_1(\mathbf{x}), u_2(\mathbf{x}), u_3(\mathbf{x})]$ is sought such that $T(\mathbf{x} + \mathbf{u}(\mathbf{x})) \approx R(\mathbf{x})$. An example of a pair of images to be registered is given in Figure 2.

The generality of the flow $\mathbf{u}(\mathbf{x})$ can be controlled by its parameterization. A general affine map in three dimensions consists of just twelve parameters, independent of the number of pixels in the image:

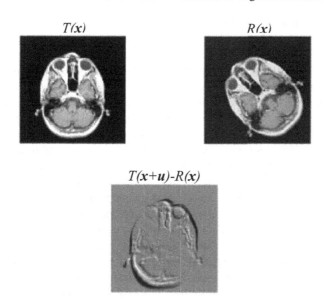

Fig. 2. $T(\mathbf{x})$ for a two-dimensional slice through the midplane of a head. $R(\mathbf{x})$, a reference image for the head. $T(\mathbf{x}+\mathbf{u}) - R(\mathbf{x})$ after construction of a coordinate flow $\mathbf{u}$.

$$
\begin{pmatrix} u_1 \\ u_2 \\ u_3 \end{pmatrix} = \begin{pmatrix} c_1 \\ c_2 \\ c_3 \end{pmatrix} + \begin{pmatrix} a_{11} & a_{12} & a_{13} \\ a_{21} & a_{22} & a_{23} \\ a_{31} & a_{32} & a_{33} \end{pmatrix} \begin{pmatrix} x_1 \\ x_2 \\ x_3 \end{pmatrix}. \tag{1}
$$

Determination of the parameters is through minimization in some norm of an objective function. A typical example is

$$
\min \frac{1}{2} ||T(\mathbf{x}+\mathbf{u}) - R(\mathbf{x})||^2 + \alpha S(\mathbf{u}), \tag{2}
$$

where S is a regularization term and α is a weighting parameter that strikes a compromise between similarity and regularity. The regularization may, for instance, penalize lack of smoothness in $\mathbf{u}$. Registration based on the minimization of distance between two images, alone, is in general ill-posed. The parameterization of the registration is also a form of regularization through the choice of basis. A subspace regularization may be employed to restrict the generality of $\mathbf{u}$, for instance

$$
\min \frac{1}{2} ||T(\mathbf{x} + Q\mathbf{z}) - R(\mathbf{x})||^2. \tag{3}
$$

Besides minimizing the distance between images, one can minimize the entropy-related concept of "mutual information" [29], or normal gradient fields [15], which is particularly useful for registration of images from two different modalities, such as CT and MRI, or a number of other objectives. Though the problem statements are simple, the solutions may not be unique.

Multilevel algorithms [14] seek to overcome the problem of multiple minima by successively registering the same pair of images at resolutions ranging from coarse to fine. While the mathematics is formal, the motivation is very intuitive and has been exploited in many areas of optimization that are plagued by multiple minima. Projections of the problem into coarse spaces obscures the local minima, which can only be differentiated at finer resolutions. As the fine structure is revealed, the registration settles into a particular local minimum, which is hopefully the global one. Figure 1 illustrates. If one imagines a properly rotationally oriented template hand being moved continuously over the reference hand, one can envision nine or more local minima, as first one, then two, then successively more fingers overlap, with the best minimum obtained in the middle when all five appendages overlap.

There are many types of registration objectives, including those based on co-locating landmarks, aligning principal axes, correlating image intensities, minimizing elastic deformation, and conserving volume. While the variety is large, and the motivations that drive selecting among the choices beyond the scope of this overview, the optimization setting provides a mathematical framework that leads to the computational data structures and the types of operations that must be executed over them.

1.2 Computational characteristics of registration

Typical contemporary registration problems may be two- or three-dimensional, and may vary widely in discrete size from tens of KB to many GB per individual pixelated or voxelated image. Inheriting contemporary tools from computational optimization, the algorithmic building blocks of importance are Newton-like nonlinear solvers [19], Krylov linear solvers [13], multilevel [3] and other linear preconditioners [25] to solve the discretized problem, and multivariate spline interpolation [2] to allow the images to be compared at chosen sets of points. Large, sparse matrix methods predominate. Domain decomposition leads to advantageous surface-to-volume communication-to-computation ratios that permit weak scaling in an implementation sense [20]; see the next section for details. Multilevel preconditioners are capable of preserving weak scaling in a convergence sense [27].

1.3 Grid-based illustration of registration

To illustrate the potential for real-time registration on the Grid in a very preliminary way that is representative of, but not pushing, the state of the art, we consider a data set of 20 three-dimensional images of pig's heart, each $128 \times 128 \times 64$ 8-bit voxels (resolved on a gray scale from 0 to 255) or 8 MB per image. The images comprise a time series. One is taken as the reference, and 19 pairwise registrations are performed to study the deformations of the heart. An SPMD code implemented in C and MPI to perform affine registration was provided by co-author Heldmann. Its input is a pair of images, the reference and one template, and the output of each execution is very compact – a set of 12 scalars describing the map. Such a compact output enables instant verification of the correct execution of the code in distributed environments.

The facility employed for the test is the Skynet cluster at ISI, a collection (at the time of writing) of 96 dual processor Intel P3 nodes, with a range of clock ratings from 800 to 1200 MHz. The Web Services Grid Resources Allocation and Management (WS-GRAM) [30] component of the Globus [12] toolkit is used to distribute the registration tasks. The GRAM service provides a single interface for requesting and using remote system resources for the execution of "jobs." The most common use of GRAM is remote job submission and control. It is designed to provide a uniform, flexible interface to job scheduling systems. GRAM does not provide scheduling or resource brokering capabilities. A wide variety of metaschedulers and resource brokers that leverage GRAM mechanisms have been developed by other projects. WS-GRAM was released in July 2006 and it is expected that the various metaschedulers and resource brokers of Globus will be integrated into it.

WS-GRAM provides rich job description and resource provisioning capabilities. Among other objectives, such as optimizing throughput by matching requirements to resources, WS-GRAM can allocate jobs so as to minimize expected overall latency, given an existing pool of resources. This is the sense in which we apply it here. Our assumption is that in medical applications, information derived from registration has time-value. If it does not return in time to enter into a physician's decision-making process, it may have little value at all. This suggests other problem formulations, which we will examine in the future, such as ordering the jobs so that the partial results of greatest value are returned first. This project (in progress) provides a preliminary demonstration of the registration application together with the WS-GRAM harness.

In the test reported here, each registration job was launched with 16-way parallelism at the MPI level, on 8 dual-procesor nodes. Up to 11 such parallel jobs could be executed at once, as mediated by the underlying PBS scheduler [23]. In the suboptimal, preliminary test reported on here, all jobs in a given batch must report complete before a subsequent batch is launched.

The result was the reduction in latency of a "sequential" processing of 19 MPI-parallel jobs that required 51.77 minutes to 6.95 minutes in the Grid environment, a speedup of 7.5.

Our near-term plans call for expansion of this registration test in many dimensions. The entire TeraGrid will be used as a resource pool. Our next data sets will be made up of images of size $512 \times 512 \times 512$, or 1GB each. Each pairwise registration job (as currently) will be run with tightly coupled SPMD parallelism. Jobs will be launched individually from a queue based on resource monitoring. A strategy will be developed for gaining the medically most relevant information first. Finally, in view of the size of the data sets, a strategy will be developed for overcoming transmission latency that is synergistic with the multilevel character of the registration algorithm, as discussed above. Specifically, coarse-grid representations of the problem can be sent before the full fine-grid representations, so that processing can begin while the fine-grid representations are still en route.

Our longer term objective includes development of parallel algorithms for registration that are sufficiently asynchronous that the Grid environment can be employed even within a single registration. This is not yet necessary for medical images of contemporary sizes, but it is a technology driver. Such algorithms would be useful for many problems besides real-time registration, which is the subject of the second part of this paper.

2 The challenge of asynchronous algorithms for Grid hosting of PDE-based systems

The image registration challenge in the first part of this paper is addressed under the relevant, but restricted paradigm of SPMD bulk synchronous processing. There are numerous applications in addition to image registration in which it is desirable to exploit the Grid to occasionally grab exceptional amounts of memory for highly resolved simulations, or in which it is desired to take over exceptional levels of processing power. As an instance of the first, an exceptional simulation might use a close to first-principles model to calibrate a multiscale model, which would then be used for the majority of production at a center. As instances of the second, flood, firespread, or pathogen transport prediction models might need to be run ahead of real time in emergencies. Or real-time control of a massive experimental device, such as ITER [18], might be allowed to take over Grid-availed resources for the exceptional experimental "shot." In these contexts, we must consider individual large jobs, not a large ensemble of small jobs. Historically, the Grid has supported very few claims for success in this realm. PDE-based simulations are naturally implemented in bulk synchronous mode, in which the work load for each processing element is carefully matched to its capabilities, so that idleness is minimized at synchronization points.

Many issues must be addressed to make PDE-simulations a reality for the dynamic environment of the Grid. One of them is fault tolerance. However, in the limited scope of this contribution, we assume that processors and networks are reliable and seek algorithmic tolerance of dynamic performance, or actual synergisms between algorithms and the dynamic performance Grid environment.

2.1 Concurrency through domain decomposition

PDE-based codes are nearly universally parallelized with domain decomposition – applying a serial algorithm that (approximately or exactly) solves a PDE on a given domain so that it solves for a subdomain's worth of data and nesting this inside of an iterative process that adjusts the values on the interfaces or overlaps between the subdomains to consistency. Such a decomposition preserves the volume(work)-to-surface(communication) ratio in the weak scaling limit as work per processor remains fixed and both the work and the number of processors are scaled in proportion. For domain decomposition methods to be weak-scalable, it is necessary that the individual problems on subdomains be well load balanced and that the number of outer iterations be bounded, independently of problem resolution and processor granularity (one implies the other) in the limit of weak scaling. Theory constructively showing how to obtain nearly resolution- and granularity-independent convergence rates is well developed for many problems [27] and freely available software exists that delivers this performance in practice [16, 24, 28]. The price of convergence-rate optimality is often the solution of auxiliary problems in reduced dimensional spaces. These auxiliary problems are not as scalable as the original union of independent fine-scale problems, and their implementation requires extreme care. Nevertheless, a families of multilevel iterative methods whose parameters can be tuned to application and architecture exist, which are mature in their analysis and software aspects. All such methods, however, presume predictable load per process since synchronization points are relatively frequent.

For nonlinear problems, a popular family of methods is Newton-Krylov-Schwarz (NKS) [5]. This is a triply-nested loop domain-decomposed algorithm, with an outer Newton loop, which evaluates a nonlinear residual vector at a given solution iterate and solves a linear system with the nonlinear residual vector as the right-hand side and the Jacobian of the residual as the system matrix. A multiple of the resulting solution is added to the current iterate. Krylov iteration is employed to solve the linear system with the Jacobian. Each Krylov loop begins with an iterate to which it applies a Jacobian-vector product and then computes some inner products, which determine coefficients with which to update the linear iterate. Both the outer Newton and inner Krylov loops are synchronous and essentially update a vector defined over the domain with AXPY operations. Inside of the Krylov loop, subspace iterations of Schwarz type are employed to precondition the linear system. The Schwarz iterations are generally a mixture of multiplicative and additive projections into subspaces, with the bulk of the work being done concurrently on each processor within subdomains. To summarize the NKS technique, within each level of the triply nested loop there is a decomposition into concurrent tasks by domain. Typically, one subdomain's worth of work is assigned to each process. Processes must communicate thin regions near their boundaries with neighbors, and they must cooperate globally in performing inner products (`AllReduce` commutatives) and in solving reduced-dimensional problems. Typically, one process is mapped to each processor, and processors synchronize at the `AllReduce` points.

2.2 Algorithmic adaptation

No computer system is well-balanced for all computational tasks since different tasks (such as concurrent neighbor communication, global reduction, concurrent local residual evaluation, concurrent local recurrences, etc.) stress different parts of the processor-memory-network system. By being aware of which algorithmic phases are limited by which aspect of hardware or system software, one can adapt algorithms to take advantage of the strengths or mitigate the weaknesses of given hardware. Detailed phase-by-phase performance analysis of an unstructured PDE-based code for aerodynamics led to the inspiration of the Gordon Bell "Special Prize," a share of which was first awarded to a subset of the co-authors in 1999 [1]. While many performance optimizations were studied in that and other papers for the massively parallel solution of PDE-based problems, one parasitic loss of performance that was noted in the strong scaling limit, but not addressed, was idleness at synchronization bottlenecks. This idleness was due to the difficulty of load balancing increasingly smaller and also increasingly less homogeneous partitions. For instance, as subdomains get smaller, the distribution of ratios of boundary and interface nodes to interior nodes gets broader. In the context of the Grid, these same synchronization points will lead to idleness for other reasons, even in weak scaling.

Historically, there have been a number of noteworthy adaptations to high latency and low bandwidth in parallel systems. Reduction of communication or replacement of communication with extra work will generally be useful adaptations in the Grid environment.

Garbey and Tromeur-Dervout [11] introduced the $C(p, j, q)$ schemes in an attempt to hide interprocessor latency by extrapolating data messages from neighboring processes in a time integration process, rather than waiting for the messages to appear before computing locally with their data as inputs. Rollbacks were used if the data upon arrival proved to be too inconsistent with the extrapolated values. Intuitively, this radical procedure has a chance of being successful, since for the problems considered, the extrapolations have to be correct in the low-spectrum eigenmodes only. Error in the the high-spectrum eigenmodes decays rapidly. For a given accuracy-work tradeoff, the technique has a payoff region.

Cai and Sarkis [6] introduced an algorithm called restricted additive Schwarz (RAS), which was discovered accidentally by turning off certain communications while debugging. Observing that not only efficiency per iteration but also convergence rate improved, the researchers were able to prove why, for many problems, the updates provided by the turned-off communication were unnecessary and even detrimental. RAS is now the default form of Schwarz preconditioning in PETSc [24].

Additive versions of algorithms are often available where multiplicative versions are the default. The additive versions may converge more slowly, but can sometimes be virtually as good as their mathematically more pedigreed cousins. The AFACx version of the asynchronous fast adaptive composite grid method is shown in [21] to be nearly as good as AFAC in practice, for instance. Such algorithms have received a bad rap historically due to theory which can be pessimistic in the worst case [8].

Cai and Keyes [7] introduced a nonlinear form of Schwarz preconditioning, called Additive Schwarz Preconditioned Inexact Newton (ASPIN), which was motivated by nonlinear convergence theory, but turns out to relax the frequency of global synchronization in Newton-Krylov methods rather dramatically, while simultaneously unbalancing domain-decomposed work. Essentially, the method introduces process-scale Newton iterations inside of the outer Newton iteration. Most of the work of the nonlinear convergence shifts from the global outer iteration to the local inner iterations, with the result that the outer iteration converges in very few Newton steps, and therefore few global synchronizations. There is often a substantial reduction of work overall, but more importantly, the work that remains occurs in local subsets of communicating processors. However, unlike the traditional Newton-Krylov-Schwarz method, whose work-per-processor can be well load-balanced up to the limit of too small the average size of the subdomains on each processor, ASPIN has an unpredictable and potentially poorly balanced distribution of subdomain work. This is because the different nonlinear systems that are iterated to convergence on each subdomain may take different numbers of internal iterations. Fortunately, these internal iterations are not synchronized with those of other subdomains. The processors governing different subdomains synchronize only at outer loops. On a tightly coupled parallel machine, ASPIN is difficult to recommend, because of this feature of unbalanced inner loop work. However, the structure of the computation lends itself well to the Grid. In the spirit of Eisenhower's maxim that "one way to solve a big problem is to make it bigger," ASPIN folds its uncertain load imbalance into the uncertain performance guarantee of the processors in a Grid-based computation, and harvests cycles when available. The tools created as part of the WS-GRAM infrastructure to monitor and predict availability and so allocate work can be combined with tools that predict the work in ASPIN processes based on recent history so that a collection of ASPIN processes can in principle share resources synergistically with other Grid-enabled jobs.

Transcending particular algorithmic inventions, we also propose an asynchronous programming style that loans itself to many bulk synchronous algorithms that must confront inefficiency through idleness at synchronization points, whether due to internal work imbalance or external dynamic availability. The synchronization in many scientific simulation codes, including PDE-based codes, is artifactual. At a synchronization point there is often lots of work ready to perform whose data needs are completely local; however conventional programming styles do not allow an independent user thread from the same overall process to begin executing while the synchronizing thread is blocked.

The critical path in a Newton-Krylov code, abstracted to a sufficiently high level is: ..., `linear_solve`, `bound_step`, `update`, `linear_solve`, `bound_step`, `update`, ... We often insert into the critical path tasks that could be performed less synchronously, on which the tasks above do not critically depend, such as refreshing the Jacobian with which the linear solver is performed, or refreshing the preconditioner for that Jacobian. It is well studied, theoretically and in practice, that Newton and Krylov methods are robust with respect to less frequent updates to these linear operators than once per step, under many circumstances. Convergence degrades if refreshing is long postponed, but for the sake of synchronization, either of these updates could be invested in to varying degrees. We also frequently insert global convergence testing and parameter adaptation on the critical path above more frequently than necessary. They can be partially completed on free cycles and thrown onto the critical path less frequently than is generally done today. Other tasks such as I/O, data compression or archiving, data visualization, or data mining, which must be or can be performed directly on the parallel cluster, represent useful work that is, to a significant degree, not tightly synchronized with respect to the solution loop above.

To take full advantage of such asynchronous algorithms, we need to develop greater expressiveness in scientific programming, by creating threads with relaxed data requirements and dynamically adjusting the relative priority of threads. This will require "associative communication" models such as the one recently addressed in [4].

3 Convergence of Grid computing and scientific computing

As illustrated in the context of medical image registration, there are numerous scientific applications today that can exploit the Grid in all of its heterogeneity without ill effect and to advantage, even in a hybrid model of nearly independent batched jobs each of which is a tightly coupled application. Tools such as WS-GRAM make it increasingly practical to schedule the independent jobs in such a way as to meet real time applications requirements, or at least to know when it is physically impractical to meet them, so that cycles are not wasted and alternatives not deferred. Many of the agendae of large-scale simulation share workflow characteristics with the image registration task considered herein. Computational science is not about individual large-scale analyses, done fast and "thrown over the wall." Both results and their sensitivities are desired; often multiple operation points to be simulated are known *a priori*, rather than sequentially. Sensitivities may be fed back into optimization process. Full PDE analyses may also be inner iterations in a multidisciplinary computation. In such contexts, "petaflop/s" may mean 1,000 analyses running somewhat asynchronously with respect to each other, each at 1 Tflop/s – clearly a less daunting challenge and one that has better synchronization properties for exploiting "The Grid" – than one analysis running at 1 Pflop/s.

However, even perfect knowledge of resource capabilities at every moment and perfect load balancers will not redeem the Grid for all SPMD implementations of PDE simulations. The cost of rebalancing is frequently too large to do on the short intervals required in the dynamic environment of the Grid, and the Amdahl penalty for failing to rebalance is fatal. A combination of better Grid monitoring and allocation tools and less synchronous algorithms is required for the greatest ultimate success.

Less synchronous algorithms for traditionally tightly coupled PDE-based simulations are highly desirable for reasons independent of the Grid. For the petascale machines of which we expect to take delivery in 2008 and beyond, consisting of 10^5 and more processors, it will be highly desirable to have such methods.

Natural forces with both the Grid community and the PDE simulation community are converging independently towards a rendezvous that it is already practical at some scale. We are cautiously optimistic about a much more significant rendezvous ahead.

Acknowledgments

This material is based upon work supported by the National Science Foundation under Grant Nos. CCF-0427464 to Columbia University, CCF-0427904 to Emory University, and CCF-0427912 to the University of Chicago.

References

1. Anderson, W. K, Gropp, W. D., Kaushik, D. K., Keyes, D. E. and Smith, B. F. (1999). *Achieving High Sustained Performance in an Unstructured Mesh CFD Application*, in "Proceedings of SC'99," IEEE Computer Society, Los Alamitos.
2. Bojanov, B., Hakopian, H. and Sahakian, B. (1993). *Spline Functions and Multivariate Interpolation*, Springer, New York.
3. Briggs, W. L., Henson, V. E. and McCormick, S. F. (2000). *A Multigrid Tutorial*, SIAM, Philadelphia.
4. Browne, J. C., Yalamanchi, M., Kane, K. and Sankaralingam, K. (2004). *General Parallel Computations on Desktop Grid and P2P Systems*, in "Proceedings of LCR 2004: Seventh Workshop on Languages, Compilers & Runtime Support for Scalable Systems," University of Houston, Houston.
5. Cai, X.-C., Gropp, W. D., Keyes, D. E. and Tidriri, M. D. (1993). *Newton-Krylov-Schwarz Methods in CFD*, in "Numerical Methods for the Navier-Stokes Equations" (F.-K. Hebeker et al., eds.), Vieweg, Braunschweig.
6. Cai, X.-C. and Sarkis, M. (1999). *A Restricted Additive Schwarz Preconditioner for General Sparse Linear Systems*, SIAM J. Sci. Comput. **21**:792–797.
7. Cai, X. C. and Keyes, D. E. (2002). *Nonlinearly Preconditioned Inexact Newton Algorithms*, SIAM J. Sci. Comp. **24**:183-200.
8. Chazan, D. and Miranker, W. (1969). *Chaotic Relaxation*, Linear Alg. Applics. **2**:199–222.
9. Chung, J., Haber, E. and Nagy, J. (2006). *Numerical Methods for Coupled Super-Resolution* Inverse Problems **22**:1261-1272.

10. Elad, M. and Feuer, A. (1997). *Numerical Methods for Coupled Super-Resolution Inverse Problems* **22**:1261-1272.
11. Garbey, M. and Tromeur-Dervout, D. (2000). *A Parallel Adaptive Coupling Algorithm for Systems of Differential Equations*, J. Comput. Phys. **161**: 401-427.
12. Globus (2006). http://www.globus.org/toolkit/.
13. Greenbaum, A. (1997). *Iterative Methods for Solving Linear Systems*, SIAM, Philadelphia.
14. Haber, E. and Modersitzki, J. (2006). *A Multilevel Method for Image Registration*, SIAM J. Sci. Comput. **27**:1594–1607.
15. Haber, E. and Modersitzki, J. (2006). *Intensity gradient based registration and fusion of multi-modal images*, Medical Image Computing and Computer-Assisted Intervention - MICCAI (2), pp. 726-733.
16. hypre (2006). http://www.llnl.gov/CASC/linear_solvers/.
17. ISI, Information Sciences Institute, University of Southern California (2006). *Breaking the Medical Image Communication Barrier*, http://www.isi.edu/news/news.php?story=152.
18. ITER (2006). http://www.iter.org/.
19. Kelley, C. T. (1995). *Iterative Methods for Linear and Nonlinear Equations*, SIAM, Philadelphia.
20. Keyes, D. E. (1998). *How Scalable is Domain Decomposition in Practice?*, in "Proceedings of the 11th Intl. Conf. on Domain Decomposition Methods" (C. H. Lai, et al., eds.), pp. 286–297, DDM.ORG, New York.
21. Lee, B., McCormick, S. F., Philip, B. and Quinlan, D. J. (2003). *Asynchronous Fast Adaptive Composite-Grid Methods: Numerical Results*, SIAM J. Sci. Comput. **25**:682–700.
22. Modersitzki, J. (2004). *Numerical Methods for Image Registration*, Oxford University Press, Oxford.
23. OpenPBS (2003). http://www.openpbs.org/.
24. PETSc (2006). http://www-unix.mcs.anl.gov/petsc/.
25. Saad, Y. (1996). *Iterative Methods for Sparse Linear Systems*, PWS Publishing, Boston.
26. Springer Verlag (2006). *Journals and New Books in Imaging*, 56 pp.
27. Toselli, A. and Widlund O. (2005). *Domain Decomposition Methods – Algorithms and Theory*, Springer, New York.
28. Trilinos (2006). http://software.sandia.gov/trilinos/.
29. Viola, P. (1995). *Alignment by Maximization of Mutual Information*, Ph.D. thesis, Massachusetts Institute of Technology.
30. WS-GRAM (2006). http://www.globus.org/toolkit/docs/3.2/gram/key/.

PART 9

CONFERENCE SUMMARY; STRATEGY FOR FUTURE ACTIVITIES

W. Gropp, *Observations on WoCo9*

B. Smith, *Future Directions for Numerical Software Research – Comments during Discussions at WoCo9*

Discussion: *What is the relevance of Grid Services to Numerical Software?* B. Smith, Session Chair/Discussant

J. Pool, *The Conference*

Observations on WoCo9

William D. Gropp

Mathematics and Computer Science Division
Argonne National Laboratory

The Ninth Working Conference on Grid-Based Problem Solving Environments brought together researchers and practitioners interested in the use of numerical software in a distributed setting. This note summarizes some of the successes and challenges in working with numerical software in a Grid environment. This is not a comprehensive list of the contributions in the meeting; rather, it provides one person's impressions of the common themes and issues. In addition, some items were noticeable by their absence, and a number of these are discussed here. Opportunities for future work also are described.

1.1 Successes

First and foremost, this meeting illustrated the many successes of numerical computing on the Grid. Grids are in everyday use for scientific applications. Examples described in this workshop included MediGrid, NAREGEI Nano, LEAD, GridSolve, and St Germain. Many of these are data-centric, bringing together data and other resources that are distributed around the world.

One interesting use of the Grid is to address the dynamic and real-time access to resources for urgent computations, such as disasters, and for fluctuating demand, such as occasional real-time data acquisition and processing.

Talks at this meeting also described the development of both superstructures and infrastructures that have been developed to ease the creation of effective Grid tools. Partly because of this wealth of tools, many Grid-based services are being provided.

Another positive note was the absence of debate about the relative advantages of the Web and the Grid—this subject was not seen as important to the users, who simply want to get their work done. In addition, there was no confusion about the differences between a specification and an implementation, and hence the discussion remained focused on appropriate issues.

Please use the following format when citing this chapter:

Gropp, W. D., 2007, in IFIP International Federation for Information Processing, Volume 239, Grid-Based Problem Solving Environments, eds. Gaffney, P. W., Pool, J.C.T., (Boston: Springer), pp. 451-453.

1.2 Challenges

The talks emphasized that many challenges remain, including the following:

Security (either the lack of it or the complexity and inconvenience of providing and dealing with it). This remains an unsolved problem in the sense that the available approaches are too cumbersome and too fragile.

Fragmentation and premature standardization. In some cases, there are clearly too many different projects (fragmentation). In others, such as the Grid RPC used in the GridSolve project, premature standardization has taken place, with the standard getting in front of thorough understanding of practical needs.

Precise syntax, semantics, and effective descriptions. These are often still missing, as systems try to "give users what they want." This is the same trap that has often made complex programming in shell languages so difficult.

Scalability of solutions. Some systems work well only because they have not been widely adopted. Part of the problem is in the implementation, but part also may be in the design; the HPC community has learned that scalability requires careful, deliberate design. This point was summed up in one comment made during the meeting: "Scalability doesn't happen by accident."

1.3 What Wasn't Discussed

Also interesting was what received little or no discussion. Like the dog that did not bark in the famous Sherlock Holmes story, the lack of discussion may indicate an unsolved problem.

In particular, numerical properties and the interactions between components received little attention. It may be important to preserve conservation laws and avoid numerical instabilities caused by exciting parasitic modes. Yet only Norris's presentation on computational quality of service explicitly addressed some of these issues; there was little discussion of the deeper mathematical issues (though some came up in Friday's presentations). The session on dynamic data-driven application systems did touch on this topic, but in terms of dynamic control of a computation, rather than the establishment of "contracts" of numerical properties between components.

Also nearly absent were quantified measures of comparison between approaches. The lack of such measures makes it hard to evaluate progress or compare different approaches. This situation is a striking contrast to that in high-performance computing, where there are many (sometimes controversial) measures of comparison. Until there is more quantification, the development of Grid- or Web-based systems will remain more of an art than a science.

1.4 Opportunities

The meeting clearly identified a number of opportunities, including the following:

1. **Develop performance models and measures of success.** How can a researcher compare different approaches? A partial ordering, perhaps a multidimensional ordering, would be helpful. This would enable researchers to quantify design decisions and address real performance issues, such as scalability, that arise when Grid applications become successful.

2. **Develop community standards and best practices.** Vouk's talk on workflow tools described a large number of current tools. This area appears to be ripe for discussing community standards that would allow the next generation of workflow tools to build on current results. Many of the other talks discussed aspects of mathematical software that could benefit from even informal community standards or best practices in software engineering.

3. **Explore collaborations in developer tools.** For example, the GAT/SAGA, NAREGI-PSE, and Java CoG project have all developed their own sets of tools for building Grid- or Web-based applications; other projects have developed their own tools based on lower-level tools, such as using Perl scripts or ssh. While concurrent development is valuable for exploring different approaches and gaining experience, we should be moving to the next generation of tools, building on a common basis. More collaborations in these tools would help in this effort.

4. **Use the Grid to develop communities.** Can we use the Grid to discover scientists who are trying to use the Grid or Web in a similar way—for example, using data-mining techniques applied to project Web pages and publications to identify people who should at least check out one another's Web sites.

As this brief summary shows, the working conference provided a stimulating and fruitful experience for the participants.

Future Directions for Numerical Software Research – Comments during Discussions at WoCo9, Prescott, AZ, July 16-21, 2006

Brian T. Smith

Numerica 21 Incorporated

Angel Fire, New Mexico, USA, carbess@swcp.com,

1   Introduction

During the discussion periods, various people expressed the concern that numerical software development had become poorly supported over the past decade, with funding agencies seeking projects that seem to ignore the development of algorithms and software for numerical computations. In the past, the community has emphasized the development of mathematical software libraries. Currently, there appears to be no interest in that mode of presentation and mode of access to our numerical software by the application community. The suggestion by Ron Boisvert and others was the Grid services may provide the new mode of access. This note discusses the relevant issues on the topic as expressed in conversation at the meeting and considered with friends since.

What is at issue here is that numerical software is hidden or buried in packages and accessed through interfaces that do not make the numerical software apparent. Because research support by the funding agencies has turned to complete application solving environments where the nature, form, and quality of the software is not directly apparent to users or those who support the development of software, support for basic numerical software has waned.

Calls for new research are for software and algorithms that work on computational grids.   Approaches that address complete applications over the computational grids are paramount. In addition, there is the need for interfaces to numerical codes that are easy to use. But, libraries, with long calling sequences that provided complete control over the algorithm, do not address these needs. Many of us believe that libraries of well-tested procedures provide the building blocks for meeting the needs, but such procedures require significant expertise to use them. However, in many cases, versions of these libraries do port across the machines of most of the grid but do not necessarily provide the top performance for all machines.

Please use the following format when citing this chapter:

Smith B. T., 2007, in IFIP International Federation for Information Processing, Volume 239, Grid-Based Problem Solving Environments, eds. Gaffney, P. W., Pool, J.C.T., (Boston: Springer), pp. 455-457.

The numerical software community has in the past, with a few exceptions, emphasized portability and transportability of our software. Portable algorithmic efficiency has been a goal but code tuning to particular architectures has not always been a major goal, although there have been well-known exceptions. As a result, high quality portable software is available to the application integrators from open source repositories, published papers, and commercial vendors such as NAG (Numerical Algorithms Group) and VNI (Visual Numerics Incorporated). The software from open source repositories and published papers typically is not tuned for high performance; notable exceptions are ATLAS (Automatically Tuned Linear Algebra Software) and FFTW (Fast Fourier Transformations from the West). The result is that many applications are "rolling their own software" from open sources because integrators have control over the software, including porting and performance, to some extent. The need for new basic numerical algorithms is not paramount. Only those application areas that recognize that their numerical codes are the bottle necks request or demand research in new and better software. And that recognition does not happen often.

2   Suggestion

Given the above scenario and to rejuvenate interest in numerical software, I made the specific suggestion described below that recommends a new tack be taken by our community. The suggestion assumes the interest and dominance of grid computing will continue and that this form of computing will provide lots of available cycles.

A major need in scientific applications, in my opinion, is software that evaluates the accuracy of the computed results or more importantly the sensitivity of the numerical results to the data and the platforms on which the computation occurs. (Recall on a computational grid that you may not know on what machine the computation occurred or be able to specify what machine it runs on.) Such software would run in tandem with the application code, giving assessments on the sensitivity of the results to small errors (rounding error, say) or errors in the data specified by the application. For certain numerical areas, we know how to do this; for example, matrix condition number estimators [1] can be used to indicate how sensitive a solution to a system of linear equations is to changes in the matrix elements or right hand sides, and similarly for the matrix eigenvalue problem [2]. Recently, Enright published two papers [3,4] describing techniques on how to verify the accuracy of approximate solutions for ordinary differential equations. Higham's book [5] covers many of the possible approaches, particularly for the optimization problem. The recent emphasis on noise estimation in optimization problems is likely to provide algorithms and software that address the problem of estimating the accuracy and reliability of computed solutions to optimization problems. Of course, this topic is not new; see [6] for an early introduction to the problem in estimating the reliability of computed solutions.

Software that propagates this sensitivity through the subsequent computations by the application would be required. Similar sensitivity estimates are available for ordinary differential equations, polynomial root finding and other computational processes. The numerical analysis and investigation of such techniques were studied by a number of early numerical analysis pioneers (e.g. Wilkinson, Kahan, Cody, etc.), often related to their experience with computing by hand machines. Review of their early papers may offer helpful starting points for present-day researchers.

What is needed then is research that provides the techniques for computing the sensitivity and propagating its effect through remaining computations. The approach of interval arithmetic may come to mind here but my belief is that such an approach should be used only when other more appropriate techniques are not available. The research I propose would lead to software that can run in tandem on available processors on the grid with the application, providing an assessment of the quality of the computed results. Ideally, one may be able to make such an assessment available as a grid service. It would no doubt use existing libraries of basic numerical procedures that we currently have and are developing, but needs to be presented to grid applications in an easy to use form.

References

[1]   Cline, A. K., Moler, C. B., Stewart, G. W., Wilkinson, J. H., An Estimate For The Condition Number Of A Matrix, SIAM Journal Of Numerical Analysis, 16:368-375, 1979.

[2]   Wilkinson, J. H, The Algebraic Eigenvalue Problem, Clarendon Press, 1965.

[3]   Enright, W. H., Tools For The Verification of Approximate Solutions To Differential Equations, in Accuracy and Reliability in Scientific Computing, Edited by Bo Einarsson, SIAM, pp. 109-121, 2005

[4]   Enright, W. H., JACM 195, pp.203-2006, 2006.

[5]   Higham, N., Accuracy And Stability Of Numerical Algorithms, SIAM 2002.

[6]   Fox, L. How To Get Meaningless Answers In Scientific Computation (and What To Do About It), IMA Bulletin, 7(1971), pp. 296-302.

What is the relevance of Grid Services to Numerical Software?

How must numeric software be structured to be incorporated as a grid service?

Date: Tuesday, 8PM, July 18, 2006

Chair/Discussant: Brian Smith

After dinner, we convened to have a discussion on the above topic.

Ron Boisvert started the discussion by making the statement that after the development of numerical software packages such as EISPACK, LINPACK, FUNPACK, MINPACK and the introduction of numerical subroutine libraries such as NAG and IMSL (now VNI), we appear to have lost the interest of the application disciplines in numerical software. He asked: "What is the smart idea/killer application that will create interest anew in the efforts of our community?"

Brian Ford responded by suggesting that applications looking for the last digit of accuracy and highest performance possible on specialized systems would continue to develop their own software but that the grid could be the catalyst to renew or rejuvenate interest in reliable robust software that computes its results reasonably accurately and in a reasonable time over the wide collection of machines inherent in a computational grid. That is, the answer was to emphasize reliability, robustness, accuracy, and power over the grid.

Brian Smith agreed with B. Ford but added that new software should be made available that accesses the accuracy of the computed solution obtained a priori, providing this additional service to the application community.

Jim Pool then compared the current application community response to the response of the application community to two similar software efforts during the late 1970s and early 1980s. One was Speakeasy by S. Cohen of ANL and the other was MATLAB by C. Moler of MathWorks, then at the University of New Mexico. Speakeasy provided very early basic functionality in numerical linear algebra and other areas and continued the development in-house into the financial area. MATLAB also initially provided the same kind of basic functionality and had a very similar content, but then developed MATLAB further by involving people from application disciplines such as engineering and physics, creating software that was developed by researchers in these other areas with a more familiar feel for physicists and engineers.

Brian Ford acknowledged the development into application areas but noted that A. Little had recognized the appeal of MATLAB in engineering, particularly for control engineering and had taken over the business development, sales and marketing of MATLAB. Together these are the reasons for the business success of MATLAB compared with SPEAKEASY.

In summary, **Jim Pool** felt that an emphasis on applications for the grid might offer real opportunity for numerical software community.

Bill Applebe thought the emphasis by the numerical software community should be on large grain applications. Object-oriented abstraction was the key to future success, using this paradigm to create dynamic structures and to facilitate the operation of the numerical software in a dynamic environment. Input/output had to be handled in a different way than it is now. Robustness and reliability were more important than speed but accuracy of the solution returned by the numerical software had to be something that was specifiable. There was a need for polyalgorithms where the user did not have to specify the method of solution and a need for representation of the data for the problems that was flexible, in the same manner as PetSc permits.

Finally, the discussion wound up with **Mladen Vouk's** comments on numerical software engineers, and other developers of scientific computing software learning from studies in the sociology of work, and in business process psychology to make their work processes much more effective, and hence their products and technologies much more attuned to current computational and scientific practice. Isometric measures of software performance and related issues of organisational efficiency had much to offer our community in the future.

Brian Smith thanked the meeting for their attendance and a worthwhile discussion.